This book is dedicated to T-Bone Burnett
and Larry Norman in memory of many
hours of Beatle talk over the years.
Also to Sean O'Mahoney, a.k.a. Johnny Dean,
who published my first article and gave me
my first job as a writer.

DEY ST.

THE COMPLETE BEATLES SONGS. Copyright © 1994, 1999, 2005, 2009, 2012, 2015 by Steve Turner.
Design copyright © 2015 by Carlton Books Limited. All rights reserved. Printed in China.
No part of this book may be used or reproduced in any manner whatsoever without
written permission except in the case of brief quotations embodied in critical articles and reviews.
For information address HarperCollins Publishers, 195 Broadway, New York, NY 10007.
HarperCollins books may be purchased for educational, business, or sales promotional use.
For information please e-mail the Special Markets Department at SPsales@harpercollins.com.

FIRST EDITION

Designed by Georgios Mardas

Library of Congress Cataloging-in-Publication Data has been applied for.

ISBN 978-0-06-244734-0

15 16 17 18 19 HH 10 9 8 7 6 5 4 3 2 1

The complete Beatles songs

THE STORIES BEHIND EVERY TRACK WRITTEN BY THE FAB FOUR

Steve Turner

DEY ST.
AN IMPRINT OF
WILLIAM MORROW *PUBLISHERS*

The complete Beatles songs

THE STORIES BEHIND EVERY TRACK WRITTEN BY THE FAB FOUR

Steve Turner

DEY ST.
AN IMPRINT OF
WILLIAM MORROW PUBLISHERS

Contents

Preface

Most books are written, get published, have short shelf lives and then disappear into personal and public libraries. This book is different. It first came out in 1994, has never been out of print since, and has gone through several updates, formats and layout changes over the years. It has expanded considerably, added new findings, and jettisoned some false information. It has also sold over 440,000 copies, making it one of the best-selling books about the Beatles.

This edition is perhaps the most significant. For the first time ever all the stories behind the Beatles' songs are available along with all the lyrics. For this new version we have changed the title from *A Hard Day's Night* (as the book has always been known) to *The Complete Beatles Songs*. This is the result of long and persistent work by my publisher Piers Murray Hill, in negotiating with the various copyright holders to bring about his dream volume. (It was Piers, then in a brand new job, who took my book on in 1993).

It has been a surprising challenge to reproduce the lyrics as they were recorded. Previously published lyric collections are riddled with errors, as are online reproductions. It's easy to understand how this has happened. During the career of the Beatles, Northern Songs, owned by Dick James, acquired lyrics either from transcriptions of early demos and 'white label' discs or from handwritten sheets used in the studio, often written up by the road managers. Failing that, a secretary would play the released record and type out what she heard.

The problem has been that the Beatles frequently changed lyrics while in the studio, sometimes as late as a final take. So even lyric sheets taken from music stands at Abbey Road after a recording session were not always reliable guides to what ended up on the singles or albums. Transcribing from a finished disc is not as easy as it sounds. Words are often sound like other words or are obscured by instruments. One obvious example is on 'Come Together' where John sings 'Holds you in his arms, yeah.' This is very often transcribed as 'Holds you in his armchair'. I was surprised to find that only once in 'Long And Winding Road' does Paul actually sing 'long and winding road.' What he sings is 'long, winding road.'

There also a lot of extraneous words not usually included in the lyrics as presented. These ranged from

RIGHT: The mock-up that was used to sell the idea of the original book to the publishers in early 1995.

count-ins and adlibs to fade-outs, exclamations, and background choruses. We've tried to include as many as possible but as they're particularly hard to pick up on we can't guarantee 100% accuracy. There's no 'authorized version' against which to compare findings and therefore you ultimately only have your ears to trust.

Although all earlier versions of the book quoted (with permission) from various songs they didn't have the advantage of having the whole text. Hopefully having all the words alongside the explanation of how the song was written will enhance the reading experience.

The point of the book from the very start was, as it said in the original subtitle, to tell 'the stories behind every Beatles' song.' It wasn't meant to detail recording procedures, list instruments used, explain the musicology or set the work in its cultural and historical context. Other writers, with better qualifications in the relevant areas, have done this. I simply wanted to recount where the songs had come from and how they came into being. Sometimes that has involved describing current events or outlining a recording trick but only as incidental information.

My ideal story was something like 'She's Leaving Home,' where a newspaper article about a particular person, had prompted Paul to image a whole scenario. In this case

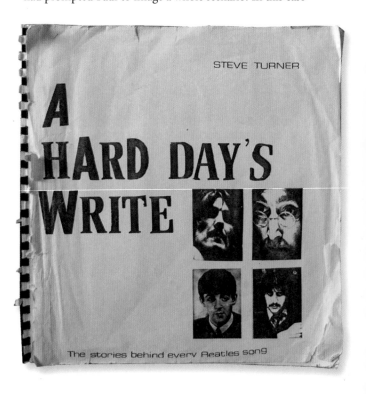

I could access the paper and trace the girl who could then tell me why she left home and how she felt when she heard the song by the Beatles. (Melanie Coe, the girl in question, actually attended the launch party for *A Hard Day's Write*.)

As you might expect, not every song had such a straightforward and colourful story. Early compositions were often written in emulation of writers they admired rather that about incidents they'd read about or had happen to them. Many later songs, like 'Get Back' for example, were built line by line in the studio and were more inspired by the sound than the sense of the words. There is no Jojo or Loretta Martin just as there had been no Vera, Chuck or Dave.

Yet even these sorts of songs often had roots in something observed. 'Lady Madonna,' I found out, was kicked off by the caption to a photo of a Vietnamese woman breastfeeding her child that was featured in a 1965 issue of *National Geographic* magazine. 'Happiness Is A Warm Gun' owed its origin to a headline of a story published in a 1968 copy of *The American Rifleman*.

For the purposes on the book a 'Beatles' song' has been defined as a song written by one or more members of the Beatles' and subsequently released on a record under the Beatles' name. I have not included songs by other writers that the Beatles' covered nor songs written by them that were only ever officially recorded by other artists. The only exception is 'Maggie Mae,' a traditional song arranged by the Beatles on *Let It Be*. I thought it worth including because the copyright isn't shared with another known writer and because it tells us something about the music that was in the Liverpool DNA before rock 'n' roll crossed the Atlantic.

It's always a great pleasure to write about the Beatles and we go back a long way together. My very first published story was about the Beatles and appeared in the *Beatles Monthly* in 1969, just before the break-up of the group and the end of this official fan magazine. It was as a result of this piece that I was offered my first job as a journalist on *Beat Instrumental* and within months of starting that job I found myself interviewing John and Yoko at the Apple HQ in Savile Row.

It was another two decades before I met Paul. Piers Murray Hill, who'd already read my pitch for *A Hard Day's Write* while at Hamlyn (and passed on it because he was 'Beatled out' having already done a number of successful Beatle books, thought of me when Linda McCartney needed a ghost writer for her photographic collection *Sixties: Portrait of a Decade*. This collaboration led to me interviewing Linda extensively and meeting the McCartneys at home as well as at their studio and office.

I can't say that meeting John and Paul helped me in the writing of this book but there is something satisfying in knowing that I have actually spoken to the key creators of this remarkable song catalogue. Paul has since told me that he likes the book and admires the extent of the research although my findings don't always tally 100% with his personal memories. Ironically, Barry Miles used the stories in an early version to prompt Paul when they were discussing the songs for the book *Many Years From Now*.

Even though this is now the fifth time that new material has been added to this book there are still songs that puzzle me or about which I think new facts could be established. The 'man with multicoloured mirrors on his hobnail boots' ('Happiness Is A Warm Gun') was apparently a football fan with a penchant for 'upskirt' reflections but who was he? 'Mean Mister Mustard' was written about someone that John read about who hid money in his bodily orifices but, again, who was he?

Not that finding any of this out would make the songs sound any better than they do already. Like anyone else, when I hear them I'm transported to that moment when I first heard them rather to any details of their composition. 'Love Me Do' takes me back to my childhood bedroom listening to Radio Luxembourg. Hearing any track from *Revolver* reminds me of discovering the Kings Road in 1966 when boutiques first began to play music. For 'Hey Jude' I'm sunbathing with friends on top of a World War II pillbox on the beach at Tal-y-bont in Wales and someone has brought along a transistor radio.

In another sense every time I hear a Beatles song feels like the first time I've ever heard it. The elements of surprise in the tunes that made them so captivating when they were first released still sound unexpected. They have a magical capacity for retaining their freshness, and they seem to have been able to do the same for succeeding generations. They are songs very much of the era and culture they were created in but also able to transcend that era and that culture.

I feel enormously privileged to have my work printed alongside the work of the Beatles but I'm under no illusions. They did their bit without me. I couldn't have done my bit without them.

Steve Turner, London 2015

The Beatles in the Backyard: an iconic shot from the early days of fame for the four boys from Liverpool, 1963.

The Beatles used magazines and newspapers as a source of inspiration for songs ranging from 'From Me to You' to 'Mean Mr. Mustard'.

Introduction

Researching a feature for the 20th anniversary of the Beatles' *Sgt. Pepper's Lonely Hearts Club Band* album, I was delighted to be able to track down Lucy, the girl who as a four-year-old had unwittingly starred in John Lennon's song 'Lucy In The Sky With Diamonds'. I soon discovered that she hadn't given much thought to her immortalization. After all, the Beatles had broken up by the time she was seven and she was well into her teens before she learned that John's inspiration had come from a nursery school drawing his son Julian had made of her floating in the sky surrounded by diamonds. Yet here she was, a girl who had been resident in my consciousness for 20 years and who therefore appeared to me to be a celebrity. She was of course an ordinary person, made extraordinary by the touch of a Beatle's pen.

Anyone who, like me, had grown up with the Beatles' music would have been similarly impressed to meet Lucy, with or without diamonds, because our memories are thronged by a cast of characters created by John Lennon, Paul McCartney and, to a lesser degree, George Harrison. The fireman with an hourglass and the banker without a mac have become as familiar to us as any incidental character in Dickens and, from Beijing to Buenos Aires, there must

be people who can sing about Dr. Robert or who can hum 'Strawberry Fields Forever' and 'Penny Lane'. It is precisely because these people and these places are now part of us, that it is fascinating to discover where they came from: the true identity of Dr. Robert, what Penny Lane really looked like, or the emotional situations that produced songs like 'And I Love Her', 'Yesterday' or 'We Can Work It Out'.

Of course, knowing the inspiration behind the songs doesn't make them any better or worse. The songs exist as creations in their own right, enhanced by the memories surrounding the time when we first heard them. If you loved 'A Hard Day's Night' in 1964, you're not going to love it any more for knowing that Ringo supplied the quip which became the title, or that John wrote it on the back of a birthday card in a small flat behind London's Cromwell Road. It is just that these songs are so much a part of us and we are so much a part of what the songs have become, that it is almost an act of self-discovery to learn the stories behind them. Looking closely at the songs also gives us an insight into the Sixties and the lives of the Beatles, who have been examined frequently as celebrities, performers and businessmen but less often as composers.

Most of the early interviewers completely ignored the Beatles as songwriters. Even after turning out the splendidly-crafted *A Hard Day's Night*, the first album to consist of nothing but Lennon and McCartney songs, no-one seemed interested in how they wrote, where the ideas came from or how much of themselves they were revealing in the lyrics. Instead, to their increasing frustration, they had to put up with questions on the level of "Do you prefer filming to making records?" or "When is Paul getting married?" No wonder they turned their backs on touring midway through their recording career and restricted the access of journalists.

It was only with the arrival of the more reflective albums (*Revolver*, *Sgt. Pepper*) and the interest of the more serious press (*The Sunday Times*, *Rolling Stone*, *Crawdaddy*), that the Beatles began to be interviewed as artists capable of discussing

LEFT: Lucy O'Donnell (later Lucy Vodden) whose picture drawn by Julian Lennon inspired a Beatles' classic.

"Picture yourself on a boat on a river..."

11

the creative process. Although they often volunteered invaluable information, no-one, as far as I know, properly followed up the clues to discover the full story. We may know, for example, that 'She's Leaving Home' was based on a newspaper story of a teenage runaway but do we know who she was? Did she ever come back home? Did she ever know that she was the subject of a Beatles' song? What about 'Ob-La-Di Ob-La-Da'? Paul has, at various times, said it was the phrase of a London night club habitué called 'Jimmy', or perhaps 'Scott', which he appropriated for his ska-inspired number. But how did this character react to having a song written around one of his catch phrases?

By the time the Beatles released their first single in 1962, there was already a considerable Lennon and McCartney catalogue because they'd been writing together for five years, meeting mostly at Paul's family home in Allerton, Liverpool, to polish off songs that they'd begun on their own. Starting a song may have meant having an idea for a melody, or arriving with an almost complete song which just needed the essential middle eight 'hook'. It may equally have meant coming up with a great title and a first line and needing help with direction, or having heard a great new rock 'n' roll song and wanting to make a version that was all their own.

From fairly early on, each song bore the distinctive signature of either John or Paul because although they were united in their love of primitive American rock 'n' roll, they were markedly different in their approaches to songwriting. Crudely put, Paul's songs were melodic and optimistic while not giving a lot away about his passions and anxieties. John's songs tended to be more rhythmic, his outlook was

pessimistic and, even before he'd heard of Bob Dylan, he was letting his feelings show.

These different styles of writing owed everything to their different backgrounds. Paul grew up in an old-fashioned working-class home where music brought people together. If you wanted to get a party going, you would persuade someone to bang out a tune on the piano and everyone would stand around and sing along. Although Paul's mother died when he was 14, his father was always encouraging and praised the values of hard work and ambition. His own tastes in music – he'd been a band leader in the Twenties – were passed on to his son and songs like 'When I'm 64', 'Your Mother Should Know' and 'Honey Pie' were Paul's affectionate tributes to the pre-war music he knew his dad loved. It was Jim McCartney who advised Paul to learn to play piano because, he said, it was people who played the piano who got invited to the best parties.

In a way, that's how Paul succeeded. He mastered several instruments learned lots of songs and became the life and soul of the party. After all, it was the fact that he could play guitar chords rather than banjo chords and knew the words to 'Be-Bop-A-Lula' and 'Twenty Flight Rock' that impressed John Lennon when he first met him at a church fete in the summer of 1957 and got him the job with John's group the Quarry Men.

Although John is often seen as the working-class Liverpudlian, a perception encouraged by his song 'Working-Class Hero', he really came from a middle-class background and his deprivations were emotional rather than material. He grew up in a semi-detached private home on one of

LEFT: John's childhood home in Menlove Avenue. 'Please Please Me' was written in the front left bedroom and early Lennon-McCartney rehearsals took place in the porch.

Liverpool's grandest suburban avenues and was an only-child whose father left him as a child and whose mother abandoned him to the care of her sister. By contrast, although Paul's father had to work hard to bring up his motherless teenage sons in a council house, there was always a lot of affection in the McCartney home. Perhaps this is what made Paul and John such a perfect match. Each of them seemed to have what the other lacked. Where Paul was sunny and uncomplicated, John was serious and brooding. Where Paul looked on the bright side, John always suspected the worst. Where Paul wanted show business with flashing lights, John wanted to be taken seriously as an artist.

It worked well for a decade. When Paul wanted "beauty queen" to rhyme with "just seventeen" in 'I Saw Her Standing There', John told him it was 'crap' and thus saved a beat music classic. When they were writing 'Getting Better', John offered the line "couldn't get much worse" and, for the similarly optimistic 'We Can Work It Out', it was he who added the contrasting middle-eight that started: "Life is very hard ..."

In curbing each other's excesses, they were both constantly reined-in to the central cause, which was always the Beatles. At the same time, Paul and John became each other's main rival. It's impossible to underestimate the creative power that was unleashed by the desire to top the other's achievements. There was always an unspoken contest to write the A-side of the next Beatle single and this pressure drove standards ever higher. The Beatles didn't really have to fear the competition of the Rolling Stones or the Byrds or even the Beach Boys, but John had to fear the competition of Paul and

vice versa. If John wrote a cracker of a song, Paul would have to go away and come back with something twice as good. This often resulted in them trying to write in the other's style just to show that they could do it. One such example, the gritty, dirty, minimalist piece 'Why Don't We Do It In The Road?' was composed by Paul and recorded without John's help. At around the same time, John was working on 'Julia', a song as tender as anything Paul had written.

Now that Beatles songs saturate the airwaves and can safely be regarded as a soundtrack for an era that started with Kennedy's assassination and ended with Neil Armstrong's moon walk, it's not easy to pinpoint the changes they ushered in. It's particularly difficult for those born and raised in the post-Beatle era to see what all the fuss was about. After all, the average rap or ambient record uses more sophisticated technology than *Sgt. Pepper* required and songwriters such as David Byrne, Morrissey and Elvis Costello all write lyrics which transcend the old Tin Pan Alley-isms of "moon and June, love and above." As T.S. Eliot responded when asked why contemporary writers knew so much more than their forebears: "Precisely, and they are that which we know." In other words, what were breakthroughs for the Beatles have become commonly accepted work practices for those who have followed.

It was the Beatles, under the guidance of producer George Martin, who pioneered multi-tracking in the studio and the idea of recording songs that were too complex to be duplicated live in concert. Before the Beatles it was rare in rock 'n' roll for songwriters to perform, or for performers to write. Indeed in Britain it was rare that performers had

anything to say at all, except perhaps to confess a love of milk shakes and steak and kidney pies, or a desire to buy a cottage for Mum and Dad. Nearly all the rock 'n' roll songs at this time were about love, fashion and adolescence. One of the great legacies of the Beatles was to extend the subject matter of the genre. Fewer than half the songs on *Revolver* were about love. The rest of the songs on this album ranged from taxation to Tibetan Buddhism.

John Lennon and Paul McCartney were the first major pop stars to have benefited from an extended education. Before the Beatles, the assumption was that a typical pop star would be an academic failure who had turned to music for a quick ride to fame and fortune. Elvis Presley had been a truck driver, Cliff Richard had worked as an office clerk, but John Lennon had been to art school in Liverpool and Paul McCartney had studied for his A-level exams at the best grammar school in the city. This was significant because it meant that for the first time rock 'n' roll had reasonably well-educated performers who were able to produce work informed by art and literature. When Paul told a story in rhyme he could see himself as working in the tradition of Chaucer. When John took the words of a Victorian poster and turned them into a lyric he would have known that he was following the tradition of *objets trouvés* started by Marcel Duchamp. As a result this led to the Beatles being ranked alongside painters, poets and novelists in the popular culture of the Sixties. Expecting more of their chosen medium than Gene Vincent or Billy Fury had ever envisioned allowed the Beatles to outgrow the teen market. Before them, no-one had managed the transition from heart throb to 'serious' artist

ABOVE: Producer George Martin, left, was the true fifth Beatle, enabling the group's aural dreams to become a reality.

but, between 1966 and 1970, the Beatles had extended their appeal to college and university students. The John Lennon look of centre-parted hair and granny glasses became the archetype of the late sixties campus radical.

The early songs were hardly profound because they were written within the limitations of the pop singles market, as well as for an increasingly adoring female audience. "We were just writing songs à la Everly Brothers, à la Buddy Holly," John once admitted. "They were pop songs with no more thought to them than … to create a sound. And the words were almost irrelevant." John would later say that he deliberately kept himself out of the early songs, channelling his personal observations and feelings into poems and short stories, some of which would eventually make up the books *In His Own Write* and *A Spaniard In The Works*. "I was already a stylized songwriter on the first album," he said. "To express myself I would write … personal stories which expressed my personal emotions. I'd have a separate songwriting John Lennon who wrote songs for the sort of meat market, and I didn't consider the lyrics to have any depth at all. They were just a joke."

Some of the songs from these days lived on to become Beatles songs. 'Love Me Do' became their first single. 'I Call Your Name', 'I'll Follow The Sun' and 'One After 909' became album tracks. Other songs such as 'Thinking Of Linking', 'Too Bad About Sorrows' and 'Just Fun' didn't make it on to record. Iris Caldwell, an early girlfriend of Paul's from Liverpool, remembered him singing a song he'd written called 'I Fancy Me Chances With You' which had a chorus of: 'I fancy me chances with you, I fancy me chances with you, When I'm at the dances, I fancy me chances, I fancy me chances with you'.

The Quarry Men became the Silver Beetles, then the Beetles, before metamorphosing into the Beatles with George Harrison joining on lead guitar and Pete Best on drums. For a while Stuart Sutcliffe, an art school friend of John's, also played bass guitar. Their repertoire was dominated by covers of songs associated with Elvis, Little Richard, Jerry Lee Lewis and other American rock 'n' rollers but gradually they became confident enough to insert Lennon and McCartney originals into the set.

In 1961, Stuart Sutcliffe left and the following year Ringo Starr, drummer with Rory Storm and the Hurricanes, replaced Pete Best. Managed by Brian Epstein and produced by George Martin, the Beatles became a national phenomenon and their musical interests expanded to include black American girl groups like the Shirelles and the Chiffons and the new Motown sound of the Miracles and Barrett Strong. They admired Gerry Goffin and Carole King who were then at their peak as a songwriting team writing pop hits such as 'Will You Still Love Me Tomorrow?', 'Chains', 'One Fine Day', 'Take Good Care Of My Baby' and 'Please Don't Ever Change' for a variety of American artists.

"First of all, Paul and I wanted to be the Goffin and King of England," said John, and in many of their early compositions you can see the hallmarks of that Brill Building style of songwriting, where hits were written to order within office hours. As with Goffin and King, they too began to write for other artists, finding themselves so prolific in 1963 and 1964 that they had material to spare. Thus, they gave 'World Without Love', 'Nobody I Know' and 'I Don't Want To See You Again' to Peter and Gordon (Peter Asher was the brother of Paul's girlfriend, Jane) and 'Bad To Me' and 'Do You Want To Know A Secret?' to Billy J Kramer (who was also managed by Brian Epstein).

These songs became hits and the rush was on to record Lennon and McCartney songs. Stephen James, son of the Beatles' original music publisher Dick James, remembers that the first task they had when the Beatles sent in a demo was to find the right act to cover the songs. By the mid-Sixties, almost every song on a Beatles album would crop up as a single by another artist, some of them like 'Michelle' by the Overlanders, 'Ob-La-Di Ob-La-Da' by Marmalade and 'Got To Get You Into My Life' by Cliff Bennett and the Rebel Rousers becoming major UK hits.

The second stage of songwriting came in 1964 when Paul and John's horizons were broadened in other ways, by other influences. Although it was Paul who first got hold of a Bob Dylan album it was John who was the most obviously affected. With songs like 'I'm A Loser', 'You've Got To Hide Your Love Away' and 'Help!', there came a new intensity and honesty which signalled that John had discovered that he could be as revealing in song as he had been in his poems and jottings. It was startling at the time for a major pop star to

BELOW: Stuart Sutcliffe, John's art school friend, was briefly the Beatles' bass player.

write songs which dealt with defeat and insecurity; songs that, for example, made statements like "I'm a loser" or "I need help" or "I don't want to spoil the party and so I'll go". The only thing that cushioned the impact was the Beatles' jaunty image, sustained particularly by films like *Help!* As the film was a rollicking romp, the title song was generally assumed to be light-hearted. It wasn't though because, as John himself admitted years later, he was desperately unhappy at the time and literally crying out for help.

Paul was affected in different ways. Through Jane Asher, his girlfriend, herself an accomplished film, television and stage actress, her brother Peter, and their mother, a professor of music, Paul was introduced to students of psychology, classical musicians, actors, theatre directors, filmmakers and members of London's fledgling 'underground' scene. He developed a fascination for the avant-garde and visited art galleries. The effect could be heard in ambitious new songs in which he developed characters and told stories like 'Eleanor Rigby', songs that used orchestral settings like 'Yesterday' and songs like 'For No One' that looked at the world through a film maker's eye. This was the period during which the Beatles began to impress those who had once dismissed them as just another noisy pop group. They weren't going to be a short-lived sensation. They had made the transition from Liverpool stars to British stars to international stars and were clearly writing songs destined to become standards.

Until 1965, the Beatles simply refined and synthesized accepted notions of rock 'n' roll. From that year on, they stretched and remodelled it, challenging all the conventions. In the mid-Sixties they were taking inspiration not from

ABOVE: Manager Brian Epstein, centre, guided the Beatles' career until his death in 1967.

Buddy Holly but from Karlheinz Stockhausen, the German electronic composer, and Ravi Shankar, the classical sitar player. They experimented with rhythms and recording techniques, reinvented the scope of the pop album and, in deserting the stage for the recording studio, changed forever the public perception of pop stars. Through their unbridled imaginations the Beatles transformed pop music. From the outset they were determined to avoid clichés, whether of lyric, rhyme or chord change. They imagined new sorts of songs and believed if they had the capacity to imagine something, then producer George Martin would be able to capture it on tape.

Their great burst of creativity in the mid-to-late Sixties came about because they accepted no limits. Accidents such as studio feedback or twisted tapes were seized upon and incorporated into their art. Random lyrics, which made no literal sense, were kept because they often sounded better than lines they would sweat over. Songs were plucked from newspaper headlines, snatches of conversation, posters, television commercials, religious tracts, dreams and letters. In the studio they demanded the impossible and usually got it. "Make me sound like a thousand chanting Buddhist monks, George", "Get me a piccolo sound like I heard last night on the Brandenburg Concerto, George", "Stick these two half-written songs together and make a new song." John and Paul had started by scrawling lyrics in old school notebooks and imagining themselves as Leiber and Stoller (the writers

ABOVE: American rocker Gene Vincent, far right, was one of the Beatles' early musical idols.

behind Elvis' 'Hound Dog' and many other early rock 'n' roll hits), or even Rodgers and Hammerstein. Now they were every bit as well-known as their heroes.

The third stage of Beatles' songwriting was influenced by drugs and eastern meditation. The phrase 'turns me on' had appeared in 'She's A Woman' but the first real fruit of the new altered states was John's song 'The Word' with its message that love can solve all our problems. Songs such as 'Tomorrow Never Knows', 'She Said She Said' and 'Strawberry Fields Forever' would never have been written without having had experience of marijuana and LSD. Equally, George Harrison's 'Within You Without You' and 'The Inner Light' wouldn't have been possible without the experience of India. John's ability to write was first enhanced and then hampered by his experimentation with drugs. He later confessed that LSD had virtually destroyed his ego and that in turn cost him the unacknowledged leadership of the Beatles. In 1964 and 1965, most of the hit singles were songs where John was the major contributor. After *Sgt. Pepper*, the hits were almost all written by Paul: 'Hello Goodbye', 'Magical Mystery Tour', 'Lady Madonna', 'Hey Jude', 'Get Back', 'Let It Be'. By 1967, the world was wondering not so much whether the Beatles could push the form of the popular song any further but where they would take it to next. The general feeling was that their recordings would be even more complex and full of tricks.

The fourth and final era of the Beatles' songwriting began in 1968. Against all expectations, it marked a return

to simplicity. They released 'Lady Madonna', as basic a rock 'n' roll song as they had ever written, and then went off to India where they composed a set of acoustic songs. The album cover this time was plain. By now the Lennon and McCartney partnership was falling apart. Although most of the songs were still credited to them as a pair, it was clear that *The Beatles* (or *The White Album* as it is popularly known) relied on solo contributions. In private life too, they were pulling in different directions. John had a new partner in Yoko. Paul had a new partner in Linda. There weren't the same reasons for being together any more.

"We cooled it because we were not playing together," Paul said at the time. "We lived together, played together, were in the same hotel, up at the same time every morning, and doing this all day. It doesn't matter what you do as long as you're this close all day. Something grows, and if you're not this close physically, something goes. You can still come together to record, but you still lose."

In 1969, the Beatles decided they had done everything they could ever do together and parted company. *Abbey Road*, with its tales of financial woes, arguments and discord was the last album the group recorded, although *Let It Be* was the final album to be released. In seven years they had gone from young Liverpudlians happy to sing about the delights of chatting up a girl in a ballroom to worldly-wise men waxing philosophical about the power of love and groaning under the weight of their business empire.

Somehow they had managed to take us along with them, particularly those of us who were 13 when they sang 'I Saw Her Standing There' and 20 when they sang

'Come Together'. They seemed to have documented the whole struggle of adolescence, from the desire to simply touch a loved one ('I Wanna Hold Your Hand'), through the feelings of loneliness ('Help!'), moving on to inquisitive experimentation with drugs and religion ('Within You Without You'), to facing up to the burdens of earning a living ('Carry That Weight') and marriage ('The Ballad Of John And Yoko').

The Beatles' songs were never as dense and poetic as Bob Dylan's or as raunchy and direct as the Rolling Stones'. At the time, however, they were taken no less seriously, because were always believed to 'mean' something. More than forty years after the band stopped playing, those songs still mean something to us. They are like old friends who we met when we were young and who made life a little more exciting and easier to cope with. Because of what they did for us, we have great affection for them. It is because we hold such affection for them that it makes sense to find out where they came from.

ABOVE: Now dressed in suits rather than leather jackets, the Fab Four at the Cavern Club in 1963.

RIGHT: Paul at the Cavern Club in 1961, at the beginning of his writing career.

Come together

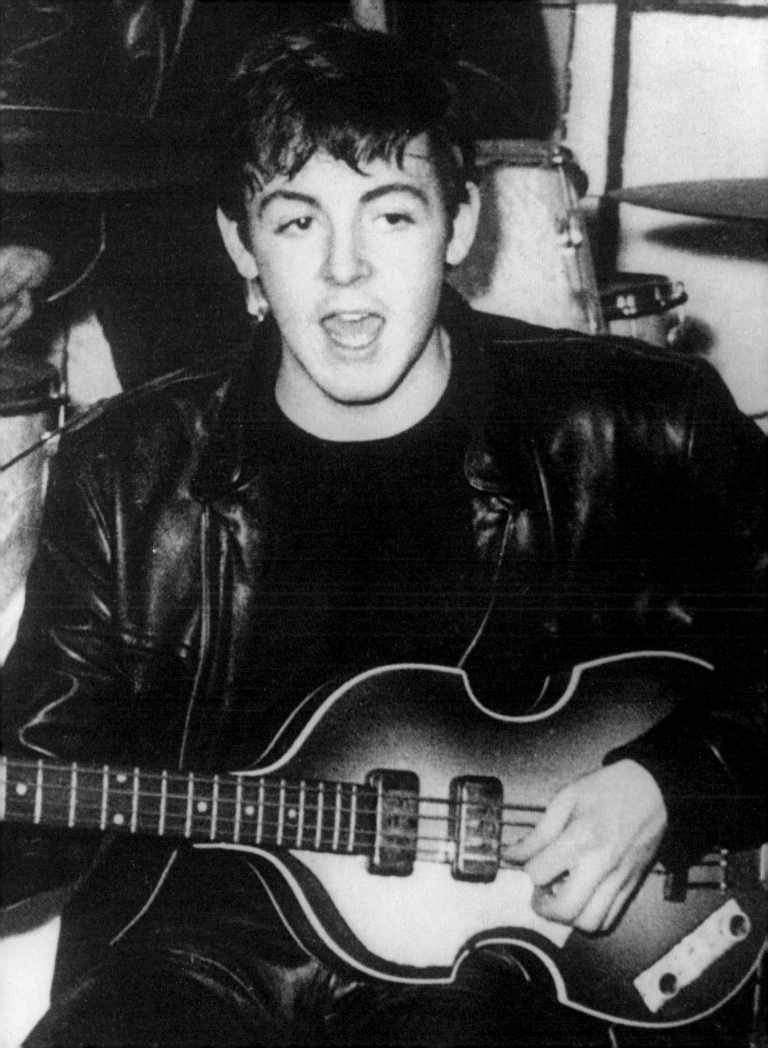

1
Please Please Me

One of the great strengths of the Beatles was that by 1962, the year they cut their first record, they were already seasoned performers who'd played over 900 shows in the previous three years alone and had a repertoire of at least 260 songs drawn from albums and singles of the artists they admired. This wealth of live experience and their intimate familiarity with a lot of the best pop, rock and R&B songs of the previous decade was to provide the foundation for their career.

From their shows they learned what worked in performance and not merely on record. Facing teenagers in Lancashire dance halls and youth clubs they discovered what stirred the passions of young girls and what made people dance. From the endless hours in red light Hamburg they found the best ways of calming the inebriated, soothing the violent and exciting the jaded. In the act of painstakingly recreating songs from repeated listens to singles and album tracks they gained a first class education into how songs were built. There were an additional 40+ songs written by John and Paul either alone or together, over 20 of which were included at one time or another in their stage act. In the early days they used about having written "over one hundred songs" but in 1966 John admitted that his was a deliberate exaggeration. "We were the only group then writing songs, so we used to say we'd written about 100, even though it was only 30."

In retrospect 1962 can be seen as a time when it was inevitable that something new would happen in the world of pop. The original rock 'n' roll movement that had started when Elvis signed with Sun Records in 1954 had largely dissipated. In 1957 Little Richard had temporarily abandoned rock 'n' roll to become a preacher and gospel singer, in 1958 Jerry Lee Lewis was extensively blacklisted after marrying his under-age cousin and Elvis joined the army, in 1959 Buddy Holly was killed in a plane crash and in 1960 Gene Vincent was injured in a car crash that killed Eddie Cochran. In the place of these original, edgy and sometimes vulgar artists came smoother singers like Ricky Nelson, Bobby Rydell and Pat Boone who often looked the part but who had little of the same creativity, wildness and magnetism.

The singer whose work they covered the most was Elvis followed by Chuck Berry, Little Richard, Buddy Holly, Carl Perkins, Jerry Lee Lewis, Ray Charles, Fats Domino and English singer Joe Brown. But they weren't adverse to covering more contemporary material. Almost a hundred of their songs were from records released since 1960 and included material by more overtly pop artists such as Chubby Checker, Freddy Cannon, Frank Ifield, Bobby Vee and The Shirelles.

The sound made by Liverpool bands like the Beatles, Gerry and the Pacemakers, the Searchers, the Big Three, and Rory Storm and the Hurricanes is often described as "Merseybeat", suggesting there was a distinctive rhythm, arrangement and approach. This wasn't so, although the Liverpool groups appeared to differ from their Southern contemporaries in preferring pop and rock 'n' roll to original blues. They all tended to favour the bass, rhythm guitar, lead guitar and drums line-up with very few groups using piano, organ or saxophone. They played no material by Muddy Waters, Howlin' Wolf, John Lee Hooker or Robert Johnson, as the Rolling Stones did, but still incorporated blues-styled songs from people like Lloyd Price, Buddy Holly and Jerry Lee Lewis. Likewise there were very few pure country songs and nothing by a gospel artist (despite John claiming in *New Musical Express* that he was a fan of gospel music). Like other Liverpool groups they found space for show tunes, some standards and a handful of instrumentals. They recognized the importance of sentimental tunes that provided a contrast to the wilder rock 'n' roll sounds.

Local groups had to fight hard to develop sets that were different from each other because everyone was fishing from the same pool of largely American material. Despite talk of seeking out "obscure B-sides" the bulk of what they performed was from singles that had been in the charts either in Britain or in America or from EP and LP tracks. There is some dispute as to whether Liverpool was particularly fortunate in being a port city with access to ships arriving from America. The traditional story has been that sailors brought back records ahead of their UK release and either gave them or sold them to musicians who quickly learned them.

It's true that there was usually a delay of up to six months between the US and UK releases of American singles. 'Blue Suede Shoes' by Carl Perkins, for example, was released in America in January 1956 but didn't make the UK charts until May. Elvis Presley's 'I Feel So Bad' was released in May 1961 but only appeared in the UK in September. But Liverpool journalist Spencer Leigh did extensive research into the subject and found that he couldn't confirm an instance of a Merseybeat group playing a song ahead of its UK release. At the same time he found that Liverpool stores stocked imports anyway.

The term "beat music", so important to the naming of the Beatles in the summer of 1960, appears to have been coined to describe music that combined elements of rock 'n' roll and pop. The first mention in the British national press was in June 1958 when the TV producer Jack Good announced to the *Daily Mirror* that his new live show *Oh Boy!* would feature "beat music". In September 1958 the producer of the rival BBC show *6.5 Special* saw "beat music" as the prevailing trend. By 1959 it was so common that in the programme of a concert at the Royal Albert Hall featuring Billy Fury and Duffy Power, the Duke of Edinburgh was quoted as saying the show featured "some of the finest examples of 'beat music'."

The UK charts of late 1962 and early 1963 show the type of sound that the Beatles would have considered commercial at the time that they began recording and writing in earnest. Their goal at the time, it needs to be remembered, was not to be progressive or speak on behalf of a generation but simply to come up with songs that would make the charts. As much as they loved the sound of early rock 'n' roll they knew that by 1962 this was considered dated in chart terms. Yet no single musical style predominated. There were dance tracks by Chubby Checker, Little Eva and Chris Montez, mock Buddy Holly songs by Adam Faith and Tommy Roe, novelty songs by Bernard Cribbens and Mike Sarne, Brill Building songs by Carole King and Neil Sedaka and even some contributions by Elvis who was now in the movie-making phase of his career. The music press constantly speculated on what the "new sound" would be – country or ballads, salsa or jazz?

Noticeably in the six months before the Beatles recorded their first LP there were only seven groups who appeared in the UK charts – from America, the Crickets, the Crystals, and the Four Seasons; from Britain, Joe Brown and the Bruvvers, the Shadows (with and without Cliff Richard), the instrumental Tornadoes (produced by Joe Meek), and the folk influenced Springfields, featuring Dusty Springfield. When the Beatles first appeared on BBC radio they sounded to many like another novelty act. When pictures of them in their suits and suede shoes were published the suspicion seemed to be confirmed.

Their training process as composers, as has already been said, was the way in which they learned songs to cover. By stripping the songs down to chords and deciphering the lyrics from repeated plays they were able to see the basic building materials of a hit single. All they needed to do was to learn how to reassemble them in a different and unique way. This was how elements of songs they loved – like the bass line of a Chuck Berry track or the phrasing of a Roy Orbison hit – would be incorporated into their own work without appearing to be stolen. It's a testament to their progress as writers that very few of the songs that they'd written over the years were considered to be good enough by the time they came to record. "There's nothing wrong with pinching ideas from other people," Paul said in 1966. "Everybody does it – Handel did it – but most people aren't as honest as Handel or us. It's the same thing as abstract art. Anybody can throw paint on canvas just like anybody can pinch bits from other songs, but not everybody can get the same result. You don't just stick it together. We go into the studio with a song, play it over and talk about what other groups it sounds like. Then we see how we want to do it, and we end up with our interpretation of their style."

Although they naturally drew on their own experiences as they wrote lyrics they did not at this time feel any compulsion to reveal their hidden selves, write words that could be judged as poetry or compose messages for alienated youth. Their key concern was to emulate those songs that had proved their worth by becoming hits. They stuck to conventional subject matter, used variations of phrases that had worked in past pop songs and deliberately targeted the emotions of their young female followers. The words of a song were deemed to "work" not simply because of what they said but because of the pleasing and appropriate sounds they made when sung. Words had to contain their own music.

Their debut album was recorded in three sessions at EMI's Abbey Road studios in London with George Martin producing. They needed only ten songs because in the manner of all albums at the time the A- and B-sides of the first two singles ('Love Me Do'/'P.S. I Love You' and 'Please Please Me'/'Ask Me Why') would be automatically included. The singles had been recorded on September 11 and November 26. Both had appeared in the UK charts.

February 11, 1963, the day of the album session, was cold. The London streets were full of snow and water pipes were freezing after Britain's most severe winter since 1947. John had a terrible cold and only survived the session through a combination of throat sweets, tea and cigarettes. It was the same day that the American poet Sylvia Plath killed herself in a house that was just less than two miles from Abbey Road. She put her head in a gas oven in the early hours while her children were asleep.

Five of the songs they intended recording were self-written and six were cover versions. The covers were 'Anna (Go To Him)' (1962) by Arthur Alexander, 'Boys' (1960) and 'Baby It's You' (1961) recorded by the Shirelles, 'Chains' (1962) recorded by the Cookies, 'A Taste Of Honey' (1962) which was the theme song from the musical version of a popular play, and the Isley Brothers' 'Twist And Shout' (1962). Of the five songs written by John and Paul one of them, 'Hold Me Tight', was held over until the next album.

It was released on March 22, 1963 and reached the top spot in the British charts. In America it was titled *Introducing The Beatles*, and released on the small Vee Jay label in Gary, Indiana. Vee Jay was better known for producing blues artists like Jimmy Reed, Memphis Slim and John Lee Hooker but had enjoyed success with its first white act, the Four Seasons, and had established a deal with EMI with an eye to breaking the Australian singer Frank Ifield ('I Remember You') in the States. The US version of the album didn't include 'Please Please Me' or 'Ask Me Why', and didn't make the charts on its initial release.

I SAW HER STANDING THERE

George Martin's first idea had been to tape one of the Beatles' shows at the Cavern Club in Liverpool, but it was eventually decided to get the group to play their live show in the studio and cut the album in a day.

'I Saw Her Standing There' was the perfect song with which to open the first album because it set the group firmly in its context of sweaty ballrooms, teenage girls and dancing. They decided to splice the 1-2-3-4 "intro" from the ninth take into the "perfect" first take to preserve the sense of immediacy and live performance. To some teenage ears in America, Paul's Liverpudlian pronunciation of the "four" sounded like another four letter word beginning with "f" and therefore provided some playground amusement.

Still titled 'Seventeen' when they made the recording, the song tells the simple story of a boy who sees a girl dancing at the local ballroom and, after deciding that her looks are "way beyond compare", determines that henceforward he will dance with no other. There's a realistic mixture of youthful arrogance and insecurity as the story unfolds, for there is no hint that the boy has considered the possibility of rejection and yet, in that unforgettable beat group rhyme, we're told that as he "crossed the room" his heart "went boom".

Paul started composing this song one night in 1962 while driving back to his home in Allerton, Liverpool. He liked the idea of writing about a 17-year-old girl because he was conscious of the need to have songs that the group's largely female audience could easily relate to. "I didn't think a lot about it as I sang it to myself," he said four years later. "Originally the first two lines were 'She was just seventeen, Never been a beauty queen'. It sounded like a good rhyme to me at the time. But when I played it through to John the next day, I realized that it was a useless line and so did John. So we both sat down and tried to come up with another line which rhymed with 17 but which meant something." After a while, John suggested "you know what I mean", which as Paul recognized, could be seen as a verbal tic or as sexual innuendo. (In 1969 Monty Python would record a sketch about innuendo best known as 'Nudge Nudge', in which Eric Idle repeatedly uses 'Nudge nudge, wink wink' and 'Know what I mean' in a pub conversation with a businessman played by Terry Jones.)

The girl's age could have been a poetic choice being the only teen number with three syllables or it could have been a knowing reference to the fact that she was safely over the UK age of sexual consent (16). In a TV interview in 1968 Paul used the song as an example of how words once casually written could later be analyzed for deeper meaning. "We'd say 'she was just seventeen' and they'd read everything into that. You know, 'she was a seventeen-year-old nymphomaniac working the streets off Broadway' whereas we meant 'she was just seventeen.' But it might mean all the other as well. I don't know!"

The two boys completed the melody on their acoustic guitars and wrote the lyrics in a Liverpool Institute exercise book. Paul later explained in an interview with *Beat Instrumental* that the bass riff was stolen from Chuck Berry's 1961 song 'I'm Talking About You' (most likely played on this recording by the great Willie Dixon, who was a star in his own right). "I played exactly the same notes as he did and it fitted our number perfectly," he confessed. "Even now, when I tell people about it, I find few of them believe me. Therefore, I maintain that a bass riff doesn't have to be original."

The theme of the song could well have been inspired by another Chuck Berry number, 'Little Queenie', in which Berry sees a girl who's "not a minute

[1,2,3,4!]

Well, she was just 17
You know what I mean
And the way she looked was way
  beyond compare
So how could I dance with another (Ooh)
When I saw her standing there

Well she looked at me, and I, I could see
That before too long I'd fall in love with her
She wouldn't dance with another (Whoo)
When I saw her standing there

Well, my heart went "boom"
When I crossed that room
And I held her hand in mine
Whoah, we danced through the night
And we held each other tight
And before too long I fell in love with her
Now I'll never dance with another (Whoo)
Since I saw her standing there

Well, my heart went "boom"
When I crossed that room
And I held her hand in mine
Well, we danced through the night
And we held each other tight
And before too long I fell in love with her
Now I'll never dance with another (Whoo)
Since I saw her standing there

I SAW HER STANDING THERE

over seventeen" standing by a "record machine" looking like a model "on the cover of a magazine". He wants to dance with her and as he sees her coming towards him he gets lumps in his throat and "wiggles in my knees." The similarities in both situation and language seem too close to be accidental, especially as it was a song that Paul performed with the Beatles.

At the time of writing 'I Saw Her Standing There', Paul was dating Iris Caldwell, sister of local beat singer Rory Storm, whose group the Hurricanes featured Ringo Starr as drummer (he joined the Beatles in August 1962). Just like the girl in the song, Iris was only 17 at the time when Paul saw her performing the twist at the Tower Ballroom in New Brighton (situated 25 minutes out of Liverpool) as part of a dance trio called the Original King Twisters. Paul was apparently impressed by her legs (she was wearing fishnet stockings) and the fact that she was already a show business professional.

Paul became a frequent guest at the Caldwell family home at 54 Broad Green Road, Liverpool 15, which, because of Rory, became known as 'Hurricaneville'. He became close to Iris' mother, Violet, and would often drop in with John to sit around and write songs. "Paul and I dated for a couple of years," says Iris. "It was never that serious. We never pretended to be true to each other. I went out with lots of people. I was working away in different theatres at the time but if I came back home then we would go out. There were never any promises made or love declared." According to Iris, Paul intended giving 'I Saw Her Standing There' to Rory to record. "He thought it would be a good song for him but it wasn't dealt out that way. Brian Epstein didn't want Rory to have it."

'I Saw Her Standing There' became part of the Beatles' stage repertoire in 1962. It's one of only two Lennon-McCartney songs recorded at the Star Club in Hamburg during December 1962 (the other being 'Ask Me Why') and was included on Live At The Star Club which tellingly included covers of Chuck Berry's 'Talking About You' and 'Little Queenie'. The first cover version of the song was by English rock 'n' roll singer Duffy Power in 1963. In America, it became the B-side of 'I Want To Hold Your Hand', the single released in January 1964 that became the Beatles' first US Number 1. It was one of five songs the Beatles performed on the celebrated *Ed Sullivan Show* of February 9, 1964, which was watched by 70 million people, then the largest US TV audience for a single programme. In November 1974, John performed the song with Elton John at Madison Square Garden.

Written: Lennon/McCartney

Length: *2'55"*

UK Release: *Please Please Me* album, March 22, 1963

US Release: December 26, 1963, as a B-side of 'I Want To Hold Your Hand'

MISERY

Having a British Top 20 hit with 'Love Me Do' was a terrific boost to the confidence of the McCartney-Lennon team (as they were initially credited) but the prospect of a 14-track LP would have seemed quite daunting in view of the fact that few of the songs they'd written to date were, in their eyes, up to scratch. The pressure was now on for them to write a string of potential hits.

Although not all the album's songs were going to be their own compositions they wanted to assert themselves as being much more than a cover band. In early 1963 this was a far from normal move for a British act. Terry Dene, Billy Fury, Tommy Steele, Marty Wilde and Adam Faith had all recorded songs written by professional "Tin Pan Alley" writers and tried to affect an American look and sound. Often they covered singles that had just become hits in America. Cliff Richard, Britain's top pop star at the

time that the Beatles began recording, and a fellow EMI artist, had broken the mould in 1958 and 1959 by recording songs written by Ian Samwell, a former member of his backing group the Drifters (not to be confused with the American vocal group), and Johnny Kidd and the Pirates had been successful in 1960 with Kidd's song 'Shakin' All Over'.

It was in this climate that Paul and John began to complete new material. Backstage at the King's Hall in Glebe Street, Stoke-on-Trent, where they were playing on January 26, 1963, they huddled together in a dressing room and wrote 'Misery', with John as the instigator and major contributor. Paul's first song on the record was the boast of a breezy optimist who knows he's going to get his girl, John's is the soul baring pain of someone who knows he's going to lose the girl and be left sad and lonely. "The world is treating me bad" was the song's portentous first line. "Allan Clarke and Graham Nash of the Hollies helped on that song," remembers Tony Bramwell, then an employee of Brian Epstein. "John and Paul were desperate to get it finished and got stuck on one of the lines and Allan and Graham began throwing in suggestions. The boys wanted to get it ready for Helen Shapiro."

Although only 16 at the time, Helen Shapiro had had five hit singles in Britain since early 1961. She was on another EMI label, Columbia, which was run by Norrie Paramor (producer for Cliff Richard) and was booked to make an album in Nashville on February 18. Before that she was due to headline the first leg of a British tour with the Kestrels, the Honeys, Danny Williams, the Red Price Band, Dave Allen, Kenny Lynch, and the Beatles as support acts. It was probably the knowledge that they would soon be touring with her and that she was, in the jargon of the time, a "hit-maker" that made her their obvious first choice. "We've called it 'Misery' but it isn't quite as slow as it sounds," Paul told *New Musical Express* reporter Alan Smith. "It moves along at quite a steady pace and we think Helen Shapiro will make quite a good job of it."

ABOVE: The Beatles with Helen Shapiro (to the left of Ringo), who was offered the Lennon-McCartney song 'Misery'.

Written: Lennon/McCartney

Length: 1'50"

UK Release: *Please Please Me* album, March 22, 1963

US Release: *Introducing The Beatles* album, July 22, 1963

"I got on great with them," remembers Helen, "and John was like a brother to me. Very protective." What's not clear is in what way the song was offered to her and why (or, whether) she personally turned it down. From what she remembers the song was demoed and sent to her A&R manager but wasn't played to her. "John and Paul certainly offered 'Misery' to me first, through Norrie, but I didn't know anything about it until I met them on the first day of the tour (February 2, Bradford, Yorks). Apparently he'd turned it down even though I hadn't heard it."

Kenny Lynch, who accepted the song to record, becoming the first artist other than the Beatles to cover a Lennon-McCartney number, remembers events differently. He says that he was recording an LP himself at the time of the tour and would come down to a London studio on his days off. "One day John and Paul called Helen up to the back of the coach and they played her 'Misery'," he says. "She listened to it and said, 'I don't like it. It's too much of a man's song.' So I said, 'I like it. I've got a free session when I go back on Tuesday. I'll do it for you.'"

Lynch had a Top 20 hit at the time with a cover of the Goffin-King song 'Up On The Roof' (a chart success in America for the Drifters), so his offer was not to be sniffed at. "I did it and brought it back on the tour," he says. "I played it to John first and he said he didn't like the guitar playing which was by Bert Weedon. He said that if I'd have asked him he'd have come and played guitar for me. He thought Bert sounded too much like Hank Marvin of the Shadows. So I got 'Misery' because Helen didn't like it and I didn't have all the songs together for my album!"

The lyric of Lynch's recording differs slightly from that released by the Beatles. Instead of "the world is treating me bad" he opens with "you've been treating me bad" and continues to use the second person singular where the Beatles used the third person. It could have been Lynch taking liberties with someone else's text in the studio but actually he was singing what was on the original sheet music supplied by Northern Songs. John must have developed the song while on the road or made last-minute changes while recording. The fact is that "The world is treating me bad" sounds more ominous than "You've been treating me bad". It verges on paranoia. It was a theme that John would return to.

Paul later described the song as he and John's "first stab at a ballad," and, as such, an exercise in song writing. In a 2000 interview he recalled that the main innovation was the half-spoken intro or "pre-verse" that is actually a synopsis of the main content of the song. "If you look at our early songs there's a lot of these little intros," he said. "We could never sustain them like the old fellows who did it but we'd do these little prelude things and then finally get to the main songs."

John used it later in 'Do You Want To Know A Secret,' 'I'm A Loser' and 'Nowhere Man' and Paul used it in 'P.S. I Love You' and 'Here, There And Everywhere'. They may have been inspired by recent songs like Dion's 'Runaround Sue' ("Here's my story, sad but true…"), Bobby Vee's 'Take Good Care of My Baby' ("My tears are falling 'cos you've taken her away…") or even Johnny Tillotson's 'Poetry in Motion' ("When I see my baby, what do I see…."). Or they may simply have noted that Helen Shapiro's biggest hit 'Walking Back To Happiness' began with a scene setting pre-verse ("Funny but it's true/ What loneliness can do/ Since I've been away/ I've loved you more each day…')

MISERY

The world is treating me bad, misery

I'm the kind of guy
Who never used to cry
The world is treating me bad, misery

I've lost her now for sure
I won't see her no more
It's gonna be a drag, misery

I'll remember all the little things
  we've done
Can't she see she'll always be
  the only one, only one

Send her back to me
Cos everyone can see
Without her I will be in misery

I'll remember all the little things
  we've done
She'll remember and she'll miss
  her only one, lonely one
Send her back to me

Cos everyone can see
Without her I will be in misery (Oh oh oh)
In misery
(Ooh ee ooh ooh)
My misery
(La la la la la la)

The Beatles at the time of their early UK hit singles.

The Beatles at the time of their early UK hit singles.

ASK ME WHY

Written in the spring of 1962, with John as the major contributor, 'Ask Me Why' was a lyrically lightweight love song belying a musically complex structure that experimented with syncopation and jazz influenced chords. There's no obvious model for the song although John's vocal delivery shares similarities with that of Smokey Robinson and the intro is almost certainly based on the guitar intro to the Miracles' 1961 track 'What's So Good About Goodbye.' As soon as it was written it was incorporated into their set, and was the first Lennon-McCartney song ever to be broadcast on radio when they performed it on a BBC programme called *Teenagers' Turn* on June 11, 1962. It was part of the set they took to Hamburg in December 1962 and features on the album *Live At The Star Club*.

It was clearly a composition they were very proud of because it was one of only three self-written songs that they took with them to their first EMI recording session on June 6, 1962 (the others being 'Love Me Do' and 'P.S. I Love You'). George Martin didn't think that it was strong enough to be the group's debut single and so it was eliminated at an early stage. The only other contender at this point was 'Tip Of My Tongue', a song that Martin didn't like, and which would end up being covered by another act managed by Brian Epstein, Tommy Quickly. However, when it came time to record 'Please Please Me' on November 26, the group tackled it again in another six takes. After being re-recorded for the album, it became the B-side of 'Please Please Me' in the UK.

PLEASE PLEASE ME

Written: Lennon/McCartney

Length: 2'27"

UK Single Release: January 11, 1963 as B-side of 'Please Please Me'

US Single Release: February 25, 1963 as B-side of 'Please Please Me'

I love you, 'cause you tell me things
 I want to know
And it's true that it really only goes
 to show
That I know that I, I, I, I
Should never, never, never be blue

Now you're mine, my happiness still
 makes me cry
And in time, you'll understand the
 reason why
If I cry, it's not because I'm sad
But you're the only love that I've
 ever had

I can't believe it's happened to me
I can't conceive of any more misery

Ask me why, I'll say I love you
And I'm always thinking of you

I love you, 'cause you tell me things
 I want to know
And it's true that it really only go
 to show
That I know that I, I, I, I
Should never, never, never be blue

Ask me why, I'll say I love you
And I'm always thinking of you

I can't believe it's happened to me
I can't conceive of any more misery

Ask me why, I'll say I love you
And I'm always thinking of you
You, you

PLEASE PLEASE ME

'Please Please Me' was one of those innocent-sounding pop songs with a possibly subversive subtext, some critics regarding it as a thinly veiled plea for orgasmic equality – please pleasure me as I have pleasured you, as they may have sung in the 16th century. Robert Christgau, one-time music editor of New York's *Village Voice*, made the more specific claim that it was about oral sex.

Iris Caldwell remembers Paul coming over to her house one night and reading her the words to the just-completed song. "He used to pick up my brother's guitar and play it but that night he didn't bother," she says. "He just read out the lyrics. They didn't seem to make any sense to me at the time and I thought they were absolutely awful." The song's origins were certainly innocuous, as the chorus was suggested by the 1932 Bing Crosby song 'Please', written by Leo Robin and Ralph Rainger, which starts off by playing with the homophones 'pleas' and 'please': "Oh please, lend your little ear to my pleas, Lend a ray of cheer to my pleas, Tell me that you love me too". Later, John recalled his mother, Julia, singing this to him as a child, adding that he'd always been fascinated by the homophone 'plez.'

When he came to write this song, in his front bedroom at 251 Menlove Avenue in Liverpool ("I remember the day and the pink eyelet on the bed"), John imagined the voice of Roy Orbison, as he'd recently heard the hit single 'Only The Lonely'. It's easy to imagine Orbison singing the original slow version of 'Please Please Me'. With his pallid, dough-like complexion and permanent shades, Orbison might have looked an unlikely pop star, but he was a brilliantly soulful singer who wrote his own songs and constantly challenged the formal verse-chorus-verse construction. He was someone whom John in particular would have connected with because his lyrics explored feelings of loss and loneliness. The "rain in my heart" is an obvious reference to Buddy Holly's 1959 single 'Raining In My Heart', which was written by Felice and Boudleaux Bryant.

Within months of 'Please Please Me' being released as a single (On January 11, 1963 in the UK), the Beatles were selected to be one of Orbison's support acts on a three-week tour of Britain. "We never talked to each other about song writing on that tour," remembered Orbison years later. "The basic thing they wanted to know at that time was how I thought they would get on in America. I told them to let people know they were British and to get on something like the *Ed Sullivan Show*. If they did that, I said they could be just as big in America as they were in Britain. I said that in an article for *New Musical Express* that came out during the tour. I thought it was important that they let people know they were British because we hadn't heard much from Britain except for the Blue Streak missile and the Profumo scandal."

His exact words, reported in May 1963, were: "The Beatles could well be tops in America. These boys have enough originality to storm our charts with the same effect as they have done here, but it will need careful handling. They have something that is entirely new even to us Americans and although we have an influx of hit groups at home I really do believe they could top the charts...It's a change to see new stars who are not just watered-down versions of Elvis Presley. This seems to be a sound they have made famous all on their own and I really think it is the greatest. Though you know it as Merseyside music, I am sure this will be hailed as the new British sound in America."

Orbison didn't know that he'd inspired 'Please Please Me' until producer George Martin told him in June 1987 at an Abbey Road celebration for the 20th anniversary of *Sgt. Pepper's Lonely Hearts Club Band*. "He told me that

Last night I said these words to my girl
I know you never even try girl
C'mon (C'mon), c'mon (C'mon),
c'mon (C'mon), c'mon (C'mon)
Please please me, whoa yeah,
Like I please you

You don't need me to show the way, love
Why do I always have to say "love"
C'mon (C'mon), c'mon (C'mon),
c'mon (C'mon), c'mon (C'mon)
Please please me, whoa yeah,
Like I please you

I don't wanna sound complaining
But you know there's always rain
 in my heart (In my heart)
I do all the pleasing with you,
It's so hard to reason
With you, whoah yeah,
Why do you make me blue

Last night I said these words to my girl
I know you never even try, girl
C'mon (C'mon), c'mon (C'mon),
c'mon (C'mon), c'mon (C'mon)
Please please me, whoa yeah,
Like I please you
(Me) Whoa yeah, like I please you
(Me) Whoa yeah, like I please you

it sounded so much like me that they had to change it a little bit," Orbison commented. "That's a nice thing to find out."

In March 1963 John revealed that the Beatles had intended 'Please Please Me' as a B-side for their first single until Martin criticized it. "He thought that the arrangement was fussy, so we tried to make it simpler," said John. "In the weeks following [the 'Love Me Do' session], we went over it again and again. We changed the tempo a little. We altered the words slightly and we went over the idea of featuring the harmonica, just as we'd done in 'Love Me Do'. By the time we came to record it, we were so happy with it that we couldn't wait to get it down."

John told Alan Smith of *NME*, "I tried to make it as simple as possible. Some of the stuff I've written has been a bit way out, but we did this one strictly for the hit parade. Now we're keeping our fingers crossed."

On November 26 they recorded 18 takes of the newly improved song at Abbey Road. Martin recalled that the session "was a joy." After the final take he spoke through the intercom in the control room and said, "Gentlemen, you've just made your first Number 1 record." His judgement was spot on. The single made the top spot in the chart of *New Musical Express* and *Melody Maker* and was second in the one published by *Record Mirror*. Its first American release on the VeeJay label had no impact but the re-release a year later went to Number 3 in the *Billboard Hot 100*.

The Beatles' fondness for Orbison was to survive the Sixties. John once described what was to be his final single, 'Starting Over', as "Elvis Orbison" and in 1988 George Harrison joined Orbison, Bob Dylan, Tom Petty and Jeff Lynne in recording the critically acclaimed *Traveling Wilburys* album.

ABOVE: The style of 'Please Please Me' was influenced by Roy Orbison, who the Beatles toured with in 1963.

Written: Lennon/McCartney

Length: 2'03"

UK Single Release: January 11, 1963

UK Chart Position: 2

US Single Release: February 25, 1963

US Chart Position: 3

LOVE ME DO

An early song written by Paul, the lyrics of 'Love Me Do' were as basic as could be, with most words consisting of only one syllable and "love" being repeated 21 times. "I'll love you forever so please love me" was the song's entire message.

What set it apart from the teen love songs of the time was a gospel-blues tinge to the singing – a feeling that was heightened by John's harmonica and the slightly mournful close harmonizing. (John listed R&B and gospel as his "tastes in music" in the *NME* of February 15, 1963).

During 1962, American star Bruce Channel had enjoyed a British hit with 'Hey Baby', a recording that featured a harmonica solo by Nashville session musician Delbert McClinton. John, who'd been given his first mouth organ as a boy, was impressed by this and when he met McClinton in June 1962 at the Tower Ballroom, New Brighton, where the Beatles were playing support for Channel, he asked him to demonstrate his technique. "John was very interested in harmonica and, when we went on to play another couple of dates with the Beatles, he and I hung out a lot together," says McClinton. "He wanted me to show him whatever I could. He wanted to know how to play. Before our time together was over he had his own harmonica ready in his pocket." It was only three months later that the Beatles recorded 'Love Me Do', in which John was able to include a distinctive harmonica break.

John went on to play harmonica on the next two singles, 'Please Please Me' and 'With Love From Me To You', as well as on six other tracks including 'Little Child' (With The Beatles) and 'I Should Have Known Better' (A Hard Day's Night). The last time he used it on record was on 'I'm A Loser' (Beatles For Sale) recorded in August 1964. By that time he reckoned it had turned into a Beatles' gimmick.

'Love Me Do' was included on the group's first four-track extended play record which had sleeve notes written by Tony Barrow, a Lancashire journalist who was then working as the Beatles' press officer. Barrow's comments on the four tracks ('From Me To You', 'Thank You Girl', 'Please Please Me' and 'Love Me Do') were remarkably prescient. "The four numbers on this EP have been selected from *The Lennon And McCartney Songbook*," he wrote. "If that description sounds a trifle pompous perhaps I may suggest you preserve this sleeve for ten years, exhume it from your collection somewhere around the middle of 1973 and write me a very nasty letter if the pop people of the Seventies aren't talking about at least two of these titles as 'early examples of modern beat standards taken from *The Lennon And McCartney Songbook*'."

In 1967, when every Beatle song was believed to be drenched in meaning and they had been elevated into "spokesmen for a generation", Paul commented to the illustrator Alan Aldridge in an interview for the *Observer* magazine "'Love Me Do' was our greatest philosophical song... for it to be simple, and true, means that it's incredibly simple."

Love, love me do
You know I love you
I'll always be true
So please, love me do
Whoa, love me do

Love, love me do
You know I love you
I'll always be true
So please, love me do
Whoa, love me do

Someone to love
Somebody new
Someone to love
Someone like you

Love, love me do
You know I love you
I'll always be true
So please, love me do
Whoa, love me do

Love, love me do
You know I love you
I'll always be true
So please, love me do
Whoa, love me do
Yeah, love me do
Whoa, oh, love me do

Written: Lennon/McCartney

Length: 2'22"

UK Single Release: October 5, 1962

UK Chart Position: 4

US Single Release: April 27, 1964

US Chart Position: 1

P.S. I LOVE YOU

Written in 1961, 'P.S. I Love You' was another early song by Paul that had been short-listed as a potential first single. In Britain, it became the B-side of 'Love Me Do'. In America, almost two years later, it became a single in its own right and made the Top 10.

There was an appetite for British rock groups in Hamburg nightclubs and German promoters and club owners would regularly visit England to scout for new talent. There was a great demand for the new American-style music in Germany but few local musicians who could make it sound authentic. In April 1961, the Beatles – John, Paul, George, Pete Best (drums) and Stuart Sutcliffe (bass) – started a gruelling 13-week residency at the Top Ten Club in Hamburg playing for over five hours, seven nights a week. It was the best apprenticeship they could have had. It gave them a deep understanding of the music they'd inherited and it taught them how to work an audience. The clientele in this port's red light district was older than the teenagers they'd been used to playing to in Liverpool and harder to please.

Paul's main girlfriend at the time was Dorothy "Dot" Rhone, an elfin Liverpool teenager who worked for a chemist and lived at home with her parents. She was a shy but sweet girl who had become a regular guest at his family home in Allerton. "She was very much in love with Paul," remembered her friend Sandra Hedges. "He in turn would jealously guard her by placing her amid the group while they were playing." Dot became close to John's art school girlfriend Cynthia Powell, and during the Easter holidays the two girls joined their boyfriends in Germany, Cynthia staying with Astrid Kirchherr, Stuart Sutcliffe's girlfriend, and Dot staying with Paul on a houseboat.

After Dot returned home, Paul wrote this song that she assumed was for

Written: Lennon/McCartney

Length: 2'05"

UK Single Release: October 5, 1962 as B-side of 'Love Me Do'

US Single Release: April 27, 1964 as B-side of 'Love Me Do'

ABOVE: George and the rest of the Beatles, whose line-up still included Pete Best and Stuart Sutcliffe, played a tough 13-week residency in Hamburg in 1961.

her – although, years later, Paul denied that he had had anyone specific in mind. Written in the form of a letter, 'P.S. I Love You' was the precursor of Paul's other letter songs, 'Paperback Writer' and 'When I'm 64'. ('From Me To You' and 'All My Loving' could also be considered as letter songs but they have no formal salutation or valediction.)

It's likely that Paul was aware that there was a song of the same name that had been written in 1934 by Gordon Jenkins (music) and Johnny Mercer (lyrics), and recorded that year by Rudy Vallee. If he didn't know the original he's likely to have heard the celebrated version by Billie Holiday released in 1954. John later claimed that Paul was trying to write his version of 'Soldier Boy', a song written by Luther Dixon and Florence Greenberg for the Shirelles which the Beatles played. When 'P.S. I Love You' was written, letter songs were in vogue with Elvis Presley's 'Return To Sender' and Brian Hyland's 'Sealed With A Kiss.'

Paul's relationship with Dot carried on after Hamburg but ended in the summer of 1962 just as the Beatles began recording. At the time, she was sharing a flat with Cynthia at 93 Garmoyle Road, Liverpool, close to Penny Lane. Paul broke the news to Dot late one night. Cynthia remembered her collapsing in tears. "Poor little defenceless Dot," she wrote in her book *A Twist Of Lennon*. "She wouldn't hurt a fly but had been hurt so much that she couldn't even tell me without renewed convulsions and outbursts of uncontrollable crying. As it happens, she didn't need to tell me anything. Only one thing would have done that to Dot and that was Paul giving her the push... he was too young to settle down. He wanted desperately to be footloose and fancy free and I suppose he let Dot down very gently under the circumstances."

As I write this letter
Send my love to you
Remember that I'll always
Be in love with you

Treasure these few words till we're together
Keep all my love forever
PS I love you
You, you, you

As I write this letter
Send my love to you
Remember that I'll always
Be in love with you

Treasure these few words till we're together
Keep all my love forever
PS I love you
You, you, you

I'll be coming home again to you, love
And till the day I do, love
PS I love you
You, you, you

As I write this letter
Send my love to you
Remember that I'll always
Be in love with you

Treasure these few words till we're together
Keep all my love forever
PS I love you
You, you, you

As I write this letter (Oh)
Send my love to you (You know I
   want you to)
Remember that I'll always (Yeah)
Be in love with you

I'll be coming home again to you, love
And till the day I do, love
PS I love you
You, you, you
You, you, you
I love you

P.S.
I LOVE
YOU

DO YOU WANT TO KNOW A SECRET

Around the time that Paul finished with Dot Rhone, Cynthia discovered that she was pregnant. As a result, she and John married at Mount Pleasant registry office in Liverpool on August 23, 1962. It was a small affair attended only by Paul, George, and a handful of relations. The best man was manager Brian Epstein, who offered the newlyweds the use of a ground floor flat he rented at 36 Faulkner Street. This wasn't his main home, but a place he kept for his homosexual liaisons.

Cynthia was delighted with the unexpected wedding gift, as the couple had given little thought to where they would live after marrying and there was no time in the busy Beatles' schedule for a honeymoon. "It was the first apartment I'd ever had that wasn't shared by 14 other art students," John later admitted.

It was while living here that John wrote 'Do You Want To Know A Secret', the secret in question being that he had just realized that he was truly in love. It had its genesis in a song from Walt Disney's 1937 film *Snow White And The Seven Dwarfs* which his mother Julia used to sing to him. In one of the scenes that opens the film, Snow White is working as a humble scullery maid in her late father's castle and, as she stands by the well, she sings to the doves: "Wanna know a secret? Promise not to tell? We are standing by a wishing well." (The song is 'I'm Wishing', words and music by Larry Morey and Frank Churchill).

In an interview with *Musician* magazine, George Harrison revealed that the musical inspiration for the song came from 'I Really Love You', a 1961 hit for the Stereos, a doo-wop group from Ohio. This could have been suggested by John or have been imported by George who liked the Stereos' song enough to record it on his 1982 album Gone Troppo.

John made a demo of 'Do You Want To Know A Secret' on an acoustic guitar while sitting in a bathroom (the flush of a toilet could be heard at the end of this recording). The finished song was offered to another artist managed by Brian Epstein, Billy J Kramer, who used it on a tour of Germany and Britain. Kramer's real name was Billy Ashton, and he was Epstein's third signing after the Beatles and Gerry and the Pacemakers. Epstein then acquired the Big Three, the Fourmost, Tommy Quickly, and Cilla Black – all of them from Liverpool.

Kramer's experience performing the song in Britain and Germany wasn't positive. The song didn't excite audiences. "Everybody hated it," he said. However, EMI liked his demo of it enough to offer him a recording contract. George Martin produced the single with the Dakotas backing Kramer. The B-side, 'I'll Be On My Way,' was written by Paul. Kramer's version, released a month after it appeared on the *Please Please Me* LP, went on to become a Number 2 hit in Britain; the first time a Lennon-McCartney song by another artist had made the hit parade.

As recorded by the Beatles it was also the first time a Beatle other than Paul or John had taken the lead vocal on a Lennon-McCartney song. "I thought it would be a good vehicle for him [George]," John said, "because it only had three notes and he wasn't the best singer in the world."

Written: Lennon/McCartney

Length: 1'59"

UK Single Release: *Please Please Me* album, March 22, 1963

US Single Release: *Introducing The Beatles* album, July 22 , 1963

You'll never know how much I really love you
You'll never know how much I really care

Listen
Do you want to know a secret
Do you promise not to tell, whoa oh, oh

Closer
Let me whisper in your ear
Say the words you long to hear
I'm in love with you

Listen
Do you want to know a secret
Do you promise not to tell, whoa oh, oh

Closer
Let me whisper in your ear
Say the words you long to hear
I'm in love with you

I've known the secret for a week or two
Nobody knows, just we two

Listen
Do you want to know a secret
Do you promise not to tell, whoa oh, oh

Closer
Let me whisper in your ear
Say the words you long to hear

I'm in love with you

DO YOU WANT TO KNOW A SECRET

RIGHT ABOVE: Billy J Kramer, behind Ringo and George, recorded 'Do You Want To Know a Secret' and had a British hit with it.

RIGHT BELOW: Brian Epstein (centre) ensured that other artists he managed benefitted from the Beatles' songs.

Written: Lennon/McCartney

Length: 1'52"

UK Single Release: *Please Please Me* album, March 22, 1963

US Single Release: *Introducing The Beatles* album, July 22 , 1963

THERE'S A PLACE

There is a place
Where I can go
When I feel low
When I feel blue
And it's my mind
And there's no time when I'm alone

I think of you
And things you do
Go 'round my head
The things you said
Like "I love only you"

In my mind there's no sorrow
Don't you know that it's so
There'll be no sad tomorrow
Don't you know that it's so

There is a place
Where I can go
When I feel low
When I feel blue
And it's my mind
And there's no time when I'm alone

There's a place
There's a place
There's a place
There's a place

OPPOSITE: Astrid Kirchherr's 1961 portrait of John captures his strength as well as his vulnerability.

THERE'S A PLACE

Just as 'Misery' introduced themes of isolation and rejection that would become so significant in John's songs, 'There's A Place' raised the connected theme of escaping into his thought world, dreams and memories. The song also hints at an idea that was to become more central to his work as the decade progressed – the desirability of an altered state of consciousness; the power of the mind to control what is deemed "real". In 'There's A Place', John deals with sorrow by retreating into his mind and, in a more sophisticated way, this thought characterized later songs such as 'Strawberry Fields Forever', 'Girl', 'In My Life', 'Rain', 'I'm Only Sleeping', 'Tomorrow Never Knows' and so many others. "The usual Lennon thing," he would comment with reference to 'There's A Place'. "It's all in your mind."

"He was a combination of introversion and extroversion," says Thelma McGough, who as Thelma Pickles dated John while they were both at Liverpool School of Art. "He appeared very extrovert and yet it was all front. He was actually very deep but he'd keep that pretty well hidden until you were on your own with him."

Although John later spoke as though the song was entirely his creation, Paul has since claimed that the original idea for it came from him, the title being derived from the *West Side Story* (1957) song 'There's A Place For Us' (music by Leonard Bernstein, lyrics by Stephen Sondheim) which he had in his Forthlin Road record collection. But whereas Sondheim looks out to the physical world to find a space free of pressure where love can grow, John retreats to his own inner world where he believes he can control what happens. For a song dashed off at a time when pop music was not a vehicle for confessional poetry it was an unusually revealing song.

Musically John claimed that 'There's A Place' was his attempt at "a sort of Motown, black thing", referring to what was then a hot new sound emerging from Detroit on Berry Gordy's fledgling independent record label. Motown hits were mostly written by production line writers and performed by groups trained in the label's own school – it was dance music driven by inventive bass lines, gospel-style shouting and harmonizing and splashes of tambourine. Among the Beatles' favourite acts were Barrett Strong, the Miracles (featuring Smokey Robinson), the Marvelettes, Marvin Gaye and "Little" Stevie Wonder.

In fact the Beatles were to play a crucial role in popularizing the Motown label, initially by recording Motown songs such as 'Please Mr Postman', 'You've Really Got A Hold On Me' and 'Money' and later by mentioning new Motown artists and records in interviews. Explaining the success of his label to *Record World* in 1964, Berry Gordy said: "It helped when we had several songs of ours recorded by the Beatles. I met them and found out that they were great fans of Motown and had been studying Motown music and they went on to become some of the greatest songwriters in history. We were absolutely delighted."

The song may have had an influence on Brian Wilson's song 'In My Room', which came out on the September 1963 album *Surfer Girl* by the Beach Boys. The opening lines are remarkably similar as is the reflection on wanting to escape from the troubles of the world. The Beach Boys and the Beatles would have a beneficial effect on each other throughout the 1960s, each pushing the other to greater heights. Wilson, the group's pained genius, shared John's melancholy but also had Paul's melodic inventiveness and an impeccable ear for harmony.

The Beatles pictured in 1963 at Abbey Road, where they recorded almost every track they released.

2 With The Beatles

The Beatles had five years to prepare for their first album and five months to prepare for their second. After years of meeting up at the McCartney home, with hours of spare time on their hands, John and Paul were now forced to write in hotel bedrooms, on tour buses and in dressing rooms – anywhere they could snatch a quiet moment together.

Such pressures cause some songwriters to freeze up, but it proved to be a positive stimulus to the Lennon and McCartney team who, as time went on, developed the ability to write Number 1 hits to order. Asked in 1963 about the writing process Paul said, "If an idea does pop into your mind, then you sit down and say, 'Let's do it.' If there are no ideas and, say, we've been told we've got a recording date in about two days time, then you have to sit down and slog it out. You normally get just a little idea that doesn't seem bad, you go on and it builds up from there. It varies every time."

Their years of playing so physically close to their audiences in Liverpool and Hamburg had given them a clear idea of who they were speaking to in their songs. Paul in particular was conscious of the public relations aspect of using personal pronouns such as 'you,' 'I' and 'your' in the songs. It made each girl listening to the song feel as though she was being addressed individually. Paul was also more likely to respond to things written to him in letters and to use them as indicators of how the fans felt.

However, if in the early days they'd been able to write for crowds they could see and for fans they knew on first name terms, everything changed after their commercial success. Now the devout followers were the other side of the footlights and the group had to be separated from overzealous fans by lines of police officers. Their entrances to and exits from hotels and concert halls had to be ingeniously planned in order to protect them. They now had fans in countries they'd yet to visit and whose languages they didn't speak.

Nevertheless even at the height of Beatlemania, often within earshot of screaming fans, they were still able to compose a string of successful singles. 'I Want To Hold Your Hand', was written with America in mind, and propelled them to the top of the *Billboard* charts, making them the first British recording artists to really conquer America, as opposed to score a handful of hits. Travel abroad and the move to London may even have stimulated their writing because it exposed them to fresh influences. People they met were eager to introduce them to new ideas. Because of his relationship with the actress Jane Asher (whose father was a medical consultant and mother a professor of music at the Guildhall School of Music), Paul was learning about musicals, plays, psychology and classical music. At the same time, John was at his Kensington flat listening to imported albums by black American groups like the Miracles, the Shirelles and the Marvelettes.

With the Beatles, their second album, was a much more considered recording than the first, with sessions spread over a three months. "We like doing stage shows because it's great to hear audiences enjoying themselves," said Paul in 1963. "But the thing we like best is going into the recording studio to make new records. What we like to hear most is one our songs taking shape and then listening to the tapes afterwards to hear how it all worked out." Telling *NME* of their work routine at Abbey Road in the same year, George said "In some cases we'd just got the general idea for a number. For instance, the middle bit might be missing. Our recording manager would pop out sometimes for a drink and we'd finish it off. When he came back we'd have added words and a bit of a tune."

It went to Number 1 in Britain shortly after its release in November 1963 and became the first pop album to sell over a million copies. A version of *With the Beatles*, titled *Meet the Beatles*, was released in America in January 1964 and also went to Number 1.

ABOVE: The Beatles with Billy J Kramer and Susan Maugham. A couple of hours later, John and Paul were in a basement club with the Rolling Stones, writing 'I Wanna be Your Man' for them.

FROM ME TO YOU

'From Me To You', the Beatles' third single, was written on February 28, 1963, while travelling by coach from York to Shrewsbury on the Helen Shapiro tour. Helen can't remember them actually writing it, but can recall the completed song being played to her when they arrived in the afternoon ready for their concert at the Granada Cinema. "They asked me if I would come and listen to two songs that they had," she says. "Paul sat at the piano and John stood next to me and they sang 'From 'Me To You' and 'Thank You Girl'. They said they sort of knew their favourite but hadn't finally decided, so they wanted me to tell them which one I thought would make the best A-side. As it happened I liked 'From Me To You' and they said, 'Great. That's the one we like.'"

The Beatles played the Odeon Cinema in Southport, Lancashire, the next day – the closest to Liverpool they would be on this tour – and here they were able to play their new song to Paul's father to get his opinion. They knew the lyrics were simple but they were worried that the music was "a bit on the complicated side" and that "it wouldn't catch on with the fans." It was Paul's dad who convinced them that it was "a nice little tune".

The title was suggested by From You To Us, the letters' column in the weekly pop newspaper *New Musical Express*. Paul and John were reading the issue dated February 22, which had their tour dates advertised on the front page and stories about Cliff Richard, Billy Fury and Elvis Presley inside. They started to "talk about one of the letters in the column", John revealed in May 1963, when asked about the origins of the song. There were only two letters and it's hard to determine which could have provoked comment. One letter complained about "maniacal laughter" on two recent limbo dance records and the other relished the fact that Cliff Richard appeared to be getting the better of Elvis Presley in the charts. Perhaps it was this last letter that fired the Beatles' own ambition.

Allegedly, John came up with the first line of the song "and after that we just took it from there." The song's vocal gimmick was the use of the high-pitched "ooooh" sound, inspired by the Isley Brothers' recording of 'Twist And Shout'. When Kenny Lynch heard them singing this on the coach, he said to them, "You can't do that. You sound like a bunch of fairies", and they replied, "It's okay, the kids will like it." In April 1963, John commented: "We were just fooling about on the guitar. This went on for a while. Then we began to get a good melody line and we really started to work at it. Before the journey was over we'd completed the lyric, everything. We were so pleased..."

A year later, again talking about how the song was written, John said: "Paul and I kicked some ideas around and came up with what we what we thought was a suitable melody line. The words weren't really all that difficult – especially as we had decided quite definitely not to do anything that was at all complicated. I suppose that is why we often had the words 'you' and 'me' in the titles of our songs. It's the sort of thing that helps the listeners to identify with the lyrics. We think this is very important. The fans like to feel that they are part of something that is being done by the performers."

From writing to recording took five days although, as John remembered, "We nearly didn't record it because we thought it was too bluesy at first, but when we'd finished it and George Martin had scored it with harmonica, it was all right." Speaking to American journalist Michael Lydon in 1966, publisher Dick James said, "'From Me To You' is a perfect Tin Pan Alley song, extremely commercial. It could have been written 30 years ago and will be listened to in another 30 years. It is simple, direct, repetitive, yet touching in an odd way. There are no frills, but it supports one idea. There is nothing special about it, but it is good a standard pop song as has ever been written."

44

FROM ME TO YOU

Da da da da da dum dum da
Da da da da da dum dum da

If there's anything that you want
If there's anything I can do
Just call on me and I'll send it along
With love, from me to you

I got everything that you want
Like a heart that's oh so true
Just call on me and I'll send it along
With love, from me to you

I got arms that long to hold you
And keep you by my side
I got lips that long to kiss you
And keep you satisfied, oooh

If there's anything that you want
If there's anything I can do
Just call on me and I'll send it along
With love, from me to you

From me, to you
Just call on me and I'll send it along
With love from me to you

I got arms that long to hold you
And keep you by my side
I got lips that long to kiss you
And keep you satisfied, oooh

If there's anything that you want
If there's anything I can do
Just call on me and I'll send it along
With love, from me to you
To you, to you, to you

RIGHT: John was on tour with Helen Shapiro when he and Paul wrote 'From Me to You'.

Written: Lennon/McCartney

Length: 1'57"

UK Single Release: April 11, 1963

UK Chart Position: 1

US Single Release: May 27,1963

US Chart Position: 1

THANK YOU GIRL

Although John and Paul claimed in the early days to have written over 100 songs together between the summer of 1957 and the summer of 1962, Paul more recently admitted that the number was probably closer to 30. Now that they were stars, they could no longer afford to compose at such a leisurely rate, as almost everything they wrote from this point on would have to aim for hit potential. Between 1963 and 1965, they released at least three singles a year and two albums, a large output for a group who were at the same time touring, filming, and meeting the press.

When the Beatles came into the industry, pop music had become formulaic and stale. The B-sides of singles tended to be throwaway songs, often written by the producer under a pseudonym in order to reap the benefits of mechanical royalties, and albums contained one or two recent hits plus a lot of filler material. The Beatles changed all this. Suddenly, every song counted. Each of their singles had a B-side which was arguably as good as the A-side and each album was full of potential singles. Only rarely did their singles appear on albums.

'Thank You Girl', originally titled 'Thank You Little Girl', was written as a follow-up to 'Please Please Me', with 'From Me To You' composed as its B-side. In the end, it was 'From Me To You' that sounded like the obvious single, and so they swapped them around. At the time, John seemed quite proud of the song but, in 1971, he dismissed it as "just a silly song that we knocked off" and, in 1980, as "one of our efforts at writing a single that didn't work." Paul appears to agree: "A bit of a hack song," he has said, "But all good practice."

Like 'From Me to You' it was apparently written on the coach during the Helen Shapiro tour, the starter idea being the girls who wrote fan letters to the Beatles. "We knew that a lot of them would take it as a genuine 'Thank you'," said Paul many years later. "A lot of our songs were directly addressed to the fans." Kenny Lynch says that he was sitting in the seat in front of them when they wrote it. "I think Paul was initially sitting with Helen and then he called to John and said, 'Shall we get on with that song?' So Helen went to the front of the coach and they got together and started writing. "I was listening to see what it was like. They got to the part that said, 'Thank you girl for loving me the way that you do,' and messed about with it for the next 20 minutes, so I said, 'I've got a good line. How about, "That's the kind of thing that's too good to be true," or something like that?' Paul said, 'That's no good' but John said, 'Yes it is' and they used a variation of that."

Oh, oh, you've been good to me
You made me glad
When I was blue
And eternally I'll always be
In love with you
And all I gotta do
Is thank you girl, thank you girl

I could tell the world
A thing or two about our love
I know little girl
Only a fool would doubt our love
And all I gotta do
Is thank you girl, thank you girl

Thank you girl for loving me
The way that you do (way that you do)
That's the kind of love
That is too good to be true
And all I gotta do
Is thank you girl, thank you girl

Oh, oh, you've been good to me
You made me glad
When I was blue
And eternally I'll always be
In love with you
And all I gotta do
Is thank you girl, thank you girl

Oh, oh, oh
Oh, oh, oh
Oh, oh

THANK YOU GIRL

Written: Lennon/McCartney

Length: 2'01"

UK Single Release: April 11, 1963 as B-side of 'From Me To You'

US Single Release: May 27, 1963 as B-side of 'From Me To You'

SHE LOVES YOU

Written: Lennon/McCartney

Length: 2'21"

UK Single Release: August 23, 1963

UK Chart Position: 1

US Single Release: September 16, 1963

US Chart Position: 1

SHE LOVES YOU

She loves you, yeah, yeah, yeah
She loves you, yeah, yeah, yeah
She loves you, yeah, yeah, yeah, yeah

You think you've lost your love
Well, I saw her yesterday
It's you she's thinking of
And she told me what to say
She says she loves you
And you know that can't be bad
Yes, she loves you
And you know you should be glad

She said you hurt her so
She almost lost her mind
But now she says she knows
You're not the hurting kind
She says she loves you
And you know that can't be bad
Yes, she loves you
And you know you should be glad, ooh

She loves you, yeah, yeah, yeah
She loves you, yeah, yeah, yeah
And with a love like that
You know you should be glad

You know it's up to you
I think it's only fair
Pride can hurt you too
Apologise to her
Because she loves you
And you know that can't be bad
Yes, she loves you
And you know you should be glad, ooh

She loves you, yeah, yeah, yeah
She loves you, yeah, yeah, yeah
With a love like that
You know you should be glad
With a love like that
You know you should be glad
With a love like that
You know you should be glad
Yeah, yeah, yeah
Yeah, yeah, yeah, yeah

SHE LOVES YOU

Although the Beatles had already topped the British singles charts twice in 1963, it was 'She Loves You' which took them to the "toppermost of the poppermost" as they used to call it. Its sales outstripped anything they'd done before and it went on to be the best-selling single of the decade, entering the Top 20 in August 1963 and staying put until February 1964. (In America, it became a hit only after the success of 'I Want To Hold Your Hand'.)

It wasn't simply a commercial triumph. In just over two minutes of vinyl, the Beatles distilled the essence of everything that made them fresh and exciting. There was the driving beat, the fine harmonizing, the girlish "wooo" sounds which had gone down so well on 'From Me To You', as well as the brimming enthusiasm illustrated by its pace. On top of this came the distinctive "Yeah, yeah, yeah" tag which became a gift to headline writers.

The rapid expansion of the hysteria around the group from can be dated to their appearance on *Sunday Night At The London Palladium*, a television show broadcast live from the heart of London on October 13, 1963. Witnessed by a national TV audience of 15 million, screaming fans mobbed the theatre and were pictured on the front page of next day's Fleet Street newspapers. It was around this time that the press coined the term "Beatlemania", based on the term "Byromania" coined in 1812 by the wife of Lord Byron to describe the hysteria that surrounded the poet.

Not only were the Beatles transforming popular music but they were also becoming an outstanding cultural phenomenon of post-war Britain. They were in music and yet they transcended music. Suddenly they found their photos plastered all over the papers, not just *Melody Maker*, *New Musical Express* and *Boyfriend*. The single that was out when the storm broke was 'She Loves You'.

John and Paul wrote the song in Newcastle after playing the Majestic Ballroom on June 26, 1963. They had a rare day off before continuing the tour in Leeds on June 28, and Paul remembered being with John in a Newcastle hotel, sitting on separate beds, playing their acoustic guitars. "God bless their cotton socks!" said Paul when reminiscing about it in 1988. "Those boys worked! Here I am talking about an afternoon off and we're sitting there writing. We just loved it so much. It wasn't work."

It had previously been thought that the Beatles stayed at the Royal Turk's Head Hotel in Newcastle but an appeal put out by the paper *The Journal* in June 1992 discovered that they'd been at the Imperial hotel, Jesmond. Local man Bernard Armstrong had drunk with them at the hotel and could remember unloading equipment with them from their van.

Their first three singles had been declarations of love with the word "me" in the title. This time, Paul suggested turning themselves into observers of a love between two other people – "she" and "you". The model song was Bobby Rydell's then current British hit 'Forget Him', written by the British songwriter Tony Hatch. The Rydell song was addressed to a girl, telling her not to waste time on an unresponsive boyfriend but to "come home" with the narrator. The Beatles' song is instead addressed to the unresponsive boyfriend, telling him to wake up to his duties.

I'LL GET YOU

'I'll Get You' (working title 'Get You In The End') was written by John and Paul together at John's home and intended as the follow-up to 'From Me To You.' It then became the B-side of 'She Loves You', a song they wrote days later but which they felt was better. The lyrics, reflective rather than cheerful, appear to owe more to John than Paul and there's a startling similarity between the opening lines ("Imagine I'm in love with you, It's easy 'cos I know") and the opening lines of his 1971 song 'Imagine' ("Imagine there's no heaven, It's easy if you try"). 'I'll Get You' is one of the earliest songs to formulate John's belief in creative visualization – the idea that by imagining changes you want to see, you can actually bring them about. For Paul, who still regards this as one of his favourite Beatles' tracks, the use of the word "imagine" evoked the beginning of a children's fairy tale and offered an invitation into a fictitious world.

Close to the time of writing, Paul said that 'I'll Get You' churned up fresh ideas which a few days later would be incorporated into 'She Loves You.' "If we write one song, then we can get going after that and get more ideas. We wrote 'I'll Get You' first and then 'She Loves You' came after that. You know, we got ideas from that. Then we recorded it."

One of the song's musical tricks, the shift from D to A minor to break the word "pretend", was suggested by Joan Baez's version of the traditional song 'All My Trials' which had been on her debut album *Joan Baez* (1960).

Released as a single in America during 1963 and again in 1964, it never made the pop charts.

Oh yeah, oh yeah
Oh yeah, oh yeah

Imagine I'm in love with you
It's easy cos I know
I've imagined I'm in love with you
Many, many, many times before

It's not like me to pretend
But I'll get you, I'll get you in the end
Yes I will, I'll get you in the end
Oh yeah, oh yeah

I think about you night and day
I need you and it's true
When I think about you, I can say
I'm never, never, never, never blue

So I'm telling you, my friend
That I'll get you, I'll get you in the end
Yes I will, I'll get you in the end
Oh yeah, oh yeah

Well, there's gonna be a time
When I'm gonna change your mind
So you might as well resign yourself to me
Oh yeah

Imagine I'm in love with you
It's easy cos I know
I've imagined I'm in love with you
Many, many, many times before

It's not like me to pretend
But I'll get you, I'll get you in the end
Yes I will, I'll get you in the end
Oh yeah, oh yeah
Oh yeah, oh yeah
Whoa yeah

ABOVE: The Beatles pictured at the start of what the British press termed "Beatlemania".

Written: Lennon/McCartney

Length: 2'04"

UK Single Release: August 23, 1963 as B-side of 'She Loves You'

US Single Release: September, 1963 as B-side of 'She Loves You'

It won't be long yeah, yeah, yeah
It won't be long yeah, yeah, yeah
It won't be long yeah, till I belong to you

Every night when everybody has fun
Here am I sitting all on my own

It won't be long yeah, yeah, yeah
It won't be long yeah, yeah, yeah
It won't be long yeah, till I belong to you

Since you left me, I'm so alone
Now you're coming, you're coming
  on home
I'll be good like I know I should
You're coming home, you're coming home

Every night the tears come down
  from my eyes
Every day I've done nothing but cry

It won't be long yeah, yeah, yeah
It won't be long yeah, yeah, yeah
It won't be long yeah, till I belong to you

Since you left me, I'm so alone
Now you're coming, you're coming
  on home
I'll be good like I know I should
You're coming home, you're coming home

So every day we'll be happy I know
Now I know that you won't leave me
  no more

It won't be long yeah, yeah, yeah
It won't be long yeah, yeah
It won't be long yeah, till I belong to you,
  woo

IT WON'T BE LONG

With the Beatles was released on November 22, 1963 as Beatlemania swept Britain and on the same day that John F. Kennedy was assassinated in Dallas. (C. S. Lewis, author of the *Narnia* books, and Aldous Huxley, author of *Brave New World*, also died on the same day.) Robert Freeman's black and white cover portraits, where half of each face was in shadow, became an iconic image of the early Beatles. Whereas the debut album had been recorded in a day, the sessions for *With the Beatles* were spread over three months, allowing the rawness of a live beat music session to give way to the beginnings of sophisticated pop. "That was when we discovered double-tracking," John later commented. "When I discovered it, I double-tracked everything. I wouldn't have anything single-tracked from then on. He (George Martin) would say, 'Please. Just this one,' and I would say, 'No.'"

'It Won't Be Long' was the album's opening track, started by John as a potential follow-up single to 'She Loves You', but discarded because, as John said, "it never really made it." Composed as a love song, this could be the story of John's early life. Lonely and rejected, he sits at home waiting for the girl who has walked out on him to come back and make him happy. As in so many later songs, he contrasts the carefree life he imagines everyone else is having with his own anguish, believing that once he's reunited with his loved one all his problems will be solved.

Thelma McGough, who started dating John a month after his mother died in July 1958, believes that his songs of rejection weren't based on broken romances but on the fact that his father had left him as a child and then his mother had effectively left him by handing him over to her sister to be brought up and had then been killed. "I lost my mother twice," he was to say. "Once as a child of five and then again at 17."

"Rejection and betrayal were his experiences of life," says Thelma. "When I met him, our first proper conversation was about this because my father had done exactly the same thing and so we felt we had something in common. It was that which helped to draw us close. Also, you have to remember that his mother was run down by a car and, although he appeared very controlled about it, you knew that he was hurting inside. We both felt very let down and abandoned. There was a big difference between Paul and John, although they'd both lost their mothers when they were teenagers. Paul had a very close-knit family with a network of cousins and aunties. His dad was absolutely wonderful. John's life was very isolated. He lived with Mimi (his mother's sister) who looked after him extremely well but there was no closeness. There was nothing tactile about the relationship."

One of the things that excited John and Paul at the time of writing was the word play around the word "belong". Although it was a small innovation for them it was to become a hallmark of their more sophisticated writing. Ironically, when George used "don't be long" in 'Blue Jay Way' four years later Charles Manson interpreted it as "don't belong" – to drop out of society.

Written: Lennon/McCartney

Length: 2'13"

UK Release: *With the Beatles* album, November 22, 1963

US Release: *With the Beatles* album, January 20, 1964

ALL I'VE GOT TO DO

Half of *With the Beatles* was written by John and Paul and most of these songs were written specifically for the album. 'All I've Got To Do', however, was an exception, having been written entirely by John in 1961. The track was, he said, an attempt "to do Smokey Robinson again". His earlier attempt had been with 'Ask Me Why', which was reminiscent of Robinson's 1961 song 'What's So Good About Goodbye'. This time he appears to have used '(You Can) Depend On Me' as his model, a song written in 1959 by Robinson and Berry Gordy. Gordy's song 'Money', found on the Miracles' first album *Hi! We're the Miracles* and Robinson's song 'You Really Got a Hold on Me', found on their 1963 album *The Fabulous Miracles*, were both covered on *With the Beatles*, showing how important the Motown sound was to them at this time.

With two other tracks on the album owing something to Robinson, this means that Smokey was the biggest outside influence on *With the Beatles*. In 1980, while he was in the studio recording his vocal track for 'Woman', Yoko commented that John sounded like a Beatle. "Actually I'm supposed to be Smokey Robinson at the moment, my dear," John answered, "because the Beatles were always supposing that they were Smokey Robinson."

William 'Smokey' Robinson was, in 1963, the 23-year-old leader of the Detroit-based Miracles, a sweet-voiced singer who could also write, arrange and produce songs. Bob Dylan, with perhaps only half of his tongue in his cheek, once referred to him as his favourite living poet. George Harrison became a huge fan of the Miracles' guitarist Marv Tarplin and in 1976 wrote the tribute song 'Pure Smokey'. "I've always liked Smokey Robinson and he's probably one of the best songwriters around," said George. "He writes great lyrics and great melodies, and he's fantastic to see in concert." Their covering of 'You Really Got A Hold On Me' provided a boost for the Miracles, whose work was subsequently introduced to a broader market. "When they recorded that, it was one of the most flattering things that ever happened to me," said Smokey. "I listened to it over and over again, not to criticize it but to enjoy it. I first met them at a private club in London, the White Elephant, and they were not only respectful of us, they were downright worshipful! Whenever reporters asked them about their influences they'd go into euphoria about Motown."

ABOVE: John being admired by his future wife Cynthia Powell (centre) during a 1959 performance at the Casbah Club in Liverpool.

Whenever I want you around, yeah
All I gotta do
Is call you on the phone
And you'll come running home
Yeah, that's all I gotta do

And when I, I wanna kiss you, yeah
All I gotta do
Is whisper in your ear
The words you long to hear
And I'll be kissing you

And the same goes for me
Whenever you want me at all
I'll be here yes I will
Whenever you call
You just gotta call on me, yeah
You just gotta call on me

And when I, I wanna kiss you, yeah
All I got to do
Is call you on the phone
And you'll come running how
Yeah, that's all I gotta do

And the same goes for me
Whenever you want me at all
I'll be here, yes I will
Whenever you call
You just gotta call on me
You just gotta call on me
Oh, you just gotta call on me

Written: Lennon/McCartney

Length: 2'04"

UK Release: *With the Beatles* album, November 22, 1963

US Release: *With the Beatles* album, January 20, 1964

ALL MY LOVING

On April 18, 1963, the actress Jane Asher was in the audience at London's Royal Albert Hall to see the Beatles and other acts in a show that was being recorded by BBC Radio. Although only 17, she was already a successful actress, having appeared in several plays, films and television dramas, besides being a regular guest on BBC Television's pop chart show *Juke Box Jury*. She had been sent to the concert as Britain's "best-known teenage girl" by the BBC magazine *Radio Times*, which wanted to record her comments.

The resulting article, designed to show the effect that the Beatles were having on young people, was published in May 1963, with a photograph of Jane early in the evening, looking mature and pensive, contrasted with one taken during the show of her feigning hysterics. Her comment on the Beatles was: "Now these I could scream for". Little did she know that she would become the best-known of all Paul McCartney's girlfriends and would consequently inspire some of the greatest love songs of the Beatles. After the show, she met up with the group at the Royal Court Hotel in Chelsea, where she and Paul soon became locked in conversation. Shortly afterwards they began dating and, before the end of 1963, Paul had moved into a room at the Ashers' family home at 57 Wimpole Street.

It was a significant change for Paul because, within a year of leaving his council house in Allerton, he was living in one of the most expensive areas of London's West End with a family that had a number of important social connections. Jane's father, Richard Asher, was a physician specializing in endocrinology and haematology, and her mother Margaret Asher, née Eliot, a professor of oboe at the Guildhall School of Music and Drama who had once taught George Martin. They had a study filled with books, paintings and scientific journals, where conversation could range from pop music and theatre to new developments in psychology and the physical basis for mental illness. It all helped to broaden Paul's horizons and this in turn would affect his song writing.

Richard Asher was not only a brilliant physician (described in the *British Medical Journal* as "one of the foremost medical thinkers of our time") but also a writer passionate about language and clear communication. He was as well known for his humorous and illuminating articles and lectures as he was for his work at the Central Middlesex Hospital. One of his best-known contributions to the *BMJ* was an article titled 'Why are Medical Journals So Dull?' In it he wrote, "I believe if a man has something to say which interests him, and he knows how to say it, then he need never be dull." He played several instruments at home and had a fine tenor voice.

In one account Paul said that the words of 'All My Loving' came to him one morning as he was shaving, but in other accounts he has said that he wrote them travelling on the bus during the Roy Orbison tour of May/June 1963. The conclusion, though, is the same; the words were completed before there was any music and this was the first time he'd written in this order. He initially imagined it would work well as a country and western song but when he arrived at the theatre and found a piano backstage, the tune that came to him was very different. "It was a good show song," he said. "It worked well live." Like so many Beatles' songs now that the group was away from home so much, it was about the pain of separation, but whereas John would have been apprehensive, Paul was confident of a happy outcome. John, who was often grudging in his praise for Paul's songs, called it "a damn good piece of work" and "one of his first biggies."

Close your eyes and I'll kiss you
Tomorrow I'll miss you
Remember I'll always be true
And then while I'm away
I'll write home every day
And I'll send all my loving to you

I'll pretend that I'm kissing
The lips I am missing
And hope that my dreams will come true
And then while I'm away
I'll write home every day
And I'll send all my loving to you

All my loving, I will send to you
All my loving, darling I'll be true

Close your eyes and I'll kiss you
Tomorrow I'll miss you
Remember I'll always be true
And then while I'm away
I'll write home every day
And I'll send all my loving to you

All my loving, I will send to you
All my loving, darling I'll be true
All my loving, all my loving
Woo, all my loving, I will send to you

ALL MY LOVING

Written: Lennon/McCartney

Length: 2'09"

UK Release: *With the Beatles* album, November 22, 1963

US Release: *With the Beatles* album, January 20, 1964

LITTLE CHILD

As the lyrics to 'Little Child' are about a "sad and lonely" boy wanting a girl to take a chance on him, the initial idea probably came from John. Asked about 'Little Child' in 1980, he would say only that it was another effort to write a song for somebody else, "probably Ringo". The fact that Ringo had a limited vocal range meant that tunes had to be kept simple.

Paul later confessed that part of the song's melody was inspired by 'Whistle My Love', a song written by American songwriters Eddie Pola and George Wyle and performed by the British singer Elton Hayes in the 1952 Disney film *The Story of Robin Hood*. Hayes, known as "the man with the small guitar", specialized in performing old folk songs and ballads and was popular on children's radio programmes. In 1950 George Martin had produced Hayes in musical versions of two of Edward Lear's nonsense poems, 'The Table And The Chair' and 'The Jumblies.'

John and Paul were now being asked to provide songs for other artists. In April 1963, John had gone on holiday to Spain with Brian Epstein, who used the opportunity to try to persuade him to write original material with Paul for the other acts he managed. They duly complied, writing 'I'll Be On My Way' and 'Bad To Me' for Billy J Kramer and the Dakotas, 'Tip Of My Tongue' for Tommy Quickly, 'Love Of The Loved' for Cilla Black, and 'Hello Little Girl' for the Fourmost.

Paul has since admitted they "knocked them out" in the belief that it was the job of a songwriting team to keep writing songs, reserving the best ones for themselves and giving the rest away.

DON'T BOTHER ME

George Harrison's first complete song was written in August 1963 while staying at the Palace Court Hotel in Bournemouth. The Beatles were playing six nights at the town's Gaumont Cinema. Photographer Robert Freeman took the celebrated album cover photographs in one of the hotel's corridors using only natural light.

"I wrote the song as an exercise to see if I could write a song," George said. "I was sick in bed. Maybe that's why it turned out to be 'Don't Bother Me'." During the *Let It Be* sessions he mentioned the song, saying: "We were on a summer season and the doctor gave me some tonic that must have had amphetamine in it, and you all drank it to get high. It just got you high. And that's when I wrote that one." Bill Harry, the founder of the Liverpool music paper *Mersey Beat*, suggested otherwise. He used to pester George whenever he saw him to see if he'd written anything since his first instrumental composition. "When George was about to go out one night, he thought he might bump into me," Harry wrote, "so he started writing a number which he called 'Don't Bother Me'."

It was an appropriately titled song for George, who became known for his independent thinking and his desire for privacy. Of all the Beatles he was the least enticed by the life of glamour and the most suspicious of fame and acclaim.

In an interview with *Mersey Beat* in February 1964, George said, "I'm still interested in trying my hand at songwriting and I've a couple of further numbers. Trouble is, I can't write lyrics. If I could write lyrics as easy as I could write melodies I would be turning them out like Paul and John. Still, with 'Don't Bother Me' I think I proved to myself I could write a song if I tried."

LITTLE CHILD

Little child, little child
Little child, won't you dance with me?
I'm so sad and lonely
Baby, take a chance with me

Little child, little child
Little child, won't you dance with me?
I'm so sad and lonely
Baby, take a chance with me

If you want someone
To make you feel so fine
Then we'll have some fun
When you're mine, all mine
So come, come on, come on

Little child, little child
Little child, won't you dance with me?
I'm so sad and lonely
Baby, take a chance with me

When you're by my side
You're the only one
Don't you run and hide
Just come on, come on
So come on, come on, come on

Little child, little child,
Little child, won't you dance with me?
I'm so sad and lonely,
Baby, take a chance with me
Baby, take a chance with me
Baby, take a chance with me

Written: Lennon/McCartney

Length: 1'48"

UK Release: *With the Beatles* album, November 22, 1963

US Release: *With the Beatles* album, January 20, 1964

DON'T BOTHER ME

ABOVE John and Paul wrote songs with a limited vocal range for Ringo.

Since she's been gone I want no one
  to talk to me
It's not the same but I'm to blame,
  it's plain to see

So go away, leave me alone,
  don't bother me
I can't believe that she would
  leave me on my own
It's just not right when every night
  I'm all alone

I've got no time for you right now,
  don't bother me
I know I'll never be the same
  if I don't get her back again
Because I know she'll always be
  the only girl for me

But 'till she's here please don't come near,
  just stay away
I'll let you know when she's come home
  Until that day

Don't come around, leave me alone,
  don't bother me

I've got no time for you right now,
  don't bother me
I know I'll never be the same
  if I don't get her back again
Because I know she'll always be
  the only girl for me

But 'till she's here please don't
  come near, just stay away
I'll let you know when she's come home
Until that day

Don't come around, leave me alone,
  don't bother me, Don't bother me
Don't bother me, Don't bother me
Don't bother me

Written: Harrison

Length: 1'48"

UK Release: *With the Beatles* album,
November 22, 1963

US Release: *With the Beatles* album,
January 20, 1964

HOLD ME TIGHT

A version of 'Hold Me Tight' had been recorded for the first album but wasn't used. Rather than return to the old tape, they re-cut it for *With The Beatles*. Paul, the main writer, considered it a "work song" and John's only comment was that it was "a pretty poor song and I was never really interested in it either way".

Musically it was influenced by the work of the Shirelles, the New Jersey vocal group who in 1961 had become the first all-girl group to make the Number 1 spot in the American charts. The Beatles were consistent champions of girl groups and girl singers, citing acts such as the Chiffons, Mary Wells, the Ronettes, the Donays, and the Crystals as influences on their close harmony vocals. Even before they arrived in London, they included Shirelles' songs in their act and had recorded 'Baby It's You' and 'Boys' for their debut album.

The Shirelles – Shirley Owens, Micki Harris, Doris Coley and Beverly Lee – had seven Top 20 hits in America and three in Britain but 1963 proved to be their last year of chart glory. Ironically, they found themselves pushed aside by the British beat group invasion spearheaded by the Beatles.

"I can't remember much about that song," Paul said in 1988. "Certain songs were just work songs. That's one of them. You just knew you had a song that would work. A good melody. It never really had that much effect on me."

Written: Lennon/McCartney

Length: 2'32"

UK Release: *With the Beatles* album, November 22, 1963

US Release: *With the Beatles* album, January 20, 1964

It feels so right now, hold me tight
Tell me I'm the only one
And then I might
Never be the lonely one
So hold me tight, to-night, to-night
It's you, you you you

Hold me tight
Let me go on loving you
To-night to-night
Making love to only you
So hold me tight, to-night, to-night
It's you, you you you

Don't know what it means to hold you tight
Being here alone tonight with you
It feels so right now

Hold me tight
Tell me I'm the only one
And then I might
Never be the lonely one
So hold me tight, to-night, to-night
It's you, you you you

Don't know what it means to hold you tight
Being here alone tonight with you
It feels so right now

Hold me tight
Let me go on loving you
To-night, to-night
Making love to only you
So hold me tight, to-night, to-night
It's you, you you you, oh, oh, oh, oh
You oh oh

"You hurt

You know you made me cry
I see no use in wondering why
I cry for you

And now you've changed your mind
I see no reason to change mine
I cry it's through, oh

You're giving me the same old line
I'm wondering why
You hurt me then
You're back again
No, no, no, not a second time

You know you made me cry
I see no use in wondering why
I cry for you, yea

And now you've changed your mind
I see no reason to change mine
I cry it's through, oh

You're giving me the same old line
I'm wondering why
You hurt me then
You're back again
No, no, no, not a second time
Not a second time
Not the second time
No, no, no, no, no
No, no no

NOT A SECOND TIME

Paul has said that the musical inspiration behind 'Not A Second Time' was again Smokey Robinson's Miracles; John claimed the main writing honours. It was another example of John allowing his feelings, in this case of being wounded, to shape his work. After having been let down and made to cry, the writer's response is to shut down his emotions because he can't face the possibility of being hurt all over again.

It was one of the first of the Beatles' songs to be subjected to critical analysis by a quality newspaper. William Mann, then music critic of *The Times* (London), compared part of it to Gustav Mahler's 'Song Of The Earth'. John would later say that this review was responsible for "starting the whole intellectual bit about the Beatles."

"Harmonic interest is typical of their quicker songs too," Mann wrote, "and one gets the impression that they think simultaneously of harmony and melody, so firmly are the major tonic sevenths and ninths built into their tunes, and the flat-submediant key-switches, so natural is the Aeolian cadence at the end of 'Not A Second Time'." John's comment on this was, "I didn't know what the hell it was all about." Another time he said that he thought Aeolian cadences sounded like exotic birds.

Written: Lennon/McCartney

Length: 2'08"

UK Release: *With the Beatles* album, November 22, 1963

US Release: *With the Beatles* album, January 20, 1964

55

You know you made me cry
I see no use in wondering why
I cry for you

And now you've changed your mind
I see no reason to change mine
I cry it's through, oh

You're giving me the same old line
I'm wondering why
You hurt me then
You're back again
No, no, no, not a second time

You know you made me cry
I see no use in wondering why
I cry for you, yea

And now you've changed your mind
I see no reason to change mine
I cry it's through, oh

You're giving me the same old line
I'm wondering why
You hurt me then
You're back again
No, no, no, not a second time
Not a second time
Not the second time
No, no, no, no, no
No, no no

NOT A SECOND TIME

Paul has said that the musical inspiration behind 'Not A Second Time' was again Smokey Robinson's Miracles; John claimed the main writing honours. It was another example of John allowing his feelings, in this case of being wounded, to shape his work. After having been let down and made to cry, the writer's response is to shut down his emotions because he can't face the possibility of being hurt all over again.

It was one of the first of the Beatles' songs to be subjected to critical analysis by a quality newspaper. William Mann, then music critic of *The Times* (London), compared part of it to Gustav Mahler's 'Song Of The Earth'. John would later say that this review was responsible for "starting the whole intellectual bit about the Beatles."

"Harmonic interest is typical of their quicker songs too," Mann wrote, "and one gets the impression that they think simultaneously of harmony and melody, so firmly are the major tonic sevenths and ninths built into their tunes, and the flat-submediant key-switches, so natural is the Aeolian cadence at the end of 'Not A Second Time'." John's comment on this was, "I didn't know what the hell it was all about." Another time he said that he thought Aeolian cadences sounded like exotic birds.

Written: Lennon/McCartney

Length: 2'08"

UK Release: *With the Beatles* album, November 22, 1963

US Release: *With the Beatles* album, January 20, 1964

55

NOT A SECOND TIME

me then"

I WANNA BE YOUR MAN

Ringo sang one number in each show and this tradition was carried on with the albums. It was with him in mind that Paul had started writing 'I Wanna Be Your Man', a basic four-chord number with a lyric that didn't progress much beyond the five words in the title.

On September 10 1963, with the song still unfinished, the Beatles attended a Variety Club Luncheon at the Savoy Hotel in the Strand, where they were given the Best Vocal Disc of the Year award for 'From Me To You' by the readers of *Melody Maker*. After posing for some photographs with Susan Maugham (Top Female Singer) and Billy J Kramer (1964 Hope), John and Paul left in a taxi. Not far away in Charing Cross Road, close to Leicester Square underground station, they spotted Andrew Oldham, manager of the Rolling Stones, who earlier in the year had being doing publicity for the Beatles. They asked the cab to stop, paid the fare and joined Oldham, who was taking a break from a rehearsal session with the Stones.

Oldham shared his concern that his group needed a good song to follow up their debut single, a cover version of Chuck Berry's 'Come On' which had sold 100,000 copies. Paul suggested that 'I Wanna Be Your Man' might be a good vehicle if it could be completed, so the three men walked to Studio 51, jazz musician Ken Colyer's club in nearby Great Newport Street, to show it to Mick, Keith, Brian, Charlie and Bill.

It was in this basement club that the song was first played to the Rolling Stones and Brian Jones, then their acknowledged leader, said that he liked it and that Decca was pressurizing them for a single. John and Paul talked it over for a moment and then John said, "Listen, if you guys really like the main part of the song, we'll finish it for you right now." They went off into a corner of the room and emerged with the completed song around 20 minutes later. "That's how Mick and Keith got inspired to write," said John in 1980. "'Look at that! They just went into a corner and wrote it and came back!' You know, right in front of their eyes we did it."

It was meant to emulate the feel of the Shirelles' song 'Boys' that Ringo sang in concert. It was the sound of the song rather than the lyrics that mattered for him. The elongated "maaaan" of the chorus was inspired by part of Benny Spellman's recording 'Fortune Teller'. "They deliberately aimed it at us," said Keith Richards. "They're songwriters, they're trying to flog their songs. It's Tin Pan Alley and they thought this song would suit us."

The Beatles recorded the song the next day, the Stones a month later on October 7, but the Stones' version would be released earlier (on November 1) and chart by the time *With The Beatles* was released three weeks later. It eventually rose to Number 12 in Britain and helped transform the Rolling Stones into a major act.

The press liked to portray the Beatles and the Stones as the deadliest of enemies but in fact they were always close friends, turning up at each other's sessions and socializing together in clubs. Before the meeting at Club 51 John and Paul had twice been to see the Stones perform. "We were a mutual admiration society," said Keith Richards. "Mick and I admired their harmonies and their songwriting capabilities; they envied our freedom of movement and our image."

Even though 'I Wanna Be Your Man' boosted the Stones, for John it was nothing more than "a throwaway song." As he said, "We weren't going to give them anything great, right?"

I WANNA BE YOUR MAN

I wanna be your lover baby
I wanna be your man
I wanna be your lover baby
I wanna be your man

Love you like no other baby
Like no other can
Love you like no other baby
Like no other can

I wanna be your man, I wanna be your man
I wanna be your man, I wanna be your man

Tell me that you love me baby
Let me understand
Tell me that you love me baby
I wanna be your man

I wanna be your lover baby
I wanna be your man
I wanna be your lover baby
I wanna be your man

I wanna be your man, I wanna be your man
I wanna be your man, I wanna be your man

I wanna be your lover baby
I wanna be your man
I wanna be your lover baby
I wanna be your man

Love you like no other baby
Like no other can,
Love you like no other baby
Like no other can

I wanna be your man, I wanna be your man
I wanna be your man, I wanna be your man
I wanna be your man, I wanna be your man

Although the Beatles were highly regarded as a teenage fad in the early days, it wasn't until William Mann reviewed 'Not A Second Time' in *The Times* that they gained the attention of senior music critics.

Written: Lennon/McCartney

Length: 1'58"

UK Release: *With the Beatles* album, November 22, 1963

US Release: *With the Beatles* album, January 20, 1964

Oh yeah I'll tell you something
I think you'll understand
When I say that something
I wanna hold your hand

I wanna hold your hand
I wanna hold your hand

Oh, please say to me
You'll let me be your man
And please say to me
You'll let me hold your hand

Now let me hold your hand
I wanna hold your hand

And when I touch you I feel happy inside
It's such a feeling that my love
I can't hide, I can't hide, I can't hide

Yeah, you got that something
I think you'll understand
When I say that something
I wanna hold your hand

I wanna hold your hand
I wanna hold your hand

And when I touch you I feel happy inside
It's such a feeling that my love
I can't hide, I can't hide, I can't hide

Yeah you, got that something
I think you'll understand
When I feel that something
I wanna hold your hand

I wanna hold your hand
I wanna hold your hand
I wanna hold your hand

I WANT TO HOLD YOUR HAND

At a piano in the basement den of the Ashers' home in Wimpole Street, John and Paul came up with 'I Want To Hold Your Hand', the song that would break them in America when it reached the Number 1 spot in January 1964.

It was a remarkable achievement; no British artists had dominated in America. In 1956 Lonnie Donegan, the "king of skiffle", had reached the Top 10 with 'Rock Island Line', but only after months of touring. Cliff Richard had toured, released movies and appeared on the *Ed Sullivan Show* but had managed only a minor hit with 'Living Doll'. The only British artists to reach Number 1 in the American charts had been Vera Lynn in 1952, Acker Bilk in 1961 and the Tornadoes in 1962. After disappointing sales on the Vee Jay and Swan labels, the Beatles were picked up by Capitol, EMI's company in America, and Brian Epstein had promised that the first single for them would be designed with an "American sound" in mind. In 1964, Paul said, "We were told we had to get down to it. We knew we really had to get this song going."

According to John, 'I Want To Hold Your Hand' materialized when Paul came up with an opening line, then hit a chord on the piano. "I turned to him and said, 'That's it! Do that again!' In those days, we really used to absolutely write like that – both playing into each other's noses." Gordon Waller, friend of Jane Asher's brother Peter (with whom he had formed the singing duo Peter and Gordon), was also there. "As far as I can remember, John was on a pedal organ and Paul was on a piano. The basement was the place where we all went to make our 'noise' and they called us down to let us hear this song they'd just written. It wasn't totally complete but the structure and the chorus were there."

Speaking close to the time of writing Paul said, "We started banging away. Suddenly a little bit came to us, the catch line. We started working on it from there. We got our pens and paper out and just wrote down the lyrics. Eventually we had some sort of song."

I WANT TO HOLD YOUR HAND

Paul and John kept Ringo's strengths and weaknesses in mind when writing for him.

The Beatles were, of course, still playing to their market, the teenage girls for whom hand holding and kissing was the ultimate in physical expression. 'I Want To Hold Your Hand' certainly wasn't indicative of their sexual reticence.

Robert Freeman, who took the cover photo for *With The Beatles*, lived in a flat beneath John, and tried to educate him about jazz and experimental music. "He [John] was intrigued by a contemporary French album of experimental music. There was one track where a musical phrase repeated, as if the record had stuck. This effect was used in 'I Want To Hold Your Hand' – at my suggestion – 'that my love, I can't hide, I can't hide, I can't hide'."

The album was most likely by Pierre Schaeffer, an engineer who developed what he termed *Musique Concrete* in the late 1940s, manipulating natural sounds and playing them back. His techniques, such as altering speeds, creating sound loops, using echo and delay and reversing chords, may have stayed with John and become an influence on *Revolver*, *Sgt. Pepper* and *The White Album*.

In January 1964 Paul told a radio journalist that 'I Want To Hold Your Hand' was written the day before it was recorded. If his memory was accurate, this would mean it was written on Wednesday October 16, a day on which they started rehearsing at 4:00 pm for BBC radio.

The Beatles were in Paris in January 1964 when they heard that the song had reached Number 1 in America. Brian Epstein's plan to let them tour America only when they had a hit single had come to pass.

ABOVE: John said that in the early days of their writing partnership, he and Paul "played into each other's noses."

Written: Lennon/McCartney

Length: 2'24"

UK Single Release: November 29, 1963

UK Chart Position: 1

US Single Release: December 26, 1963

US Chart Position: 1

That boy took my love away
He'll regret it someday
But this boy wants you back again

That boy isn't good for you
Though he may want you too
This boy wants you back again

Oh, and this boy would be happy
Just to love you, but oh my
That boy won't be happy
Till he's seen you cry

This boy wouldn't mind the pain
Would always feel the same
If this boy gets you back again

This boy, this boy, this boy

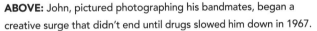

ABOVE: John, pictured photographing his bandmates, began a creative surge that didn't end until drugs slowed him down in 1967.

THIS BOY

'This Boy' was written by John and Paul in a hotel bedroom, as an exercise in three-part harmony, which they had never attempted on record before, and was inspired, as so much else was at the time, by Smokey Robinson and the Miracles. "The middle eight," said George, "was John trying to do Smokey." The lyrics, John claimed, amounted to nothing. All that was important was "sound and harmony". Harmony was integral to the early Beatles' work, and the influence of the Everly Brothers in particular is evident in this song. They'd become familiar with three-part harmonizing by singing Phil Spector's 'To Know Him Is To Love Him', a 1959 hit for the Teddy Bears. Saying that the lyrics amounted to nothing was not the same as saying that they were without meaning, for again John was portraying himself here as a loser waiting for his lover to come back.

THIS BOY

Written: Lennon/McCartney

Length: 2'12"

UK Release: November 29, 1963 as a B-side of 'I Want To Hold Your Hand'

US Release: *Meet the Beatles* album, January 20, 1964

I CALL YOUR NAME

John reckoned that he wrote 'I Call Your Name' back when "there was no Beatles and no group." As the Quarry Men, his first group, was formed shortly after buying his first guitar in March 1957, he must have either written it as he was learning to play or before that, when he could only play banjo. However, Paul can remember working on it in John's bedroom at Menlove Avenue, suggesting that it may have been written at a later date.

The Quarry Men was initially a skiffle group composed of friends from Quarry Bank High School for Boys. Rod Davis, who played banjo with them, can't recall John writing songs in those days. "What we did was to listen to the latest singles when they were played on the radio and try to copy the words down," he says. "The trouble was, if you couldn't make them out, or couldn't write quickly enough, you were stuck. So what John used to do was to add his own words to these tunes. No-one ever seemed to notice because they didn't know the words either. There was a song called 'Streamline Train' which John rewrote as 'Long Black Train'. He also put new words to the Del Vikings' hit 'Come Go With Me' and I didn't realize what he'd done until I heard the original version many years later."

If the song was written as long ago as John thought, it's interesting that even as a teenager he was writing about despair. The lines "I never weep at night, I call your name" are close to his 1971 lines "In the middle of the night, I call your name" in 'Oh Yoko' on the *Imagine* album.

It was first of all given to Billy J Kramer who recorded in June 1963 and released it as the B-side of 'Bad to Me', which got to Number 1 in the UK charts in August of that year. The Beatles didn't record it until March 1964. It was released on the US LP *The Beatles' Second Album* in April and then on the UK EP 'Long Tall Sally' in June. It was the first track to feature George playing his Rickenbacker guitar.

John added the Jamaican blue beat instrumental break for the Beatles' recording. Blue beat and ska music, brought to Britain by West Indian immigrants, were becoming popular with British mods. The Blue Beat label, founded by Ziggy Jackson in 1961, had released 213 singles in the previous three years. John wasn't unfamiliar with music from the Caribbean, though. Tony Carricker, an art school friend, remembers that at the time John only owned two records; *The Chirping Crickets*, the 1957 debut album by Buddy Holly and his group, and an album of risqué calypsos called *Calypsos Too Hot To Handle* which had tracks like 'Don't Touch Me Nylon' by the Charmer, 'I Left Her Behind For You' by Duke of Iron and Lord Kitchener's 'Muriel & De Bug'.

Two weeks after the recording of 'I Call Your Name', the *New Musical Express* asked whether ska and blue beat were going to be the major new talking point in pop music. With the Beatles around, there was no chance of that.

I call your name
But you're not there
Was I to blame
For being unfair?

Oh, I can't sleep at night
Since you've been gone
I never weep at night
I can't go on

Don't you know I can't take it?
I don't know who can
I'm not gonna make it
I'm not that kind of man

Oh, I can't sleep at night
But just the same
I never weep at night
I call your name

Don't you know I can't take it?
I don't know who can
I'm not gonna make it
I'm not that kind of man

Oh, I can't sleep at night
But just the same
I never weep at night
I call your name
I call your name
I call your name

Written: Lennon/McCartney

Length: 2'09"

UK Release: On 'Long Tall Sally' EP, June 19, 1964

US Release: *The Beatles' Second* album, April 10, 1964

The Beatles were in Paris when they were given the news of their first American Number 1 hit.

The Beatles' first feature film captured the freshness and excitement of Beatlemania and combined it with a zany surrealism.

YOU MAY TELE
FROM HE

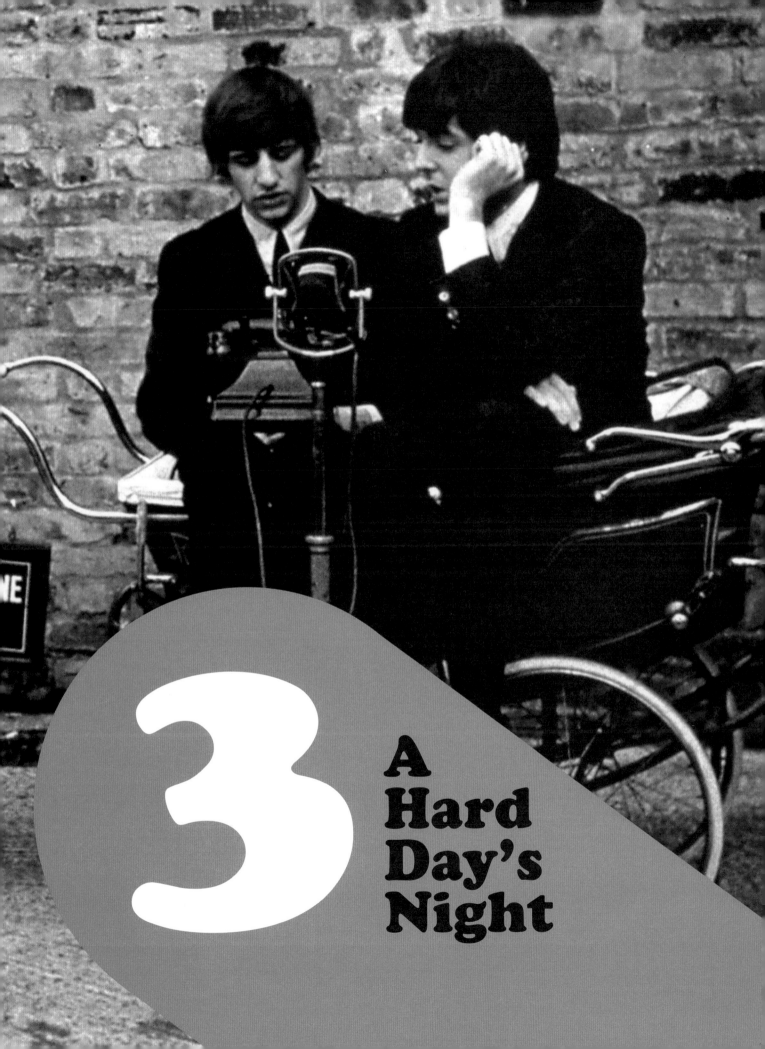

3

A Hard Day's Night

A *Hard Day's Night* was a breakthrough album in that it was the first to consist only of self-composed songs. The songwriter Roger Greenaway, who toured with the Beatles in 1963 as part of the Kestrels, recalls a decision being made during the autumn tour of Britain. "We were all in the same dressing room and Brian Epstein came in. By this time the group was very, very successful. He said that from now on they were only going to be recording Beatles' songs. They wouldn't be recording songs written by outsiders. Paul said to him 'You're mad.'" If Paul did say this he couldn't have meant that it was economic madness because it certainly wasn't. He must have meant that it was madness to think that he and John could compose the A- and B-sides of three or four singles a year plus two 14-track albums, which was the rate at which were releasing material at the time. He had a point. The two albums following *A Hard Day's Night* did include covers, but from *Rubber Soul* onwards they stuck to their own compositions.

A Hard Day's Night was a *tour de force* for John, the major contributor to 10 of the album's 13 tracks. Being the oldest in the group and the founder member of the Quarry Men, John was the de facto leader at the time. Walter Shenson, producer of the film, called him "the spiritual head of the Beatles." Although Paul was more musically accomplished – he had mastered guitar and piano ahead of John – the same junior-to-senior-pupil relationship that existed when they met in 1957 was still in place.

Later in his life John later acknowledged that this was the period of his dominance in the Beatles and it was only when, in his own words, that he became "self-conscious and inhibited" that Paul began to take over. The majority of the group's singles up to this point, John claimed, had either been written by him, or featured him as lead vocalist. The only reason Paul sang parts of the lead vocal in the track 'A Hard Day's Night' was because John couldn't reach the high notes.

Seven songs were written for the film *A Hard Day's Night* although one of them, 'I'll Cry Instead', was subsequently removed from the fire escape scene in favour of 'Can't Buy Me Love,' a single Paul had written under pressure. They were still writing pop songs to order but injecting more of their actual feelings into the lyrics. 'And I Love Her' was one of Paul's most personal songs yet and 'If I Fell' was an insight into John's insecurities. At the time, few people knew how or why the songs had been written because the Beatles were rarely quizzed about the stories behind their songs and details about John's emotional scarring were not widely known.

Initially the film of *A Hard Day's Night* was thought of as a vehicle to sell a soundtrack album but, as with everything the Beatles touched in 1964, it turned into a great commercial success, recouping its production costs almost 30 times over. The idea was to capture the delirium of Beatlemania in the style of a black and white television documentary. The story was little more than a way of stitching together a series of essential scenes – concert, television recording, journey, fan mobbing – and, because of this, the Beatles were provided with undemanding roles and a strong supporting cast of character actors to cover any weaknesses.

"I was with the Beatles in Paris when they played there in January 1964," said screenwriter Alun Owen. "I was also around them in an unofficial capacity on a lot of other occasions. The biggest nonsense that has been written about the film is that it was ad-libbed. It wasn't. They were at the time 22 or 23 years old. They had never acted before. If you go through the script, you'll see that no sentence is longer than six words, because they

A HARD DAY'S NIGHT

It's been a hard day's night,
And I've been working like a dog
It's been a hard day's night,
I should be sleeping like a log
But when I get home to you
I find the things that you do
Will make me feel alright

You know I work all day
To get you money to buy you things
And it's worth it just to hear you say
You're going to give me everything
So why on earth should I moan,
'Cause when I get you alone
You know I feel OK

When I'm home
Everything seems to be right
When I'm home feeling you
holding me tight, tight

It's been a hard day's night,
And I've been working like a dog
It's been a hard day's night,
I should be sleeping like a log
But when I get home to you
I find the things that you do
Will make me feel alright, oww

So why on earth should I moan,
'Cause when I get you alone
You know I feel OK

When I'm home
Everything seems to be right
When I'm home feeling you
holding me tight, tight

It's been a hard day's night,
And I've been working like a dog
It's been a hard day's night,
I should be sleeping like a log
But when I get home to you
I find the things that you do
Will make me feel alright
You know I feel alright
You know I feel alright

couldn't have handled any more. The only ad-libs were made by John."

The Beatles were pleased with the final result. Although they knew it only showed one side of their personalities and wasn't as realistic as it could have been, they recognized that *A Hard Day's Night* avoided the clichés of most pop movies. The album was released in Britain in July 1964 and a month earlier in America, making the Number 1 spot in both countries. The American version was substantially different, featuring only the seven soundtrack songs and 'I'll Cry Instead'. It was made up to a 12-track album by including several of George Martin's orchestral versions of Lennon and McCartney's songs.

A HARD DAY'S NIGHT

In the early Sixties, it was customary for British pop stars to make a film after only a few hits, just as Elvis Presley had done in America. *The Young Ones* (1961) and *Summer Holiday* (1962) were big box office hits in the UK for Cliff Richard, and even lesser names such as Tommy Steele (*The Tommy Steele Story*, 1957) Terry Dene (*The Golden Disc*, 1958), Adam Faith (*Beat Girl*, 1960) and Billy Fury (*Play It Cool!*, 1962) had made it to the cinema screen.

The typical rock 'n' roll film story was of a poor boy discovered in a coffee bar and launched as a star. The Beatles wanted to do something from a different angle and were fortunate in being introduced to director Dick Lester, who was not only a musician himself (he played piano) but was as creative visually as they were musically. The freshness, excitement and humour of his style was a perfect match for the Beatles and their songs. Negotiations over the film began in October 1963 and, in November, Liverpool-born writer Alun Owen, who had an ear for the Beatles' natural speech patterns, accompanied the group to Dublin and Belfast to observe them at work and catch the flavour of Beatlemania.

Without having seen the script, the Beatles had to write seven songs for the soundtrack. Two were written in Paris in January 1964, some were written the next month in Miami during one two-hour burst, and the title track was written in London in April. "All of the songs, except for 'A Hard Day's Night', were written independently of what I was writing," said Alun Owen. "Paul and John wrote them and they were woven into the script as things came up. None of them bear any relation to the story. They were just numbers."

For two-thirds of the filming (which took place between March 2 and April 24, 1964) there was no finalized title for the film. Working titles *On The Move*, *Let's Go* and *Beatlemania* had all been rejected as unsuitable. On April 14, the Beatles were at Twickenham Film Studios and after filming a sequence that wasn't used in the final film John, Paul, Dick Lester and Walter Shenson discussed possible titles. Either John or Paul mentioned a malapropism of Ringo's. He was well known for misplacing words. "I came up with the phrase 'a hard day's night,'" Ringo said in 1964. "It just came out. We went to do a job and we worked all day and then we happened to work all night. I came out, still thinking it was day and said, 'It's been a hard day...' looked around, saw that it was dark and added '...'s night.'"

The story was put out that Ringo had made the comment after a hard day on the set but John had already used it in his book *In His Own Write*, so it must have been said at least the year before. Who then thought it was a great title for the film is a matter of dispute. Shenson went to his grave believing it was he who decided. John said that Dick Lester told him while driving back to London that night. Paul has said that it was the group's decision. Whoever decided, Dick Lester liked it as a title because it summed up the frenetic pace of the film as well as the humour of the Beatles and, as he was driving him home, he asked John to start writing a song with that title that could be used in the opening sequence. The next day John brought in a lyric and the day after that the Beatles recorded it at Abbey Road.

Evening Standard journalist Maureen Cleave, who had been one of the first London journalists to write about the Beatles, can recall John coming into the studio on April 16, 1964, with the lyrics written on the back of a card to his son Julian, who had just had his first birthday. The card had a colour illustration of a boy in a yellow jumper sitting in a green toy train engine. The words were in black ink with some crossing out. Initially part of the lyric read: "But when I get home to you, I find my tiredness is through, and I feel all right." Cleave told him that she thought "my tiredness is through" was a weak line. John crossed it out and substituted it with: "I find the things that you do, they make me feel all right". Maureen said, "The song seemed to materialize as if by magic. It consisted of John humming to the others, then they would all put their heads together and hum and three hours later they had this record."

John's other major change was altering "When I'm home everything's right from the start" to "When I'm home everything seems to be right". The "everything seem to be right" is a thought that would come up two years later in 'She Said She Said' with the line "When I was a boy everything was right". Another small addition was the word "just" in "it's worth it just to hear you say." In 1967 when he was writing 'A Little Help From My Friends' Cynthia suggested that John use the line "I just feel fine" and he remarked, "No. You never use the word 'just'. It's meaningless. It's a fill-in word."

The song was recorded in nine takes with the lyric hardly altered throughout other than the uses of "OK" and "alright" being changed round and the eventual dropping of "all through the night" after "holding me tight" in favour of repeating the word "tight" and adding "yeh". This may have been because the "tight/night" rhyme had already been used in both 'I Saw Her Standing There' and 'Hold Me Tight'. Before the eighth take John can be heard saying. "I wish we had the words written out properly."

When promoting the film in America, Paul was asked about the song and explained how it was put together. "It seemed a bit ridiculous writing a song called 'A Hard Day's Night'," he said, "because it sounded a funny phrase at the time, but the idea came of saying that it had been a hard day's night and we'd been working all day and you get back to a girl and everything's fine. So it was turned into one of those songs."

'A Hard Day's Night' was featured over the opening and closing credits of the film. It was the first cut on the soundtrack album and became a Number 1 single in Britain and America. The actor Peter Sellers, once a member of John's favourite radio comedy group the Goons, did a spoken version of 'A Hard Day's Night' where he enunciated every word as if he were Laurence Olivier delivering a Shakespearean monologue. It made the British Top 20 in December 1965.

A HARD DAY'S NIGHT

Written: Lennon/McCartney

Length: 2'32"

UK Release: June 10, 1964

UK Chart position: 1

US Release: *A Hard Day's Night* album, June 26, 1964

A Hard Day's Night **was based on the group's frenetic lifestyle in 1963–64.**

I SHOULD HAVE KNOWN BETTER

Released as the flip side of 'A Hard Day's Night' in America, 'I Should Have Known Better' was the first song heard in the film after the title track and was performed in a sequence where the Beatles and Paul's 'grandfather' (played by Wilfred Brambell) are on a train and banished to the mail van. They start playing cards and, a few shots later, appear with guitars, harmonica and drums. "It just seemed the natural place to have the first number," said Alun Owen.

Although much of the filming took place on trains travelling between London and the West Country, the 'I Should Have Known Better' sequence was actually filmed in a van in Twickenham with crew members providing the rocking motion.

As it was recorded three days after returning from America it's likely that it was one of three songs completed "while we were soaking up the sun on Miami Beach" – as John put it at the time. The group had been staying at the Deauville Hotel on Collins Avenue to record their second appearance for the *Ed Sullivan Show* on February 16 and stayed on for four additional nights after the performance. They borrowed the nearby home of a millionaire to sunbathe and swim.

Surprisingly for a song by John it is very optimistic: he loves her, she loves him and everything is fine. However, Paul has since suggested that this and other songs John wrote for the film may have disguised his marital troubles. In 1980 John said of 'I Should Have Known Better', "It's just a song. It doesn't mean a damn thing", yet in 1964 he chose it as one of four songs in the film that "I really go for".

I should have known better
  with a girl like you
That I would love everything that you do
And I do, hey, hey, hey, and I do

Whoa, oh, I never realised what a kiss
  could be
This could only happen to me
Can't you see, can't you see

That when I tell you that I love you, oh
You're gonna say you love me too, oh
And when I ask you to be mine
You're gonna say you love me too

So I should have realised a lot of things
  before
If this is love you've got to give me more
Give me more, hey hey hey, give me
  more

Whoa, oh, I never realised what a kiss
  could be
This could only happen to me
Can't you see, can't you see

That when I tell you that I love you, oh
You're gonna say you love me too, oh
And when I ask you to be mine
You're gonna say you love me too
You love me too, you love me too
You love me too

Written: Lennon/McCartney

Length: 2'44"

UK Release: *A Hard Day's Night* album,
June 10, 1964

US Release: *A Hard Day's Night* album,
June 26, 1964

RIGHT: Although John and Cynthia had not long been married, John was restless and open to other relationships.

IF I FELL

Although this is a love song, John had to sing it to Ringo in the film because the already written script didn't include any romance. "We're in the television studio and Ringo is supposed to be sulking a bit," Paul explained in 1964. "John starts joking with him and then sings the song as though we're singing it to him. We got fits of the giggles just doing it."

'If I Fell' is one of John's most beautiful songs and one of his most revealing. It's about an illicit relationship. He is asking the woman in question for an assurance that if he leaves his partner for her that she'll love him more than he's ever been loved. It is the story of someone keen to avoid confrontation and also someone who fears being let down. He knows that if he walks out of his relationship he will cause pain and so he only wants to do it if he gets a guarantee of commitment from his lover. Paul later said that he was sure some on the songs John had written at this time "may have been based in real experiences or affairs John was having, or arguments with Cynthia or whatever," but that at the time it never occurred to them to delve deeper into what was being hinted at.

John later admitted that the song was "semi-autobiographical" – it is known that he was unfaithful to his wife Cynthia although, at the time, she was oblivious to what was going on. "Of course I'm a coward," he said in 1968 when discussing his first marriage. "I wasn't going to go off and leave Cynthia and be by myself."

Early demos show that John had almost all the words and the tune together before he went in the studio on February 27, 1964. The only significant change was that during the writing stage he was toying with both "I hope that she will cry" and "I hope that she won't cry" referring to his partner's response when she hears of his new relationship. The first assumes that even though he's walking out on her he still wants assurance that he meant something to her. He eventually settled for a modification of the second, less selfish option. He also planned to play out by repeating "Too much in love/ Too, too much in love" but didn't use it on the recording.

John saw this as his first proper ballad and a precursor to 'In My Life', his song about growing up, which used the same chord sequence.

If I fell in love with you
Would you promise to be true
And help me understand
Cos I've been in love before
And I found that love was more
Than just holding hands

If I give my heart to you
I must be sure
From the very start
That you would love me more than her

If I trust in you oh please
Don't run and hide
If I love you too oh please
Don't hurt my pride like her
Cos I couldn't stand the pain
And I would be sad if our new love
Was in vain

So I hope you see that I
Would love to love you
And that she will cry
When she learns we are two
Cos I couldn't stand the pain
And I would be sad if our new love
Was in vain

So I hope you see that I
Would love to love you
And that she will cry
When she learns we are two
If I fell in love with you

IF I FELL

Written: Lennon/McCartney

Length: 2'22"

UK Release: *A Hard Day's Night* album, June 10, 1964

US Release: *A Hard Day's Night* album, June 26, 1964

AND I LOVE HER

For Paul rock 'n' roll was never a means of scorning the popular music that had preceded it. He loved the big band music of the Twenties and Thirties which his father had played, the Victorian music hall songs that his relatives would sing around the piano and the show tunes of the Forties and Fifties.

Even in the days of Hamburg and the Cavern Club in Liverpool, Paul had performed 'Till There Was You', a song from the 1957 Broadway musical *The Music Man*, later popularized by Peggy Lee, and this was included on *With The Beatles*. From these early performances Paul must have realized that ballads enriched the Beatles' show, and wrote 'And I Love Her' as a first attempt to fill this space. John said it was Paul's first 'Yesterday'. Paul said it was, "the first song that I impressed myself with."

The initial exercise was to write a song with a title that began mid-sentence. Paul then wrote the verses in the basement music room of the Ashers' home in Wimpole Street where Margaret Asher gave her oboe lessons and came to John for help with the middle eight. It didn't escape Paul's notice that almost a decade later Perry Como recorded a song titled 'And I Love You So'.

Recording on the song began in February 1964 and it was the first Beatle track to feature only acoustic instruments (Ringo played bongos). In the film they are shown recording it for a television show.

Only the month before recording, Jane Asher commented to American writer Michael Braun: "The trouble [with Paul] is that he wants the fans' adulation and mine too. He's so selfish. That's his biggest fault. He can't see that my feelings for him are real and that the fans' [feelings for him] are fantasy." Paul has since said that it wasn't written with anyone in mind but it's hard to believe that in his first flush of love with Jane Asher he was writing such tender songs to an imaginary girl.

AND I LOVE HER

I give her all my love
That's all I do
And if you saw my love
You'd love her too
I love her

She gives me everything
And tenderly
The kiss my lover brings
She brings to me
And I love her

A love like ours
Could never die
As long as I
Have you near me

Bright are the stars that shine
Dark is the sky
I know this love of mine
Will never die
And I love her

Bright are the stars that shine
Dark is the sky
I know this love of mine
Will never die
And I love her

Written: Lennon/McCartney

Length: 2'31"

UK Release: *A Hard Day's Night* album, June 10, 1964

US Release: *A Hard Day's Night* album, June 26, 1964

LEFT: Jane Asher, pictured here with Paul in 1967, was the perfect Beatles girlfriend – attractive, discreet and professionally accomplished.

Before this dance is through
I think I'll love you too
I'm so happy when you dance with me

I don't want to kiss or hold your hand
If it's funny try and understand
There is really nothing else I'd rather do
Cos I'm happy just to dance with you

I don't need to hug or hold you tight
I just want to dance with you all night
In this world there's nothing I would
  rather do
Cos I'm happy just to dance with you

Just to dance with you
Is everything I need
Before this dance is through
I think I'll love you too
I'm so happy when you dance with me

If somebody tries to take my place
Let's pretend we just can't see his face
In this world there's nothing I would
  rather do
Cos I'm happy just to dance with you

Just to dance with you
Is everything I need
Before this dance is through
I think I'll love you too
I'm so happy when you dance with me

If somebody tries to take my place
Let's pretend we just can't see his face
In this world there's nothing I would
  rather do
I've discovered I'm in love with you
Cos I'm happy just to dance with you

I'M HAPPY JUST TO DANCE WITH YOU

John and Paul wrote 'I'm Happy Just To Dance With You' for George to sing in the film "to give him a piece of the action" and it was filmed on stage at the Scala Theatre in Charlotte Street, London. As the youngest member of the Beatles, George was at the time living in the shadow of Paul and John. When he started writing his own songs, he became resentful that more of them weren't considered for the albums.

John was equally hurt in 1980 when George published his biography *I Me Mine* and made no mention of his influence on his songwriting. Paul has admitted that 'I'm Happy Just To Dance With You' was a "formula song" that played with some chord changes that they knew from experience were guaranteed to stir up some excitement.

73

A HARD DAY'S NIGHT

I'M HAPPY JUST TO DANCE WITH YOU

Written: Lennon/McCartney

Length: 1'58"

UK Release: *A Hard Day's Night* album,
July 10, 1964

US Release: *A Hard Day's Night* album,
June 26, 1964

TELL ME WHY

'Tell Me Why' was written to provide an "upbeat" number for the concert sequence in A Hard Day's Night. John thought of something the Chiffons or the Shirelles might do and "knocked it off."

It's a typical John scenario. He has been lied to and deserted. He's crying. He appeals to his girl to let him know what he's done wrong so that he can put it right. Children whose parents either leave them or die suddenly are often left with a feeling that they must in some way be responsible. "If there's something I have said or done, Tell me what and I'll apologize," John sang. Paul later assumed that there was an element of autobiography to it.

It was only when he underwent Primal Therapy in 1970 that John came to terms with these subconscious fears. Therapist Arthur Janov set him the exercise of looking back through all his Beatles' songs to see what they revealed of his anxieties. On his first post-therapy album, *John Lennon/Plastic Ono Band*, he was able to sing about these traumas in their original context in songs such as 'Mother', 'Hold On', 'Isolation' and 'My Mummy's Dead'.

Written: Lennon/McCartney

Length: 2'10"

UK Release: *A Hard Day's Night* album, June 10, 1964

US Release: *A Hard Day's Night* album, June 26, 1964

Tell me why you cried,
And why you lied to me
Tell me why you cried,
And why you lied to me

Well I gave you everything I had
But you left me sitting on my own
Did you have to treat me oh so bad
All I do is hang my head and moan

Tell me why you cried,
And why you lied to me
Tell me why you cried,
And why you lied to me

If it's something that I've said or done
Tell me what and I'll apologise
If you don't I really can't go on
Holding back these tears in my eyes

Tell me why you cried,
And why you lied to me
Tell me why you cried,
And why you lied to me

Well, I'm beggin' on my bended knees
If you'll only listen to my pleas
Is there anything I can do
Cos I really can't stand it, I'm so in love
  with you

Tell me why you cried,
And why you lied to me
Tell me why you cried,
And why you lied to me

LEFT: Out and about in Paris, in the company of fans and photographers.

RIGHT: The "freedom" sequence from *A Hard Day's Night* over which 'Can't Buy Me Love' was played.

Can't buy me love, love
Can't buy me love

I'll buy you a diamond ring my friend if it
makes you feel alright
I'll get you anything my friend if it makes
you feel alright
Cause I don't care too much for money
money can't buy me love

I'll give you all I got to give if you say
you'll love me too
I may not have a lot to give but what I got
I'll give to you
I don't care too much for money
money can't buy me love

Can't buy me love, everybody tells me so
Can't buy me love, no no no, no

Say you don't need no diamond rings and
I'll be satisfied
Tell me that you want the kind of things
that money just can't buy
I don't care too much for money,
money can't buy me love
Owww

Can't buy me love, everybody tells me so
Can't buy me love, no no no, no

Say you don't need no diamond rings and
I'll be satisfied
Tell me that you want the kind of things
that money just can't buy
I don't care too much for money, money
can't buy me love

Can't buy me love, love
Can't buy me love

Written: Lennon/McCartney

Length: 2'14"

UK Release: March 20, 1964

UK chart position: 1

US Release: March 16, 1964

US chart position: 1

CAN'T BUY ME LOVE

In January 1964, the Beatles went to Paris for 18 days of concerts at the Olympia Theatre. They stayed at the five-star George V hotel, in the centre of Paris not far from the Arc de Triomphe, and had a Caveau console piano installed in one of their suites so that they could work. It was here that John and Paul wrote 'One And One Is Two' for fellow Liverpool group the Strangers and Paul wrote 'Can't Buy Me Love'.

With a new single due in March, and the news that 'I Want To Hold Your Hand' had gone to the top of the American charts, the pressure for new material was on. After the song was written George Martin came to the Pathé Marconi Studios in Paris to record it along with German language versions of 'I Want to Hold Your Hand' and 'She Loves You.' It was George's idea to restructure the song and start it with the chorus. Although 'She Loves You', 'I Wanna Be Your Man', 'Don't Bother Me' and 'All My Loving' were all used in *A Hard Day's Night*, 'Can't Buy Me Love' was the only previously released song to be included on the soundtrack album. This was because it was a late replacement for 'I'll Cry Instead', which director Dick Lester didn't think was right for the film.

'Can't Buy Me Love' was used over a scene where the group ran down a fire escape at the back of the theatre (actually the Odeon in Hammersmith, London) and fooled around on some open ground (partly playing fields in Isleworth). It was the group's first experience of freedom in the film after having been locked for days in cars, trains, dressing rooms and hotels. Screenwriter Alun Owen remembered: "My stage direction at this point was very simple. It read: 'The boys come down the fire escape. It is the first time they have been free. They run about and play silly buggers'."

The lyric suggests it was in part an answer song to Berry Gordy's 'Money', a number the Beatles had started performing in 1960 and had recorded on *With The Beatles*. Gordy's song argued that money could get you anything whereas Paul made the point that it could get you anything but love. "All these material possessions are all very well but they won't buy me what I want," said Paul. "It was a very hooky song."

American journalists asked Paul in 1966 whether 'Can't Buy Me Love' was a song about prostitution. He replied that all the songs were open to interpretation but that suggestion was going too far.

CAN'T BUY ME LOVE

...atles played
...eks of shows in
...g the days they
...g songs for the
...ding the follow-
...ant To Hold Your
...and planning
...r US debut.

ANY TIME AT ALL

ANY TIME AT ALL

Having written the songs that would be used in the film, the race was on to come up with songs for what would be the non-film side of the album.

John was obviously the more prolific songwriter at the time, having written five of the seven songs in the film and going on to write all but one of the tracks on the other side. This had not been achieved without some difficulty. 'Any Time At All', he later admitted, was a rewriting of his earlier song 'It Won't Be Long', using the same chord progression from C to A minor and back and, when it came to recording, employing the same bawling vocal style.

In January 1964 he spoke about some of the changes in his songwriting techniques. "If I found a new chord [I used to] write a song around it," he said. "I thought that if there were a million chords I'd never run out. Sometimes the chords got to be an obsession and we started to put unnecessary ones in. We then decided to keep the songs simple and it's the best way. It might have sounded okay for us but the extra chords wouldn't make other people like them any better. That's the way we've kept it all along."

There were only three other occasions when John claimed Beatles' songs had been recycled. 'Yes It Is', he said, was a rewrite of 'This Boy', 'Paperback Writer' was "son of 'Day Tripper'" and 'Get Back' was a "potboiler rewrite" of 'Lady Madonna'.

Written: Lennon/McCartney

Length: 2'13"

UK Release: *A Hard Day's Night* album,
June 10, 1964

US Release: *Something New* album,
July 10, 1964

Any time at all, any time at all
Any time at all, all you've gotta do is call
And I'll be there

If you need somebody to love
Just look into my eye
I'll be there to make you feel right

If you're feeling sorry and sad
I'd really sympathise
Don't you be sad, just call me tonight

Any time at all, any time at all
Any time at all, all you've gotta do is call
And I'll be there

If the sun has faded away
I'll try to make it shine
There is nothing I won't do
When you need a shoulder to cry I hope
 it will be mine
Call me tonight, and I'll come to you

Any time at all, any time at all
Any time at all, all you've gotta do is call
And I'll be there
Any time at all, any time at all

Any time at all, all you've gotta do is call
And I'll be there
Any time at all, all you've gotta do is call
And I'll be there

I've got every reason on earth to be mad
Cos I've just lost the only girl I had
And if I could get my way
I'd get myself locked up today
But I can't so I'll cry instead

I've got a chip on my shoulder that's
  bigger than my feet
I can't talk to people that I meet
And if I could see you now
I'd try to make you sad somehow
But I can't so I'll cry instead

Don't want to cry when
  there's people there
I get shy when they start to stare
I'm gonna hide myself away, ay hay
But I'll come back again someday
And when I do you'd better
  hide all the girls
I'm gonna break their hearts
  all 'round the world
Yes, I'm gonna break them in two
And show you what your
  loving man can do
Until then I'll cry instead

Don't want to cry when
  there's people there
I get shy when they start to stare
I'm gonna hide myself away, ay hay
But I'll come back again someday
And when I do you'd better
  hide all the girls
Cos I'm gonna break their hearts
  all 'round the world
Yes, I'm gonna break them in two
And show you what your
  loving man can do
Until then I'll cry instead

I'LL CRY INSTEAD

I'LL CRY INSTEAD

'I'll Cry Instead' was the song which was going to be used over the fire escape sequence in *A Hard Day's Night* but which was then dropped in favour of the already released 'Can't Buy Me Love'. However, when the film was re-mastered for video release in 1986, the song was used over a collage sequence preceding the opening credits.

John had written about crying in many of his songs to date but 'I'll Cry Instead' marked a difference in that he was saying that once he'd finished crying he would return to seek vengeance. He imagined coming back and breaking girls' hearts around the world, as if by causing people to fall for him and then spurning them, he would be able to punish everyone who had ever rejected him. He would later admit having been violent at times and in 'Getting Better' he was able to write about his cruelty to women as something he had overcome.

This was also the first song in which John admitted having a chip on his shoulder, an indication that he was entering a period of intense self-examination, which was to continue until his first solo albums, after the break-up of the Beatles.

Written: Lennon/McCartney

Length: 1'47"

UK Release: *A Hard Day's Night* album,
June 10, 1964

US Release: *Something New* album,
July 10, 1964

BELOW: *A Hard Day's Night* was the only Beatles album to be written entirely by John and Paul, seen here in New York during February 1964.

THINGS WE SAID TODAY

In May 1964, having completed the filming of *A Hard Day's Night* and after fulfilling some performing commitments in England and Scotland, the Beatles and their partners took off for a holiday break. John and George made a round-the-world trip with stop-offs in Holland, Polynesia, Hawaii and Canada, while Paul and Ringo went to France and Portugal before taking off for the Virgin Islands.

While in the Caribbean, Paul chartered a 50ft yacht called *Happy Days* and it was while on board with Ringo, Maureen and Jane that he wrote 'Things We Said Today' on his acoustic guitar. He started the song in one of the cabins but found the smell of engine oil too nauseating, so he came on deck to complete it.

The song was a reflection of his relationship with Jane in light of the fact that he knew, by the nature of their work, that times together would be few. When they were apart, he explained, he would take comfort from the memory of the things they'd said in the recent past.

THINGS WE SAID TODAY

Written: Lennon/McCartney

Length: 2'38"

UK Release: July 10, 1964 as B-side of '*A Hard Day's Night*'

US Release: *Something New* album, July 20, 1964

You say you will love me
If I have to go
You'll be thinking of me
Somehow I will know
Someday when I'm lonely
Wishing you weren't so far away
Then I will remember
Things we said today.

You say you'll be mine, girl
Till the end of time
These days such a kind girl
Seems so hard to find
Someday when we're dreaming
Deep in love, not a lot to say
Then we will remember
Things we said today

Me, I'm just the lucky guy
Love to hear you say that love is love
And though we may be blind
Love is here to stay and that's enough

To make you mine, girl
Be the only one
Love me all the time, girl
We'll go on and on
Someday when we're dreaming
Deep in love, not a lot to say
Then we will remember
Things we said today

Me, I'm just the lucky guy
Love to hear you say that love is love
Though we may be blind
Love is here to stay and that's enough

To make you mine, girl
Be the only one
Love me all the time, girl
We'll go on and on
Someday when we're dreaming
Deep in love, not a lot to say
Then we will remember
Things we said today

ABOVE LEFT: Paul and Jane returning from their holiday in the Virgin Islands during which he wrote 'Things We Said Today'.

WHEN I GET HOME

Whoa-I, whoa-I
I got a whole lot of things to tell her
When I get home
Come on, out my way
Cos I'm gonna see my baby today
I've got a whole lot of things I've gotta say
To her

Whoa-I, whoa-I
I got a whole lot of things to tell her
When I get home
Come on if you please
I've got no time for trivialities
I've got a girl who's waiting home for me
Tonight

Whoa-I, whoa-I
I got a whole lot of things to tell her
When I get home
When I'm getting home tonight
I'm gonna hold her tight
I'm gonna love her till the cows come home
I bet I'll love her more
Till I walk out that door
Again

Come on, let me through
I've got so many things I've got to do
I've got no business being here with you
This way

Whoa-I, whoa-I
I've got a whole lot of things to tell her
When I get home, yeah
I've got a whole lot of things to tell her
When I get home

WHEN I GET HOME

'When I Get Home' was described by John as a "four-in-the-bar cowbell song," influenced by his love of Motown and American soul music. Around the time it was recorded, he was asked what song he wished he had written and he said his first choice would be Marvin Gaye's 'Can I Get A Witness'. "Then there's other stuff on Tamla Motown that we like," he went on. "It's harder to write good 12-bar numbers because so much has been done before with them. I'd rather write a song with chords all over the place."

An unusually optimistic song for John, the lyric revealed his thoughts about what he was going to say and do to his girl, when he got home. With slightly similar subject matter to the single 'A Hard Day's Night' ("when I get home to you…") it shows that he still thought of home as the place where true love should be waiting. Despite his image as the "lad" in the group, John was really a homebody who liked nothing more than to curl up in front of a television with a supply of books and magazines. Knowing this makes it less surprising that he spent much of his final decade as a house husband, happy to be confined to his rooms in the Dakota Building in New York.

Written: Lennon/McCartney

Length: 2'18"

UK Release: *A Hard Day's Night* album, June 10, 1964

US Release: *Something New* album, July 10, 1964

I got something to say that might cause
 you pain
If I catch you talking to that boy again
I'm gonna let you down
And leave you flat
Because I told you before, oh
You can't do that

Well, it's the second time
 I've caught you talking to him
Do I have to tell you one more time,
 I think it's a sin
I think I'll let you down (Let you down)
Leave you flat (Gonna let you down and
 leave you flat)
Because I've told you before, oh
You can't do that

Everybody's green
Cos I'm the one who won your love
But if they'd seen
You talking that way they'd laugh
 in my face

So please listen to me,
 if you wanna stay mine
I can't help my feelings,
 I'd go out of my mind
I'm gonna let you down (Let you down)
And leave you flat (Gonna let you down
and leave you flat)
Because I've told you before
Oh, you can't do that
You can't do that
You can't do that
You can't do that
You can't do that
You can't do that

YOU CAN'T DO THAT

In both Britain and America 'You Can't Do That' became the B-side of 'Can't Buy Me Love'. In this song, instead of passively weeping, John tries actively threatening. He tells his girl that he'll leave her if he catches her talking to another boy. He knows what it feels like to be spurned and he's determined that it won't happen again.

The musical influence, John later said, was Wilson Pickett, the soul artist from Alabama who at the time had released only five singles although he'd had earlier success as a gospel singer. John may have been inspired by B-sides such as 'I Can't Stop' and 'I'm Gonna Love You' which had more of the pace of 'You Can't Do That' than his slower A-sides or he may have been wrong about Pickett's influence on this song. It wasn't until 1965, his contract then having been acquired by Atlantic Records, that Pickett became known as one of the great soul singers of the Sixties with hits such as 'Mustang Sally', '634-5789' and 'In The Midnight Hour'. It was at the suggestion of guitarist Duane Allman that Pickett recorded 'Hey Jude' in 1969 and had a hit with it at the same time that the Beatles' version was in the charts.

On the recording of 'You Can't Do That', John played lead on his Rickenbacker, while George played 12-string guitar for the first time on a Beatles' record. "I find it a drag to play rhythm guitar all the time," John told *Melody Maker*, "I like to work out something interesting to play. The best example is what I did on 'You Can't Do That'. There wasn't really a lead guitarist and a rhythm guitarist on that because...rhythm guitar is too thin for records. Anyway, it would drive me potty to play chunk-chunk rhythm all the time. I never play anything as lead guitarist that George couldn't do better. But I like playing lead sometimes, so I do it."

It was recorded after returning from America and earmarked for the concert sequence in the film but wasn't used.

Everybody's green
Cos I'm the one who won your love
But if they'd seen
You talking that way they'd laugh
 in my face

So please listen to me,
 if you wanna stay mine
I can't help my feelings,
 I'd go out of my mind

I'm gonna let you down (Let you down)
And leave you flat (Gonna let you down
 and leave you flat)
Because I've told you before, oh
You can't do that

Written: Lennon/McCartney

Length: 2'37"

UK Release: March 20, 1964 as B-side of 'Can't Buy Me Love'

US Release: March 16, 1964 as B-side of 'Can't Buy Me Love'

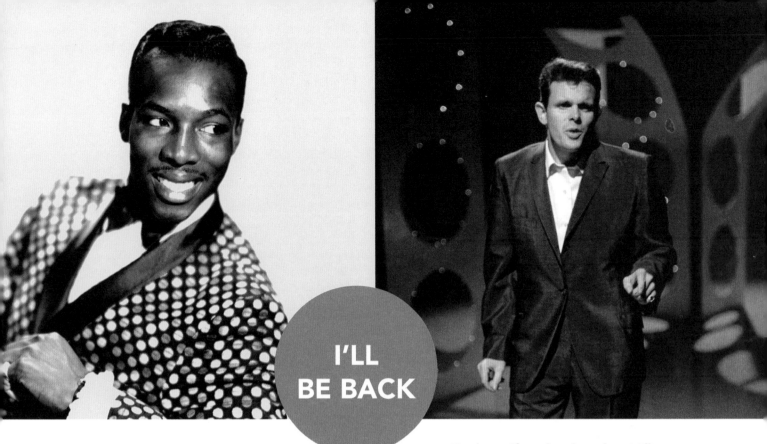

I'LL BE BACK

John found the chords for 'I'll Be Back' while playing a Del Shannon song. This was probably 'Runaway' which the Beatles had performed in their early shows and which also starts in a minor chord and has a descending bass line.

Shannon had hits in 1961 and 1962 with 'Runaway', 'Hats Off To Larry', 'So Long Baby' and 'Hey Little Girl'. In 1963, after a hit with 'Little Town Flirt', he played London's Royal Albert Hall (April 18) with the Beatles and suggested to them that he could help expose their work in America by covering one of their songs as a single.

The Beatles agreed and Shannon went back home and recorded a version of 'From Me To You' which, although it only reached Number 77, was the first Lennon and McCartney composition to feature in the American charts.

Written: Lennon/McCartney

Length: 2'37"

UK Release: March 20, 1964 as B-side of 'Can't Buy Me Love'

US Release: March 16, 1964 as B-side of 'Can't Buy Me Love'

ABOVE LEFT: Soul Singer Wilson Pickett, who John later credited as an influence on 'You Can't Do That'.

ABOVE RIGHT: Del Shannon was the first performer to take one of their songs into the US charts. John returned the compliment, reworking the chords of a Shannon hit into 'I'll Be Back'.

You know if you break my heart I'll go
But I'll be back again
Cos I told you once before goodbye
But I came back again

I love you so
I'm the one who wants you
Yes, I'm the one who wants you, oh ho,
  oh ho, oh

You could find better things to do
Than to break my heart again
This time I will try to show that I'm
Not trying to pretend

I thought that you would realise
That if I ran away from you
That you would want me too
But I got a big surprise
Oh ho, oh ho, oh

You could find better things to do
Than to break my heart again
This time I will try to show that I'm
Not trying to pretend

I wanna go but I hate to leave you
You know I hate to leave you, oh ho,
  oh ho, oh
You, if you break my heart I'll go
But I'll be back again

The Beatles' fourth album was put together either side of their first full American tour in the summer of 1964.

4
Beatles For Sale

The *Beatles For Sale* sleeve revealed the flip side of Beatlemania – the exhaustion, bewilderment and loneliness of life at the top. John, Paul, George and Ringo look frazzled and world-weary in Robert Freeman's cover photographs, and the same pressurized feeling coloured their new songs. They only had time to write eight of the album's 14 tracks. Covers of early rock 'n' roll, rockabilly and R&B favourites were used to supplement their originals.

The songs they composed showed all the signs of having been written in the hot house of fame. Although 'Eight Days A Week' was a love song, its title was inspired by a comment about overwork. John's songs were bleaker than anything he'd written before, with 'I'm A Loser' offering a foretaste of his confessional style of song writing. For 'I'll Follow The Sun', Paul had to go back through his old school notebooks to polish up a song he hadn't played since the group's appearances at the Cavern.

Bob Dylan was starting to become an influence: Paul and John had both heard and met for the first time during 1964. In the early days, the Beatles had concentrated mainly on mastering the musical side of the songs – chord changes, arrangements, harmonies and delivery. Dylan was the first recording artist to affect them primarily as lyricists. Initially, Paul was the big Dylan fan, but John soon caught up. He'd been writing poems and short stories for years, mostly for the amusement of friends. Some of these were published in his book *In His Own Write* in 1964, which caused the press to hail him as "the literary Beatle" and compare his work to that of Lewis Carroll, Edward Lear and the James Joyce of *Finnegan's Wake*. Dylan, and later the British journalist Kenneth Allsop, caused him to question the difference between his literary outpourings and his lyric writing. "Instead of projecting myself into a situation," said John, "I would try to express what I felt about myself [as I had done] in my book."

In the way that the previous albums were influenced by such American music as Motown, Memphis soul and the New York girl groups, *Beatles For Sale* seems to have been influenced by country music. This could have been because it provided the right tone for the more melancholy songs they were writing or simply because their two tours of America had exposed them to the sound of Nashville. Ringo was already a fan of country and in 1963 George told his sister Louise in a letter that Chet Atkins was one of his favourite guitar players. Two of the cover songs ('Everybody's Trying To Be My Baby' and 'Honey Don't') were written by Tennessean Carl Perkins, another ('Words Of Love') was by Texan Buddy Holly, and all had a rockabilly feel to them. 'I Don't Want To Spoil The Party,' 'Baby's In Black' and 'I'm A Loser' appear to owe both sound and sentiment to country.

The group's press officer Derek Taylor was surely right when he wrote in the sleeve notes; "The kids of AD 2000 will draw from the music much the same sense of well being and warmth as we do today. For the magic of the Beatles is, I suspect, timeless and ageless…it is adored by the world."

Beatles For Sale took two and a half months to record and was released in December 1964, reaching Number 1 in Britain. The American equivalent, *Beatles '65*, also hit the top spot and sold a million copies in the first week.

I FEEL FINE

The Beatles completed the album *A Hard Day's Night* in June 1964 and by mid-August were recording *Beatles For Sale*. On August 19, they left to tour America but returned a month later and picked up where they'd left off. *A Hard Day's Night* had been the first album to consist solely of Lennon and McCartney songs but, with so little time between projects, they found it impossible to come up with enough original material to fill *Beatles For Sale*.

On October 6, while recording 'Eight Days A Week', John was working out the guitar riff that would become the basis of 'I Feel Fine', a song they recorded only 12 days later. It was inspired by the riff on Bobby Parker's 1961 track 'Watch Your Step'. "I actually wrote 'I Feel Fine' around the riff which is going on in the background," John said in December 1964. "I tried to get that effect into every song on the LP, but the others wouldn't have it."

"I told them that I'd write a song specially for this riff so they said, 'Yes. You go away and do that,' knowing that we'd almost finished the album. Anyway, going into the studio one morning I said to Ringo, 'I've written this song but it's lousy', but we tried it, complete with riff, and it sounded like an A-side, so we decided to release it just like that." After one of the early takes John told press agent Derek Taylor, "It's gear, except for one thing. We've got the phrase 'diamond rings' in again, but we can always change that." No alternative was found and 'diamond rings' remained.

In 1990 George Harrison told *Musician* magazine that the genesis of the song lay in a three-part harmony that he Paul and John had made up to the Carl Perkins' song 'Matchbox' when the Beatles were touring Scotland. "It turned into 'I Feel Fine,'" he said. However, the Scottish visits closest to the recording date are either over five months before or a day after. It may be that John had developed the chorus prior to the rest of the song or that what George remembered was singing the words of a new song to the tune of an old favourite.

Apart from the riff, the distinctive feature of 'I Feel Fine' was the sound of feedback from John's guitar that blends into the opening chords. It was an accident that they decided to make part of the song. John's semi-acoustic Gibson guitar was leaning against an amplifier after a take and an electronic whine resulted. This, along with other innovations on *Beatles For Sale*, was a significant development in their approach to recording. Having mastered the studio basics, they wanted George Martin to take more risks and were open to incorporating the sounds produced by such mistakes as twisted tapes and electronic interference. Feedback was to become a familiar part of recording – used by artists such as Jimi Hendrix and the Who – and John remained proud of the fact that the Beatles were the first group to purposely include it on a record. In 1980 he said, "I defy anybody to find a record – unless it's some old blues record from 1922 – that uses feedback that way. So I claim it for the Beatles. Before Hendrix, before the Who, before anybody. The first feedback on record."

'I Feel Fine', John's most optimistic song to date, became a Number 1 single in both Britain and America.

Baby's good to me you know
She's happy as can be you know
She said so
I'm in love with her and I feel fine

Baby says she's mine you know
She tells me all the time you know
She said so
I'm in love with her and I feel fine

I'm so glad that she's my little girl
She's so glad, she's telling all the world

That her baby buys her things you know
He buys her diamond rings you know
She said so
She's in love with me and I feel fine

Baby says she's mine you know
She tells me all the time you know
She said so
I'm in love with her and I feel fine

I'm so glad that she's my little girl
She's so glad, she's telling all the world

That her baby buys her things you know
He buys her diamond rings you know
She said so
She's in love with me and I feel fine
She's in love with me and I feel fine

Written: Lennon/McCartney

Length: 2'20"

UK Release: November 27, 1964

UK chart position: 1

US Release: November 23, 1964

US chart position: 1

SHE'S A WOMAN

'She's A Woman' was conceived by Paul on the streets of St John's Wood on October 8, 1964 and was recorded on the same day. He wanted to bring a more bluesy sound and used his Little Richard voice to sing it. Some lines of the lyric, and the middle eight, were added by John. "We needed a real screaming rocker for the live act," said Paul. "It was always good if you were stuck for something to close with or if there was a dull moment."

On the early takes Paul improvised extensively. The seventh take, for example, lasted almost six and a half minutes, and contained lots of ad-libs and screams. At the end Paul can be heard saying, "We've got a song and an instrumental there!" Unfortunately the song also contained one of the most strained rhymes in the Beatles songbook when "present" was matched with "she's no peasant".

'She's A Woman' was also the first Beatles' song to contain a veiled drug reference. John later confessed that they were quite proud to have inserted the line "turns me on when I get lonely" and for it to have escaped the attention of the broadcast censors. When they used the phrase "turn you on" three years later (in 'A Day In The Life'), it led to a radio ban: by then, the authorities had become aware of the growing drug culture and its terminology.

Significantly, it was just five weeks before recording 'She's A Woman' that the Beatles had smoked marijuana for the first time. Until then, their only experience of drugs had been Drinamyl and Preludin tablets that they'd discovered in Hamburg and the strips from Benzedrine inhalers that they'd been shown in Liverpool. They were introduced to marijuana in the company of Bob Dylan, who met them for the first time in their suite at the Delmonico Hotel in New York City. The Beatles were happy to drink cheap wine into the small hours, but Dylan wanted to smoke a joint and assumed that they were all dope smokers because he mistakenly thought they had sung "I get high", instead of "I can't hide" in 'I Want To Hold Your Hand'.

My love don't give me presents
I know that she's no peasant
Only ever has to give me
Love forever and forever
My love don't give me presents

Turns me on when I get lonely
People tell me that she's only fooling
I know she isn't

She don't give boys the eye
She hates to see me cry
She is happy just to hear me
Say that I will never leave her
She don't give boys the eye

She will never make me jealous
Gives me all her time as well as loving
Don't ask me why

She's a woman who understands
She's a woman who loves her man

My love don't give me presents
I know that she's no peasant
Only ever has to give me
Love forever and forever
My love don't give me presents

Turns me on when I get lonely
People tell me that she's only fooling
I know she isn't, woo

She's a woman who understands
She's a woman who loves her man

My love don't give me presents
I know that she's no peasant
Only ever has to give me
Love forever and forever
My love don't give me presents

Turns me on when I get lonely
People tell me that she's only fooling
I know she isn't

She's a woman
She's a woman
She's a woman

The Beatles were apprehensive about joining in at first, but before long the lights were lowered, candles and incense were lit and towels were stuffed along the bottoms of the doors. For the next few hours, the musicians were "legless with laughing" as George Harrison later put it. Paul thought that he'd suddenly been blessed with amazing insights and asked road manager Mal Evans to take notes.

'She's A Woman' was released as the B-side of 'I Feel Fine' in Britain and America. "At first, it wasn't so well received," said Paul in 1965. "A lot of people thought that I was just singing too high and that I'd picked the wrong key. It sounded as though I was screeching, but it was on purpose. It wasn't a mistake."

ABOVE: The Beatles at the Delmonico Hotel in New York with Ed Sullivan (top left) and Peter Yarrow, Mary Travers and Paul Stockley of Peter, Paul and Mary.

Written: Lennon/McCartney

Length: 2'57"

UK Release: November 27, 1964 as B-side of 'I Feel Fine'

US Release: November 23, 1964 as B-side of 'I Feel Fine'

She's a woman who loves her man

EIGHT DAYS A WEEK

John always claimed that 'Eight Days A Week' was written by Paul as a potential title track for the Beatles' follow-up film to *A Hard Day's Night*.

Director Dick Lester denied this, pointing out that 'Eight Days A Week' was recorded in October 1964, whereas filming on *Help!* didn't begin until late February 1965. It's unlikely that they were considering film music this far in advance. "The film was always supposed to be called *Help* but there was a copyright problem in that someone else had registered this title," says Lester. "So we originally called it *Beatles II* and then *Eight Arms To Hold You*, but the possibility of having to write a song called 'Eight Arms To Hold You' had everyone throwing their hands in the air and saying that it was impossible. It was because of this that we thought, sod it, we'll take the chance, because the laws of registration were so vague. We decided to stick in an exclamation mark because the one that was registered didn't have one."

Paul heard the phrase "eight days a week" from a chauffeur that drove him to John's home in Weybridge for a writing session (Paul had been banned from driving after a traffic offence). Asked if he had been busy lately the chauffeur replied, "Busy? I've been working eight days a week." When they arrived in Weybridge Paul immediately informed John that he had a title for the song they would write that day. American radio DJ Larry Kane, who accompanied the Beatles on their 1964 US tour, claims in his book that he heard the group running through the tune on a flight between Dallas and New York on September 20.

ABOVE: In November 1965, the Beatles performed for their first promotional films at Twickenham Film Studios, a move that anticipated the pop video revolution. Although it had been released a year earlier, their hit single 'I Feel Fine' was one of the five songs filmed.

EIGHT DAYS A WEEK

Ooh I need your love babe
Guess you know it's true
Hope you need my love babe
Just like I need you
Hold me, love me, hold me, love me
I ain't got nothin' but love babe
Eight days a week

Love you every day girl
Always on my mind
One thing I can say girl
Love you all the time
Hold me, love me, hold me, love me
I ain't got nothing but love girl

Eight days a week
I love you
Eight days a week
Is not enough to show I care

Ooh I need your love babe
Guess you know it's true
Hope you need my love babe
Just like I need you
Hold me, love me, hold me, love me
Ain't got nothin' but love babe
Eight days a week

Eight days a week
I love you
Eight days a week
Is not enough to show I care

Love you every day girl
Always on my mind
One thing I can say girl
Love you all the time
Hold me, love me, hold me, love me
I ain't got nothin' but love babe
Eight days a week
Eight days a week
Eight days a week

John never liked the song, saying it was "lousy" and that they'd struggled to make it into a song and then struggled to record it.

'Eight Days A Week', the first track to be recorded with a fade-in, was under consideration as a single in Britain until John came up with 'I Feel Fine'. In America, it was released as the follow-up to 'I Feel Fine' and made the Number 1 spot.

Written: Lennon/McCartney

Length: 2'45"

UK Release: *Beatles For Sale* album, December 4, 1964

US Release: February 15, 1965

US chart position: 1

ABOVE: Music publisher Dick James (left) took a close interest in John and Paul's development as writers.

I'M A LOSER

Two events during 1964 had a profound effect on John's writing. The first was hearing Bob Dylan's music in Paris during January, when Paul acquired *The Freewheelin' Bob Dylan* from an interviewer at a local radio station. Paul had heard Dylan's music before through his student friends in Liverpool but it was the first time John had heard it. After hearing *Freewheelin'*, Dylan's second album, they bought his debut album *Bob Dylan* and, according to John, "for the rest of our three weeks [in Paris] we didn't stop playing them. We all went potty on Dylan."

The second event to affect John was meeting journalist Kenneth Allsop, a writer for the *Daily Mail* and a regular interviewer on BBC Television's news magazine programme *Tonight*. John was interviewed by him about his book *In His Own Write* on March 23. Allsop, a Yorkshireman, was 44 years old at the time. He had been in journalism since 1938, with a brief interruption caused by the war when he served in the Royal Air Force. In 1958 he had written a book called *The Angry Decade* with the subtitle "A survey of the cultural revolt of the nineteen fifties".

It was in the "green room", the hospitality suite at the BBC's Lime Grove Studios, that Allsop spoke to John about his songwriting, encouraging him not to hide his true feelings behind the conventions of the pop song. It was obvious to Allsop from reading *In His Own Write* that John had much more to give if he explored his deeper feelings and developed the surrealism and wordplay he so obviously loved.

Years later, John told his confidant Elliot Mintz that this meeting marked a significant turning point in his writing. "He told me that he was very nervous that day and, because of this, became very talkative and engaged Allsop in conversation," says Mintz. "Allsop had in essence said to him that he wasn't terribly enamoured with Beatles' songs because they all tended to be 'she loves him', 'he loves her', 'they love her' and 'I love her'. He suggested to John that he try to write something more autobiographical, based on personal experience rather than these abstract images. That struck a chord with him."

Although recorded five months later, 'I'm A Loser' was the first evidence of this change. It would be wrong to say it was something completely new, because from the beginning John had written songs in which he revealed himself as lonely, sad and abandoned, but in 'I'm A Loser' he let a little more of his true self show. On the surface, it's another song about having lost a girl but the lines which announce that beneath his mask he is "wearing a frown", suggest that he considers himself a loser in more ways than one. He's not just a loser in love; he feels that he's a loser in life.

All this would be idle speculation if not for the fact that 'I'm A Loser' can now be seen as an early stage in John's journey towards candid self-revelation. He was quick to credit the effect Bob Dylan had on 'I'm A Loser'. "Anyone who is one of the best in his field – as Dylan is – is bound to influence people," he said at the time. "I wouldn't be surprised if we influenced him in some way." However, the sound of the song is more country than folk and the confessional nature of the song is closer to such blues laments of Hank Williams as 'I'm So Tired of it All', 'Never Been So Lonesome' and 'You Win Again' than it is to the confident, often acerbic songs that Dylan was writing at this time.

Kenneth Allsop went on to present the television news programme *24 Hours*. In May 1973, he was found dead at his home after taking an overdose of painkillers. Because there was no suicide note the inquest into the death recorded an open verdict.

I'm a loser
I'm a loser
And I'm not what I appear to be

Of all the love I have won or have lost
There is one love I should never have
  crossed
She was a girl in a million, my friend
I should have known she would win in
  the end

I'm a loser
And I lost someone who's near to me
I'm a loser
And I'm not what I appear to be

Although I laugh and I act like a clown
Beneath this mask I am wearing a frown
My tears are falling like rain from the sky
Is it for her or myself that I cry

I'm a loser
And I lost someone who's near to me
I'm a loser
And I'm not what I appear to be

What have I done to deserve such a fate
I realize I have left it too late
And so it's true, pride comes before
  a fall
I'm telling you so that you won't lose all

I'm a loser
And I lost someone who's near to me
I'm a loser
And I'm not what I appear to be

Written: Lennon/McCartney

Length: 2'33"

UK Release: *Beatles For Sale* album,
December 4, 1964

US Release: *Beatles '65* album,
December 15, 1964

NO REPLY

'No Reply' was a typical John song about betrayal and jealousy; a story of a girl taking off with another guy. It wasn't based on his experience, he once said, but on 'Silhouettes', a big hit in 1957 for the Rays on Philadelphia's independent Cameo label. Written by Bob Crewe and Frank Slay Jr., who went on to write hits for Freddy Cannon, 'Silhouettes' put a new twist on the old love cheat story: the boy discovers he is being two-timed when he notices the silhouettes of his girlfriend and her lover on the curtains of a bedroom window.

"It's amusing, if true," says Crewe of the story that John told. "Regarding the genesis of 'Silhouettes' – I was travelling home to New York City in 1957 from my brother's graduation in Annapolis when I heard one of those old time detective stories on my car radio. The mystery revolved around someone's mistaken identity, having been 'spotted' but only in silhouette through a window. The version by the Rays was produced by Frank Slay and I. Years later it was a hit for Herman's Hermits on a single produced by Mickie Most."

In John's version of the scenario, the boy becomes suspicious when his girl doesn't answer the door and, when he calls her on the phone, her parents tell him she's not at home. As in 'Silhouettes', he returns to her house and, watching from the shadows, sees her go in "with another man". His repetition of the line "I saw the light", referring to the light behind the curtain but also to the revelation that he was being two-timed, could be an allusion to Hank Williams' well-known song of personal salvation 'I Saw The Light' (1948) given that he appears to have been influenced by country music during this period. (John was apparently a fan of Williams even before coming across Elvis and used to play a version of 'Honky Tonk Blues' when with the Quarry Men. When recording *Let It Be* he played the Williams' number 'You Win Again'.)

Ever since 'Please Please Me', the Beatles' compositions had been published by Northern Songs, a company set up by John, Paul, Brian Epstein and music publisher Dick James, who was a friend of George Martin. James had experience both as singer and songwriter before getting into publishing and, when he heard 'No Reply', he said to John: "That's the first complete song you've written, the first song which resolves itself. It's a complete story."

It was almost certainly written during May when John and Cynthia went on a three-week holiday in Hawaii and Tahiti with George and Pattie. A week after John arrived back in England the song was recorded as a demo by Tommy Quickly, another singer managed by Brian Epstein.

This happened once before
When I came to your door
No reply
They said it wasn't you
But I saw you peep through
Your window

I saw the light, I saw the light
I know that you saw me
Cos I looked up to see your face

I tried to telephone
They said you were not home
That's a lie
Cos I know where you've been
I saw you walk in your door

I nearly died, I nearly died
Cos you walked hand in hand
With another man in my place

If I were you I'd realise that I
Love you more than any other guy
And I'll forgive the lies that I
Heard before when you gave me
no reply

I've tried to telephone
They said you were not home
That's a lie
Cos I know where you've been
I saw you walk in your door

I nearly died, I nearly died
Cos you walked hand in hand
With another man in my place
No reply, no reply

Written: Lennon/McCartney

Length: 2'17"

UK Release: *Beatles For Sale* album,
December 4, 1964

US Release: *Beatles '65* album,
December 15, 1964

I DON'T WANT TO SPOIL THE PARTY

The Beatles briefly visited America in February 1964, playing in Washington DC and New York City to promote 'I Want To Hold Your Hand' and doing live TV shows for Ed Sullivan in New York and Miami. It wasn't until August 1964 that they arrived for their first full-fledged tour, a month-long trek that would take them to 20 US cities plus three in Canada. Playing 12 songs per show, they were supported by four American acts – the Bill Black Combo, the Exciters, Jackie DeShannon and the Righteous Brothers.

It is highly likely that John wrote 'I Don't Want To Spoil The Party' in Los Angeles the night of August 24, 1964. Of the eight self-written songs on the album two had already been written before the tour ('Baby's In Black' and 'I'm A Loser') and two were written in Britain on their return ('Eight Days A Week' and 'She's A Woman'). That leaves four songs that must have been written on the tour. Paul told an interviewer that he had written two of them when staying at the Marquis de Lafayette Hotel on Cape May, New Jersey. The remaining two songs, for which John would have been the primary writer, must have been 'No Reply' and 'I Don't Want To Spoil The Party'.

Evidence for 'I Don't Want To Spoil The Party' being written in LA is that we know from contemporary accounts that John had been invited to a party at Burt Lancaster's house on August 24 but turned down the invite in order to stay in and write a song. George, Paul and Ringo went to the party. It makes sense that John's mind would turn to the subject of being a party pooper.

The two days in LA had been particularly stressful for the Beatles. They had arrived the day before at 3:55 am, flown in from Vancouver, and had been housed in a mansion owned by British actor Reginald Owen, at 356 St. Pierre Road. They gave a press conference for over 200 journalists on the first day and then in the evening played at the Hollywood Bowl. Later there had been a party at the mansion where John had spoken at length with Joan Baez.

On the following day the Beatles had to shake hands for an hour at a charity garden party for the Haemophilia Foundation. Adults could attend only if they brought a child. It was just the sort of event that John hated because he would have been expected to play the role of the cheerful Beatle. This might have put him in just the mood to write a song about his inability to pretend that he's enjoying himself. Discussing the song later he said it was "deeply personal".

Written: Lennon/McCartney

Length: 2'36"

UK Release: *Beatles For Sale* album, December 4, 1964

UK Release: February 15, 1965 as B-side of 'Eight Days A Week'

I don't want to spoil the party so I'll go
I would hate my disappointment to show
There's nothing for me here
  so I will disappear
If she turns up while I'm gone please let
  me know

I've had a drink or two and I don't care
There's no fun in what I do if she's not
  there
I wonder what went wrong
I've waited far too long
I think I'll take a walk and look for her

Though tonight she's made me sad
I still love her
If I find her I'll be glad
I still love her

I don't want to spoil the party so I'll go
I would hate my disappointment to show
There's nothing for me here
  so I will disappear
If she turns up while I'm gone
  please let me know

Though tonight she's made me sad
I still love her
If I find her I'll be glad
I still love her

Though I've had a drink or two and I
  don't care
There's no fun in what I do if she's not
  there
I wonder what went wrong
I've waited far too long
I think I'll take a walk and look for her

I DON'T WANT TO SPOIL THE PARTY

I'LL FOLLOW THE SUN

One day you'll look to see I've gone
For tomorrow may rain, so
  I'll follow the sun
Some day you'll know I was the one
But tomorrow may rain, so
  I'll follow the sun

And now the time has come
And so my love I must go
And though I lose a friend
In the end you will know, oooh

One day you'll find that I have gone
But tomorrow may rain, so
  I'll follow the sun
Yea, tomorrow may rain, so
  I'll follow the sun

And now the time has come
And so my love I must go
And though I lose a friend
In the end you will know, oooh

One day you'll find that I have gone
But tomorrow may rain, so
  I'll follow the sun

I'LL FOLLOW THE SUN

The contrast between John and Paul's outlooks on life and love could hardly have been greater. Whereas John usually saw himself as a victim, Paul felt himself to be in charge of life. In 'If I Fell', John demanded a promise that love would last. In 'I'll Follow The Sun', Paul accepts that no such guarantee is possible. He knows that stormy weather may hit his relationship and so he makes plans to follow the sun. A selfish song in a way, because it doesn't consider how the abandoned girl might find her own sunshine, it was nonetheless an accurate reflection of Paul's romantic life.

Polished up for use when the pressure was on for the Beatles to come up with their own material, it was originally written in 1959. There was a wave of interest in Buddy Holly following his death, which gave him four hit singles in Britain before the year was out, and 'I'll Follow The Sun' was written during this period. Holly was a significant influence on the Beatles because, unlike Elvis, he wrote all his own songs and had a permanent, identifiable backing group. John (who was short-sighted) was heartened to find a bespectacled singer who had become a rock 'n' roll star and the "Beetles" group name was a homage to Buddy's Crickets.

In 1988 Paul said, "I wrote that in the front room (at Forthlin Road). It was one of those very early ones. I seem to remember writing it just after I'd had flu. I remember standing looking out through the lace curtains of the window and writing it. We had this rough R&B image in Liverpool, so songs like 'I'll Follow The Sun' got pushed back."

Beatles For Sale included a Chuck Berry track ('Rock And Roll Music'), a Leiber and Stoller ('Kansas City'), a Little Richard ('Hey, Hey, Hey'), a Buddy Holly ('Words Of Love') and two songs by Carl Perkins ('Honey Don't' and 'Everybody's Trying To Be My Baby'), all of them recorded hurriedly towards the end of the sessions. "There are still one or two of our very early numbers which are worth recording," Paul explained to *Mersey Beat* at the time. "Every now and then we remember one of the good ones we wrote in the early days and one of them, 'I'll Follow The Sun', is on the LP."

In the Seventies, Paul McCartney's company MPL Communications bought Holly's publishing catalogue and has since been responsible for organizing an annual Buddy Holly Day.

Written: Lennon/McCartney

Length: 1'51"

UK Release: *Beatles For Sale* album, December 4, 1964

US Release: *'Beatles '65'* album, December 15, 1964

BABY'S IN BLACK

A simple song with a simple story: boy loves girl, girl loves other boy, other boy doesn't love girl. Girl is sad and therefore dresses in black.

By 1964, Lennon and McCartney rarely sat together and wrote a song from start to finish as they had done so often in the past. Even though many songs were still collaborations, this now usually meant that an unfinished song was given a middle eight by the other partner or awkward lines were improved. The nose-to-nose writing that had happened in Liverpool and during the early days in London was coming to an end. "It would be daft to sit around waiting for a partner to finish your song off with you," explained Paul at the time. "If you happen to be on your own, you might as well get it finished yourself. If I get stuck on the middle eight of a new number, I give up, knowing that when I see John he will finish it off for me. He'll bring a new approach to it and that particular song will finish up half and half, Lennon and McCartney."

'Baby's In Black' was a genuine joint effort, the first since 'I Want To Hold Your Hand' almost a year before, with John and Paul writing the song together in the same room at Kenwood. Ian MacDonald has suggested that the session may have started off with them fooling around with the nursery rhyme 'Johnny's So Long At The Fair' which has a chorus of "Oh dear! What can the matter be/Johnny's so long at the fair." According to Paul it was another attempt to write something "a little bit darker, bluesy…" It was the first song recorded for *Beatles For Sale*.

Written: Lennon/McCartney

Length: 2'07"

UK Release: *Beatles For Sale* album,
December 4, 1964

US Release: *Beatles '65* album,
December 15, 1964

Oh dear, what can I do?
Baby's in black and I'm feeling blue
Tell me, oh what can I do?

She thinks of him
And so she dresses in black
And though he'll never come back,
She's dressed in black
Oh dear, what can I do?
Baby's in black and I'm feeling blue
Tell me, oh what can I do?

I think of her
But she thinks only of him
And though it's only a whim,
She thinks of him
Oh how long will it take
Till she sees the mistake she has made?
Dear what can I do?
Baby's in black and I'm feeling blue
Tell me, oh what can I do?

Oh how long will it take
Till she sees the mistake she has made?
Dear what can I do?
Baby's in black and I'm feeling blue
Tell me, oh what can I do?

She thinks of him and so
She dresses in black
And though he'll never come back,
She's dressed in black
Oh dear, what can I do?
Baby's in black and I'm feeling blue
Tell me, oh what can I do?

EVERY LITTLE THING

'Every Little Thing' was written by Paul for Jane Asher and had much the same theme as 'Things We Said Today'. Reflecting the values of the era, it tells the tale of a lucky guy whose girl loves him so much she does everything for him. The girl's needs are not even considered, the assumption being that she should find her fulfilment in serving her man. Ironically, it was the attitudes expressed in this song that Jane Asher later challenged when she told Paul that it wasn't enough for her to be simply the girlfriend of one of the world's most desirable pop stars; she wanted to make her own mark as an actor.

In 1964 Paul remembered "John and I got this one written in Atlantic City" where the Beatles had played on August 30 and stayed for a couple of extra nights at the ocean-front Marquis de Lafayette Hotel at Cape May, New Jersey. (Thirty years later he told his biographer Barry Miles that it was written at Wimpole Street but I prefer to trust memories recounted closer to the event.) It was predominantly a Paul song although John remembered that he might have "thrown something in" too. It was an attempt at writing a single, he said, but became an album track because "it didn't quite have what was required."

BELOW: John and Paul's writing practices began to change. Instead of starting songs together from scratch, they began to write separately and come together to polish the core.

EVERY LITTLE THING

When I'm walking beside her
People tell me I'm lucky
Yes, I know I'm a lucky guy
I remember the first time
I was lonely without her
Can't stop thinking about her now

Every little thing she does
She does for me, yeah
And you know the things she does
She does for me, oooh

When I'm with her I'm happy
Just to know that she loves me
Yes, I know that she loves me now
There is one thing I'm sure of
I will love her forever
For I know love will never die

Every little thing she does
She does for me, yeah
And you know the things she does
She does for me, oooh

Every little thing she does
She does for me, yeah
And you know the things she does
She does for me, oooh
Every little thing
Every little thing

97

BEATLES FOR SALE

Written: Lennon/McCartney

Length: 2'04"

UK Release: *Beatles For Sale* album, December 4, 1964

US Release: *Beatles '65* album, December 15, 1964

BEATLES FOR SALE

WHAT YOU'RE DOING

Although 'What You're Doing' tells the straightforward story of a boy being given the run-around by his girl, the lyric contains some inventive rhyming with "doing" and "blue an'", "running" and "fun in". The most memorable part of the arrangement was the Beatles shouting the first word of each verse, with Paul completing the phrases. Like 'Every Little Thing', it was written while staying outside Atlantic City at Cape May. "It's not that Atlantic City is particularly inspiring," said Paul, "It's just that we happened to have a day off on the tour there."

In *Tell Me Why*, Tim Riley praised the track for its pop ingenuity, saying that the addition of piano only for the guitar solo and final fade-out suggested a love of detail that they were later to develop more fully: "The Beatles' conception for what the studio allowed them to do in altering textures and changing musical colours is emerging as a stylistic trait, not just a gimmick." Paul, the main contributor, didn't have such a high opinion of his work, saying that it was "a bit of a filler." He said it sounded too much as though everything had been built on the first line. "You sometimes start a song and hope the best bit will arrive by the time you get to the chorus. Sometimes that's all you get, and I suspect this was one of them."

'What You're Doing' was written specifically for *Beatles For Sale*. The process of recording was painstaking, beginning in September 1964 and picking up again in late October, at which time the track was completely re-made. Paul's final verdict was that it was a better recording than it was a song.

ABOVE: It was their debut on the *Ed Sullivan Show* that alerted America to the Beatles. They are pictured here in rehearsal.

WHAT YOU'RE DOING

Look what you're doing,
I'm feeling blue and lonely
Would it be too much to ask of you
What you're doing to me?

You got me running
And there's no fun in it
Why should it be so much to ask of you
What you're doing to me?

I've been waiting here for you
Wond'ring what you're gonna do
Should you need a love that's true
It's me

ABOVE: John Lennon relaxing after a performance at the
Metropolitan Stadium, Bloomington, Minnesota, 1965.

Please stop your lying,
You've got me crying, girl
Why should it be so much to ask of you
What you're doing to me?

I've been waiting here for you
Wond'ring what you're gonna do
Should you need a love that's true
It's me

Please stop your lying,
You've got me crying, girl
Why should it be so much to ask of you
What you're doing to me?
What you're doing to me?
What you're doing to me?

Written: Lennon/McCartney

Length: 2'34"

UK Release: *Beatles For Sale* album,
December 4, 1964

US Release: *Beatles VI* album,
June 14, 1964

5

Help!

The Beatles' second feature film, produced by Walter Shenson and directed by Dick Lester, was shot between February and May 1965, mainly in the Bahamas, the Austrian Alps and at Twickenham Film Studios. The Bahamas and Austria were not chosen to add to the story but because John, Paul, George and Ringo fancied some holiday time in exotic places.

The original script was by American Marc Behm, who wanted Ringo to play a man who mistakenly signs his own death warrant and is pursued by a homicidal maniac played by Peter Sellers. "We were just about to begin shooting when I learned that Philip de Brocca was filming the very same story – *The Troubles of a Chinaman in China* starrring Jean-Paul Belmondo. I rushed to my pads and pencils and in a day or so wrote another script, *The Indian Giver*. It was this script that Richard Lester asked Charles Wood to do an 'English draft' of because he considered mine too American!"

Ringo was still the main protagonist in the rewrite, cast as the inheritor of a magic ring of great value to an evil cult that decides to pursue him for its return. Again all the songs, apart from the title track, were written without having seen the screenplay and were dropped into the film at appropriate points. Dick Lester was given a tape of the songs and chose the six that he considered would best fit.

In retrospect *Help!* (the album) can be seen as the last "beat music" album of the Beatles. Everything from now on would be more introspective, socially aware and experimental. The seeds of this can be seen in John's 'Help!', his great song of honest self-examination, and Paul's 'Yesterday', a classic ballad using instruments never before used on a Beatles' album. Otherwise this album had more than the usual number of "fillers" on it. This was probably not done out of cynicism but because of the pressures of writing to a deadline and also because they felt they had exhausted the boy-girl love formula and were ready for a new phase in their writing.

It was during the recording of *Help!* that John and George were introduced to LSD, although its effects can only be heard on one of the songs. The drug of choice for the period was pot, which they never smoked openly in the studio but did use off the film set when no-one was looking. According to John this resulted in so much hilarity that many of the scenes had to be scrapped because the boys couldn't stop laughing.

Help!, the album, was released in August 1965 and topped the charts in Britain and America. As with *A Hard Day's Night*, the American version consisted only of the songs in the film plus a few tracks by George Martin and his orchestra.

YES
IT IS

YES IT IS

John spoke about having once written love songs purely for "the meat market" and yet it's hard to find the ones he was referring to. 'Yes It Is', though, was a song he felt particularly embarrassed about in later years, scoffing at the line "for red is the colour that will make me blue". John claimed that it was nothing more than an attempt to rewrite 'This Boy', as it had the same chords, harmonies and "double-Dutch words".

The lyric is a warning to a girl not to wear red, not because it's the colour traditionally associated with sexual temptation but because it is the favoured colour of his "baby". The implication is not that he's cheating but that he's still getting over a broken relationship. The idea of blue moods either contrasting with or being confirmed by the colour of a girl's dress had already been explored by John recently in 'Baby's In Black'.

Back in 1965 John thought of it as the slowest track they'd ever put out, Paul thought it "sounded very weird... unusual for us," George thought "it should have been the major side", and Cynthia Lennon considered it her "favourite Beatles' track so far". Thirty years later Paul declared it "a fine song of John's."

It was released as the B-side to 'Ticket To Ride' in both Britain and America during April 1965.

Written: Lennon/McCartney

Length: 2'42"

UK Release: April 9, 1965 as B-side of 'Ticket To Ride'

US Release: April 19, 1965 as B-side of 'Ticket To Ride'

If you wear red tonight
Remember what I said tonight
For red is the colour that my baby wore
And what's more, it's true
Yes it is

Scarlet were the clothes she wore
Everybody knows I'm sure
I would remember all the things we
   planned
Understand it's true
Yes it is, it's true
Yes it is

I could be happy with you by my side
If I could forget her, but it's my pride
Yes it is, yes it is, oh, yes it is, yea

Please don't wear red tonight
This is what I said tonight
For red is the colour that will make me
   blue
In spite of you, it's true
Yes it is, it's true
Yes it is

I could be happy with you by my side
If I could forget her, but it's my pride
Yes it is, yes it is, oh, yes it is, yeah

Please don't wear red tonight
This is what I said tonight
For red is the colour that will make me
   blue
In spite of you, it's true
Yes it is, it's true
Yes it is, it's true

I'M DOWN

The B-side of the single 'Help!', 'I'm Down' is an unashamed attempt by Paul to write a Little Richard style of song with which to replace 'Long Tall Sally' in the Beatles' set. "We spent a lot of time trying to write a real corker – something like 'Long Tall Sally'," Paul said in October 1964. "It's very difficult. 'I Saw Her Standing There' was the nearest we got to it. We're still trying to compose a Little Richard sort of song. I'd liken it to abstract painting. People think of 'Long Tall Sally' and say it sounds so easy to write. But it's the most difficult thing we've attempted. Writing a three-chord song that's clever is not easy."

'She's A Woman', although not as frenetic, was a similar attempt to get into the little Richard mode but Paul always felt culturally disadvantaged because he hadn't been exposed to gospel music during his formative years. Church of England choirs and Salvation Army bands didn't provide the same sort of musical education for writing barnstorming rock 'n' roll. "It's like an out-of-body experience," Paul has said of when he sings in the Little Richard style. "You have to leave your current sensibilities and go about a foot above your head to sing it."

Little Richard, who'd had his first British hit with 'Rip It Up' in 1956, met the Beatles when they shared a bill at the Tower Ballroom, New Brighton, on October 12, 1962, one week after the release of 'Love Me Do'. It was a great moment for the group, who had featured 'Rip It Up', 'Good Golly Miss Molly', 'Tutti Frutti', and 'Lucille' among several Little Richard numbers in their shows.

"I met them in Liverpool before the world ever knew about them," says Little Richard. "Paul especially was into my music and had been playing it since he was in high school. He was impressed with my hollerin' and when I was on stage in Liverpool, and later in Hamburg (at the Star Club the following month), he used to stay in the wings and watch me sing. I felt honoured that they liked my music. My style is very dynamic. It's full of joy, it's full of fun and it's alive. There is nothing dead about it. There's never a dull moment. It keeps you on your toes, it keeps you movin' and I think that's what everybody gets from my music. People know that if they sing one of my songs on stage, they're gonna light up the house."

It's hard to believe but on June 14, 1965 Paul completed the seven takes of 'I'm Down' at 5:30 pm and then an hour and a half later began work on 'Yesterday'.

Fittingly, the Beatles used 'I'm Down' to close the show during the 1965 and 1966 tours. The last song they ever played live in concert though, at San Francisco's Candlestick Park on August 29, 1966, was 'Long Tall Sally'.

You tell lies thinking I can't see
You can't cry 'cause you're laughing at me
I'm down (I'm really down)
I'm down (Down on the ground)
I'm down (I'm really down)

How can you laugh,
When you know I'm down?
How can you laugh,
When you know I'm down?

Man buys ring, woman throws it away
Same old thing happen every day
I'm down (I'm really down)
I'm down (Down on the ground)
I'm down (I'm really down)

How can you laugh,
When you know I'm down?
How can you laugh,
When you know I'm down?

We're all alone and there's nobody else
You'll still moan, "Keep your hands to
    yourself"
I'm down (I'm really down)
Ah babe I'm down (Down on the ground)
I'm down (I'm really down)

How can you laugh,
When you know I'm down?
How can you laugh,
When you know I'm down? Whoa-ow

Ah babe you know I'm down
  (I'm really down)
I guess I'm down (I'm really down)
I'm down on the ground (I'm really down)
I'm down (I'm really down)
Ah, baby I'm upside down
Oh yeah, yeah, yeah, yeah, yeah, yeah

(I'm really down)
Oh baby I'm down (I'm really down)
I'm feeling upside down (I'm really down)
Ohh, I'm down (I'm really down)
Oh baby I'm down, yeah
Oh baby I'm down, yeah

Oh baby I'm down (I'm really down)
Oh baby I'm down (I'm really down)
Oh baby, baby, baby (I'm really down)
Oh baby I'm down (I'm really down)

Written: Lennon/McCartney

Length: 2'31"

UK Release: June 23, 1965 as B-side
of 'Help!'

US Release: June 19, 1965 as B-side
of 'Help!'

ABOVE: Filming a scene for *Help!* in Ailsa Avenue,
Twickenham on April 14, 1965. In the film, the
modest front doors opened into a single luxury
suite.

HELP!

'Help!' was one of John's proudest achievements, a song he would refer to as one of his favourites right up to his death. He included it with songs like 'In My Life' and 'Strawberry Fields Forever' as being "real."

It was written with Paul at Kenwood. From what he later said he didn't fully understand just how autobiographical the song was when he was writing it. "I just wrote the song because I was commissioned to write it for the movie. But later, I knew I really was crying out for help. So it was my Fat Elvis period. You see the movie. He – I – is very fat, very insecure, and he's completely lost himself. And I'm singing about when I was so much younger and all the rest, looking back at how easy it was."

For a brief period the film was known as *Eight Arms To Hold You* but neither Paul nor John were keen to write a song with that title (especially after having written 'Eight Days A Week'). "We didn't like it," said Paul in 1965. "We thought it was a bit daft." (The eight arms were not a reference to the goddess Kaili created for the film, who in fact had ten arms, but to the arms of John, Paul, George and Ringo.) "Another call to the lawyers resulted in the question 'Does your title have an exclamation mark in it?'" recalls Lester. "We said, 'If it helps we can have one.' Since the other title didn't, we were in the clear. John later said that 'Help!' was a very personal and emotional song for him. All thanks to an exclamation mark."

There may have been an even deeper level to the song that even John never discussed. Judging by available documentation the song was written over the weekend of Friday April 2. In a letter to a fan cited in Philip Norman's biography *John Lennon: A Life*, Aunt Mimi wrote of having spoken to John on the Monday following the Beatles' appearance on *Thank Your Lucky Stars* (April 3) and remarked that "he has written another very good song … (which) he thinks is a much better one (than the just about to be released 'Ticket To Ride') but it's for the film. Title for the film is just one word up to now."

This would mean that it was almost certainly the first song written after his first experience with LSD, which he was given at a dinner party in Bayswater without his knowledge. Although John became a huge fan of the drug, the initial trip was disorientating, particularly because he hadn't been primed for it. He told *Rolling Stone* in 1970 that he found the experience both terrifying and fantastic. "I was pretty stunned for a month or two." (John Riley, the dentist who spiked the drinks of George, Pattie, John and Cynthia, turned up in the Bahamas for the filming of *Help!* and became an extra, playing a member of the "Thug Army" in the climactic scene.)

If 'Help!' was composed while in this state of mind it would throw new light on the lyric. When he got to George's home after the dinner party he felt the house was " a big submarine" and he was the captain. When everyone else had retired to bed the submarine appeared to "float above his wall." Could that have been why he wanted his "feet back on the ground"? Was this why he felt that his life had changed? Was the insecurity and loss of independence referred to in the song a reference to the loss of ego he experienced while on LSD?

If this was the first Beatles' drug song, the phrase "changed my mind" takes on new meaning. It no longer refers to having his opinion changed but to having his consciousness changed. So too the phrase "opened up the doors." This may not be the doors of opportunity, as it might seem, but the doors of perception. It may have been a knowing reference to Aldous Huxley's book *The Doors Of Perception*, its title borrowed from poet William Blake ("If the doors of perception were cleansed everything would appear to man as it is, infinite."),

Help! I need somebody
Help! Not just anybody
Help! You know I need someone
Help!

When I was younger
  so much younger than today
I never needed anybody's
  help in any way
But now these days are gone,
  I'm not so self assured
Now I find I've changed my mind
  I've opened up the doors

Help me if you can, I'm feeling down
And I do appreciate you being 'round
Help me get my feet back on the ground
Won't you please, please help me

And now my life has changed
  in oh so many ways
My independence seems to
  vanish in the haze
But every now and then
  I feel so insecure
I know that I just need you
  like I've never done before

Help me if you can, I'm feeling down
And I do appreciate you being 'round
Help me get my feet back on the ground
Won't you please, please help me

When I was younger
  so much younger than today
I never needed anybody's
  help in any way
But now these days are gone,
  I'm not so self assured
Now I find I've changed my mind
  I've opened up the doors

Help me if you can, I'm feeling down
And I do appreciate you being 'round
Help me get my feet back on the ground
Won't you please, please help me,
 help me, help me, ooh

HELP!

Written: Lennon/McCartney

Length: 2'21"

UK Release: July 23, 1965

UK Chart position: 1

US Release: July 19, 1965

US Chart position: 1

which was a key text for users of hallucinogenics. It's surely significant that he used the plural "doors" rather that the singular "door" which would have been the most natural rhyme for "before". (Jim Morrison's LA group was named the Doors in 1965 as a tribute to Huxley and Blake.)

Maureen Cleave, the *Evening Standard* journalist who'd helped with the words to 'A Hard Day's Night', was visiting Cynthia at Kenwood while 'Help!' was being written and said to John, "Why don't you ever write songs with (words of) more than one syllable?". John obliged with "self-assured", "appreciate", "independence" and "insecure". He later said, "I very proudly showed them to her and she still didn't like them."

In the film, 'Help!' was used in the title sequence where black and white footage of the Beatles performing the song is shown in the temple of the goddess Kaili as followers of the cult throw darts with coloured flights at the screen.

Released as a single in July 1965, it reached the top spot in both Britain and America.

ABOVE: 'Help!' sounded like another jolly Beatles song but contained John's thoughts about insecurity and possibly his first attempts to describe LSD.

We said our goodbyes,
   ah, the night before
Love was in your eyes,
   ah, the night before
Now today I find
You have changed your mind
Treat me like you did the night before

Were you telling lies,
   ah, the night before?
Was I so unwise, ah, the night before?
When I held you near
You were so sincere
Treat me like you did the night before

Last night is a night
   I will remember you by
When I think of things
   we did it makes me wanna cry

We said our goodbyes,
   ah, the night before
Love was in your eyes,
   ah, the night before
Now today I find
You have changed your mind
Treat me like you did the night before

When I held you near
You were so sincere
Treat me like you did the night before

Last night is a night
   I will remember you by
When I think of things
   we did it makes me wanna cry

Were you telling lies,
   ah, the night before?
Was I so unwise,
   ah, the night before?
When I held you near
You were so sincere
Treat me like you did
   the night before
Like the night before

THE NIGHT BEFORE

'The Night Before' was written mainly by Paul, probably at Wimpole Street, and featured him playing both bass and lead while George played rhythm and John played electric piano (a 1964 Hohner Pianet). In 1965 Paul commented that the sound of the track "was one of the best [we] had got on record, instrumentally." John pointed out that Paul and George were playing the same breaks exactly "but in different octaves."

It could have been about the tumultuous nature of his relationship with Jane Asher but might just as easily have been about an invented situation. As with *A Hard Day's Night*, the songs used in *Help!* owed nothing to the script. "I think all the songs in *Help!* were written before the screenplay was even completed," confirms Dick Lester. "I was given a demo tape with about eleven songs and I chose six of them in a rather arbitrary way, thinking that they were ones which I could do something with. It was as casual as that and I fitted the songs into the film in places where I thought I could do something with them."

Three months after it was recorded Paul was filmed singing 'The Night Before' on Salisbury Plain while surrounded by troops and tanks. The plain, which is mostly in Wiltshire, is the site of the Army Training Estate, a 150 square mile area that is used 340 days a year as a firing range.

Written: Lennon/McCartney

Length: 2'33"

UK Release: *Help!* album, August 6, 1965

US Release: *Help!* album, August 13, 1965

THE
NIGHT
BEFORE

YOU'VE GOT TO HIDE YOUR LOVE AWAY

Bob Dylan's music – (the acoustic *Another Side Of Bob Dylan* had been his most recent album) – directed John towards a more intense and personal style of writing. He began to compose songs using his current state of mind, whatever it might be, as the starting point. This can be seen in later songs as varied as 'Nowhere Man', 'Good Morning Good Morning' and 'I'm So Tired'. "Instead of projecting myself into a situation I would try to express what I felt about myself, which I had done with my books," he explained. "I think Dylan helped me realize that." In the first lines of 'You've Got To Hide Your Love Away', the image of John standing facing a wall with his head in his hands was probably a perfect description of a mild case of writer's block. It also appears to have been lifted from Dylan's song 'I Don't Believe You (She Acts Like We Never Have Met)' where the narrator has been stood up by his girl and is left "facing the wall." On its surface the song is about being left by a girl and the love that he needs to hide away is his unrequited feeling.

However, there are alternative explanations. Tony Bramwell, friend and employee of the Beatles, suggests that it may have been written with Brian Epstein in mind, urging him to be discreet about his homosexual relationships (which, at the time, were illegal in Britain). It could also have been about a secret affair of John's – in other words, John talking to himself.

Written at Kenwood, it was used in the film during a scene in which British actress Eleanor Bron visits the group in their terraced house in an attempt to retrieve the ring.

John's childhood friend, Pete Shotton, was with him as it was being composed and remembered that in the original version he had sung that he felt "two foot tall". However when he sang it to Paul, he mistakenly sang "two foot small", which Paul liked better and so it was kept. Shotton went to the recording on February 18, 1965, and added some "heys" to the chorus.

Here I stand head in hand
Turn my face to the wall
If she's gone I can't go on
Feeling two-foot small

Everywhere people stare
Each and every day
I can see them laugh at me
And I hear them say

Hey, you've got to hide your love away
Hey, you've got to hide your love away

How can I even try
I can never win
Hearing them, seeing them
In the state I'm in

How could she say to me
Love will find a way
Gather round all you clowns
Let me hear you say

Hey, you've got to hide your love away
Hey, you've got to hide your love away

LEFT: The Beatles with British soldiers on the Army Training Estate in Wiltshire, May 1965.

Written: Lennon/McCartney

Length: 2'11"

UK Release: *Help!* album, August 6, 1965

US Release: *Help!* album, August 13, 1965

I NEED YOU

A formulaic love song, 'I Need You' was written by George for his girlfriend Pattie Boyd, and was one of two of his Beatles' songs that he didn't comment on in his 1980 book *I Me Mine* (the other was 'You Like Me Too Much').

Prior to 'I Need You', George had only contributed one song to a Beatles' album. The previous two albums had had nothing by him. In later years he complained that his contributions were overlooked by John and Paul but at this point his lack of exposure may have had more to do with the length of time he took to complete songs. In 1965 he told the American radio journalist Larry Kane, "If I get something going, then I'll tape it. I'll leave it for about five weeks, then I'll suddenly remember. Then I add a bit more to it, so it will probably take me about three months until I finish one song."

It was also the only George song to be featured in the film *Help!* (in the Salisbury Plain sequence) and the first to use a tone pedal to distort the guitar sound. He must have been proud that it was included in the film because his voice can be heard over the 'Overture' from Rossini's *Barber of Seville* announcing his credit at the moment it comes on screen – "'I Need You' by George Harrison."

Some books have claimed that George wrote it in the Bahamas while apart from Pattie, but this can't be true, as recording began on February 15, 1965, and the Bahamian scenes weren't shot until the following week. Tom Petty performed the song at the Concert For George that took place at London's Royal Albert Hall on November 29, 2002, a year after George's death.

Written: Harrison

Length: 2'31"

UK Release: *Help!* album August 6, 1965

US Release: *Help!* album August 13, 1965

You don't realise how much I need you
Love you all the time and never leave you
Please come on back to me
I'm lonely as can be
I need you

Said you had a thing or two to tell me
How was I to know you would upset me?
I didn't realise as I looked in your eyes
You told me, oh yes, you told me,
    you don't want my lovin' anymore
That's when it hurt me and feeling like this
    I just can't go on anymore

Please remember how I feel about you
I could never really live without you
So, come on back and see
Just what you mean to me
I need you

But when you told me,
    you don't want my lovin' anymore
That's when it hurt me and feeling like this
    I just can't go on anymore

Please remember how I feel about you
I could never really live without you
So, come on back and see
Just what you mean to me
I need you
I need you
I need you

ABOVE RIGHT: The Beatles with Eleanor Bron on the set of *Help!* where John sang 'You've Got To Hide Your Love Away'.

BELOW RIGHT: Apparently carefree but actually posing for photographers while in Miami, Florida during their first visit to America, February 1964.

For I have got another girl,
Another girl
You're making me say that
I've got nobody but you
But as from today, well,
  I've got somebody that's new
I ain't no fool and I don't take
  what I don't want
For I have got another girl,
Another girl
She's sweeter than all the girls
  and I met quite a few
Nobody in all the world can
  do what she can do
And so I'm telling you,
  "This time you'd better stop"
For I have got another girl,
Another girl
Who will love me till the end
Through thick and thin
She will always be my friend

I don't want to say that
  I've been unhappy with you
But, as from today, well,
  I've seen somebody that's new
I ain't no fool and I don't take
  what I don't want
For I have got another girl,
Another girl
Who will love me till the end
Through thick and thin
She will always be my friend

I don't want to say that
  I've been unhappy with you
But, as from today, well,
  I've seen somebody that's new
I ain't no fool and I don't take
  what I don't want
For I have got another girl,
Another girl
Another girl

ANOTHER GIRL

'Another Girl' was written by Paul during a ten-day holiday in Tunisia and used in a scene filmed on Balmoral Island in the Bahamas.

In this song, Paul talks about being under pressure to commit long-term to his girlfriend but says he's not going to do this, mainly because he's already got himself another girl. This may have been a reference to the fact that although he was still firmly linked to Jane Asher in the public imagination he was also seeing other women. He told his biographer Barry Miles. "I had a girlfriend and I would go with other girls. It was a perfectly open relationship."

In the same book – *Many Years From Now* – Paul wrongly identified the villa as British Embassy property. It was actually Villa Sebastian built in the coastal resort of Hammamet in the 1920s by a wealthy Romanian, Georges Sebastian. Surrounded by 14 acres of botanical gardens, the Moorish style building was later described by the great American architect Frank Lloyd Wright as "the most beautiful house I know." It was visited by such writers and artists as Ernest Hemingway, F. Scott Fitzgerald, Paul Klee, Cecil Beaton, and Jean Cocteau. During the war it was requisitioned by Rommell and, when peace returned, Winston Churchill stayed there. In 1959 it was gifted to the Tunisian state and in 1964 an amphitheatre was added in the grounds. In the tiled bathroom there was a sunken cross-shaped bath capable of seating four. Paul found the acoustics here ideal for song writing. There was also a huge swimming pool surrounded by colonnades. Paul heard about the property from the raconteur, writer and actor Peter Ustinov, who had stayed there. Villa Sebastian is now Hammamet's International Cultural Centre and a popular tourist destination.

John once said that the Beatles' songs were like signatures; even when they weren't trying to give anything away they would betray their most fundamental attitudes. "It was always apparent – if you looked below the surface – what was being said. Resentfulness or love or hate, it's apparent in all our work."

'Another Girl' was recorded the day after Paul returned from his holiday.

Written: Lennon/McCartney

Length: 2'08"

UK Release: *Help!* album, August 6, 1965

US Release: *Help!* album, August 13, 1965

ANOTHER GIRL

ABOVE RIGHT: Filming the Buckingham Palace scene at Cliveden House, Cliveden, Maidenhead, May 1965.

You're going to lose that girl
You're going to lose that girl

If you don't take her out tonight
She's going to change her mind
And I will take her out tonight
And I will treat her kind
You're going to lose that girl
You're going to lose that girl

If you don't treat her right, my friend
You're going to find her gone
Cos I will treat her right, and then
You'll be the lonely one
You're going to lose that girl
You're going to lose that girl

I'll make a point
  of taking her away from you, yeah
The way you treat her what else can I do?

You're going to lose that girl
You're going to lose that girl
I'll make a point
  of taking her away from you, yeah
The way you treat her what else can I do?

If you don't take her out tonight
She's going to change her mind
And I will take her out tonight
And I will treat her kind
You're going to lose that girl
You're going to lose that girl
You're going to lose that girl

YOU'RE GOING TO LOSE THAT GIRL

YOU'RE GOING TO LOSE THAT GIRL

The Beatles performed 'You're Going To Lose That Girl' in a recording studio scene in the film, which was actually filmed at Twickenham Film Studios. The song is interrupted when the gang chasing Ringo cut a hole around his drum kit in the ceiling of the room below. Written mainly by John but completed with Paul at Weybridge, it is a warning to an unidentified male that if he doesn't start treating his girlfriend right, he (John) is going to make a play for her – a theme he first outlined in 'She Loves You'.

Written: Lennon/McCartney

Length: 2'20"

UK Release: *Help!* album, August 6, 1965

US Release: *Help!* album, August 13, 1965

TICKET TO RIDE

'Ticket To Ride' was written by John and Paul as a single and was described by John as "one of the earliest heavy metal records made." Although it had been preceded by the Kinks' 'You Really Got Me', which charted in Britain the previous summer, this was the first Beatles' track to feature an insistent, clanking riff underpinned by a heavy drum beat and it used an innovative fade-out with an altered melody. "It was pretty heavy for (the time) if you go back and look in the charts for what other music people were making," said John in 1970. "And you hear it now and it doesn't sound too bad." Paul confessed to his biographer Barry Miles that the apparently loopy suggestion made by some American Beatles' fans at the time that the song was referring to a British Railways ticket to the town of Ryde on the Isle of Wight was partly right. Paul's cousin Betty Robbins and her husband Mike ran the Bow Bars in Union Street, Ryde, and Paul and John had visited them. Although the song was primarily about a girl riding out of the life of the narrator, they were conscious of the potential for a double meaning. (Blow-ups of rail tickets were used in the background when they recorded a promotional film for the single.)

Don Short, a show business journalist who travelled extensively with the Beatles in the Sixties, was told by John that the phrase had yet another meaning. "The girls who worked the streets in Hamburg had to have a clean bill of health and so the medical authorities would give them a card saying that they didn't have a dose of anything," says Short. "I was with the Beatles when they went back to Hamburg in June 1966 and it was then that John told me that he had coined the phrase 'a ticket to ride' to describe these cards. He could have been joking – you always had to be careful with John like that – but I certainly remember him telling me that."

The phrase "ticket to ride" has been used in spirituals and gospel songs. A familiar spiritual is titled 'If I Got My Ticket Lord, Can I Ride' and in

ABOVE: The Beatles perform for *Help!*.

I think I'm gonna be sad
I think it's today, yeah
The girl that's driving me mad
Is going away

She's got a ticket to ride
She's got a ticket to ride
She's got a ticket to ride
But she don't care

She said that living with me
Is bringing her down, yeah
For she would never be free
When I was around

She's got a ticket to ride
She's got a ticket to ride
She's got a ticket to ride
But she don't care

I don't know why she's riding so high
She ought to think twice
She ought to do right by me
Before she gets to saying goodbye
She ought to think twice
She ought to do right by me

I think I'm gonna be sad
I think it's today, yeah
The girl that's driving me mad
Is going away, yeah

Oh, she's got a ticket to ride
She's got a ticket to ride
She's got a ticket to ride
But she don't care

I don't know why she's riding so high
She ought to think twice
She ought to do right by me
Before she gets to saying goodbye
She ought to think twice
She ought to do right by me

She said that living with me
Is bringing her down, yeah
For she would never be free
When I was around

Ah, she's got a ticket to ride
She's got a ticket to ride
She's got a ticket to ride
But she don't care

My baby don't care, my baby don't care
My baby don't care, my baby don't care
My baby don't care, my baby don't care
(fade out)

1941 Alan and John Lomax did a field recording of Vera Hall and Dock Reed singing a folk song called 'Low Down Chariot', one verse of which went "Got a ticket to ride, oh let me ride/Got a ticket to ride, oh let me ride/Got a ticket to ride, oh let me ride/Oh, low down chariot let me ride."

Speaking in April 1965 Beatles' music publisher Dick James said that John had told him in December 1964 that he had a line "she's got a ticket to ride" that he planned to work into a song. "I liked the phrase," said James. "It was a slightly more original idea than usual for expressing goodbye and parting. I encouraged John to work at it." Two months later John was playing 'Ticket To Ride' on his winter holiday in Switzerland. George Martin, who was with John in Switzerland, said, "I liked it straightaway. John said he would get together with Paul as soon as he got back to London and finish it off." John returned on February 7, Paul and Jane returned from Tunisia on February 14, and the song was recorded on February 15.

'Ticket To Ride' was released on April 9 1965 in Britain and on April 19 in America. It was also used on the film soundtrack over scenes of the Beatles playing on the ski slopes in Austria.

TICKET
TO RIDE

Written: Lennon/McCartney

Length: 3'12"

UK Release: April 9, 1965

UK Chart position: 1

US Release: April 19, 1965

US Chart position: 1

She's got a ticket

TELL ME WHAT YOU SEE

'Tell Me What You See' was another "work song" mainly by Paul, who asks his girl to give her heart to him because he's utterly trustworthy and will brighten up her life. If she doesn't believe him, he suggests that she take a look in his eyes and tell him what she sees.

John told American journalist Michael Lydon that the lines that begin "Big and black the clouds may be" and end "I'll make bright your day" were based on a religiously inspired verse that hung on the wall of his childhood home in Woolton. The original words were:

> However black the clouds may be
> In time they'll pass away
> Have faith and trust and you will see
> God's light makes bright your day.

In his first book *In His Own Write* he parodied the lines as:

> However Blackpool tower may be
> In time they'll bass away
> Have faith and trump and BBC
> Griff's light make bright your day.

The track was recorded before the filming of *Help!* and offered to Dick Lester for the soundtrack, but was rejected. Tim Riley notes that it is one of the album's weaker songs, suggesting that it became a working draft for the altogether stronger track 'I'm Looking Through You'. Speaking to Barry Miles, Paul commented, "Not awfully memorable. Not one of the better songs but they did a job, they were very handy for albums or B-sides. You need those kinds of sides."

If you let me take your heart
 I will prove to you
We will never be apart
 if I'm part of you
Open up your eyes now,
 tell me what you see
It is no surprise now,
 what you see is me

Big and black the clouds may be,
 time will pass away
If you put your trust in me
 I'll make bright your day
Look into these eyes now,
 tell me what you see
Don't you realise now,
 what you see is me
Tell me what you see

Listen to me one more time,
 how can I get through?
Can't you try to see that I'm
 trying to get to you?
Open up your eyes now,
 tell me what you see
It is no surprise now,
 what you see is me
Tell me what you see

Listen to me one more time,
 how can I get through?
Can't you try to see that I'm
 trying to get to you?
Open up your eyes now,
 tell me what you see
It is no surprise now,
 what you see is me

Written: Lennon/McCartney

Length: 2'39"

UK Release: *Help!* album, August 6, 1965

US Release: *Beatles VI* album, June 14 1965

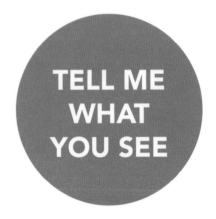

TELL ME WHAT YOU SEE

YOU LIKE ME TOO MUCH

'You Like Me Too Much' was written and recorded by George for the soundtrack and recorded before filming started on *Help!* It was eventually relegated to the non-film side of the album.

George chose not to discuss 'You Like Me Too Much' in his otherwise comprehensive account of his songwriting, *I Me Mine*, presumably because there was nothing much to say. A standard love story, the song describes how having been jilted, the lover feels everything will turn out all right in the end, as the girl simply loves him too much. If this song had been written by John, he would undoubtedly have dismissed it as one of his throwaways.

Written: Harrison

Length: 2'38"

UK Release: *Help!* album, August 6, 1965

US Release: *Beatles VI* album, June 14 1965

BELOW: Filming the snow scenes for *Help!* in Obertauern, Austria.

Though you've gone away this morning
You'll be back again tonight
Telling me there'll be no next time
If I don't just don't treat you right
You'll never leave me
  and you know it's true
Cos you like me too much and I like you

You've tried before to leave me
But you haven't got the nerve
To walk out and make me lonely
Which is all that I deserve
You'll never leave me
  and you know it's true
Cos you like me too much and I like you

I really do,
And it's nice when you believe me
If you leave me
I will follow you
  and bring you back where you belong
Cos I could't really stand it
  I'd admit that I was wrong
I wouldn't let you leave me cos it's true
Cos you like me too much and I like you

Cos you like me too much and I like you
I really do,
And it's nice when you believe me
If you leave me
I will follow you and bring you back
  where you belong
Cos I could't really stand it
  I'd admit that I was wrong
I wouldn't let you leave me cos it's true
Cos you like me too much and I like you
Cos you like me too much and I like you

IT'S ONLY LOVE

John wrote 'It's Only Love' as an upbeat number, and filled it with the most clichéd rhymes and images. In the lyric, he describes how his girl lights up the night for him and yet he's suffering from butterflies in his stomach. The only problem is that he is in love.

It was one of the few Beatles' songs that John really hated. "I was always ashamed of that because of the abominable lyrics," he admitted in 1969. All the songs that John came to hate were condemned on the grounds of their lyrics rather than their melodies, usually because he felt that he had produced platitudes rather than genuine insights.

In this case, the song's shortcomings could have been a result of having to produce a further side of songs to complete the soundtrack album.

George Martin and his orchestra recorded the composition as an instrumental using John's original working title of 'That's A Nice Hat'.

IT'S ONLY LOVE

Written: Lennon/McCartney

Length: 1'58"

UK Release: *Help!* album, August 6, 1965

US Release: *Rubber Soul* album, December 6 1965

HELP!

I get high when I see you go by
My oh my
When you sigh, my, my inside just flies
Butterflies
Why am I so shy when I'm beside you?

It's only love and that is all
Why should I feel the way I do?
It's only love, and that is all
But it's so hard loving you

Is it right that you and I should fight
Every night?
Just the sight of you makes
  nighttime bright
Very bright
Haven't I the right to make it up girl?

It's only love and that is all
Why should I feel the way I do?
It's only love, and that is all
But it's so hard loving you
Yes it's so hard loving you, loving you

LEFT: George, pictured with Pattie, was nowhere near as prolific a songwriter as Paul and John, and when he did get started, felt that his contributions were overlooked.

I've just seen a face
I can't forget the time or place
Where we just met
She's just the girl for me
And I want all the world to see
We've met, mmm-mmm-mmm-m'mmm-
mmm

Had it been another day
I might have looked the other way
And I'd have never been aware
But as it is I'll dream of her
Tonight, di-di-di-di'n'di
Falling, yes I am falling
And she keeps calling
Me back again

I have never known
The like of this, I've been alone
And I have missed things
And kept out of sight
But other girls were never quite
Like this, da-da-n'da-da'n'da
Falling, yes I am falling
And she keeps calling
Me back again

Falling, yes I am falling
And she keeps calling
Me back again

I've just seen a face
I can't forget the time or place
Where we just met
She's just the girl for me
And I want all the world to see
We've met,
mmm-mmm-mmm-da-da-da
Falling, yes I am falling
And she keeps calling
Me back again
Falling, yes I am falling
And she keeps calling
Me back again
Oh, falling, yes I am falling
And she keeps calling
Me back again

I'VE JUST SEEN A FACE

'I've Just Seen A Face' was a tune that Paul had been playing on piano for some time. He played it at family get-togethers back in Liverpool and his Auntie Gin (his dad's sister) loved it so much that it was dubbed 'Auntie Gin's Theme'. The George Martin Orchestra went on to record an instrumental version under this title. Auntie Gin, born Jane Virginia McCartney, was the youngest sister of Paul's father Jim and would later get a mention in 'Let 'Em In', recorded by Wings. Paul also played 'I've Just Seen A Face' with Wings. "It was slightly country and western from my point of view. It was faster, though. It was a strange uptempo thing. I was quite pleased with it. The lyric works: it keeps dragging you forward, it keeps pulling you to the next line. There's an insistent quality to it that I liked."

Written: Lennon/McCartney

Length: 2'07"

UK Release: *Help!* album, August 6, 1965

US Release: *Rubber Soul* album, December 6, 1965

ABOVE: Jane Asher was often present when Paul was inspired to write. This photo shows them on holiday in Portugal in 1965.

For many months, what was to become Paul's best-known song was titled 'Scrambled Eggs', much to the annoyance of everyone he cared to play it to.

Yesterday all my troubles seemed
 so far away.
Now it looks as though they're
 here to stay.
Oh, I believe in yesterday.

Suddenly I'm not half the man
 I used to be.
There's a shadow hanging over me.
Oh, yesterday came suddenly.

Why she had to go, I don't know,
 she wouldn't say.
I said something wrong,
 now I long for yesterday.

Yesterday love was such
 an easy game to play.
Now I need a place to hide away.
Oh, I believe in yesterday.

Why she had to go, I don't know,
 she wouldn't say.
I said something wrong,
 now I long for yesterday.

Yesterday love was such
 an easy game to play.
Now I need a place to hide away.
Oh, I believe in yesterday.

Mm mm mm mm mm mm mm

YESTERDAY

YESTERDAY

Paul woke up one morning in his top floor room at the Ashers' home in Wimpole Street with the tune for 'Yesterday' in his head. There was a piano by the bed and he went straight to it and started playing. "It was just all there," he said. "A complete thing. I couldn't believe it."

Although at that point it had no lyric, Paul was worried that the tune itself might have been unconsciously plagiarized, and that what had seemed like a flash of inspiration may only have been a surge of recollection. "For about a month, I went round to people in the music business and asked them whether they had ever heard it before," he said. "Eventually it became like handing something in to the police. I thought that if no-one claimed it after a few weeks then I would have it."

He then came up with the provisional title 'Scrambled Eggs' and began singing "Scrambled eggs, Oh you've got such lovely legs", simply to get a feel for the vocal. This was a common practice and sometimes "dummy lyrics" gave rise to interesting lines that were kept in the final version. The first lyric was:

Scrambled eggs, Have an omelette with some Muenster cheese,
Put your dishes in the wash bin please
So I can clean the scrambled eggs.

Join me do, There are lots of eggs for me and you,
I've got ham and cheese and bacon too,
So go get two and join me, do.

Fried or sunny side,
Just aren't right,
The mix-bowl begs,
Quick, go get a pan.
And we'll scramble up some eggs, eggs, eggs, eggs.

Scrambled eggs, Good for breakfast, dinner-time or brunch,
Don't buy six or twelve, buy a bunch,
and we'll have lunch on scrambled eggs.

"We were shooting *Help!* in the studio for about four weeks," remembers Dick Lester. "At some time during that period, we had a piano on one of the stages and he was playing this 'Scrambled Eggs' all the time. It got to the point where I said to him, 'If you play that bloody song any longer I'll have the piano taken off stage. Either finish it or give it up!'"

Paul must have conceived the tune late in 1964 because Eric Clapton, then with the Yardbirds, can recall him playing the tune backstage at the Hammersmith Odeon during the time of the Beatles' Christmas shows. It wasn't until June 1965, when Paul took a brief holiday in Portugal at the villa of the Shadows' rhythm guitarist Bruce Welch, that he'd completed the lyric. It was then he hit on the idea of using a one word title – 'Yesterday'.

"I was packing to leave and Paul asked me if I had a guitar," says Welch. "He'd apparently been working on the lyrics as he drove to Albufeira from the airport at Lisbon. He borrowed my guitar and started playing the song we all now know as 'Yesterday'."

Two days after returning from Portugal, Paul recorded it at Abbey Road. The song startled pop fans at the time because it featured a string quartet with

LEFT: The tune to 'Yesterday' came to Paul in his sleep and he went straight to his piano on waking up.

Paul as the only Beatle on the session. In America, it became a single and reached the Number 1 spot but, in Britain, it was never released as either an A- or a B-side during the group's career. It rapidly became a pop standard, covered by everyone from Frank Sinatra to Marianne Faithfull. Nowadays, more than half a century later, it is still one of the most played tracks on American radio.

Although John claimed that he never wished that he had written it, he did admit that it was a "beautiful" song with "good" lyrics but argued that the lyrics were never resolved. However, others have felt that its strength lies in its vagueness. All the listener needs to know is that it's about someone wanting to turn back the clock, to retreat to a time before an unwelcome and life-changing event. The application is universal.

There has been speculation that in Paul's case the death of his mother was the event alluded to and the regret was about his inability to express appropriate grief at the time. "It does say 'why she had to go I don't know, she wouldn't say' and 'I believe in yesterday', so it may subconsciously something to do with the death of my mother," Paul has admitted.

Iris Caldwell remembered an interesting incident in connection with the song. She had broken up with Paul in March 1963 after a silly argument over her dogs (Paul wasn't too keen on dogs at the time) and, when he later called up to speak to Iris, her mother told Paul that her daughter didn't want to speak to him because he had no feelings. Two and a half years later, on Sunday August 1, 1965, Paul was scheduled to sing 'Yesterday' on a live television programme, *Blackpool Night Out*. During that week, he phoned Mrs Caldwell and said, "You know that you said that I had no feelings? Watch the telly on Sunday and then tell me that I've got no feelings."

In July 2003 the Liverpool writer Spencer Leigh made the discovery that there were both musical and lyrical similarities between 'Yesterday' and the Nat King Cole song 'Answer Me' (1953). The Cole song even has the lines "Yesterday I believed that love was here to stay/Won't you tell me that I've gone astray?" When this news broke the response from Paul's office was that the two songs were as alike as 'Get Back' and 'God Save The Queen'.

Written: Lennon/McCartney

Length: 2'03"

UK Release: *Help!* album August 6, 1965

US Release: (single) September 13, 1966

US chart position: 1

6 Rubber Soul

Although there had been hints of a new direction on the preceding albums, *Rubber Soul* marked a major period of transition. John would later call it the beginning of the group's "self-conscious" period; the end of the Beatles' "tribal child-like" stage.

The cover, with its deliberately distorted photograph of the Beatles hinted at the perception shifts of LSD and marijuana. It was a hint to listeners that all was not the same. The music inside explored new sounds, new rhythms and new subject matter. It introduced Paul on fuzz bass and George on sitar. When producer George Martin played a piano solo back at double-speed to create a baroque sound, it was the first time that they'd tampered with tapes to create an effect. "We found out a lot technically," John said in 1965. "Things have come into focus."

There was a playfulness to *Rubber Soul* exemplified by the wordplay of the title (Paul had seen a record review referring to an inauthentic sounding single as "plastic soul") and the "beep beeps" and "tit tits" of the backing vocals. Paul was quoted saying that they were now into humorous songs and both 'Drive My Car', with its role reversal, and 'Norwegian Wood', with its clumsy seduction scene, are songs he could have had in mind. For a group that had only ever sung about love, 'Nowhere Man', a song about lack of belief, was a breakthrough. Other songs like 'The Word' and 'In My Life' were only tangentially about boy-girl relationships.

The love songs of this album evidenced a new maturity. Paul's 'We Can Work It Out', stemming from his own increasingly troubled relationship with Jane Asher, was a long way from the simple hope expressed in 'She Loves You' or 'I Saw Her Standing There'. There is a recognition that relationships often involve game playing, that the role of women was changing and that true love involves hard work to maintain. John's 'The Word' pointed in the direction of the universal love that would later be the basis of songs like 'Within You Without You' and 'All You Need Is Love'.

They were also experimenting with different types of narrative – dialogue in 'Drive My Car', sermonizing in 'The Word', bilingualism in 'Michelle'. They were growing in confidence as lyricists and were for the first time recognizing their position as cultural leaders. John later acknowledged that 'The Word' was the first song of the Beatles that offered instruction to the audience.

Speaking to Norman Jopling of *Record Mirror*, Paul said, "I think John and I are writing different sorts of songs to what we were a couple of years back. I can't say whether they're better or worse but they're certainly different. And that's OK by us because we wouldn't want to stand still, to stagnate musically." To another writer he said, "We are so well established now that we can bring the fan along with us and stretch the limits of pop. We don't have to follow what everyone else is doing." To Michael Lydon he said, "If someone saw a picture of you taken two years ago and said that was you, you'd say it was a load of rubbish and show them a new picture. That's how we feel about the early stuff and *Rubber Soul*. That's who we are now. People have always wanted us to stay the same, but we can't stay in a rut. No one else expects to hit a peak at 23 and never develop, so why should we? *Rubber Soul* for me is the beginning of my adult life." John neatly summarized the advance when speaking to Loraine Alterman. "Beatles' music," he said, "has progressed and got more like Beatles' music. Before, it was more of anyone else's music."

Recorded over a four-week period in the autumn of 1965, *Rubber Soul* was released in December and became a chart-topping album in Britain and America. Four of the British tracks were left off the American album and were replaced by two tracks from *Help!*.

DAY TRIPPER

Written: Lennon/McCartney

Length: 2'49"

UK Release: December 3, 1965 as double A-side with 'We Can Work It Out'

UK Chart position: 1

US Release: December 6, 1965 as double A-side with 'We Can Work It Out'

US Chart position: 5

* Although 'Day Tripper'/'We Can Work It Out' was a double A-side single, US chart compilers calculated their sales separately

DAY TRIPPER

'Day Tripper' was written under pressure when the Beatles needed a new single for the 1965 Christmas market. John wrote most of the lyric and the basic guitar break, coming up with a riff that he later admitted was derived from 'I Feel Fine'. Paul helped on the verses and his bass riff owed something to the bass riff on Roy Orbison's 'Oh Pretty Woman' (1964).

In August, 1965, while in America, John and George took LSD of their own free will for the first time and from then on John confessed that he "just ate it all the time." 'Day Tripper' was a play on words by John, who wanted to reflect the influence of the growing drug culture within a Beatles' song. It was his way of referring to those who couldn't, like him, afford the luxury of being almost permanently tripped out. "It's just a rock 'n' roll song," he commented. "Day trippers are people who go on a day trip, right? Usually on a ferryboat or something. But (the song) was kind of...you're just a weekend hippie. Get it?"

The song is also about a girl who leads the singer on. His oblique description of the girl as a "big teaser", was an allusion to the term "prick teaser", a phrase sometimes used by British men about women who encouraged sexual arousal with no intention of following through.

'Day Tripper' was released in both Britain and America as a double A-sided single with 'We Can Work It Out'. It was the more popular song in Britain, reaching Number 1, but in America it peaked at 5. The Beatles later said that 'We Can Work It Out' was their choice for the A-side.

DAY TRIPPER

Got a good reason
For taking the easy way out
Got a good reason
For taking the easy way out now

She was a day tripper
One way ticket, yeah
It took me so long to find out
And I found out

She's a big teaser
She took me half the way there
She's a big teaser
She took me half the way there now

She was a day tripper
One way ticket, yeah
It took me so long to find out
And I found out
Ah, ah, ah, ah, ah, ah

Tried to please her
She only played one night stands
Tried to please her
She only played one night stands now

She was a day tripper
Sunday driver, yeah
It took me so long to find out
And I found out

Day tripper, day tripper, yeah
Day tripper, day tripper, yeah
Day tripper

LEFT: John and Cynthia photographed at Weybridge in May 1965. Elements of Surrealism were creeping in.

WE CAN WORK IT OUT

In October 1965, Jane Asher decided to join the Bristol Old Vic Company, which meant moving from London to the west of England just at the time the Beatles were recording tracks for *Rubber Soul*. Her departure upset Paul and caused the first major rift in their relationship. As had been suggested in his songs, Paul's notion of a good woman at this time was someone who would be happy just to be around him. Jane's outlook was more liberated. She was not content to be a rock star's "chick". She was well educated, independently minded and wanted, above all, to establish a career.

The opening line of the song, "Try and see it my way", may have been inspired by dialogue from the Bond film *Goldfinger* (the Beatles were given a private pre-release screening by producer Cubby Broccoli). James Bond asks Pussy Galore, "What would it take for you to see things my way?", to which she answers, "A lot more than you've got." The Bond film franchise came about at around the same time that the Beatles took off and tapped into similar aspirations. George Martin produced the title track 'Goldfinger' by Shirley Bassey, although in the film Bond is revealed as a Beatles-hater. "My dear girl," he says at one point, "there are some things that just aren't done, such as drinking Dom Perignon '53 above a temperature of 38 degrees Fahrenheit. That's as bad as listening to the Beatles without earmuffs."

In 'We Can Work It Out', Paul doesn't try to argue the merits of his case, but simply pleads with his woman to share his perspective for no other reason than that he believes he is right and she is wrong. It was typical of Paul that, faced with what could be the end of a relationship, he didn't retreat sobbing to his room, but emerged with the positive slogan "we can work it out". The slightly downbeat middle eight, with its intimations of mortality, was added by John. "The middle eight is the best," said Paul at the time. "It changes the beat to a waltz in the middle. The original arrangement was terrible – very skiffley. Then at the session George Martin had the idea of splitting the beat completely. The words go charging at double speed against this slow waltz music."

In 2006 the former *Daily Mirror* editor Piers Morgan revealed that he had heard a voice mail message left by Paul on the answerphone of his wife Heather McCartney during a rift in the marriage. Heather had gone to India and Paul was pleading for her to return. "He sounded lonely, miserable and desperate," Morgan wrote. "He even sang 'We Can Work It Out'."

It was a song that perfectly combined the opposite personalities of John and Paul. "You've got Paul writing 'we can work it out'," said John. "Real optimistic, and me, impatient, [with] 'Life is very short, And there's no time, For fussing and fighting my friend.'" The song was written at Paul's father's house in Heswall, Cheshire. The harmonium "wash" was an afterthought added in the studio, and George Harrison suggested changing the middle-eight to waltz time.

Try to see it my way
Do I have to keep on talking
Till I can't go on?

While you see it your way
Run the risk of knowing that
Our love may soon be gone
We can work it out
We can work it out

Think of what you're saying
You can get it wrong and still
You think that it's all right

Think of what I'm saying
We can work it out and
Get it straight or say good night
We can work it out
We can work it out

Life is very short
And there's no time
For fussing and fighting, my friend

I have always thought
That it's a crime
So I will ask you once again

Written: Lennon/McCartney

Length: 2'15"

UK Single Release: December 3, 1965 as double A-side with 'Day Tripper'

UK Chart position: 1

US Single Release: December 6, 1965 as double A-side with 'Day Tripper'

US Chart position: 1

Try to see it my way
Only time will tell
If I am right or I am wrong

While you see it your way
There's a chance that we might
Fall apart before too long
We can work it out
We can work it out

Life is very short
And there's no time
For fussing and fighting, my friend

I have always thought
That it's a crime
So I will ask you once again

Try to see it my way
Only time will tell
If I am right or I am wrong

While you see it your way
There's a chance that we might
Fall apart before too long
We can work it out
We can work it out

RIGHT: Paul's natural optimism was challenged by his emotionally turbulent relationship with Jane Asher. As a result his songs began to have more bite.

DRIVE MY CAR

Asked a girl what she wanted to be
She said baby, "Can't you see
I wanna be famous, a star of the screen
But you can do something in between"

Baby you can drive my car
Yes I'm gonna be a star
Baby you can drive my car
And maybe I'll love you

I told a girl that my prospects were good
And she said "Baby, it's understood
Working for peanuts is all very fine
But I can show you a better time"

Baby you can drive my car
Yes I'm gonna be a star
Baby you can drive my car
And maybe I'll love you
Beep beep'n beep beep yeah

Baby you can drive my car
Yes I'm gonna be a star
Baby you can drive my car
And maybe I'll love you

I told that girl I can start right away
And she said, "Listen baby
I got something to say
I got no car and it's breaking my heart
But I've found a driver and that's a start"

Baby you can drive my car
Yes I'm gonna be a star
Baby you can drive my car
And maybe I'll love you
Beep beep'n beep beep yeah
Beep beep'n beep beep yeah
Beep beep'n beep beep yeah
Beep beep'n beep beep yeah

DRIVE MY CAR

A first hearing of 'Drive My Car' might suggest that the Beatles are telling some "baby" to drive their car, but closer inspection of the lyric reveals that it's the male narrator who is being asked to do the driving. He's trying to chat someone up, using that well-worn line, "Well, what do you want to be?" – suggesting sexual favours in return for promises of career advancement.

The woman tells him that she wants to be a movie star – but then reverses the roles by saying that she might (and it is only might) agree to give him some love if he agrees to be her chauffeur. By the second verse it's the man who is pleading his case, arguing that his "prospects are good". It's a good twist, inspired perhaps by the tougher breed of woman that the Beatles were meeting in America.

It could also have been inspired by early blues songs such as Robert Johnson's 'Terraplane Blues' where a woman's body is compared to the engine of a car, although unlike the blues songs it doesn't push the metaphor. It's theme is very close in many ways to that of 'Me And My Chauffeur Blues' which was made popular by Memphis Minnie, and is appropriate because over 75 per cent of the words in 'Drive My Car' are those of the woman.

Going to let my chauffeur
Going to let my chauffeur drive me around
Then he can be my little boy –
Yes, I'll be his little girl.
'Me And My Chauffeur Blues'

Paul remembered 'Drive My Car' as the only song on the album that he got stuck on, the storyline being pulled together at the last minute with some help from John. When he arrived at Abbey Road on October 20, 1965, to record the song, the chorus was "I can give you golden rings, I can give you anything, Baby I love you". John dismissed this as "crap" and so the two of them worked together to create an alternative and came up with "Baby, you can drive my car", a tougher, more sexually charged image which in turn gave rise to the "Beep beep'n beep beep yeah" background vocal. This was, of course, a playful reference to the "yeah, yeah, yeah" that had become their signature shout and a gift to headline writers but it may also have been a nod to 'Beep Beep' by the Playmates (1958), a song that was a fixture on BBC's radio programming for children at the time that the Beatles started out. "The idea of the bitchy girl was the same," said Paul, "but it gave the song a better story line, and made the key line much more effective."

John always agreed it was Paul's song with a bit of last-minute tuning and Paul said: "The idea of the girl being a bitch was the same but [the change]

made the key line better." Two days after recording 'Drive My Car', Paul told a music magazine, "We've written some funny songs – songs with jokes in. We think that comedy numbers are the next thing after protest songs." The bass line was patterned after Donald 'Duck' Dunn's playing on Otis Redding's 'Respect' (1965), which had been released the month before. They had clearly been inspired by Memphis soul that year. John even suggested to one journalist that he would have liked guitarist Steve Cropper, the key session guitarist with Stax Records, to produce the Beatles and Brian Epstein even went to Memphis in March 1966 to investigate the possibility.

ABOVE: With *Rubber Soul* came lyrical subtlety. 'Drive My Car' sounded macho on the surface but was actually aboudt role reversal.

Written: Lennon/McCartney

Length: 2'30"

UK Release: *Rubber Soul* album, December 3, 1965

US Release: *Yesterday And Today* album, June 20, 1966

NORWEGIAN WOOD

Although John was famous as the married Beatle he was not happily married. Nor was he faithful. He took advantage of backstage groupies, admitted to having been photographed on his hands and knees outside a Dutch brothel, and confessed to Cynthia in 1968 that he had had affairs. 'Norwegian Wood' was about one such entanglement. In language John later described as "gobbledygook", the song details a seduction scene where again the woman appears to be the one in control.

The lyrics open with a boast about a girl John has "had", but he quickly corrects himself by saying that it was she who "had" him. She takes him back to her apartment and asks him to admire the furnishings that are made out of cheap (but then fashionable) Norwegian pine. After talking and drinking until two in the morning, she says it's time for bed. In the song, he makes his excuses and leaves for a night in the bathroom, but in reality the story obviously had a different ending because he said it had been written about an act of unfaithfulness, "without letting my wife know I was writing about an affair." John's friend Pete Shotton has said that it was about a female journalist that John was close to and it was widely assumed that this referred to Maureen Cleave. However, Cleave never had an affair with John and the most likely candidate was revealed by Philip Norman in his biography *John Lennon: The Life* as being Sonnhild "Sonny" Freeman, then the wife of photographer Robert Freeman, who lived in a wood-panelled flat beneath the Lennons' in South Kensington.

John began 'Norwegian Wood' in February 1965 while on a skiing holiday in St Moritz, Switzerland, with Cynthia, George Martin and George's future wife, Judy but only came up with the basic tune and an opening couplet. "'Norwegian Wood' started as a guitar bit," he explained to Michael Lydon in 1966. "I was just fiddling when it came to me. It almost never got written." He later asked Paul for help and Paul suggested that he should develop a story about a girl who leads a man on and ends with the man setting the apartment on fire as an act of revenge. Pete Shotton thought this could have referred to John's habit of burning furniture in the fireplace at Gambier Terrace in Liverpool when the weather turned cold and there was no money for coal. While he was there, John would sometimes ask guests to sleep in the bath, the memory of which may have prompted the line in 'Norwegian Wood' about sleeping in the bath.

Paul saw the song as a complete fantasy. He assumed the Norwegian wood of the title was suggested by the decoration of Peter Asher's room in Wimpole Street but it was almost certainly a reference to the wood panelling in the Freeman's flat at Emperor's Gate and Sonny Freeman's habit of referring to herself as Norwegian rather than German. She certainly took it as an oblique reference to the affair between them that was conducted behind the backs of their respective spouses.

The track stood out on *Rubber Soul* for its use of sitar – it was the first time the Indian instrument had appeared on a pop record. George Harrison had become fascinated with the sitar after coming across one while filming the Indian restaurant scene for *Help!*, at Twickenham Film Studios in April, and would later study under the Indian master Ravi Shankar.

I once had a girl, or should I say,
  she once had me
She showed me her room, isn't it good,
Norwegian wood?

She asked me to stay
  and she told me to sit anywhere
So I looked around and I noticed
  there wasn't a chair

I sat on the rug, biding my time,
  drinking her wine
We talked until two and then she said,
"It's time for bed"

She told me she worked in the morning
and started to laugh
I told her I didn't and crawled off
  to sleep in the bath

And when I awoke I was alone,
  this bird had flown
So I lit a fire, isn't it good,
Norwegian wood?

NORWEGIAN WOOD

Written: Lennon/McCartney

Length: 2'05"

UK Release: *Rubber Soul* album,
December 3, 1965

US Release: *Rubber Soul* album,
December 6, 1965

When I call you up
Your line's engaged
I have had enough
So act your age
We have lost the time
That was so hard to find
And I will lose my mind
If you won't see me (You won't see me)
You won't see me (You won't see me)

I don't know why you
Should want to hide
But I can't get through
My hands are tied
I won't want to stay
I don't have much to say
But I can turn away
And you won't see me (You won't see me)
You won't see me (You won't see me)

Time after time
You refused to even listen
I wouldn't mind
If I knew what I was missing

Though the days are few
They're filled with tears
And since I lost you
It feels like years
Yes, it seems so long
Girl, since you've been gone
And I just can't go on
If you won't see me (You won't see me)
You won't see me (You won't see me)

Time after time
You refused to even listen
I wouldn't mind
If I knew (no I wouldn't)
What I was missing (no I wouldn't)

Though the days are few
They're filled with tears
And since I lost you
It feels like years
Yes, it seems so long
Girl, since you've been gone
And I just can't go on
If you won't see me (You won't see me)
You won't see me (You won't see me)

YOU WON'T SEE ME

'You Won't See Me' was another song written by Paul during the crisis in his relationship with Jane Asher. By now, he was suffering the indignity of unanswered phone calls and other forms of rejection. The dip in his romantic fortunes raised his writing to new heights because he now found himself in the vulnerable position. Paul had never viewed life from this perspective. Throughout *Beatles For Sale* and *Help!*, he'd been dreaming up situations for his love songs but now, perhaps for the first time, he was writing from the heart.

It was written as a two-note progression and Paul had the Motown sound in mind, particularly the melodic bass playing of James Jamerson, the legendary studio musician. Ian MacDonald in *Revolution In The Head* suggests that the specific model might have been 'It's The Same Old Song' by the Four Tops.

'You Won't See Me' was recorded during the last session for Rubber Soul, by which time Jane was playing the title role in the Frank Marcus play *Cleo* at the Theatre Royal, Bristol.

Written: Lennon/McCartney

Length: 3'22"

UK Release: *Rubber Soul* album, December 3, 1965

US Release: *Rubber Soul* album, December 6, 1965

NOWHERE
MAN

NOWHERE MAN

Recorded on October 21 and 22, 1965, 'Nowhere Man' has the distinction of being the first Beatles' song that wasn't about love. John wrote it early one morning after a night out and it marked the beginning of his overtly philosophical musings.

'Nowhere Man' was always assumed to be either about a specific person (in her Hollywood exposé *You'll Never Eat Lunch In This Town Again*, Julia Phillips speculated that it was written about an entrepreneur called Michael Brown) or about an archetypal member of "straight" society whose life seems directionless.

John said that he was the 'Nowhere Man' in question, and that desperation had driven him to it after he'd been writing solidly for over five hours, feeling that he wouldn't be able to complete another song for the album. "I'd actually stopped trying to think of something," he told Beatles' biographer Hunter Davies. "Nothing would come. I was cheesed off and went for a lie-down, having given up. Then I thought of myself as Nowhere Man – sitting in his nowhere land."

The Nowhere Man has potential – the world is said to be at his command – but his perception is limited. He just sees what he wants to see. He can only be rescued by having his mind expanded. This is a theme picked up in other songs of the period, such as 'The Word' and 'Rain' ,and became central to the outlook of the Beatles.

Like 'Help!', it was about John's lack of self-worth and probably also about the fact that he felt trapped both in his marriage and in the suburbs. It was released as a single in America in February 1966 and was later included in the animated film *Yellow Submarine*.

Written: Lennon/McCartney

Length: 2'44"

UK Release: *Rubber Soul* album, December 3, 1965

US Release: February 21, 1966

US chart position: 3

134

RUBBER SOUL

He's a real Nowhere Man
Sitting in his nowhere land
Making all his nowhere plans for nobody

Doesn't have a point of view
Knows not where he's going to
Isn't he a bit like you and me?

Nowhere Man, please listen
You don't know what you're missing
Nowhere Man
The world's at your command

He's as blind as he can be
Just sees what he wants to see
Nowhere Man can you see me at all?

Nowhere Man, don't worry
Take your time, don't hurry
Leave it all till somebody else
Lends you a hand

Doesn't have a point of view
Knows not where he's going to
Isn't he a bit like you and me?

Nowhere Man, please listen
You don't know what you're missing
Nowhere Man
The world is at your command

He's a real Nowhere Man
Sitting in his nowhere land
Making all his nowhere plans for nobody
Making all his nowhere plans for nobody
Making all his nowhere plans for nobody

John's lyrics changed when he began to explore his exact feelings at the time of writing. 'Nowhere Man' was not so much about society's loss of faith but his own loss of belief.

I've got a word or two
To say about the things that you do
You're telling all those lies
About the good things that we can have
If we close our eyes

Do what you want to do
And go where you're going to
Think for yourself
I won't be there with you

I left you far behind
The ruins of the life that you have in
  mind
And though you still can't see
I know your mind's made up
You're gonna cause more misery

Do what you want to do
And go where you're going to
Think for yourself
Cos I won't be there with you

Although your mind's opaque
Try thinking more if just for
  your own sake
The future still looks good
And you've got time to rectify
All the things that you should

Do what you want to do
And go where you're going to
Think for yourself
Cos I won't be there with you

Do what you want to do
And go where you're going to
Think for yourself
Cos I won't be there with you
Think for yourself
Cos I won't be there with you

ABOVE: As the youngest Beatle, George always
felt that he lived in the shadow of John and Paul.
He was the first Beatle to tire of touring.

THINK FOR YOURSELF

THINK FOR YOURSELF

'Think For Yourself', a song written by George Harrison, is an admonition against listening to lies. Recorded just a few months before his engagement to Pattie Boyd, it was presumably not about his wife-to-be. "It must be about somebody from the sound of it," he wrote in his book *I Me Mine*. "But all this time later, I don't quite recall who inspired that tune. Probably the government."

Taking into account the period in which it was written, it appears to be another song – like 'Rain', 'The Word' and 'Nowhere Man' – that is about mind expansion. Just as John accuses people of being blind, George accuses them of having closed eyes and "opaque" minds and urges them to "try thinking more". The "closed eyes" image is similar to one later used by John in 'Strawberry Fields Forever'. George revealed to Maureen Cleave in 1966 that he'd bought a copy of *Roget's Thesaurus* to help with his lyric writing. It was while looking up a synonym for "thick" (as in "dense" or "stupid") that he'd come across the word "opaque".

Written: Harrison

Length: 2'19"

UK Release: *Rubber Soul* album, December 3, 1965

US Release: *Rubber Soul* album, December 6, 1965

ABOVE: John, pictured with Paul and Beatles' assistant Neil Aspinall, considered 'The Word' to be his first "message" song (*see* overleaf).

THE WORD

THE WORD

Recorded two years after 'She Loves You' (July 1963) and two years before 'All You Need Is Love' (June 1967), 'The Word' marks the transition between the boy-meets-girl love of Beatlemania and the peace-and-harmony love of the hippie era.

Understood at the time as just another Beatles' love song, it was actually sprinkled with clues pointing to a song of a different kind. The love that John was now singing about offered "freedom" and "light". It even offered "the way". He may have been thinking of 'The Word' in the evangelistic sense of "preaching the word". Speaking to British writer Francis Wyndham, Paul said "This could be a Salvation Army song. 'The word is love.' But it could be Jesus (it isn't, mind you, but it could be.) … It's so much more original than our old stuff, less obvious. 'Give the world the chance to say/That the word is just the way.' Then the organ comes in, just like the Sally Army."

In their classic study *The Varieties Of Psychedelic Experience*, Masters and Houston found that not only did LSD often produce experiences of a religious nature, but it could provide people with the idea that "a universal or brotherly love is possible and constitutes man's best if not only hope." It was for this reason that "love" became such a buzz-word within the drug culture of the mid- to late Sixties, John being one of the first songwriters to catch the mood. He later recalled the song as one of the Beatles' first "message songs" and the beginnings of the group's role as cultural leaders expected to supply answers to social and spiritual questions.

John told *Playboy* that it was a song about "getting smart", meaning the state of realization which users of marijuana and LSD were claiming to have achieved. "It's love," he said. "It's the marijuana period. It's the love and peace thing. The word is 'love', right?"

Appropriately when John and Paul had finished writing it at Kenwood they rolled joints and wrote out a psychedelically decorated lyric sheet that John later presented to the composer John Cage for his 50th birthday. A reproduction can be seen in Cage's book *Notations*, in which he published a number of different contemporary music scores collected from composers over the years.

Written: Lennon/McCartney

Length: 2'43"

UK Release: *Rubber Soul* album, December 3, 1965

US Release: *Rubber Soul* album, December 6, 1965

RUBBER SOUL

Say the word and you'll be free
Say the word and be like me
Say the word I'm thinking of
Have you heard the word is love?
It's so fine, it's sunshine
It's the word, love

In the beginning I misunderstood
But now I've got it, the word is good

Spread the word and you'll be free
Spread the word and be like me
Spread the word I'm thinking of
Have you heard the word is love?
It's so fine, it's sunshine
It's the word, love

Everywhere I go I hear it said
In the good and bad books that I have read

Say the word and you'll be free
Say the word and be like me
Say the word I'm thinking of
Have you heard the word is love?
It's so fine, it's sunshine
It's the word, love

Now that I know what I feel must be right
I'm here to show everybody the light

Give the word a chance to say
That the word is just the way
It's the word I'm thinking of
And the only word is love
It's so fine, it's sunshine
It's the word, love

Say the word, love
Say the word, love
Say the word, love
Say the word, love

Michelle, ma belle
These are words that go together well
My Michelle

Michelle, ma belle
Sont les mots qui vont tres bien
* ensemble*
Tres bien ensemble

I love you, I love you, I love you
That's all I want to say
Until I find a way
I will say the only words I know
That you'll understand

Michelle, ma belle
Sont les mots qui vont tres bien
* ensemble*
Tres bien ensemble

I need to, I need to, I need to
I need to make you see
Oh, what you mean to me
Until I do I'm hoping you will
Know what I mean

I love you

I want you, I want you, I want you
I think you know by now
I'll get to you somehow
Until I do I'm telling you
So you'll understand

Michelle, ma belle
Sont les mots qui vont tres bien
* ensemble*
Tres bien ensemble

I will say the only words I know
That you'll understand, my Michelle

MICHELLE

'Michelle' dates back to Liverpool days when Paul went to parties thrown by one of John's art tutors, Austin Mitchell. This was at a time when the intellectual and artistic life of the Parisian Left Bank was fashionable among students and bohemianism was signalled by berets, beards and Gitanes cigarettes. John and Paul had travelled to Paris for the first time in October 1961 using money given to John for his 21st birthday. They were both enchanted by the city and it was while they were there that they had their first "Beatle haircuts", given to them by their Hamburg friend Jurgen Vollmer, who was working with a French photographer.

"Back in those days people would point at you in the street in Liverpool if you had a beard," remembers Rod Murray, who shared the Gambier Terrace flat with John and Stuart Sutcliffe. "If you had a beret, they would call you a beatnik. We liked Juliette Greco and everyone fancied getting in with Brigitte Bardot."

At one of Austin Mitchell's parties, a student with a goatee beard and a striped T-shirt was hunched over his guitar singing what sounded like a French song. Soon after, Paul began to work a comical imitation to amuse his friends. It remained a party piece with nothing more than cod-French vocals as accompaniment until, in 1965, John suggested that Paul should write proper words for it and include it on the album.

Radio presenter Muriel Young, then working for Radio Luxembourg, could remember Paul visiting her at her holiday home in Portugal while he was working on it. This was probably in September 1965 when the Beatles took a month off between the American tour, which had finished on August 31, and the new album which was due to begin recording on October 12. "He sat on our sofa with Jane Asher and he was trying to find the words," Muriel said. "It wasn't 'Michelle, ma belle' then. He was singing 'Goodnight sweetheart' and then 'Hello my dear', just looking for something that would fit the rhythm."

Eventually, Paul chose to go with the French feel and to incorporate a French name and some real French words. He spoke to Jan Vaughan, the wife of his old friend Ivan Vaughan (the person responsible for introducing Paul to John), who taught French. "I asked her what sort of things I could say that were French and which would go together well," said Paul. "It was because I'd always thought that the song sounded French that I stuck with it. I can't speak French properly, so that's why I needed help in sorting out the actual words."

Jan remembers that Paul first spoke to her about it when she and Ivan were visiting him at the Ashers' London home. "He asked me if I could think of a French girl's first name, with two syllables, and then a description of the girl which would rhyme. He played me the rhythm on his guitar and that's when I came up with 'Michelle, ma belle', which wasn't actually that hard to think of! I think it was some days later that he phoned me up and asked if I could translate the phrase 'these are words that go together well' and I told him that it should be 'sont les mots qui vont tres bien ensemble'."

When Paul played the song to John he suggested the "I love you" in the middle section, specifying that the emphasis should fall on the word "love" each time. He was inspired by Nina Simone's recording of 'I Put A Spell On You', a hit in Britain during August 1965, where she had used the same phrase but placed the emphasis on the "you". "My contribution to Paul's songs was always to add a little bluesy edge to them," John said. "Otherwise 'Michelle' is a straight ballad."

Instrumentally Paul was inspired by the finger picking style of Chet Atkins as exemplified on 'Trambone' (1961) and was proud to have introduced the new chord of F7#9 that he had been taught by Jim Gretty, the regular musical demonstrator at Frank Hessy's Musical Store in Liverpool. "I remember George and I were in the shop when Gretty played it," said Paul. "We said 'wow! What was that man?' And he answered, 'It's just basically an F, but you barre the top two strings at the fourth fret with your little finger. We immediately learned that and for a while it was the only jazz chord we knew."

Of the bass line Paul later said, "I'll never forget putting the bass on 'Michelle', because it was a kind of Bizet thing. It really turned the song around."

ABOVE: Although 'Michelle' was Paul's song, John made a contribution to the middle eight that was inspired by a version of 'I Put A Spell On You' by Nina Simone.

Written: Lennon/McCartney

Length: 2'42"

UK Release: *Rubber Soul* album, December 3, 1965

US Release: *Rubber Soul* album, December 6, 1965

WHAT GOES ON

What goes on in your heart?
What goes on in your mind?
You are tearing me apart
When you treat me so unkind
What goes on in your mind?

The other day I saw you
As I walked along the road
But when I saw him with you
I could feel my future fold
It's so easy for a girl like you to lie
Tell me why

What goes on in your heart?
What goes on in your mind?
You are tearing me apart
When you treat me so unkind
What goes on in your mind?

I met you in the morning
Waiting for the tides of time
But now the tide is turning
I can see that I was blind
It's so easy for a girl like you to lie
Tell me why

What goes on in your heart?

I used to think of no one else
But you were just the same
You didn't even think of me
As someone with a name
Did you mean to break my heart
  and watch me die
Tell me why

What goes on in your heart?
What goes on in your mind?
You are tearing me apart
When you treat me so unkind
What goes on in your mind?

WHAT GOES ON

'What Goes On' was one of the four songs that the Beatles played to George Martin on March 5, 1963, as possible follow-ups to 'Please Please Me'. (The other three were 'From Me To You', 'Thank You Girl' and 'The One After 909').

Written by John, it was the only song Martin chose not to record that day and was forgotten until November 4, 1965, when it was brought back into service as Ringo's vocal number. A new middle eight was added by Paul and Ringo, giving the drummer his first composer's credit. Asked in 1966 what his precise contribution to the song had been, Ringo replied: "About five words."

"This was 'early Lennon'," said John in 1980. It was written before the Beatles when we were Quarry Men or something like that. It was resurrected, probably with Paul's help, to give Ringo a song, and also because I never liked to waste a song."

In America, it was released as the B-side of 'Nowhere Man' in February 1966.

141

Written: Lennon/McCartney

Length: 2'50"

UK Release: *Rubber Soul* album, December 3, 1965

US single Release: February 21, 1966 as B-side to 'Nowhere Man'

US chart position: 3

GIRL

Is there anybody going to listen to
  my story
All about the girl who came to stay?
She's the kind of girl you want so much
  it makes you sorry
Still, you don't regret a single day
Ah girl, girl

When I think of all the times I've tried
  so hard to leave her
She will turn to me and start to cry
And she promises the earth to me
And I believe her
After all this time I don't know why
Ah girl, girl

She's the kind of girl who puts you down
When friends are there, you feel a fool
When you say she's looking good
She acts as if it's understood
She's cool, ooh, ooh, ooh
Girl, girl

Was she told when she was young
That pain would lead to pleasure?
Did she understand it when they said
That a man must break his back to earn
  his day of leisure?
Will she still believe it when he's dead?

Ah girl, girl, girl
Ah girl, girl, girl

GIRL

Asked who the girl was in 'Girl', John said that she was a figure from a dream, the ideal woman who had not yet appeared in his life. "I always had this dream of this particular woman coming into my life," he said. "I knew it wouldn't be someone buying Beatles' records. I was hoping for a woman who could give me what I get from a man intellectually. I wanted someone I could be myself with."

However, the girl in the song seems far from his ideal. She's heartless, conceited and humiliates him. Perhaps there are two girls in the song: the dream girl in the first half, whom he appears to be mesmerized by, and the nightmare girl in the second half who ridicules him.

When John spoke in depth about the song, he remembered it more for its comment on the church than its comment on a particular woman. In 1970, he revealed to *Rolling Stone* that the verse which asks whether she had been taught that pain would lead to pleasure, and that a man must break his back to earn his leisure, was a reference to, "the Catholic/Christian concept – be tortured and then it'll be all right." He added, "I was...trying to say something or other about Christianity, which I was opposed to at the time." He was referring to the Genesis account of the effects of Adam and Eve's disobedience, where Eve is told by God "with pain you will give birth to children" and Adam is told that "cursed is the ground because of you; through painful toil you will eat of it all the days of your life."

Christianity, and in particular Jesus Christ, seemed to bother John. At the time of writing 'Girl', he was avidly reading books about religion, a subject that preoccupied him until his death, and four months later he gave the interview to Maureen Cleave that contained his controversial comment about the Beatles having become "more popular than Jesus".

Paul explained to Francis Wyndham just before *Rubber Soul* was released "John's been reading a book about pain and pleasure, about the idea behind Christianity that to have pleasure you have to have pain. The book says that's all rubbish; it often happens that pain leads to pleasure but you don't have to have it. That's all a drag. So we've written a song about it. Listen to John's breath on the word 'girl'. We asked the engineer to put it on treble, so you get this huge intake of breath and it sounds just like a percussion instrument."

It's likely that the book John was reading was *Masochism in Modern Man* by Theodor Reik, a disciple of Freud. Reik argued that the teachings of Christ appealed to a masochistic tendency. The command to love our enemies and pray for those who persecute us was "a translation of masochistic behaviour modelled into a religious format." He concluded, "The dying Saviour had found a new way of enjoyment. The steps of suffering became rungs of the ladder to heaven. The warrior ideal is by and by replaced by the ideal of the saint or martyr. The late Jewish faith and the Christian faith bring the glorification of masochism."

Written: Lennon/McCartney

Length: 2'33"

UK Release: *Rubber Soul* album, December 3, 1965

US Release: *Rubber Soul* album, December 6, 1965

The bouzouki style of guitar playing could have been suggested by the recent hit single 'Zorba's Dance' by Marcello Minerbi taken from the soundtrack of the film *Zorba The Greek*. The background vocals emulated the "la la la la" chorus used by the Beach Boys on 'You're So Good To Me' (July 1965) but for a joke they sang "tit tit tit tit" in the studio rather than the scheduled "dit dit dit dit". These borrowings show that the Beatles were as influenced by current chart music as they were by rare B-sides and Fifties R&B hits.

I'M LOOKING THROUGH YOU

Jane Asher's move to Bristol continued to preoccupy Paul. It meant that she was no longer readily at hand even though he continued to use her family home in Wimpole Street as his London base. As a young working-class man from Liverpool, he found it hard to come to terms with a girl who put her career before romance.

He later admitted to Hunter Davies that his whole existence so far revolved around living a carefree bachelor's life. He hadn't treated women as most people did. He'd always had a lot around him, even when he had steady girlfriends. "I knew I was selfish," he said. "It caused a few rows. Jane went off and I said, 'OK then. Leave. I'll find someone else. It was shattering to be without her. That was when I wrote 'I'm Looking Through You'."

This was Paul's most bitter song so far. Rather than question his own attitudes (as he obviously did later), Paul accuses his woman of changing and holds out the thinly veiled threat of withdrawing his affection. Love has a habit, he warns, of disappearing overnight. He would later remember the song as having served to get rid of "some emotional baggage".

Written: Lennon/McCartney

Length: 2'27"

UK Release: *Rubber Soul* album,
December 3, 1965

US Release: *Rubber Soul* album,
December 6, 1965

I'm looking through you,
Where did you go?
I thought I knew you, what did I know?
You don't look different,
But you have changed
I'm looking through you,
You're not the same

Your lips are moving, I cannot hear
Your voice is soothing,
But the words aren't clear
You don't sound different,
I've learned the game
I'm looking through you,
You're not the same

Why, tell me why,
Did you not treat me right?
Love has a nasty habit
Of disappearing overnight

You're thinking of me, the same old way
You were above me, but not today
The only difference is you're down there
I'm looking through you,
And you're nowhere

Why, tell me why,
Did you not treat me right?
Love has a nasty habit
Of disappearing overnight

I'm looking through you,
Where did you go
I thought I knew you, what did I know
You don't look different,
But you have changed
I'm looking through you,
You're not the same

Yeah
Oh baby I'm changed
Ah I'm looking through you
Yeah I'm looking through you

IN MY LIFE

Although John had been writing more obviously autobiographical songs for over a year now, it was with 'In My Life' that he felt he'd made the breakthrough that Kenneth Allsop had encouraged him to make in March 1964, when he suggested writing more about his personal feelings.

Recorded in October 1965, the song was a long time in gestation. It started, John said, as a long poem in which he reflected on favourite childhood haunts by tracing a journey from his home on Menlove Avenue down to the Docker's Umbrella, the overhead railway which ran along Liverpool's dockside until 1958 and beneath which dockers would shelter from the rain.

Elliot Mintz, who was hired by Yoko Ono to carry out an inventory of all John's personal possessions after his death, remembers seeing the first handwritten draft of the song. "It was part of a large book in which he kept all his original Beatles' compositions," says Mintz. "He had already told me about how the song was written and that he considered it a significant turning point in his writing and, just as he had described to me, the song went on at great length and included lots of place names including Penny Lane."

In a later single-page draft of this rambling lyric, John listed Penny Lane, Church Road, the clock tower, the Abbey Cinema, the tram sheds, the Dutch Cafe, St Columbus Church, the Docker's Umbrella and Calderstones Park. Although this fulfilled the requirement of being autobiographical, John must have known that it was more of a travelogue. The tram sheds were now "without trams" and the Docker's Umbrella had been "pulled down". "It was the most boring sort of 'what I did on my holidays' bus trip song and it wasn't working at all..." he said. "Then I lay back and these lyrics started coming to me about the places I remember."

John jettisoned all the specific place names, and worked up the sense of mourning for a disappeared childhood and youth, turning what would otherwise have been a song about the changing face of Liverpool into a universal song about death and decay. Here was a tough guy, who had been known to laugh at cripples and who poured scorn on the middle-class nature of his upbringing, but who was also a sentimentalist. Throughout his life, he kept a box of childhood mementos in his apartment and in the 1970s wrote to his Aunt Mimi from New York asking her to send him his Quarry Bank school tie.

He later told Pete Shotton that when he wrote the line about friends in 'In My Life', some of whom were dead and some of whom were living, he was thinking specifically of Shotton and former Beatle Stuart Sutcliffe, who had died of a brain tumour in April 1962.

The lyric bears a surprising resemblance to Charles Lamb's 18th century poem 'The Old Familiar Faces' which John could well have come across in the popular poetry anthology *Palgrave's Treasury*. The poem starts:

I have had playmates, I have had companions,
In my days of childhood, in my joyful schooldays:
All, all are gone, the old familiar faces.

Six verses later it concludes with:

How some they have died, and some they have left me,
And some are taken from me; all are departed;
All, all are gone, the old familiar faces.

IN MY LIFE

There are places I remember
All my life though some have changed
Some forever not for better
Some have gone and some remain
All these places have their moments
With lovers and friends I still can recall
Some are dead and some are living
In my life I've loved them all

But of all these friends and lovers
There is no one compares with you
And these memories lose their meaning
When I think of love as something new
Though I know I'll never lose affection
For people and things that went before
I know I'll often stop and think about them
In my life I love you more

Though I know I'll never lose affection
For people and things that went before
I know I'll often stop and think about them
In my life I love you more

In my life I love you more

Written: Lennon/McCartney

Length: 2'27"

UK Release: *Rubber Soul* album, December 3, 1965

US Release: *Rubber Soul* album, December 6, 1965

The source of the melody to 'In My Life' remains in dispute. John has said that Paul helped out with a section on which he was stuck. Paul still believes he wrote it all. "I remember that he had the words written out like a long poem and I went off and worked something out on the Mellotron," he said. "The tune, if I remember rightly, was inspired by the Miracles." He was almost certainly referring to 'You Really Got A Hold On Me'.

The instrumental break was created by George Martin who recorded himself on piano and then, in order to create a baroque sound, played it back at twice the speed. John's opinion on the finished result was that it was his "first real major piece of work".

WAIT

The Beatles don't appear to have had any great affection for 'Wait'. It was first recorded for *Help!* in June 1965, but not used, and was taken up again as the *Rubber Soul* sessions finished – but only because the album was a song short.

Written mostly by Paul, it's an all-purpose song about a couple that has been separated and now that they're back together everything's going to be all right. Paul's recollection is that it was written in the Bahamas during filming and that the late Brandon de Wilde, the child star of *Shane*, had watched him write it. The Beatles stayed in cottages on the grounds of the Balmoral Club (now Sandals) close to Cable Beach, which is probably where it was written.

It's been a long time
Now I'm coming back home
I've been away now
Oh how, I've been alone

Wait till I come back to your side
We'll forget the tears we've cried

But if your heart breaks
Don't wait, turn me away
And if your heart's strong
Hold on, I won't delay

Wait till I come back to your side
We'll forget the tears we've cried

I feel as though
You ought to know
That I've been good
As good as I can be
And if you do
I'll trust in you
And know that you
Will wait for me

It's been a long time
Now I'm coming back home

I've been away now
Oh how, I've been alone

Wait till I come back to your side
We'll forget the tears we've cried

I feel as though
You ought to know
That I've been good
As good as I can be
And if you do
I'll trust in you
And know that you
Will wait for me

But if your heart breaks
Don't wait, turn me away
And if your heart's strong
Hold on, I won't delay

Wait till I come back to your side
We'll forget the tears we've cried

It's been a long time
Now I'm coming back home
I've been away now
Oh how, I've been alone

Written: Lennon/McCartney

Length: 2'16"

UK Release: *Rubber Soul* album, December 3, 1965

US Release: *Rubber Soul* album, December 6, 1965

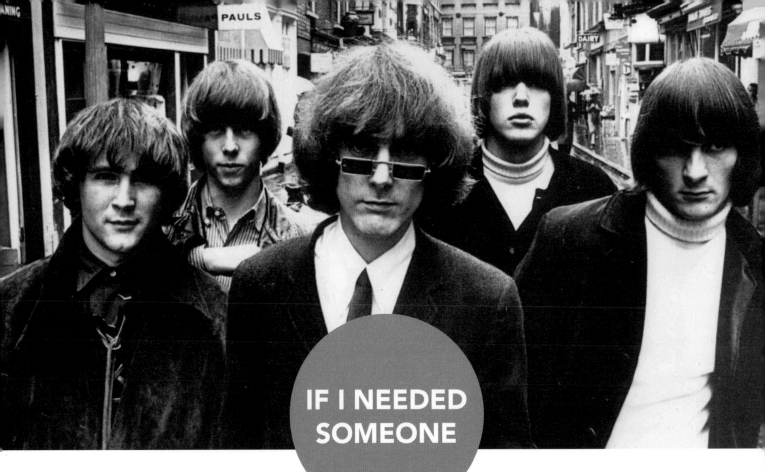

IF I NEEDED SOMEONE

'If I Needed Someone' was written by George for girlfriend Pattie, and grew out of a musical exercise using the D chord. "That guitar line, or variations on it, is found in many a song and it amazes me that people still find new permutations of the same notes," he said. Beatles' press officer Derek Taylor had moved to Los Angeles and began to represent the Byrds, so George sent an advanced pressing of *Rubber Soul* to Byrds' guitarist Roger McGuinn via Taylor along with a message saying that the tune to 'If I Needed Someone' had been inspired by two Byrds' tracks – 'The Bells Of Rhymney' and 'She Don't Care About Time'. 'The Bells of Rhymney,' written by Pete Seeger with words based on a 1938 poem by Welsh poet Idris Davies, had been a track on the Byrds' first album, *Mr Tambourine Man*, which had come out in August 1965. 'She Don't Care About Time', written by vocalist Gene Clark, was the B-side of the single 'Turn! Turn! Turn!' released in October 1965, the same month that 'If I Needed Someone' was recorded.

Written: Harrison

Length: 2'23"

UK Release: *Rubber Soul* album, December 3, 1965

US Release: *Yesterday and Today* album, June 20, 1966

If I needed someone to love
You're the one that I'd be thinking of
If I needed someone

If I had some more time to spend
Then I guess I'd be with you my friend
If I needed someone

Had you come some other day
Then it might not have been like this
But you see now I'm too much in love

Carve your number on my wall
And maybe you will get a call from me
If I needed someone
Ah, ah, ah, ah

If I had some more time to spend
Then I guess I'd be with you my friend
If I needed someone

Had you come some other day
Then it might not have been like this
But you see now I'm too much in love

Carve your number on my wall
And maybe you will get a call from me
If I needed someone
Ah, ah

RUN FOR YOUR LIFE

John developed 'Run For Your Life' from the line "I'd rather see you dead little girl than see you with another man", which features in Elvis Presley's 1955 Sun single 'Baby, Let's Play House'. John referred to this as "an old blues song that Presley did once" but in fact it dates back only to 1954 and was written by a 28-year-old preacher's son from Nashville named Arthur Gunter.

Gunter in turn had based his song on a 1951 country hit by Eddy Arnold, 'I Want To Play House With You', and had recorded it for the Excello label in late 1954. It wasn't a national hit but Elvis heard it and recorded it on February 5, 1955. When 'Baby, Let's Play House' reached Number 10 in Billboard's country chart in July 1955, it became the first Elvis record to chart nationally in America. Gunter's song was one of devotion. He wanted the girl to move in with him and the line that caught John's attention was an indication of the depths of his feelings for her.

However, in John's mouth the lines become threatening. If he sees his girl with anyone else she'd better run because he's going to bump her off. It was another revenge fantasy in the mould of 'I'll Cry Instead'. The singer explains his behaviour by saying that he's "wicked" and that he was born with "a jealous mind" – lines which contain intimations of later songs such as 'Jealous Guy' and 'Crippled Inside'. It stands in complete contrast to 'The Word' and its message of love and reveals the side of John that he felt needed controlling. Later on in his life he admitted, "I am a violent man who has learned not to be violent and has learned to control his violence."

Although it was the first track recorded for *Rubber Soul*, John always cited 'Run For Your Life' as an example of his worst work. It was written under pressure, he said and, as such, was a "throwaway song".

Written: Lennon/McCartney

Length: 2'18"

UK Release: *Rubber Soul* album,
December 3, 1965

US Release: *Rubber Soul* album,
December 6, 1965

LEFT ABOVE: The Byrds in 1965, with Roger McGuinn (centre). McGuinn's guitar playing was an influence on George Harrison.

Well I'd rather see you dead, little girl
Than to be with another man
You better keep your head, little girl
Or I won't know where I am

You better run for your life if you can,
  little girl
Hide your head in the sand little girl
Catch you with another man
That's the end, ah, little girl

Well I know that I'm a wicked guy
And I was born with a jealous mind
And I can't spend my whole life
Trying just to make you toe the line

You better run for your life if you can,
  little girl
Hide your head in the sand little girl
Catch you with another man
That's the end, ah, little girl

Let this be a sermon
I mean everything I've said
Baby, I'm determined
And I'd rather see you dead

You better run for your life if you can,
  little girl
Hide your head in the sand little girl
Catch you with another man
That's the end, ah, little girl

I'd rather see you dead, little girl
Than to be with another man
You better keep your head, little girl
Or you won't know where I am

You better run for your life if you can,
  little girl
Hide your head in the sand little girl
Catch you with another man
That's the end, ah, little girl
Nah nah nah
Nah nah nah
Nah nah nah
Nah nah nah

7 Revolver

Revolver marked a significant development in the Beatles' sound, as well as the end of an era. It was the first time they had recorded an album without having to consider whether the songs could be reproduced in concert. The art was in the sounds they could create in the studio and the record was an end in itself. This had an immediately liberating effect by turning them into recording artists in the truest sense of that description. "Unlike our previous LPs," said Paul, "this one is intended to show our versatility rather than being a haphazard collection of songs."

They were also energized by contact with the hippie movement in America and the British underground scene. The lyrics touched on ever more serious issues and the music absorbed inspiration not only from other pop and rock records but from Asian, classical and avant garde music. Drug use was making them question previously sacrosanct boundaries and heightening their awareness of sounds.

In a March 1966 interview with British DJ Alan Freeman, Paul spoke enthusiastically about George's interest in Indian music and his own recent exploration of theatre, painting, film making and electronic music. "As far as the Beatles are concerned, we can't just stop where we are or there's nothing left to do," he said. "We can go on trying to make popular records and it can get dead dull if we're not trying to expand at all and move onto other things. Unless you're careful you can be successful and unsuccessful at the same time."

It was an album brimming with ideas. Until this time the conventional wisdom was that you developed an identifiable "sound" and stuck to it, but on *Revolver* the Beatles went in 14 different directions, all of them fruitful. All that 'Eleanor Rigby' had in common with 'Tomorrow Never Knows' – or 'And Your Bird Can Sing' had in common with 'Yellow Submarine' – was authorship. Yet, despite the experimentation, *Revolver* was not so "far out" that it lefts its audience behind. It was wonderfully accessible. 'Eleanor Rigby', 'For No One' and 'Here, There And Everywhere' were three of the most beautiful and popular songs Paul ever wrote. 'Taxman' and 'I Want To Tell You' were George's best compositions so far and John's dream-like 'I'm Only Sleeping' and 'She Said She Said' were perfect evocations of the mood of the times.

After the final session for the album the Beatles would play only 32 more concerts and none of the songs from *Revolver* would be played. They were becoming ever more dissatisfied with touring despite the increasingly large crowds they were attracting. Not only were their threats of violence and a backlash because of John's reported remarks about the popularity of Jesus and the Beatles but the screaming was drowning out their sound. They felt that they could no longer develop as musicians in such an environment.

Appropriately their final concert, on August 29, 1966 was in San Francisco, where the hippie movement was about to make itself known to the rest of the world. *Revolver* was released in the same month and topped in album charts in Britain and America. This was the last Beatles' album to have different track listings for the US market. Three of John's songs – 'I'm Only Sleeping', 'And Your Bird Can Sing' and 'Doctor Robert' – had already appeared in the US in June on the album *Yesterday And Today*.

Paperback writer, writer, writer
Dear Sir or Madam, will you read
my book?
It took me years to write, will you take
a look?
It's based on a novel by a man named
Lear
And I need a job, so I want to be a
paperback writer
Paperback writer

It's a dirty story of a dirty man
And his clinging wife doesn't understand
His son is working for the Daily Mail
It's a steady job but he wants to be a
paperback writer
Paperback writer

Paperback writer

It's a thousand pages, give or take a few
I'll be writing more in a week or two
I can make it longer if you like the style
I can change it round and I want to be a
paperback writer
Paperback writer

If you really like it you can have the rights
It could make a million for you overnight
If you must return it, you can send it here
But I need a break and I want to be a
paperback writer
Paperback writer

Paperback writer
Paperback writer, paperback writer
Paperback writer, paperback writer
Paperback writer, paperback writer
Paperback writer, paperback writer

PAPERBACK WRITER

The Beatles' first single not to have a love theme ('Nowhere Man' had been the first album track), 'Paperback Writer' was the story of a novelist begging a publisher to take on his thousand-page book. Written by Paul in the form of a letter, it was startling at the time to hear a pop single on such an unusual topic.

British disc jockey Jimmy Savile, who then worked for Radio Luxembourg as well as BBC Television's *Top Of The Pops*, claims he was backstage after a show when Paul first conceived the idea for the song. John had been principal writer of the Beatles' last five singles and so it was generally agreed that it was Paul's turn to come up with something. Savile recalled John asking Paul what he was going to do because there were only a few days left before they were due to record. "Paul told him that one of his aunts had just asked if he could ever write a single that wasn't about love," remembers Savile. "With that thought obviously still in his mind, he walked around the room and noticed that Ringo was reading a book. He took one look and announced that he would write a song about a book."

In an interview of the period Paul said: "We like to do something different. The idea's a bit different. Years ago, my Auntie Lil said to me, 'Why do you write songs about love all the time? Can't you ever write about a horse or the summit conference or something interesting? So I thought, 'All right, Auntie Lil.' And recently, we've not been writing all our songs about love."

Paul has said that he had always liked the sound of the words "paperback writer" and decided to build his story round them. The epistolary style of the song came to him as he drove down to Weybridge for a day's writing with John. "As soon as I arrived I told him that I wanted us to write it as if it was a letter," he said. Tony Bramwell believes that the inspiration for much of the lyric came from an actual letter written to Paul by an aspiring novelist.

Paperbacks had caused a publishing revolution in the 1930s, making books available to people who would have found hardbacks too expensive to

PAPERBACK WRITER

buy. Poet Royston Ellis, the first published author the Beatles had ever met when they played music backing his poetry in 1960, is convinced that Paul latched on to the phrase "paperback writer" from his conversations with the group. "Although I was writing poetry books then, if they asked me what I wanted to be I would always say "a paperback writer" because that's what you had to be if you wanted to reach a mass market," says Ellis, who went on to become a writer of travel books and plantation novels. "My ambition was to be a writer who sold his books and made money out of it. It was my equivalent of their ambition of making a million-selling single."

As with many of Paul's songs, the lyric was driven more by the sound of the words than the logic of the story. Taken literally, it's about a writer who has composed a novel based on a novel about a paperback writer. In other words, it's a novel based on a novel about the writing of a novel. The "man named Lear" is probably a reference to Edward Lear, the Victorian painter who, although he never wrote a novel, did write nonsense poems and songs that John read after being compared to him in reviews of *In His Own Write*. The *Daily Mail* gets a mention because it was John's regular newspaper and a copy often would be on the table at Weybridge as they were writing. Stories from the *Daily Mail* would later be used as inspiration for two songs on *Sgt. Pepper*.

The main musical innovation on 'Paperback Writer' was the boosted bass sound that allowed it to be used as a lead instrument for the first time. Paul was now playing a Rickenbacker and, through some studio innovations made by engineer Ken Townsend, the bass became the most prominent instrument on the track, bringing it into line with recent American recordings by Otis Redding and Wilson Pickett. The background harmonies were inspired by the Beach Boys' album *Pet Sounds*, which had been completed by the end of March 1966. An advance pressing had been brought to London by Kim Fowley in order to get it "talked up" by influential people like the Beatles. John and Paul were given a preview at the Waldorf Hotel in the Aldwych. During part of the harmonies on 'Paperback Writer' the Beatles can be heard singing 'Frère Jacques' as a subliminal exercise in evoking childhood memories.

'Paperback Writer' was a Number 1 single in many countries including Britain, America, Germany and Australia.

Written: Lennon/McCartney

Length: 2'18"

UK Single Release: June 10, 1966 UK

UK Chart position: 1

US Single Release: May 30, 1966

US Chart position: 1

RIGHT: Poet and pop music critic Royston Ellis first met the Beatles in 1960, and was the first published author they'd known.

LEFT: A promotional film for 'Paperback Writer' was made in the grounds of Chiswick House, London, on May 20, 1966.

RAIN

In 'There's A Place' on the Beatles' first album, John had voiced the opinion that state of mind mattered more than events "out there". In 'Rain', he returned to the theme, but this time with the experience of psychedelic drugs behind him. On one level, it was a simple song about "people moaning because ... they don't like the weather," as he once explained, but at a deeper level it was a song that argued for a new consciousness capable of transcending good and evil. He claimed to have reached a condition where such external events no longer affected him. As with 'The Word', this was a song where he took on the mantle of the preacher or spiritual leader as is evidenced by the phrases "I can show you" and "Can you hear me?"

'The Word' was about the feelings of universal love stirred up by LSD and therefore didn't have an obvious musical correlative. Because 'Rain' was about altered perceptions, there was an opportunity to explore music that suggested this state of mind. The mournful vocal, the slowed-down instruments and the backward tape at the end were intimations of music to come.

Backward taping became a controversial issue in the rock industry during the Seventies and Eighties when some artists were accused of concealing hidden messages within their recordings. The Beatles had not done it to conceal messages but simply to suggest a mind free of conventional logic.

George Martin has said that he came up with the idea while experimenting on his own after the Beatles had left the studio. He played back his new effects to the group the next day. John, who wrote 'Rain' at Kenwood, always claimed that he'd discovered the process trying to thread a demo tape of the song on his home recorder while high on marijuana. He was in such a disoriented state that he got the tape twisted and when he heard what sounded like an eastern religious chant coming from his headphones, he knew he had found a sound that accurately reflected his stoned consciousness. Speaking to *Detroit Free Press* journalist Loraine Alterman on August 13, 1966 he said, "After we recorded it, it wasn't long enough. I took it home. It was four in the morning and I played it backwards. I was knocked out."

'Rain' was released as the reverse side of 'Paperback Writer'.

Written: Lennon/McCartney

Length: 3'02"

UK Release: June 10, 1966 as B-side to 'Paperback Writer'

US Release: May 30, 1966 as B-side to 'Paperback Writer'

If the rain comes they run
  and hide their heads
They might as well be dead
If the rain comes, if the rain comes

When the sun shines
  they slip into the shade
(When the sun shines down)
And drink their lemonade
(When the sun shines down)
When the sun shines,
When the sun shines

Rain, I don't mind
Shine, the weather's fine

I can show you that when it starts to rain
(When the rain comes down)
Everything's the same
(When the rain comes down)
I can show you, I can show you

Rain, I don't mind
Shine, the weather's fine

Can you hear me,
  that when it rains and shines
(When it rains and shines)
It's just a state of mind?
(When it rains and shines)
Can you hear me, can you hear me?

Sdaeh rieht edih dna nur yeht semoc
  niar eht fl
(Rain)
niaR
(Rain)
niaR, enihsnuS

TAXMAN

'Taxman' was written by George Harrison after he found himself apparently paying 19 shillings and three pence in every pound (a pound was then made up of 20 shillings) to the government in the form of tax. A top tax rate payer would be paying a basic rate plus a 10 shilling in the pound surtax plus a 10% surcharge on surtax (another one shilling in the pound).

Until 1966, the Beatles' touring schedule had been so hectic that there had been no time to sit down and examine their accounts in detail. When they did get round to it, they discovered that they didn't have as much money as they had imagined. "We were actually giving most (of our money) away in taxes," said George. "It was, and still is, typical. Why should this be so? Are we being punished for something we have forgotten to do?" Ironically, in light of his conversion to religious views that stressed the futility of materialism, George was always the Beatle in the early days to mention money when asked about his ambitions.

John later said that he had a hand in the writing of 'Taxman' and he was bitter that George had neglected to mention this in the account of the song's composition in his autobiography, *I Me Mine*. John claimed that George phoned him up as he was writing it. "I threw in a few one-liners to help the song along, because that's what he asked for," he said. "I didn't want to do it... but because I loved him... I just sort of bit my tongue and said OK."

Certainly the recorded version was an improvement on George's rough draft, in which "get some bread" was rhymed with "before you're dead". On the first take the background chorus was "Anybody gotta lotta money? Anybody gotta lotta money? Anybody gotta lotta money?", sung at breakneck speed, but this was later changed to include references to Prime Minister Harold Wilson and Leader of the Opposition Edward Heath. These two politicians shared the distinction of being the first living people to be named in a Beatles' song. Although they had never met Heath, they had met Wilson (a fellow Northerner and MP for the Liverpool district of Huyton) on several occasions and had each received MBEs in the honours list that Wilson approved after leading Britain's Labour Party to victory in 1964.

The Beatles – four enterprising young people with regional accents who came from mainly working-class backgrounds – were just the sort of people Wilson wanted to encourage as part of his vision for a new classless Great Britain.

The theme music to the then-new TV series *Batman* may have been an influence – the "taxman" chorus at the end of the song bearing a resemblance to the 'Batman' chorus. The first series starring Adam West as Batman started in January 1966 although it wasn't shown in Britain until May 1966.

When the Trappist monk, poet and spiritual writer Thomas Merton (*Seven Storey Mountain*) heard 'Taxman' he wrote in his diary (June 10, 1967): "The Beatles' 'Taxman' is running through my head. They are good. Good beat, independence, wit, insight, voice, originality. They take pleasure in being Beatles and I do not resent the fact that they are multi-millionaires, for that is part of it. They have to contend with that sneaky tax man."

Written: Harrison

Length: 2'39"

UK Release: *Revolver* album, August 5, 1966

US Release: *Revolver* album, August 5, 1966

1234, 1234
Let me tell you how it will be
There's one for you, nineteen for me

Cos I'm the taxman
Yeah, I'm the taxman

Should five per cent appear too small
Be thankful I don't take it all
Cos I'm the taxman, yeah I'm the taxman

If you drive a car, I'll tax the street
If you try to sit, I'll tax your seat
If you get too cold I'll tax the heat
If you take a walk, I'll tax your feet

Taxman!
Cos I'm the taxman, yeah I'm the taxman

Don't ask me what I want it for
(Aha, Mr. Wilson)
If you don't want to pay some more
(Aha, Mr. Heath)
Cos I'm the taxman
Yeah, I'm the taxman

Now my advice for those who die
Declare the pennies on your eyes
Cos I'm the taxman
Yeah, I'm the taxman

And you're working for no one but me
Taxman!

TAXMAN

ELEANOR RIGBY

As was the case in so many of Paul's songs, the melody and first words of 'Eleanor Rigby' came to him as he sat playing his piano. By asking himself what type of person would be picking up rice in a church where a wedding had been, he was eventually led to his protagonist. She was originally named Miss Daisy Hawkins, as this name fitted the rhythm.

Paul started by imagining Daisy as a young girl but soon realized that anyone who cleaned up after weddings was likely to be older. He speculated that if she was older she might be a spinster and the empty church became a metaphor for her missed marriage opportunities. Her character then became based on his memories of old people he'd met and listened to while running errands as a Boy Scout in Liverpool. "I couldn't think of any more, so I put it away," he remembered.

Paul continued to mull over the song but wasn't happy with the name of Miss Daisy Hawkins. It didn't sound "real" enough. Sixties folksinger Donovan remembered Paul playing him a version of the song where the protagonist was called Ola Na Tungee. "The words hadn't yet come out right for him," says Donovan

He has always said that he arrived at the name of Eleanor because of Eleanor Bron, the leading actress in *Help!*. Songwriter Lionel Bart, however, was convinced that the choice was inspired by a gravestone in Putney Vale Cemetery in London that he saw as they walked through it together one afternoon. "The name on the gravestone was Eleanor Bygraves," said Bart, "and Paul thought that would fit his song. He came back to my office and began playing it on my clavichord."

There is no such dispute about the surname. Paul came across the name Rigby in January 1966, while in Bristol visiting Jane Asher, who was playing the role of Barbara Cahoun in John Dighton's *The Happiest Days Of Your Life*. The Theatre Royal, home of the Bristol Old Vic, is at 35 King Street and, as Paul was waiting for Jane to finish, he strolled past Rigby & Evens Ltd, Wine & Spirit Shippers, which was then on the opposite side of the road at Number 22. Rigby was the surname of two syllables that he was looking for to go with Eleanor.

The song was completed at Kenwood when John, George, Ringo and John's boyhood friend Pete Shotton went into the music room where Paul played it through. They each contributed ideas to flesh out the story. One of them suggested an old man rifling through garbage cans whom Eleanor Rigby could have a romance with, but it was decided that would complicate the story. A priest called Father McCartney was considered. Ringo suggested that he could be darning his socks, an idea that Paul liked. George came up with a line about "lonely people". Paul thought that calling the priest Father McCartney would lead people to think he was referring to his dad. A local phone directory was flipped open and McKenzie picked as an alternative.

"Wearing the face that she keeps in a jar by the door", one of the song's most striking images, may have been inspired by a line in the 1920 poem 'The Love Song of J. Alfred Prufrock' where T. S. Eliot wrote of the time when it's necessary "to prepare a face to meet the faces that you meet." (Jane Asher was a distant relative of Eliot through her mother, Margaret Eliot.)

Paul was then stuck for a conclusion to his story. Pete Shotton suggested that the two lonely people, Rigby and McKenzie, should be brought together in the final verse as Father McKenzie takes Eleanor Rigby's funeral and stands beside her grave. The idea was rejected by John, who thought that Shotton had

ELEANOR RIGBY

Ah, look at all the lonely people
Ah, look at all the lonely people

Eleanor Rigby picks up the rice in the
  church where a wedding has been
Lives in a dream
Waits at the window, wearing the face
  that she keeps in a jar by the door
Who is it for?

All the lonely people
Where do they all come from?
All the lonely people
Where do they all belong?

Father McKenzie writing the words of a
  sermon that no one will hear
No one comes near
Look at him working, darning his socks
  in the night when there's nobody there
What does he care?

All the lonely people
Where do they all come from?
All the lonely people
Where do they all belong?

Ah, look at all the lonely people
Ah, look at all the lonely people

Eleanor Rigby died in the church and was
  buried along with her name
Nobody came
Father McKenzie wiping the dirt from his
  hands as he walks from the grave
No one was saved

All the lonely people (Ah, look at all the
  lonely people)
Where do they all come from?
All the lonely people (Ah, look at all the
  lonely people)
Where do they all belong?

missed the point but Paul, who said nothing at the time, eventually used it.

Extraordinarily, sometime in the Eighties the gravestone of an Eleanor Rigby was discovered in the churchyard of St Peter's Parish Church, Woolton, within yards of the spot where John and Paul had met at the church's annual summer fête in 1957. It's certain that Paul didn't get his idea directly from this gravestone, but possible that he saw it as a teenager and the name registered in his subconscious. The fact that, as he said, "Eleanor Rigby sounded natural" could have been because it was already there.

This Eleanor Rigby was born at 8 Vale Road, Woolton, in August 1895 as Eleanor Whitfield but took the name Rigby from her maternal grandfather. She married at the age of 35 but had no children and died of a brain haemorrhage in October 1939 at the house where she had been born. She was 44. There are no known photographs of her.

In a further coincidence, the firm of Rigby and Evens Ltd, whose sign had inspired Paul in Bristol in 1966, had originally been established in Dale Street, Liverpool, by local man Frank Rigby.

At the time of its release George Harrison thought the song was so unusual that it would "probably only appeal to Ray Davies types", a reference to the chief Kinks' knack of writing songs like 'Well Respected Man' and 'Dedicated Follower of Fashion' which told stories about ordinary people. As a single 'Eleanor Rigby' reached the top of the British hit parade but peaked at Number 11 in America.

Written: Lennon/McCartney

Length: 2'30?

UK Release: *Revolver* album, August 5, 1966

US Release: *Revolver* album, August 5, 1966

ABOVE LEFT: The gravestone of an Eleanor Rigby in the churchyard of St. Peter's Parish Church, Woolton, where John was a parishioner as a child.

ABOVE: A 1966 street directory for Bristol shows Rigby and Evens at 22 King Street and the Old Vic offices at 19 and 35.

LEFT: Jamaican rum imported by Rigby and Evens Ltd., the company whose name provided part of the inspiration for Eleanor Rigby's name.

I'M ONLY SLEEPING

I'M ONLY SLEEPING

The first draft of John's lyric for 'I'm Only Sleeping', then titled 'I'm Sleeping', was scribbled on the back of a letter from the Post Office, dated April 25, 1966, reminding him that he owed them 12 pounds and three shillings for an outstanding radio-phone bill. Two days later the Beatles started to record it. It's clear from this first draft that he was writing about the joys of staying in bed rather than about a drug-induced dream state. His original opening line was "Try to sleep again, got to get to sleep".

John loved his bed. When he wasn't sleeping in it, he would be lying on it, propped up by pillows writing or watching television. 'I'm Only Sleeping' celebrated the bed and its value as a place for contemplation. It also prefigured 'Watching The Wheels' on the *Double Fantasy* album. The more disturbing truth, however, was that he was losing his grip on the Beatles, spending too much time either in bed or lazing around Kenwood. This indolent behaviour allowed Paul to assume control, something that was easier for him to do anyway because of his lack of family commitments and the fact that he lived close to Abbey Road in his newly purchased London home.

It was the month before this recording that the *Evening Standard* ran Maureen Cleave's famous interview with John where he declared that "We're more popular than Jesus now; I don't know which will go first – rock 'n' roll or Christianity." In the story Cleave noted: "He can sleep almost indefinitely, is probably the laziest person in England. 'Physically lazy,' he said. 'I don't mind writing or reading or watching or speaking, but sex is the only physical thing I can be bothered with any more'."

When I wake up early in the morning
Lift my head, I'm still yawning
When I'm in the middle of a dream
Stay in bed, float up stream (Float up
  stream)
Please, don't wake me, no,
  don't shake me
Leave me where I am, I'm only sleeping

Everybody seems to think I'm lazy
I don't mind, I think they're crazy
Running everywhere at such a speed
Till they find there's no need (There's no
  need)
Please, don't spoil my day,
I'm miles away
And after all I'm only sleeping

Keeping an eye on the world
  going by my window
Taking my time
  lying there and staring at the ceiling
Waiting for a sleepy feeling

Please, don't spoil my day,
I'm miles away
And after all I'm only sleeping

Ooh yeah

Keeping an eye on the world
  going by my window
Taking my time
When I wake up early in the morning
Lift my head, I'm still yawning
When I'm in the middle of a dream
Stay in bed, float up stream (Float up
  stream)

Please, don't wake me, no,
  don't shake me
Leave me where I am,
I'm only sleeping

Written: Lennon/McCartney

Length: 3'01"

UK Release: *Revolver* album, August 5, 1966

US Release: *Yesterday And Today* album,
June 20, 1966

LOVE YOU TO

Although 'Norwegian Wood' had featured sitar, it had been added as an afterthought. 'Love You To' was the first song written by George with the instrument specifically in mind. He'd recently become a member of the Asian Music Circle in London, which was run by musician Ayana Deva Angadi, who had promoted Ravi Shankar's first UK concerts. On this recording, he also featured Anil Bhagwat, a tabla player recommended to him by Angadi.

In his biography, *I Me Mine*, George recollected that he had used tabla and sitar on the basic track, overdubbing vocals and guitar at a later stage. However, Mark Lewisohn, author of *The Complete Beatles Recording Sessions*, discovered that the sitar didn't appear until the third take and the tabla wasn't added until the sixth.

The song's working title was 'Granny Smith' – after the apple variety – simply because George couldn't think of anything better. As the words "love you to" don't appear in the song, the eventual title is rather puzzling: perhaps "love me while you can" might have been more appropriate as this sums up what the song is saying.

Written: Harrison

Length: 3'01"

UK Release: *Revolver* album, August 5, 1966

US Release: *Revolver* album, August 8, 1966

LOVE YOU TO

Each day just goes so fast
I turn around, it's past
You don't get time to hang a sign on me

Love me while you can
Before I'm a dead old man

A lifetime is so short
A new one can't be bought
But what you've got means such a lot to me

Make love all day long
Make love singing songs

Make love all day long
Make love singing songs

There's people standing round
Who'll screw you in the ground
They'll fill you in with all their sins, you'll see

I'll make love to you
If you want me to

To lead a better life
I need my love to be here...

Here, making each day of the year
Changing my life
   with the wave of her hand
Nobody can deny that there's
   something there

There, running my hands
   through her hair
Both of us thinking how good it can be
Someone is speaking but she doesn't
   know he's there

I want her everywhere
And if she's beside me
I know I need never care
But to love her is to need
   her everywhere
Knowing that love is to share

Each one believing that love never dies
Watching her eyes and hoping I'm
   always there

I want her everywhere
And if she's beside me
I know I need never care
But to love her is to need
   her everywhere
Knowing that love is to share

Each one believing that love never dies
Watching her eyes and hoping I'm
   always there

I will be there and everywhere
Here, there and everywhere

HERE, THERE AND EVERYWHERE

With things starting to look up again in his romance with Jane Asher, Paul wrote one of his most powerful love songs. Both John and Paul declared that it was one of their favourite Beatles' songs, Paul eventually re-recording it for use in his film *Give My Regards To Broad Street*.

Paul wrote 'Here, There And Everywhere' in June 1966 while sitting by John's outdoor pool. He'd arrived early for a writing session, and finding that John was still in bed began composing alone. Wanting to set himself a structural challenge he built each verse of the song around the three adverbs in the title. When he recorded it he imagined the ethereal voice of Marianne Faithfull, who was then going out with Peter Asher's friend John Dunbar.

Beatles' road manager Mal Evans claimed that Paul played him a version that had the final line missing. "The line I came up with was 'Watching her eyes and hoping I'm always there'. I'm very eye conscious."

The opening line of "I need my love to be there" appears more urgent in light of what we now know about Jane's plans to work away from London and Paul's dissatisfaction with this arrangement.

This was the *Revolver* track most obviously influenced by *Pet Sounds* by the Beach Boys. Paul had been particularly impressed with the shimmering quality of 'God Only Knows' and wanted to write a number that captured the same mood. Ironically, *Pet Sounds* had been composed under the influence of *Rubber Soul*. "The first mind-blowing Beatles' album I heard was *Rubber Soul*," said Brian Wilson. "I was so blown away that I went to my piano and wrote some of the melody to 'God Only Knows'. It wasn't about competition. It was admiration."

Written: Lennon/McCartney

Length: 2'25"

UK Release: *Revolver* album, August 5, 1966

US Release: *Revolver* album, August 8, 1966

YELLOW SUBMARINE

The idea of writing a children's song about different coloured submarines came to Paul as he was drifting asleep at the Ashers' home one night. This was to develop into 'Yellow Submarine', the tale of a boy who listens to the tall stories of an old sailor about his exploits in the "land of submarines" and decides to go sailing and see for himself.

Between 1962 and 1965, the Beatles had obeyed the unwritten rules for writing pop singles: they should have love as the central theme, last less than three minutes and be easily reproducible in concert. They were now enjoying seeing how many of these rules could be broken while still retaining the immediacy and excitement of commercial pop. 'Paperback Writer' had been their first non-love single; 'Eleanor Rigby' and 'Rain' were the first of their singles never to be played at a Beatles' concert; 'Yellow Submarine' was their first children's song.

Paul used only short words in the lyric because he wanted it to be learned quickly and sung by children. While writing it, he visited Donovan at his flat in Maida Vale. "We were in the habit of just dropping in on each other," remembers Donovan. "I was just waiting for the release of my album *Sunshine Superman* and so we played each other our latest songs. One of the songs Paul played me was about a yellow submarine but he said he was missing a line or two. He asked me if I'd like to make a contribution. I left the room for a bit and came back with 'Sky of blue and sea of green, In our yellow submarine'. It wasn't an earth-shattering creation but Paul liked it enough to use it on the eventual recording."

The earliest takes of the song include the sound of marching feet before the song proper begins and Ringo intoning a spoken introduction. The Stanley Unwin inspired wordplay in this section suggests that it was written by John. "And we will march 'til three the day/ to see them gathered there/ from Land O'Groats to John O'Greer with Stepney do we tread/ To see us yellow submarine/ We love it".

The song was released as the flip side of 'Eleanor Rigby' in August 1966, the same month that *Revolver* came out, and the rumour quickly spread that the yellow submarine was a veiled reference to drugs. In New York, Nembutal capsules started to be known on the street as "yellow submarines". Paul denied the allegations and said that the only submarine he knew that you could eat was a sugary sweet he'd come across in Greece while on holiday. These had to be dropped in water and were known as "submarines". "I knew 'Yellow Submarine' would get connotations," said Paul, "but it really was a children's song."

Written: Lennon/McCartney

Length: 2'40"

UK Release: *Revolver* album, August 5, 1966

US Release: *Revolver* album, August 8, 1966

In the town where I was born
Lived a man who sailed to sea
And he told us of his life
In the land of submarines

So we sailed on to the sun
Till we found the sea of green
And we lived beneath the waves
In our yellow submarine

We all live in a yellow submarine
Yellow submarine, yellow submarine
We all live in a yellow submarine
Yellow submarine, yellow submarine

And our friends are all aboard
Many more of them live next door
And the band begins to play

We all live in a yellow submarine
Yellow submarine, yellow submarine
We all live in a yellow submarine
Yellow submarine, yellow submarine

[Full speed ahead, Mr. Captain,
 full speed ahead!
Full speed over here, sir!
Action station! Action station!
Aye, aye, sir, fire!
Captain! Captain!]

As we live a life of ease (A life of ease)
Everyone of us (Everyone of us) has all
 we need (Has all we need)
Sky of blue (Sky of blue) and sea of
 green (Sea of green)
In our yellow (In our yellow) submarine
 (Submarine, ha, ha)

We all live in a yellow submarine
Yellow submarine, yellow submarine
We all live in a yellow submarine
Yellow submarine, yellow submarine
We all live in a yellow submarine
Yellow submarine, yellow submarine
We all live in a yellow submarine
Yellow submarine, yellow submarine

'Yellow Submarine' started as a children's song and ended up, three years later, as the main inspiration for an animated film.

"IT'S ALL IN THE MIND Y'KNOW!"
—George Harrison

APPLE FILMS presents a KING FEATURES production

The Beatles

"Yellow Submarine"

ELEVEN BEATLE SONGS

Starring
SGT. PEPPER'S LONELY HEARTS CLUB BAND

Produced by
AL BRODAX · GEORGE DUNNING · LEE MINOFF

Directed by

From an original story by

Based upon a song by
JOHN LENNON and PAUL McCARTNEY

Screenplay by
LEE MINOFF and AL BRODAX JACK MENDELSOHN and ERICH SEGAL

Design
HEINZ EDELMANN COLOR by DeLuxe

United Artists
Entertainment from Transamerica Corporation

SHE SAID SHE SAID

When the Beatles visited Los Angeles in August 1965, they rented a house at 2850 Benedict Canyon for a week while they played dates in Portland, San Diego, the Hollywood Bowl and San Francisco.

One afternoon they threw a party and Neil Aspinall, Roger McGuinn and David Crosby from the Byrds, actor Peter Fonda and *Daily Mirror* show business correspondent Don Short were among the guests. "Neil Aspinall was sent to escort me downstairs to the pool room," remembers Short, "because I was the only journalist on the premises. His job was to divert my attention from the fact that everyone else was taking acid."

Upstairs, out of Short's sight, everyone (except Paul), was indeed tripping out on LSD. It was the first time John and George had deliberately taken the drug, and they were anxious to have a good experience after the disturbing visions of their first, unintentional trip. Fonda had tripped out many times and saw his role as that of a guide. "I remember sitting out on the deck of the house with George, who was telling me that he thought he was dying," says Fonda. "I told him that there was nothing to be afraid of and that all he needed to do was to relax. I said that I knew what it was like to be dead because when I was ten years old I'd accidentally shot myself in the stomach and my heart stopped beating three times while I was on the operating table because I'd lost so much blood. John was passing by at the time and heard me saying, 'I know what it's like to be dead'. He looked at me and said, 'You're making me feel I've never been born. Who put all that shit in your head?'"

Roger McGuinn felt that Fonda's comment had upset John because he was feeling insecure. "We were all on acid and John couldn't take it," McGuinn said. "John said, 'Get this guy out of here.' It was morbid and bizarre. We'd just finished watching *Cat Ballou* with Jane Fonda in it and John didn't want anything to do with any of the Fondas. He was holding the movie against Peter and then what he said just added to it."

Indeed, the earliest demo of the song (where it is called 'He Said, He Said') is far more aggressive than the final recording: "I said, who put all that crap in your head?/I know what it's like to be mad/ And it's making me feel like my trousers are torn". But John felt that as a song this was leading nowhere and abandoned it. Although it came out of a real experience it meant nothing, he said. It was just a sound. But days later he picked it up again and tried to find a middle eight. "I wrote the first thing that came into my head," said John, "and it was 'when I was a boy', in a different beat. But it was real, because it had just happened."

Peter Fonda has no doubt about the origins of the song. "When I heard *Revolver* for the first time I knew exactly where the song had come from, although John never acknowledged it to me and I never mentioned it to anyone."

Written: Lennon/McCartney

Length: 2'37 "

UK Release: *Revolver* album, August 5, 1966

US Release: *Revolver* album, August 8, 1966

SHE SAID SHE SAID

She said "I know what it's like to be dead
I know what it is to be sad"
And she's making me feel like
  I've never been born

I said "Who put all those things
  in your head
Things that make me feel that I'm mad
And you're making me feel like
I've never been born"

She said "You don't understand
  what I said"
I said "No, no, no, you're wrong
When I was a boy everything was right
Everything was right"

I said "Even though you know
  what you know
I know that I'm ready to leave
Cos you're making me feel like
  I've never been born"

She said "You don't understand
  what I said"
I said "No, no, no, you're wrong
When I was a boy everything was right
Everything was right"
I said "Even though you know
  what you know
I know that I'm ready to leave
Cos you're making me feel like
  I've never been born"

She said "I know what it's like to be dead
I know what it is to be sad
I know what it's like to be dead"

Good day sunshine, good day sunshine,
Good day sunshine

I need to laugh and when the sun is out
I've got something I can laugh about
I feel good in a special way
I'm in love and it's a sunny day

Good day sunshine, good day sunshine,
Good day sunshine

We take a walk, the sun is shining down
Burns my feet as they touch the ground

Good day sunshine, good day sunshine,
Good day sunshine

Then we'd lie beneath the shady tree
I love her and she's loving me
She feels good, she knows she's looking
  fine
I'm so proud to know that she is mine.

Good day sunshine, good day sunshine,
Good day sunshine
Good day sunshine, good day sunshine,
Good day sunshine
Good day sunshine, good day sunshine,
Good day sunshine
Good day...

GOOD DAY SUNSHINE

'Good Day Sunshine' was written by Paul at John's house on a particularly sunny day. Paul admitted in 1984 that it had been influenced by the Lovin' Spoonful, the New York-based folk-rock group that had scored two American hits with 'Do You Believe In Magic?' and 'You Didn't Have To Be So Nice'. The group was distinguished by the lyrical folk music of founder member John Sebastian who, later as a solo artist, turned in a memorable performance in the Woodstock movie with 'The Younger Generation'.

The specific song that inspired Paul that day was 'Daydream', the Spoonful's first British hit, which was in the Top 20 when the Beatles began recording *Revolver* in May 1966. Like 'Good Day Sunshine', 'Daydream' starts off with a choppy guitar beat before launching into a story of love-induced bliss heightened by beautiful weather: "I'm blowin' the day to take a walk in the sun, And fall on my face on somebody's new mown lawn".

"One of the wonderful things the Beatles had going for them," says Sebastian, "is that they were so original that when they did cop an idea from somebody else it never occurred to you. I thought there were one or two of their songs which were Spoonful-oid but it wasn't until Paul mentioned it in a *Playboy* interview that I specifically realized we'd inspired 'Good Day Sunshine'."

'Daydream' itself was inspired by the Tamla beat on songs such as 'Where Did Our Love Go?' and 'Baby Love' that the Lovin' Spoonful heard while touring America with the Supremes. "I said, we gotta have a tune like 'Baby Love'," Sebastian remembers. "I wrote the song while trying to approximate the 'Baby Love' feel on one guitar. Sometimes you attempt to cop something and what you come up with is something very much your own."

The Lovin' Spoonful owed its foundation to a meeting between Sebastian and fellow guitarist Zal Yanovsky which took place at (Mama) Cass Elliot's house where the two men had been invited independently to see the Beatles debut on the *Ed Sullivan Show* in February 1964. "Seeing the Beatles that night crystallized the idea for us both of wanting to be part of a self-contained unit which wrote its own music," remarks Sebastian. "I eventually got to meet them in April 1966 (April 18). John, Paul and George came to see us at the Marquee Club in London's Soho and it was that night that George had his first proper meeting with Eric Clapton. Unfortunately we never got to play together because everyone was just so busy in those days. We had other meetings but we always seemed to be together because we were waiting for something else to happen."

"When they played Shea Stadium in New York in August 1966 I went backstage and had a few laughs with John, who was beginning to look a lot like me. He was getting a lot of ribbing from the other Beatles about copying me. I always wished I could have spent more time with them."

Written: Lennon/McCartney

Length: 2'09"

UK Release: *Revolver* album, August 5, 1966

US Release: *Revolver* album, August 8, 1966

Written: Lennon/McCartney

Length: 2'01"

UK Release: *Revolver* album, August 5, 1966

US Release: *Yesterday And Today* album, June 20, 1966

AND YOUR BIRD CAN SING

AND YOUR BIRD CAN SING

John dismissed this song of his as "a horror" (1971) and "a throwaway" (1980) although it's difficult to see what caused his dissatisfaction. The lyric was one of his most enigmatic and was probably a dig at Paul cloaked in poetry. After all, there had only been one previous Beatles' song title beginning with the word "And" – Paul's 'And I Love Her'. Was John mocking this innovation and at the same time giving us a clue as to the target of his put-down?

The song is about someone who doesn't "get" John, someone who does all the things that hip people do but who isn't himself naturally hip. This was an accusation that he often made about Paul. The line "You say you've seen seven wonders" could therefore be a reference to the first time the Beatles smoked pot in New York when Paul thought he had discovered the answer to all of life's big questions and wrote his insight on a piece of paper. When he read it the next morning, all it said was "there are seven levels."

The period during which *Revolver* was recorded coincided with a time when Paul had a ravenous appetite for new cultural experiences and this made John feel uneasy because he felt that, as an ex-art student, this was his territory. In April 1966 Paul was commenting about the different forms of music he was getting into – Indian, classical, electronic – and bemoaning the fact that there simply wasn't time to listen to everything he wanted to. "The only thing to do is to listen to everything and then make your mind up about it." Could talk like this have led John to write, "Tell me that you've heard every sound there is"?

If this was a put-down, Paul was unaware of it. During a session to add vocal overdubs he breaks up in hysterics when John deliberately mis-quotes his own lines and sings "When your bike has broken" instead of "When your bird has broken" and then whistles the tune instead of singing.

You tell me that you've got
  everything you want
And your bird can sing
But you don't get me, you don't get me

You say you've seen seven wonders
  and your bird is green
But you can't see me, you can't see me

When your prized possessions
Start to weigh you down
Look in my direction, I'll be 'round,
I'll be 'round

When your bird is broken will it bring
  you down
You may be awoken, I'll be 'round,
I'll be 'round

You tell me that you've heard every
  sound there is
And your bird can swing
But you can't hear me,
you can't hear me

FOR NO ONE

With its haunting melody and horn section, this was one of Paul's most beautiful songs. 'For No One' was written in a rented chalet half a mile outside the Swiss ski resort of Klosters, where he and Jane Asher spent a brief holiday in March 1966. He returned from Switzerland to work on *Revolver* and Jane began rehearsals for her role as the young Ellen Terry in *Sixty Thousand Nights* at the Royal Theatre, Bristol.

Through a series of flashbacks of their life together, the song captures the dawning realization that someone's feeling of love has disappeared. In an early interview, Paul said that it was all about his own experience of living with a woman when he was fresh from leaving home. The working title was 'Why Did It Die?' and he later admitted that it was probably written about "another argument" with Jane. It can be contrasted with his 1964 song 'And I Love Her' with its belief that "a love like ours could never die".

Written: Lennon/McCartney

Length: 2'01"

UK Release: *Revolver* album, August 5, 1966

US Release: *Revolver* album, August 8, 1966

Your day breaks, your mind aches
You find that all her words of kindness
  linger on
When she no longer needs you

She wakes up, she makes up
She takes her time and doesn't feel she
  has to hurry
She no longer needs you

And in her eyes you see nothing
No sign of love behind the tears
Cried for no one
A love that should have lasted years

You want her, you need her
And yet you don't believe her when she
  says her love is dead
You think she needs you

And in her eyes you see nothing
No sign of love behind the tears
Cried for no one
A love that should have lasted years

You stay home, she goes out
She says that long ago she knew
  someone but now he's gone
She doesn't need him

Your day breaks, your mind aches
There will be times when all the things
  she said will fill your head
You won't forget her

And in her eyes you see nothing
No sign of love behind the tears
Cried for no one
A love that should have lasted years

LEFT: The light folk-rock of the Lovin' Spoonful was the musical inspiration behind 'Good Day Sunshine'.

Ring my friend,
I said you call Doctor Robert
Day or night he'll be there
    any time at all, Doctor Robert
Doctor Robert, you're a new
    and better man
He helps you to understand
He does everything he can,
Doctor Robert

If you're down he'll pick you up,
    Doctor Robert
Take a drink from his special cup,
    Doctor Robert
Doctor Robert, he's a man you
    must believe
Helping everyone in need
No one can succeed like Doctor Robert

Well, well, well, you're feeling fine
Well, well, well, he'll make you...
Doctor Robert

My friend works for the National Health,
    Doctor Robert
Don't pay money just to see yourself
    with Doctor Robert
Doctor Robert, you're a new
    and better man
He helps you to understand
He does everything he can,
Doctor Robert

Well, well, well, you're feeling fine
Well, well, well, he'll make you...
Doctor Robert

Ring my friend, I said you'd call
    Doctor Robert
Ring my friend, I said you'd call
    Doctor Robert
Doctor Robert

REVOLVER

Written: Lennon/McCartney

Length: 2'15"

UK Release: *Revolver* album, August 5, 1966

US Release: *Yesterday And Today* album,
June 20, 1966

DOCTOR ROBERT

On their American visits the Beatles heard about a chic New York doctor who gave mysterious "vitamin" injections. "We'd hear people say, 'You can get anything off him, any pills you want'," said Paul. "It was a big racket. The song was a joke about this fellow who cured everyone of everything with all these pills and tranquillizers. He just kept New York high."

Dr Robert was almost certainly Dr Robert Freymann, a 60-year-old German-born physician with a practice on East 78th Street. (The Dr Charles Roberts cited in some Beatles' books didn't exist. It was an alias used by the biographer of Warhol actress Edie Sedgwick, Jean Stein, to conceal the identity of another "speed doctor".) Known as Dr Robert or the Great White Father (he had white hair), Freymann was well connected with the city's vibrant arts scene. He had helped, among others, Theolonius Monk and Charlie Parker (whose death certificate he signed in 1955), and had a reputation for being generous with amphetamines. "I have a clientele that is remarkable, from every sphere of life," he once boasted. "I could tell you in ten minutes probably 100 famous names who come here." John, who wrote 'Dr Robert', was one of these famous names, according to Freymann's daughter Sarah Jane.

Initially prescribed as anti-depressants, amphetamines soon became a recreational drug for hip New Yorkers. One former patient of Dr Robert Freymann's, quoted in the *New York Times* in 1973, said: "If you want to make a big night of it you'd go over to Max's [Dr Max Jacobson] and then over to Freymann's and then down to Bishop's [Dr John Bishop]. It was just another kind of bar hopping." Film director Joel Schumacher, who used speed doctors in the Sixties, agrees: "We thought of them as vitamin injections but then became speed freaks."

Administering amphetamines was not illegal at the time although regulations warned against prescribing "excessive quantities" or giving the drug when it wasn't necessary. Dr Robert Freymann lost his licence to practise for six months in 1968 and, in 1975, was expelled from the New York State Medical Society for malpractice. Asked by the *New York Times* in March 1973 to defend his actions, he said "the addicts killed a good drug." His notoriety didn't stop him from writing a book, *What's So Bad About Feeling Good?*, which was published in 1981. He died in 1987.

RIGHT: Dr. Robert Freymann, New York-based 'speed doctor', who became the subject of a drug song written by John.

WHAT'S SO BAD ABOUT FEELING GOOD?

A world-famous physician who has practiced medicine for half a century and has successfully diagnosed and treated thousands of patients for both mystifying and familiar diseases reviews his most memorable cases from drug addiction and hepatitis to obesity and tension.

DR. ROBERT FREYMANN
WITH LESLIE HOLZER

GOT TO GET YOU INTO MY LIFE

'Got To Get You Into My Life' was written by Paul in emulation of the sound recently developed by the Motown writer-producer team of Holland-Dozier-Holland for the Supremes. It was the first time the Beatles had used brass.

John believed Paul was alluding to his drug experiences in the words of the song. "I think this was one of his best songs because the lyrics are good and I didn't write them," said John. "It actually describes his experiences taking acid. I think that's what he's talking about. I couldn't swear to it, but I think it was the result of that."

Paul has since confirmed that he was alluding to drugs but he (mistakenly) thought it was "one I wrote when I had first been introduced to pot... (it's) really a song about that, it's not a person, it's actually about pot … So, it's actually an ode to pot, like someone else might write an ode to chocolate or good claret." However, Paul had been introduced to pot in New York on August 24, 1965, over 18 months before. It seems unlikely that he would have waited so long to pen a tribute. The almost certain truth is that it was, as John suspected, a song to LSD.

Paul was more reticent that John and George to sample LSD. He was naturally cautious about taking a drug that was surrounded by rumour and suspicion. For a while this caused a rift between him and John and George, with them feeling that he was too conservative. In his co-written biography, *Many Years From Now*, he told Barry Miles that he didn't take the drug until 1966 and implies that this was after *Revolver* but before *Sgt. Pepper*. He took it, he said, in the company of socialite Tara Browne (later to be referenced in 'A Day In The Life') and Pretty Things' drummer Viv Prince.

Prince can remember the night well. It was in December 1965. He knows that he'd just returned from substituting for Keith Moon at a Who gig in Norfolk and that he met Paul at the Scotch of St James club where Browne's wife, Nicky, invited him, John and Paul to come back to their place at 18 Eaton Row in Belgravia. John wanted to get back home, so just he and Paul went. It was while they were there that they were both administered their first trips.

"I'd heard about LSD before because Brian Jones had been taking it," says Prince, "but neither Paul or I knew what the effects would be. It was pure LSD. That was put into a dropper and then put on to a sugar cube. Nicky made some tea and she just said, 'One lump, or two?'. The trip went on until 11 o clock the next morning. Paul was sitting there looking at this book of art. I remember him looking at one particular page for what must have been over an hour."

The exact date was the night of December 13, 1965. Prince had been playing with the Who after playing The Federation Club in Norwich. The night before the Beatles had played what would be their final British concert at the Capitol Cinema in Cardiff. The next Paul McCartney song to be recorded, on April 7, 1966, was 'Got to Get You into My Life'. This means that all of Paul's songs on *Revolver* were written after his introduction to LSD although, if his memory is correct, he didn't take it again until March 21, 1967, during the recording of *Sgt. Pepper*.

What was a bit galling for John and George was that although Paul had taken his first trip nine months after theirs he became the first pop star to go public about it when in June 1967 he admitted his usage to a reporter from *Life* magazine. It subsequently became headline news around the world. Sunday newspaper *The People* led with "Beatle Paul's Amazing Confession"

I was alone, I took a ride
I didn't know what I would find there
Another road where maybe I could see
 another kind of mind there
Ooh, then I suddenly see you
Ooh, did I tell you I need you
Every single day of my life

You didn't run, you didn't lie
You knew I wanted just to hold you
And had you gone you knew in time
 we'd meet again
For I had told you
Ooh, you were meant to be near me
Ooh, and I want you to hear me
Say we'll be together every day

Got to get you into my life

What can I do, what can I be
When I'm with you I want to stay there
If I'm true I'll never leave
And if I do I know the way there
Ooh, then I suddenly see you
Ooh, did I tell you I need you
Every single day of my life

Got to get you into my life
Got to get you into my life

I was alone, I took a ride
I didn't know what I would find there
Another road where maybe I could see
 another kind of mind there
Then suddenly I see you
Did I tell you I need you
Every single day of my life?

on June 18. In a "remarkable, frank interview" Paul admitted to having taken the drug four times in the past year. He said of his first trip, "It was quite an incredible experience. Impossible to put into words. It lasted about six hours. In that time you realize things as if you were having a lesson. This opened my eyes to the fact that there is a God. A similar experience would probably do some of our clergy some good. It is obvious that God isn't in a pill but it explained the mystery of life. It was truly a religious experience."

Just as John's first post-acid song 'Help!' spoke of having his mind changed, so Paul's first post-acid song spoke of taking "a ride" (a "trip" would have been too obvious) along another road where he might see "another kind of mind". The song was as enthusiastic and optimistic about the drug experience as he would be over a year later when speaking to the press. When a British television news reporter asked whether it wouldn't have been better if he'd kept his drug-taking private, he answered, "I was asked a question by a newspaper and the decision was whether to tell a lie or tell the truth. I decided to tell him the truth but … if I'd had my way, I wouldn't have told anyone because I'm not trying to spread the word about this … I'll keep it a personal thing if he does too. But he wanted to spread it, so it's his responsibility for spreading it. Not mine."

A recording of the song by Cliff Bennett and the Rebel Rousers entered the British Top Ten in September 1966.

ABOVE: Cliff Bennett (in the silver grey suit) with his Rebel Rousers. They had a hit with Paul's drug song 'Got To Get You Into My Life'.

Written: Lennon/McCartney

Length: 2'30 "

UK Release: *Revolver* album, August 5, 1966

US Release: *Revolver* album, August 8, 1966

I WANT TO TELL YOU

'I Want To Tell You', written by George, was about the frustrations of having things to say but being unable to articulate them. "It's about the avalanche of thoughts that are so hard to write down or say or transmit," he later said, adding that if he were to write the song again he would amend the bridge section which says: "But if I seem to act unkind, It's only me, it's not my mind, That's confusing things" so that it was clear that his mind was responsible for the confusion. "The mind is the thing that hops about telling us to do this and do that. What we need is to lose the mind," explained George.

Appropriately for a song which was about not knowing what to say, 'I Want To Tell You' was recorded under the nonsensical title 'Laxton's Superb', a name of an English apple, first suggested by engineer Geoff Emerick. It later became known as 'I Don't Know', after George Martin had asked George what he wanted to title it and had been given this negative answer.

ABOVE: Timothy Leary, known as the 'High Priest of LSD', called the Beatles "inspired revealers of the great vibration". His book *The Psychedelic Experience* provided the words that John adapted for use in 'Tomorrow Never Knows'.

I WANT TO TELL YOU

I want to tell you
My head is filled with things to say
When you're here
All those words, they seem to slip away

When I get near you
The games begin to drag me down
It's alright
I'll make you maybe next time around

But if I seem to act unkind
It's only me, it's not my mind
That is confusing things

I want to tell you
I feel hung up but I don't know why
I don't mind
I could wait forever, I've got time

Sometimes I wish I knew you well,
Then I could speak my mind and tell you
Maybe you'd understand

I want to tell you
I feel hung up but I don't know why
I don't mind
I could wait forever, I've got time,
 I've got time, I've got time

Written: Harrison

Length: 2'29"

UK Release: *Revolver* album, August 5, 1966

US Release: *Revolver* album, August 8, 1966

TOMORROW NEVER KNOWS

Turn off your mind, relax
and float down stream
It is not dying, it is not dying

Lay down all thought,
surrender to the void
It is shining, it is shining

That you may see the meaning of within
It is being, it is being

That love is all and love is everyone
It is knowing, it is knowing

That ignorance and haste may mourn
the dead
It is believing, it is believing

But listen to the colour of your dreams
It is not living, it is not living

Or play the game existence to the end
Of the beginning, of the beginning
Of the beginning, of the beginning
Of the beginning, of the beginning
Of the beginning, of the beginning

REVOLVER

Written: Lennon/McCartney

Length: 2'57"

UK Release: *Revolver* album, August 5, 1966

US Release: *Revolver* album, August 8, 1966

TOMORROW NEVER KNOWS

As the last track on the album, and the clearest signpost of things to come, it's often assumed that 'Tomorrow Never Knows' was the last track recorded. In fact, it was the first. Certainly the most unusual and most experimental piece of music to appear under the Beatles' name at the time, this was John's attempt to create in words and sounds a suitable guide track for the LSD experience.

Some of the words were borrowed from Timothy Leary's 1964 book *The Psychedelic Experience*, which was itself a poetic reinterpretation of the ancient *Tibetan Book Of The Dead*. Barry Miles, then running Indica Books in Southampton Row and an influential figure on the British underground scene, had sent the book to John. He had an arrangement with the Beatles to send them significant books, magazines and newspapers to keep them up-to-date.

Leary, known as the "High Priest of LSD", had spent seven months in the Himalayas studying Tibetan Buddhism under Lama Govinda. *The Psychedelic Experience* was a direct result of this period of study. "I would ask Lama Govinda questions," says Leary, "and then I tried to translate what he said into something useful for people. *Book Of The Dead* really means 'Book Of The Dying' but it's your ego rather than your body that is dying. The book is a classic. It's the bible of Tibetan Buddhism. The concept of Buddhism is of the void and of reaching the void – that is what John captured in the song."

The words of the *Tibetan Book Of The Dead* were written to be spoken to a dying person in order to guide them through the states of delusion that come with the approach of death. Many people experienced ego death while on LSD so the words could be employed to keep trippers on track and protect them from the horrors. John is believed to have made a tape of Leary's words to listen to on headphones while tripping at home. Part of the 'First Bardo Instructions' for use during a psychedelic session said, "You are about to be set face to face with the Clear Light. You are about to experience it in its reality. In the ego-free state, wherein all things are like the void and cloudless sky, And the naked spotless intellect is like a transparent vacuum; At this moment, know yourself and abide in that state".

The working title of the track was 'The Void'. Its eventual title was a Ringo-ism which John decided the use because it added some deceptive levity to what otherwise might have sounded like a bleak journey into nothingness. The sound of the piece, which consists of 16 tape loops made by each of the Beatles fading in and out, grew out of Paul's home tape recorder experimentation. "He had this little Grundig," says George Martin. "He found by moving the erase head and putting a loop on he could actually saturate the tape with a single noise. It would go round and round and eventually the tape couldn't absorb any more and he'd bring it in and play it."

For the vocal track, John wanted the vocals to sound like a chorus of Tibetan monks chanting on a mountaintop (sometimes he specified the Dalai Lama alone chanting). "He said he wanted to hear the words but he didn't want to hear him," says George Martin. The result, which sounds as if John is singing at the end of a long tunnel, was achieved by feeding his voice through a Leslie speaker.

John, George and Paul with future British Prime Minister Harold Wilson in 1964. Two years later, feeling squeezed by the tax system, George would give him a none-too-flattering name check in 'Taxman'.

John at home in Weybridge reading the "underground" newspaper *International Times*. Journalist Maureen Cleave called him "probably the laziest man in England".

Although Paul was a cautious user of drugs, he was the brains behind the concept of the *Sgt. Pepper* album in 1967.

8

Sgt. Pepper's Lonely Hearts Club Band

Sgt. Pepper, along with 'Penny Lane' and 'Strawberry Fields Forever' was the first fruit of the Beatles' decision not to tour. The public's expectations for the album were huge, especially as news leaked out of the unprecedented amount of time they were putting in at Abbey Road. The two sides of the single took 105 hours to record and another five months were spent on the album.

Sgt. Pepper was the brainchild of Paul, who conceived the album as a show staged by a fictional Edwardian brass band transported through time into the psychedelic age and played, of course, by the electronically equipped Beatles. "Basically Sgt. Pepper was McCartney's album, not Lennon's," says Barry Miles, who was the group's main contact on the London underground scene at the time. "People make the mistake of thinking it must have been Lennon's because he was so hip. Actually, he was taking so many drugs and trying to get rid of his ego that it was much more McCartney's idea."

Released in June 1967, it became the album of The Summer of Love – a brief season when the hippie ethic generated in San Francisco seemed to pervade the whole of the Western world. For anyone who was young at the time, the music automatically evokes the sight of beads and kaftans, the sound of tinkling bells and the aroma of marijuana masked by joss sticks. Yet only four songs on Sgt. Pepper – 'Lucy In The Sky With Diamonds', 'She's Leaving Home', 'Within You Without You' and 'A Day In The Life' – even alluded to the social upheaval caused by the changing youth culture. The rest of it was timeless in subject matter but musically very much of its era. The Beatles and George Martin were consciously trying to push the boundaries of what could be achieved in the studio, putting the energy that had until then been used in performing on stage into creating songs that sounded different to anything heard before.

The Beatles had for a long time worked this way but they now had the luxury of time. They were the first pop musicians to concentrate solely on recording and they approached the task with the attitude that if they could conceive of a sound or style then George Martin should be able to enable it to happen.

Almost all the conventions of album making were overturned. Sgt. Pepper was one of the first records to have a gatefold sleeve, printed lyrics, decorated inner bag, free gift and a cover designed by a celebrated artist. Its reputation as the first "concept album", though, is undeserved. Firstly, all that was conceptual about the album was the concept of the Lonely Hearts Club Band evident in the title, the photos and the 'Sgt. Pepper' song. The songs weren't written to explore a single topic and nor did they link together in any way. Secondly, there had been already been albums whose songs were held together by a theme such as Merle Travis's Folk Songs From the Hills (1947), Frank Sinatra's In The Wee Small Hours (1955) and Johnny Cash's Blood Sweat and Tears (1963) and Bitter Tears (1965).

Sgt. Pepper was a tremendous commercial and critical success, reaching Number 1 in the album charts in Britain and America. Almost 30 years later, it still regularly tops critics' polls as the greatest rock album ever made. It is also still regarded as one of the most influential pop albums of all time.

PENNY LANE

In Penny Lane there is a barber
 showing photographs
Of every head he's had the
 pleasure to know
And all the people that come and go
Stop and say hello

On the corner is a banker with a
 motorcar
The little children laugh at him
 behind his back
And the banker never wears
 a mac in the pouring rain
Very strange

Penny Lane is in my ears and in my eyes
There beneath the blue suburban skies
I sit and meanwhile back in
Penny Lane there is a fireman
 with an hourglass
And in his pocket is a portrait
 of the Queen
He likes to keep his fire engine clean
It's a clean machine

PENNY LANE

John and Paul had long wanted to write songs about Liverpool. Very early on in their career there were vague plans to write a musical but these were kiboshed when Lionel Bart, hot on the heels of *Oliver!*, wrote *Maggie May* (1964), a musical set in the Merseyside docks with a book by Alun Owen, the screenwriter of *A Hard Day's Night*. John initially tackled his home city when writing 'In My Life,' which had a reference to Penny Lane in its first draft, but it wasn't until 1967 that they incorporated actual Liverpool places into their songs.

Paul has said that they were partly inspired by hearing 'Club-A-Gogo,' the B-side of the Animals' hit single 'Don't Let Me Be Misunderstood' released in Britain in January 1965. The song, written by Eric Burdon and Alan Price, was about a Newcastle club on Percy Street where the Animals used to play. The song may not sound exceptional in retrospect, but early in 1965 it was novel for a British group to write and record a song about the streets of their own city.

Paul's 'Penny Lane' is based on a real location in Mossley Hill – an area where the street of Penny Lane forms a junction with Smithdown Road – but, as with 'Strawberry Fields Forever', it's also about a state of mind. It details a place that he remembered from his childhood but he's re-enchanted it, perhaps with the 'other kind of mind' that he discovered after taking LSD. This is not Penny Lane as experienced by local people going about their daily business but Penny Lane with every colour intensified, every sound magnified and every sense heightened. It's pouring with rain and yet the skies are blue. The beauty of Penny Lane is inside his head, it's "in my ears and in my eyes". (The street was most likely named after James Penny, an 18th-century slave trader who worked out of Liverpool.)

The scene that Paul unveiled could have been in a children's picture book; the barber and his photographs, the banker with his car, the fireman with his clean fire engine, the nurse with her poppies. They were, as Paul once described, "Part fact and part nostalgia." It was a fact that there was a barber's shop, owned by a Mr Bioletti, who'd had the pleasure of cutting hair for John, Paul and George when they were young. "I wrote that the barber had photographs of every head he'd had the pleasure of knowing," said Paul. "Actually he just had photos of different hairstyles. But all the people who come and go, do stop and say hello."

It was also a fact that there was a fire station (in Mather Avenue), an old tram stop shelter in the middle of the roundabout and two banks (Barclays and Lloyds). In 2004 an old school friend of John's, Stan Williams, claimed that the "pretty nurse" in the song was a girl called Beth Williams, who later married Quarry Man Pete Shotton. "As soon as I heard 'Penny Lane' I thought, 'That's Beth!'" he said. "I'm absolutely certain it was her they were singing about. She was a cadet nurse and I can remember her selling poppies out of a tray like they sell ice creams from in the theatre. The reference to being in a play could be because she loved performing and the father of one of her friends built a stage complete with lights and seats in the back yard so the girls could act and invite an audience." Beth died at the age of 35.

The idea that the nurse was "in a play" could also have been a reference to the idea promoted by Timothy Leary that the ego is a "sham" and that all we think of as "reality" is in fact an illusion. In 1967 George referred to Shakespeare's observation that "all the world's a stage" and said, "He was right because we're Beatles and it's a little scene and we're pretending to be Beatles, like Harold Wilson's pretending to be Prime Minister … They're all playing."

Penny Lane is in my ears and in my eyes
A four of fish and finger pies
In summer meanwhile back
Behind the shelter in the
  middle of the roundabout
A pretty nurse is selling
  poppies from a tray
And though she feels as if she's in a play
She is anyway

Penny Lane, the barber
  shaves another customer
We see the banker sitting
  waiting for a trim
And the fireman rushes
  in from the pouring rain
Very strange

Penny Lane is in my ears and in my eyes
There beneath the blue suburban skies
I sit and meanwhile back
Penny Lane is in my ears and in my eyes
There beneath the blue suburban skies
Penny Lane

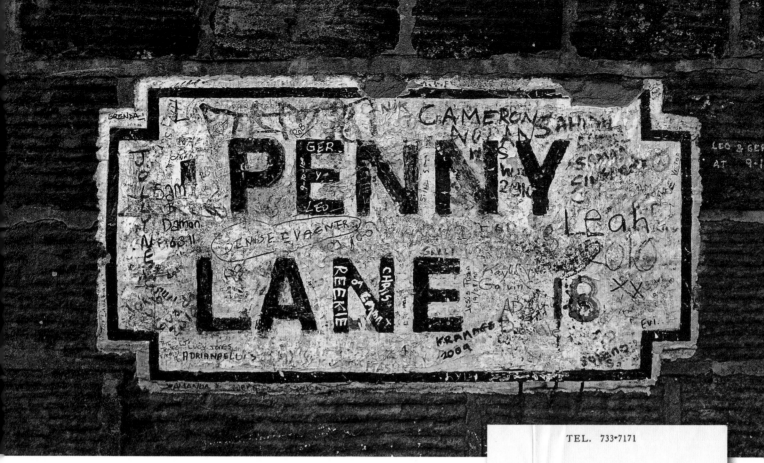

Finger pie was a Liverpudlian sexual reference included in the song to amuse the locals. "It was just a nice little joke for the Liverpool lads who like a bit of smut," said Paul. "For months afterwards, girls serving in local chip shops had to put up with requests for 'fish and finger pie'."

Liverpool poet Roger McGough, who was in the music and satire group Scaffold with Paul's brother Mike, believes that 'Penny Lane' and 'Strawberry Fields' were significant because, it was the first time that places other than American cities, and roads other than Route 66 or Highway 61, had been celebrated in rock. "The Beatles were starting to write songs about home," McGough says. "They began to draw on things like the rhymes we used to sing in the streets and old songs our parents remembered from the days of the music halls. Liverpool didn't have a mythology until they created one."

Today, because of the song, Penny Lane is a Liverpool tourist attraction and this itself has altered the area. The original street signs were stolen years ago and their replacements have had to be placed beyond easy reach. The barber's shop remains under new ownership, the shelter became a bistro which, at the time of writing, is now empty. All the Beatles coach tours now stop at Penny Lane.

Both 'Strawberry Fields Forever' and 'Penny Lane' were intended for the new album, but Capitol Records in America were pushing for a single, and it was released as a double A-side. In America it took the top spot, but in Britain it was kept at Number 2 by Engelbert Humperdinck's hit, 'Please Release Me'.

TEL. 733·7171

Bioletti's,
OF PENNY LANE.

GENTLEMEN'S
HAIRDRESSING, STYLING & COLOURING.

PRIVATE CUBICLE FOR TOUPEE FITTING
AND APPOINTMENTS

11, SMITHDOWN PLACE,   ESTABLISHED
LIVERPOOL, 15   1859

ABOVE: The business card of Harry Bioletti, who ran the barber shop mentioned in 'Penny Lane' until his death in 1976.

Written: Lennon/McCartney

Length: 3'03"

UK Single Release: February 17, 1967 as double A-side with 'Strawberry Fields Forever'

UK Chart position: 2

US Single Release: February 13, 1967 as double A-side with 'Strawberry Fields Forever'

US Chart position: 1

ABOVE LEFT: Penny Lane has become one of the best-known areas of Liverpool, thanks to a song by Paul McCartney.

STRAWBERRY FIELDS FOREVER

In the autumn of 1966, John went to the south of Spain to film the role of Private Gripweed in Dick Lester's *How I Won The War*. While relaxing on the beach at Almeria between scenes he began composing 'Strawberry Fields Forever', a song he conceived as a slow talking-blues. Further work on the song took place in a large gated 13-room house called Santa Isabel, which he was renting on the outskirts of the town. His fellow actor Michael Crawford was a guest in the house at the time and Cynthia flew out from London to join John.

The song began with what would become the second verse in the recorded version. It was a meditation on the conviction he'd had since he was a child that he was somehow different from everyone else; that he saw and felt things that other people didn't. In the earliest preserved version of his Spanish tapes he starts, "No-one is on my wavelength", later changing the line to "No-one I think is in my tree", presumably to disguise what would otherwise have been seen as arrogance. He was saying that he believed that no-one could tune in to his way of thinking, and that he must therefore either be a genius ("high") or a fool ("low"). "I seem to see things in a different way to most people," he once said. It was only on take four of the songwriting tape that he introduced Strawberry Fields (but without the "forever") and on take five he added the line "nothing to get mad about" that was latter amended to "nothing to get hung about". He was already using the deliberate hesitant language of "er", "that is", "I mean", "I think" to underline the difficulty of putting this vision into words.

On his return to England the final verse was added when he polished the song off at home. It wasn't until he went into the studio that it was completed by the addition of the opening verse, which helps explain why the sentiment of the introduction seems out of joint with the rest of the song.

In the completed version a place is made to represent a state of mind, just as Wordsworth used his experience above Tintern Abbey to represent "The joy/

Written: Lennon/McCartney

Length: 4'10"

UK Release: February 17, 1967 as double A-side with 'Penny Lane'

UK Chart position: 2

US Release: February 13, 1967 as double A-side with 'Penny Lane'

UK Chart position: 8*

* Although 'Penny Lane'/'StrawberryFields Forever' was a double A-side single, US chart compilers calculated the two songs' sales separately

Of elevated thoughts; a sense sublime/ Of something more deeply interfused". Strawberry Field (John added the 's') was a huge Victorian building in Gothic style on Beaconsfield Road, Woolton, a five-minute walk from his home in Menlove Avenue, which had been bought by the Salvation Army in 1936. Set in wooded grounds with flowerbeds containing rhododendrons, brambles and exotic plants it was a place of majesty, beauty and mystery. Evangeline Booth, daughter of Salvation Army founder William Booth, visited the property shortly before it opened as an orphanage and commented, "There is something else not of this world, already in the place. The wings of the Almighty, promised to gather over the heads of those who save the little ones, are already here." It was a place where John would go with his Aunt Mimi for summer fêtes, but also somewhere that he would sneak into during evenings and at weekends with friends such as Pete Shotton, David Ashton and Ivan Vaughan. "To grow up in Woolton was a near-religious experience in itself," said Ashton. "There were just so many beautiful things around it."

These illicit visits were, to John, like Alice's escapades down the rabbit hole and through the looking glass. He felt that he was entering another world, a world that more closely corresponded to his inner world, and as an adult he would associate these moments of bliss with his lost childhood and also with a feeling of ego loss. His comment in the opening verse that living is easy "with eyes closed" reiterates the idea put forward in 'Nowhere Man' and 'The Word' that the unenlightened consciousness is blind, ignorant and doomed to misunderstanding. With the enlightened mind there is nothing to get hung up about because the old categories no longer exist (they are "just a state of mind" as he said in 'Rain') and "nothing is real".

In his *Playboy* interview of 1980, John told David Sheff that he would "trance out into alpha" as a child, seeing "hallucinatory images" of his face when looking into a mirror. He said it was only when he later discovered the work of artists like the surrealists that he came to believe that he wasn't mad but a part of "an exclusive club that sees the world in those terms".

Let me take you down, cos I'm going to
Strawberry Fields
Nothing is real
And nothing to get hung about
Strawberry Fields forever

Living is easy with eyes closed
Misunderstanding all you see
It's getting hard to be someone
  but it all works out
It doesn't matter much to me
Let me take you down, cos I'm going to
Strawberry Fields
Nothing is real
And nothing to get hung about
Strawberry Fields forever

No one I think is in my tree
I mean it must be high or low
That is you can't, you know, tune in but
  it's all right
That is I think it's not too bad
Let me take you down, cos I'm going to
Strawberry Fields
Nothing is real
And nothing to get hung about
Strawberry Fields forever

Always, no sometimes, think it's me
But you know I know when it's a dream
I think I know I mean, er, yes but it's all
  wrong
That is I think I disagree
Let me take you down, cos I'm going to
Strawberry Fields
Nothing is real
And nothing to get hung about
Strawberry Fields forever
Strawberry Fields forever
Strawberry Fields forever

STRAWBERRY
FIELDS
FOREVER

SGT. PEPPER'S LONELY HEARTS CLUB BAND

SGT. PEPPER'S LONELY HEARTS CLUB BAND

Success meant that the public expected the Beatles to deliver not only another artistic masterpiece but a prophetic statement. To relieve this pressure, Paul developed the personae of Sgt. Pepper and his musicians, a new identity that would allow the band more creative freedom. They had become self-conscious as the Beatles but as the Lonely Hearts Club Band they would have nothing to live up to.

Paul conceived the idea on a flight back home to London from Nairobi on in November 19, 1966. During an earlier part of this holiday when he was in France he had used a facial disguise in order to get around incognito. This had led him to consider how free the Beatles would be if they as a group could adopt a disguise.

The conceit, however, wasn't sustained beyond the opening track and the reprise, although it succeeded in giving the impression to many people that *Sgt. Pepper's Lonely Hearts Club Band* was a "concept album". "The songs, if you listen to them, have no connection at all," George Martin admits. "Paul said 'Why don't we make the band 'Pepper' and Ringo 'Billy Shears' because it gives a nice beginning to the thing? It wasn't really a concept album at all. It was just a question of me trying to make something coherent by doing segues as much as possible." Later, Martin came up with the idea for a reprise, which helped to wrap it all up.

Sgt. Pepper and his band achieved the feat of being very "West Coast 1967" (you could just as easily picture their name on a psychedelic poster for the Avalon Ballroom in San Francisco) at the same time as remaining quintessentially English (you could imagine them playing on an Edwardian summer lawn). Paul had intended to play it both ways, writing old-fashioned lyrics delivered with a satirical psychedelic intensity, and using a title that appealed to the late Sixties vogue for long and surreal band names – Jefferson Airplane, Quicksilver Messenger Service, Incredible String Band, Big Brother and the Holding Company. "They're a bit of a brass band in a way," Paul said at the time, "but they're also a rock band because they've got that San Francisco thing."

The origin of the name Sgt. Pepper is disputed. The Beatles' former road manager Mal Evans is sometimes cited as having created it as a jokey substitute for "salt 'n' pepper". Others suggest that the name was derived from the popular American soft drink Dr Pepper.

It was twenty years ago today
Sgt. Pepper taught the band to play
They've been going in and out of style
But they're guaranteed to raise a smile

So may I introduce to you
The act you've known for all these years
Sgt. Pepper's Lonely Hearts Club Band

We're Sgt. Pepper's Lonely Hearts
  Club Band
We hope you will enjoy the show
Sgt. Pepper's Lonely Hearts Club Band
Sit back and let the evening go
Sgt. Pepper's lonely, Sgt. Pepper's lonely
Sgt. Pepper's Lonely Hearts Club Band

It's wonderful to be here
It's certainly a thrill
You're such a lovely audience
We'd like to take you home with us
We'd love to take you home

I don't really want to stop the show
But I thought that you might like
  to know
That the singer's going to sing a song
And he wants you all to sing along

So let me introduce to you the one
  and only Billy Shears
And Sgt. Pepper's Lonely Hearts Club
Band

Written: Lennon/McCartney

Length: 2'02"

UK Release: *Sgt. Pepper's Lonely Hearts Club Band* album, June 1, 1967

US Release: *Sgt. Pepper's Lonely Hearts Club Band* album, June 2, 1967

WITH A LITTLE HELP FROM MY FRIENDS

Journalist Hunter Davies, then working for London's *Sunday Times* newspaper, was granted a unique insight into the Beatles' writing methods when authoring their eponymous 1968 biography. On the afternoon of March 29, 1967, he went to Paul's house in Cavendish Avenue and watched as Paul and John worked on 'With A Little Help From My Friends'. It was one of the first times a journalist had witnessed Lennon and McCartney composing. "They wanted to do a Ringo-type song," remembers Davies. "They knew it would have to be for the kids, a sing-along type of song. That was what they thought was missing on the album so far. I recorded them trying to get all the rhymes right and somewhere I've got a list of all the ones they didn't use."

At the beginning of the afternoon, the writers only had a chorus line and a bit of a melody. For the first two hours, they thrashed away on guitars, neither of them getting very far. It was John who eventually suggested starting each verse with a question. The line "Do you believe in love at first sight?" didn't have the right number of syllables and so it became "Do you believe in *a* love at first sight?". John's answer to this was "Yes, I'm certain that it happens all the time". This was then followed by "Are you afraid when you turn out the light?" but rephrased as "What do you see when you turn out the light?".

Cynthia Lennon then came in and suggested a sentence ending in "I'm just fine" as an answer, but John dismissed it saying that "just" was a meaningless word only ever used as a filler. Instead he tried "I know it's mine", eventually coming up with the more substantial "I can't tell you, but I know it's mine".

After a few hours of playing around in this way, their minds began to wander from the task. They began fooling around, singing 'Can't Buy Me Love' and playing 'Tequila' (a 1958 instrumental hit for the Champs) on the piano. "When they got stuck, they would go back and do a rock 'n' roll song," remembers Davies. "Sometimes they would sing an Englebert Humperdinck song and just bugger around and then get back to the job in hand."

A recording session was due to begin at seven o'clock and they called Ringo to tell him that his song was ready, even though the words were incomplete. The final improvements were made in the studio, where ten takes of the song were recorded that night. As John had an injured finger at the time he came up with the tune on the piano, he had christened it 'Bad Finger Boogie'. (Badfinger was later given as a group name to Apple signing the Iveys).

'With A Little Help From My Friends' become a huge hit for Joe Cocker, who gave a passionate performance of it at the Woodstock Festival in 1969.

Written: Lennon/McCartney

Length: 2'44"

UK Release: *Sgt. Pepper's Lonely Hearts Club Band* album, June 1, 1967

US Release: *Sgt. Pepper's Lonely Hearts Club Band* album, June 2, 1967

WITH A LITTLE HELP FROM MY FRIENDS

What would you think if I sang out of tune
Would you stand up and walk out on me?
Lend me your ears and I'll sing you a song
And I'll try not to sing out of key
Oh I get by with a little help from my friends
Mm I get high
  with a little help from my friends
Mm gonna try
  with a little help from my friends

What do I do when my love is away?
(Does it worry you to be alone?)
How do I feel by the end of the day?
(Are you sad because you're on your own?)
No I get by with a little help from my friends
Mm get high
  with a little help from my friends
Mm gonna try
  with a little help from my friends

(Do you need anybody?)
I need somebody to love
(Could it be anybody?)
I want somebody to love

(Would you believe in a love at first sight?)
Yes I'm certain that it happens all the time
(What do you see when you turn out the
  light?)
I can't tell you, but I know it's mine
Oh I get by with a little help from my friends
Mm get high
  with a little help from my friends
Oh I'm gonna try
  with a little help from my friends

(Do you need anybody?)
I just need someone to love
(Could it be anybody?)
I want somebody to love

Oh I get by with a little help from my friends
Mm gonna try
  with a little help from my friends
Oh I get high
  with a little help from my friends
Yes I get by
  with a little help from my friends
With a little help from my friends

LUCY IN THE SKY WITH DIAMONDS

One afternoon early in 1967, Julian Lennon came home from his nursery school with a coloured drawing that he said was of his classmate, four-year-old Lucy O'Donnell. Explaining his artwork to his father, Julian said it was of "Lucy – in the sky with diamonds."

This poetry of the phrase struck John and triggered off the associations that led to the writing of the dream-like 'Lucy In The Sky With Diamonds', one of three tracks on the album that were supposed to be "about drugs". Although it's unlikely that John would have written such a piece of reverie without ever having experimented with hallucinogenics, this song was equally affected by his love of surrealism, word play and the works of Lewis Carroll.

That the song was a description of an LSD trip seemed to be substantiated when it was noted that the initials of the key words in the title spelt LSD. Yet John consistently denied this both in public and in private, although he was never hesitant to discus songs that did refer to drugs. He insisted that the title was taken from what Julian had said about his painting. Julian recalls, "I don't know why I called it that or why it stood out from all my other drawings but I obviously had an affection for Lucy at that age. I used to show Dad everything I'd built or painted at school and this one sparked off the idea for a song about Lucy in the sky with diamonds."

Lucy O'Donnell lived near the Lennon family in Weybridge and she and Julian were pupils at Heath House, a nursery school in a rambling Edwardian house run by two ladies known to the pupils as Miss Sylvia and Miss Delta. "I can remember Julian at school," said Lucy, who didn't discover that she'd been immortalized in a Beatles' song until she was 13. "I can remember him very well. I can see his face clearly. We used to sit alongside each other in proper old-fashioned desks. The house was enormous and they had heavy curtains to divide the classrooms. Julian and I were a couple of little menaces from what I've been told."

John claimed that the hallucinatory images in the song were inspired by the 'Wool And Water' chapter in Lewis Carroll's *Through The Looking Glass*, where Alice is taken down a river in a rowing boat by the Queen, who has changed into a sheep.

As a child, *Alice's Adventures In Wonderland* and *Through The Looking Glass* were two of John's favourite books. They'd been given to him as birthday presents and in a 1965 interview he claimed that he read both books once a year. In a later interview he claimed that it was partly through reading them that he realized the images in his own mind weren't indications of insanity. "Surrealism to me is reality," he said. "Psychedelic vision is reality to me and always was."

For similar reasons, John was attracted to *The Goon Show*, the British radio comedy show programme featuring Spike Milligan, Harry Secombe and Peter Sellers which were broadcast by the BBC between June 1952 and January 1960. *The Goon Show* scripts, principally written by Milligan, lampooned establishment figures, attacked post-war stuffiness and popularized surreal humour. The celebrated Beatle "wackiness" owed a lot to the Goons, as did John's poetry and writing. He told Spike Milligan that 'Lucy In The Sky With Diamonds' and several other songs had been partly inspired by his love of *Goon Show* dialogue. "We used to talk about 'Plasticine ties' in *The Goon Show* and this crept up in Lucy as 'Plasticine porters with looking glass ties'," said Milligan who, as a friend of George Martin, sat in on some of the *Sgt. Pepper* sessions. "I knew Lennon quite well. He used to talk a lot about comedy. He

Picture yourself in a boat on a river
With tangerine trees and marmalade skies
Somebody calls you, you answer quite slowly
A girl with kaleidoscope eyes

Cellophane flowers of yellow and green
Towering over your head
Look for the girl with the sun in her eyes
And she's gone

Lucy in the sky with diamonds
Lucy in the sky with diamonds
Lucy in the sky with diamonds
Aaaaahhhhh...

Follow her down to a bridge by a fountain
Where rocking horse people eat
  marshmallow pies
Everyone smiles as you drift past the flowers
That grow so incredibly high

Newspaper taxis appear on the shore
Waiting to take you away
Climb in the back with your head in
  the clouds
And you're gone

Lucy in the sky with diamonds
Lucy in the sky with diamonds
Lucy in the sky with diamonds
Aaaaahhhhh...

Picture yourself on a train in a station
With Plasticine porters with looking-glass ties
Suddenly someone is there at the turnstile
The girl with kaleidoscope eyes

Lucy in the sky with diamonds
Lucy in the sky with diamonds
Lucy in the sky with diamonds
Aaaaahhhhh...
Lucy in the sky with diamonds
Lucy in the sky with diamonds
Lucy in the sky with diamonds
Aaaaahhhhh...
Lucy in the sky with diamonds
Lucy in the sky with diamonds
Lucy in the sky with diamonds

Julian Lennon's drawing of Lucy (with diamonds) which was first published in this book in 1994.

LUCY IN THE SKY WITH DIAMONDS

Written: Lennon/McCartney

Length: 3'28"

UK Release: *Sgt. Pepper's Lonely Hearts Club Band* album, June 1, 1967

US Release: *Sgt. Pepper's Lonely Hearts Club Band* album, June 2, 1967

ABOVE: Lucy O'Donnell pictured around the time that she became the subject of Julian Lennon's drawing, which in turn led to John's composition 'Lucy In The Sky With Diamonds'.

was a *Goon Show* freak. It all stopped when he married Yoko Ono. Everything stopped. He never asked for me again."

When Paul arrived at Weybridge to work on the song, John had only completed the first verse and the chorus. For the rest of the writing they traded lines and images; Paul coming up with "newspaper taxis" and "cellophane flowers", John with "kaleidoscope eyes".

When she was 32, Lucy married her childhood sweetheart Ross Vodden, but her life was then blighted by a series of serious health problems starting with psoriatic arthritis which saw her confined to a wheelchair, and then continuing with kidney, liver and spleen problems. At the age of 39 she was diagnosed with lupus and several other auto-immune diseases which eventually confined her to bed. She died in September 2009 and her death was reported in news media around the world.

Despite the catalogue of illnesses and the repeated visits to hospital for pain relief treatment she remained incredibly positive and cheerful, used her fame as Lucy from the Beatles' song to draw attention to the underfunded work of St Thomas' Lupus Trust in London, and was more concerned to find out how other people were doing than to detail her own suffering.

Weeks before she died she wrote me a long email – a remarkable achievement in itself, as her eyesight was badly affected – during which she mentioned that Julian had recently contacted her. "He really is such a lovely, kind person," she wrote. "I was blown away when he got in touch and sent me the biggest flower arrangement I have ever seen." In December 2009 Julian wrote and recorded a song called 'Lucy' in her memory and a year later became patron of St Thomas' Lupus Trust.

It's getting better all the time

I used to get mad at my school
  (Now I can't complain)
The teachers that taught me weren't cool
  (Now I can't complain)
You're holding me down (Oh),
Turning me round (Oh)
Filling me up with your rules (Foolish rules)

I've got to admit it's getting better (Better)
A little better all the time
(It can't get no worse)
I have to admit it's getting better (Better)
It's getting better since you've been mine

Me used to be angry young man
Me hiding me head in the sand
You gave me the word, I finally heard
I'm doing the best that I can

I've got to admit it's getting better (Better)
A little better all the time
(It can't get more worse)
I have to admit it's getting better (Better)
It's getting better since you've been mine

Getting so much better all the time
It's getting better all the time
Better, better, better
It's getting better all the time
Better, better, better

I used to be cruel to my woman
I beat her and kept her apart from the
  things that she loved
Man I was mean
  but I'm changing my scene
And I'm doing the best that I can (Ooh)

I admit it's getting better (Better)
A little better all the time
(It can't get more worse)
Yes I admit it's getting better (Better)
It's getting better since you've been mine
Getting so much better all the time
It's getting better all the time
Better, better, better
It's getting better all the time
Better, better, better
Getting so much better all the time

GETTING BETTER

Much of *Sgt. Pepper* was written as the album was being recorded, with John and Paul snatching ideas from whatever was happening around them. Hunter Davies was with Paul on one such occasion – when he was struck by the phrase that became the basis of 'Getting Better'. "I was walking around Primrose Hill with Paul and his dog Martha," he says. "It was bright and sunny – the first spring-like morning we'd had that year. Thinking about the weather Paul said, "It's getting better". He was meaning that spring was here but he started laughing and, when I asked him why, he told me that it reminded him of something."

The phrase took Paul back to drummer Jimmy Nicol, who briefly became a Beatle in June 1964, after substituting on tour for a sick Ringo. Nicol was an experienced musician who had worked with the Spotnicks and Georgie Fame's Blue Flames, but he had to learn to be a Beatle overnight. Called in by George Martin on June 3, he met John, Paul and George that afternoon and was on stage with them in Copenhagen the following night. A week later in Adelaide, after playing just five dates, Nicol was given his fee, together with a jokey "retirement present", a gold watch. "After every concert, John and Paul would go up to Jimmy Nicol and ask him how he was getting on," says Davies. "All that Jimmy would ever say was, 'It's getting better.' That was the only comment they could get out of him. It ended up becoming a joke phrase and whenever the boys thought of Jimmy they'd think of 'it's getting better'."

After the walk on Primrose Hill, Paul drove back to his home in St John's Wood and sang the phrase over and over, while picking out a tune on his guitar. Then he worked it out in his music room on a piano that had a strange tone that made it sound out of tune. "That evening John came round," remembers Davies. "Paul suggested writing a song called 'It's Getting Better'. Now and again, they'd write whole songs individually, but mostly one of them had half a song and the other one would finish it off. That's how it was with this one. Paul played what he'd come up with to John and together they finished it."

'Getting Better' proved an interesting example of how they curbed each other's excesses when they worked together. The optimism of Paul's chorus, where everything is improving because of love, is counterbalanced by John's confession that he was once a schoolboy rebel, an angry young man and a wife beater. When Paul sings that things are getting better all the time, John chimes in with "it couldn't get no worse".

Asked about the song years later, John admitted it referred to his aggressive tendencies, "I sincerely believe in love and peace. I am a violent man who has learned not to be violent and regrets his violence."

Written: Lennon/McCartney

Length: 2'47"

UK Release: *Sgt. Pepper's Lonely Hearts Club Band* album, June 1, 1967

US Release: *Sgt. Pepper's Lonely Hearts Club Band* album, June 2, 1967

RIGHT: Jimmy Nicol became a Beatle overnight in June 1964 when Ringo fell ill. His phrase "it's getting better" provided the title and chorus of a Beatles song three years later.

FIXING A HOLE

'Fixing A Hole' was another *Sgt. Pepper* song assumed to refer to drugs. People assumed that Paul was talking about 'fixing' with heroin. But the song was about renovating his life, allowing himself the freedom to close up the cracks and holes through which the enemies of creativity seeped in. "It's the hole in your make up which lets the rain in and stops your mind from going where it will," as he put it.

Although it wasn't about DIY, Paul may have drawn the images from High Park, the Scottish hideaway surrounded by 400 acres of grazing land he had bought in June 1966 on the advice of his accountants. Situated on the Mull of Kintyre, the house hadn't been lived in for five years and was in poor condition from the regular battering of rain and sea winds. The brown walls were dark with damp, the only furniture consisted of potato boxes and there was no bath.

Paul decorated this property "in a colourful way" as recalled by Alistair Taylor, Brian Epstein's assistant, who accompanied Paul and Jane on their first visit to High Park. "The brown paint made the farmhouse look like the inside of an Aero bar," he wrote in his book *Yesterday: My Life With The Beatles*. "Paul decided he'd had enough of it, so he went into Campbeltown and bought lots of packets of coloured pens. The three of us spent the next few hours just doodling in all these colours, spreading them all over the wall and trying to relieve the gloom."

In 1967, in an interview with artist Alan Aldridge, Paul was probed on the drug associations: "If you're a junky sitting in a room and fixing a hole, then that's what it will mean to you, but when I wrote it I meant if there's a crack, or the room is uncolourful, then I'll paint it."

FIXING A HOLE

Written: Lennon/McCartney

Length: 2'36"

UK Release: *Sgt. Pepper's Lonely Hearts Club Band* album, June 1, 1967

US Release: *Sgt. Pepper's Lonely Hearts Club Band* album, June 2, 1967

I'm fixing a hole where the rain gets in
And stops my mind from wandering
Where it will go

I'm filling the cracks that ran through
  the door
And kept my mind from wandering
Where it will go

And it really doesn't matter
If I'm wrong I'm right
Where I belong I'm right
Where I belong
See the people standing there
Who disagree and never win
And wonder why they don't get in my door

I'm painting the room in the colourful way
And when my mind is wandering
There I will go
Ooh ooh ooh ah ah
Hey, hey, hey, hey

And it really doesn't matter
If I'm wrong I'm right
Where I belong I'm right
Where I belong
Silly people run around
They worry me and never ask me
Why they don't get past my door

I'm taking the time for a number of things
That weren't important yesterday
And I still go
Ooh ooh ooh ah ah

I'm fixing a hole where the rain gets in
Stops my mind from wandering
Where it will go oh
Where it will go oh

I'm fixing a hole where the rain gets in
And stops my mind from wandering
Where it will go

SHE'S LEAVING HOME

SHE'S LEAVING HOME

In February 1967, Paul came across a newspaper article about a 17-year-old London schoolgirl studying for her A-level GCE exams who'd been missing from home for over a week. Her distressed father was quoted as saying, "I cannot imagine why she should run away. She has everything here."

The subject of teenage runaways was a topical one in 1967. As part of the creation of an alternative society, counter-culture guru Timothy Leary had urged his followers to "drop out" – to abandon education and "straight" employment. Many young people took his advice and headed for San Francisco, centre of Flower Power. The FBI announced that there had been a record 90,000 runaways that year.

With only the newspaper facts to guide him, Paul created a moving song about a young girl sneaking away from her claustrophobically respectable home in search of fun and romance in the swinging Sixties. What he didn't know at the time was how accurate his speculation was. He also had no idea that he had met the girl in question just three years before.

The runaway in the story was Melanie Coe, the daughter of John and Elsie Coe, who lived in a luxury apartment block on Amhurst Park, Stamford Hill, north London. The only differences between her story and the story told in the song are that she met a man from a gambling casino rather than from "the motor trade" (a jokey reference to the Beatles' Liverpool friend Terry Doran), and that she walked out in the afternoon while her parents were at work, rather than in the morning while they were asleep. "The amazing thing about the song was how much it got right about my life," says Melanie. "It quoted the parents as saying, 'we gave her everything money could buy', which was true in my case. I had two diamond rings, a mink coat, hand-made clothes in silk and cashmere and even my own car.

"Then there was the line 'after living alone for so many years', which really struck home to me because I was an only child and I always felt alone," Melanie continues. "I never communicated with either of my parents. It was a constant battle. I left because I couldn't face them any longer. I heard the song when it came out and thought it was about someone like me but never dreamed it was actually about me. I can remember thinking that I didn't run off with a man from the motor trade, so it couldn't have been me! I must have been in my twenties when my mother said she'd seen Paul on television and he'd said that the song was based on a story in a newspaper. That's when I started telling my friends it was about me."

Melanie's case was a textbook example of the generational friction of the late sixties. Melanie wanted a freedom she'd heard about but could not find at home. Her father was a successful executive with the Metal Box Company and her mother a hairdresser, but their marriage was

Wednesday morning at five o'clock
  as the day begins
Silently closing her bedroom door
Leaving the note that she hoped would
  say more
She goes downstairs to the kitchen
  clutching her hankerchief
Quietly turning the backdoor key
Stepping outside she is free

She (We gave her most of our lives)
Is leaving (Sacrificed most of our lives)
Home (We gave her everything
  money could buy)
She's leaving home after living alone
For so many years (Bye bye)

Father snores as his wife gets
  into her dressing gown
Picks up the letter that's lying there
Standing alone at the top of the stairs
She breaks down and cries to her
  husband "Daddy our baby's gone
Why would she treat us so thoughtlessly?
How could she do this to me?"

She (We never thought of ourselves)
Is leaving (Never a thought for ourselves)
Home (We struggled hard all
  our lives to get by)
She's leaving home after living alone
For so many years (Bye bye)

Friday morning at nine o'clock
  she is far away
Waiting to keep the appointment
  she made
Meeting a man from the motor trade

She (What did we do that was wrong)
Is having (We didn't know it was wrong)
Fun (Fun is the one thing that money
  can't buy)
Something inside that was always denied
For so many years (Bye bye)

She's leaving home
Bye bye

characterized by dissatisfaction. They had no religious beliefs. The most important things in life were success, respectability and money. "My mother didn't like any of my friends," says Melanie. "I wasn't allowed to bring anyone home. She didn't like me going out. I wanted to act but she wouldn't let me go to drama school. She wanted me to become a dentist. She didn't like the way I dressed. She didn't want me to do anything that which I wanted to do. My father was weak. He just went along with whatever my mother said, even when he disagreed with her. The Sixties were exciting times and I was a natural extrovert with an artistic temperament. I think that if I had been allowed to study drama I would have found the outlet that I needed to express myself."

Instead it was in music and nightlife that Melanie found an outlet. At the age of 13, she began clubbing in the West End of London and, when the legendary live television show *Ready Steady Go!* started in late 1963, she became one of its regular dancers. Her parents would often scour the clubs and drag her back home. If she came back late, she would be hit. "When I went out, I could be me," she said. "In fact, in the clubs I was encouraged to be myself and to have a good time. Dancing was my passion. I was crazy for the music of the time and couldn't wait until the next single came out. When the song says 'Something was denied', that something was me. I wasn't allowed to be me. I was looking for excitement and affection. My mother wasn't affectionate at all. She never kissed me."

On Friday, October 4, 1963, Melanie won a *Ready Steady Go!* competition where she and three other female contestants had to mime to Brenda Lee's 'Let's Jump The Broomstick'. By coincidence, it happened to be the first time the Beatles were on the show and Paul McCartney presented her with her award. Each of the Beatles then gave her a signed message. "I spent that day in the studios going through rehearsals," she says, "so I was around the Beatles most of that time. Paul wasn't particularly chatty and John seemed distant but I did spend time talking to George and Ringo."

Melanie's flight from home took her, first of all, by bus to a friend's flat on the Holloway Road and then into the arms of David, a croupier from a casino of Finchley Road whom she had met previously in a club. After a brief stay in St John's Wood they rented a flat around the corner from Sussex Gardens in Paddington and, while out walking one afternoon, she saw her photo on the front page of an evening newspaper. "I immediately went back to the flat and put on dark glasses and a hat," she said. "From then on, I lived in terror that they'd find me. They did discover me after about ten days, because I think I'd let it slip where my boyfriend worked. They talked to his boss who persuaded me to call them up. When they eventually called to see me, they bundled me into the back of their car and drove me home."

To escape from her parents, Melanie married at 18. The marriage didn't last much more than a year and by the age of 21 she had moved to America to live in an ashram, and tried to make it as an actress in California. She now lives in Granada, Spain, with her two adult children following the sudden departure of her partner of 27 years. After several years in the Spanish property business she is looking to start a new venture. "If I had my life to live over again, I wouldn't choose to do it the same way," she says. "What I did was very dangerous but I was lucky. I suppose it is nice to be immortalized in a song but it would have been nicer if it had been for doing something other than running away from home."

A-level girl dumps car and vanishes

By DAILY MAIL REPORTER

THE FATHER of 17-year-old Melanie Coe, the schoolgirl who seemed to have everything, spent yesterday searching for her in London and Brighton.

Melanie had her own car, an Austin 1100. It was left, unlocked, outside her home when she vanished.

She had a wardrobe full of clothes. She took only those she was wearing—a cinnamon trouser suit and black patent leather shoes.

She left her cheque book and drew no money from her account.

Melanie, who has long blonde hair and is 5ft. 1in. tall, was studying for her A-level examinations. She planned to go to university or drama school.

She has been missing from her home at Amhurst Park, Stamford Hill, N, for a week.

Search

Her father, businessman Mr. John Coe, said yesterday: "I cannot imagine why she should run away. She has everything here. She is very keen on clothes but she left them all, even her fur coat.

"We have spoken to her friends and visited the places where she goes, but there is no trace of her. I only wish that she would telephone us."

Melanie is a pupil at Skinner's Grammar School, Stamford Hill.

MELANIE COE ... PICTURED THE DAY SHE VANISHED

ABOVE: The story of teenage runaway Melanice Coe was published in London's *Daily Mail* on February 27, 1967.

OVERLEAF: Melanie Coe, standing to the left, at a *Ready Steady Go!* rehearsal in October 1963. In 1967 she inspired 'She's Leaving Home'.

Written: Lennon/McCartney

Length: 3'35"

UK Release: *Sgt. Pepper's Lonely Hearts Club Band* album, June 1, 1967

US Release: *Sgt. Pepper's Lonely Hearts Club Band* album, June 2, 1967

ABOVE: John standing beside the Victorian poster which supplied the names and phrases for his song. The poster now hangs in Sean Lennon's room at the Dakota Building in New York.

RIGHT: The real Pablo Fanque, photographed around 1855. His Circus Royal would become the subject of John's song 'Being For The Benefit Of Mr Kite!'.

BEING FOR THE BENEFIT OF MR. KITE!

BEING FOR THE BENEFIT OF MR KITE!

In January 1967, the Beatles went to Knole Park near Sevenoaks in Kent to make a promotional film to accompany 'Strawberry Fields Forever'. "There was an antique shop close to the hotel we were using in Sevenoaks," says former Apple employee Tony Bramwell. "John and I wandered in and John spotted this framed Victorian circus poster and bought it."

Printed in 1843, the poster proudly announced that Pablo Fanque's Circus Royal would be presenting the "grandest night of the season" at Town Meadows, Rochdale, Lancashire. The production was to be "for the benefit of Mr. Kite" and would feature "Mr J. Henderson the celebrated somerset thrower" who would "introduce his extraordinary trampoline leaps and somersets over men and horses, through hoops, over garters and lastly through a hogshead of real fire. In this branch of the profession Mr H challenges the world'. Messrs Kite and Henderson were said to assure the public that 'this night's production will be one of the most splendid ever produced in this town, having been some days in preparation".

John began to compose a song using based on the poster's words. It now hung on the wall of his music room and Pete Shotton saw him squinting at the words while he picked out a tune on his piano. John changed a few facts to fit the song. On the poster it was Mr Henderson who offered to challenge the world, not Mr Kite: the Hendersons weren't "late of Pablo Fanque's Fair" anyway, it was Kite who was "late of Wells's Circus". In order to rhyme with "don't be late", John had events moved from Rochdale to Bishopsgate, London, and to rhyme with "will all be there" he changed the circus to a fair. The original horse was named Zanthus rather than Henry.

Pablo Fanque, Mr Kite and the Hendersons were never more than colourful names to John but records show that, 150 years ago, they were stars in the circus world. Mr Kite was William Kite, son of circus proprietor, James

For the benefit of Mr. Kite
There will be a show tonight
On trampoline
The Hendersons will all be there
Late of Pablo Fanque's Fair,
What a scene!
Over men and horses hoops and garters
Lastly through a hogshead of real fire!
In this way Mr. K will challenge the world!

The celebrated Mr. K
Performs his feat on Saturday
At Bishopsgate
The Hendersons will dance and sing
As Mr. Kite flys through the ring,
Don't be late!
Messrs. K and H assure the public
Their production will be second to none
And of course Henry The Horse dances
  the waltz!

The band begins at ten to six
When Mr. K performs his tricks
Without a sound
And Mr. H will demonstrate
Ten somersets he'll undertake
On solid ground
Having been some days in preparation
A splendid time is guaranteed for all
And tonight Mr. Kite is topping the bill!

Kite, who founded Kite's Pavilion Circus around 1810. William appears to have been born around 1825 in Lambeth, London, and to have become an all-round circus performer specializing in equestrianism. He was with Lord Sanger's Circus and then Wells's Circus and worked in Pablo Fanque's Circus from 1843 to 1845. He married Ann Deveraux and they had a daughter Elizabeth in 1875.

Pablo Fanque was a multi-talented performer, who became the first black circus proprietor in Britain. His real name was William Darby and he was born in Norwich in 1796 to John and Mary Darby. He started calling himself Pablo Fanque in the 1830s when he was principally a rope walker. He died in Stockport in May 1871 and was buried in Woodhouse Lane Cemetery, Leeds, which is now within the grounds of Leeds University.

The Hendersons were John (wire-walker, equestrian, trampolinist and clown) and his wife Agnes, who was the daughter of celebrated circus owner Henry Hengler. The couple travelled all over Europe and Russia during the 1840s and 1850s. The "somersets" which Mr Henderson performed on "solid ground" were somersaults, "garters" were banners held between two people and a "trampoline" in those days was a wooden springboard rather than stretched canvas attached to springs.

It was common for well-known circus performers of the time to have benefits thrown for them and they would receive all the proceeds from the event. An established and popular act like William Kite could expect at least one benefit a year.

At the time, John saw 'Being For The Benefit Of Mr. Kite!' as a throwaway, telling Hunter Davies, "I wasn't proud of that. There was no real work. I was just going through the motions because we needed a new song for *Sgt. Pepper* at that moment." However, in framing the words of an advertisement as a popular song he was doing in popular music what Marcel Duchamp had done in art in 1917 when he took a urinal and put it in an exhibition. William Burroughs and Bryon Gysin did a similar thing by incorporating the words of adverts, journals and newspapers into their poetry and fiction. By 1980, John had radically revised his opinion. He told *Playboy* interviewer David Sheff: "It's so cosmically beautiful... The song is pure, like a painting, a pure watercolour."

Written: Lennon/McCartney

Length: 2'37"

UK Release: *Sgt. Pepper's Lonely Hearts Club Band* album, June 1, 1967

US Release: *Sgt. Pepper's Lonely Hearts Club Band* album, June 2, 1967

WITHIN YOU WITHOUT YOU

George first became interested in Eastern thought as a consequence of discovering the sitar in 1965. He studied the instrument under Ravi Shankar, who gave him a copy of the book *Autobiography Of A Yogi* by Paramhansa Yogananda in September 1966 when George went to India straight after the final Beatles' concert in San Francisco. His first explicit statement about his new-found philosophy came in 'Within You Without You'.

Written as a remembered conversation, the song put forward the view that individualism – the idea that we each have our own separate identity and existence – is based on an illusion created by the ego and that it encourages disharmony and division. To draw closer to each other and get rid of the "space between us all", we need to give up this illusion produced by the ego and realize that we are essentially "all one". Although the view expressed in 'Within You Without You' was drawn from Hindu teaching, it was close to the LSD-inspired ideas that John had expressed in 'The Word,' 'Rain' and 'Strawberry Fields Forever'. Through a chemically induced dissolution of ego, acid trippers often felt as if they had been absorbed into a greater 'cosmic consciousness'. The line about gaining the world but losing your soul is taken from a warning given by Jesus and recorded in two of the gospels (Matthew 16 v 26, Mark 8 v 36).

George began to compose the song one night after a dinner party at the home of Klaus Voormann, a German artist and musician he had first met in Hamburg and who had designed the cover for *Revolver*. Voormann was now living in London, married to former *Coronation Street* actress Christine Hargreaves and playing bass for Manfred Mann. Also present at the party were Tony King and Pattie Harrison. King had known the Beatles since they arrived in London in 1963 and he would later work for Apple. "Klaus had this pedal harmonium and George went into an adjoining room and started

ABOVE: Paul, John, George and partners listening to Maharishi Mahesh Yogi at the Hilton Hotel, London, August 24, 1967.

fiddling around on it," remembers King. "It made these terrible groaning noises and, by the end of the evening, he'd worked something out and was starting to sing snatches of it to us. It's interesting that the eventual recording of 'Within You Without You' had the same sort of groaning sound that I'd heard on the harmonium because John once told me that the instrument you compose a song on determines the tone of a song. A number originally written on the piano sounds totally different to one worked out on a guitar."

King's recollection of the evening is of a typical hip Sixties affair with joints being smoked and lots of cosmic ideas being discussed. "We were all on about the wall of illusion and the love that flowed between us but none of us knew what we were talking about. We all developed these groovy voices. It was a bit ridiculous really. It was as if we were sages all of a sudden. We all felt as if we had glimpsed the meaning of the universe.

"When I first met George in 1963, he was Mr Fun, Mr Stay Out All Night," King continues. "Then all of a sudden, he found LSD and Indian religion and he became very serious. Things went from rather jolly weekends, where we'd have steak and kidney pie and sit around giggling, to these rather serious weekends where everyone walked around blissed out and talked about the meaning of the universe. It was never really my cup of tea but we all got caught up in it because we were young, easily influenced, and around famous people. I remember when the Dutch artists Simon and Marijke, who later painted the Apple shop front, were at George's, I got fed up with it all and went down the pub. Just as I was walking down George's drive, Simon and Marijke floated past in yards of chiffon and said in their groovy voices 'Ooh. Where are you going man?' I told them I was going for a Guinness. They said. 'Oh. Say something beautiful for me, will you?'"

In an interview with *International Times* in 1967, George said: "We're all one. The realization of human love reciprocated is such a gas. It's a good vibration which makes you feel good. These vibrations that you get through yoga, cosmic chants and things like that, I mean it's such a buzz. It buzzes you out of everywhere. It's nothing to do with pills. It's just in your own head, the realization. It's such a buzz. It buzzes you right into the astral plane."

None of the other Beatles were present when 'Within You Without You' was recorded. George and Neil Aspinall played tambouras while session musicians played an assortment of instruments including dilruba, tabla, violin, swordmandel and cello. "The Indian musicians on the session weren't hard to organize," remembers George Martin. "What was difficult, though, was writing a score for the cellos and violins that the English players would be able to play like the Indians. The dilruba player, for example, was doing all kinds of swoops and so I actually had to score that for strings and instruct the players to follow."

"The laugh at the very end of the track was George Harrison. He just thought it would be a good idea to go out on it," recalls Martin.

For many people it was the least enjoyable track on the album but it was also the track that most explicitly declared the group's philosophical viewpoint and one of the clearest expositions of the hippie outlook of 1967.

Written: Harrison

Length: 5'05"

UK Release: *Sgt. Pepper's Lonely Hearts Club Band* album, June 1, 1967

US Release: *Sgt. Pepper's Lonely Hearts Club Band* album, June 2, 1967

WITHIN YOU WITHOUT YOU

We were talking
  about the space between us all
And the people who hide themselves
  behind a wall of illusion
Never glimpse the truth, then it's far too
  late, when they pass away
We were talking
  about the love we all could share
When we find it, to try our best to hold
  it there with our love
With our love, we could save the world,
  if they only knew

Try to realise it's all within yourself
No one else can make you change
And to see you're really only very small
And life flows on within you
  and without you

We were talking
  about the love that's gone so cold
And the people who gain the world
  and lose their soul
They don't know, they can't see,
  are you one of them?

When you've seen beyond yourself
  then you may find
Peace of mind is waiting there
And the time will come when you see
  we're all one
And life flows on within you
  and without you

WHEN I'M SIXTY-FOUR

Paul has said that the melody to 'When I'm Sixty-Four' was composed on the piano at Forthlin Road, Liverpool, "when I was about 15". This places it in either 1957 or 1958, shortly after he joined John in the Quarry Men. By 1960, Paul was playing a version of it at gigs when the amplification broke down. At the time, he thought of it as "a cabaret tune", written out of respect for the music of the Twenties and Thirties, which his father had played as a young man.

In the midst of psychedelia, the fashions of Jim McCartney's younger days were being revived and it made sense for Paul to dust off his teenage song. Twenties pastiche song 'Winchester Cathedral' had been a UK hit for the New Vaudeville Band in September 1966, and *Bonnie and Clyde*, the movie that started a craze for Thirties clothing, was released in 1967.

Although the song was written with his father in mind, it was coincidental that he was 64 when it was eventually released. "My dad was probably only 56 when I wrote it," Paul said, "Retirement age in Britain is 65, so maybe I thought 64 was a good prelude. But probably 64 just worked well as a number."

The song is written as a letter from a socially inept young man trying to coax a female he hardly knows into promising him long-term devotion. The official tone of the letter ("drop me a line, stating point of view") paints a convincing picture of this formal young gent who wants to get it all in writing before he signs on the dotted line. "It was a kind of pastiche," says George Martin. "It was a send-up of the old stuff. The words are slightly mocking. It was also something of his father's music coming out because his father had been a musician in the Twenties. Paul always had that sneaking respect for the old rooty-tooty music."

John claimed that he wouldn't have dreamt of writing anything like 'When I'm Sixty-Four'. "John sneered at a lot of things," says Martin. "But that was part of the collaborative style. They tended to be rivals. They were never Rodgers and Hart. They were more like Gilbert and Sullivan. One would do one thing and the other would say, 'Yeah. I can do better than that,' and go and do better than that. At the same time, he was thinking, 'That was bloody good. I wish I could do it.'"

When I get older losing my hair
Many years from now
Will you still be sending me a Valentine
Birthday greetings, bottle of wine?
If I'd been out till quarter to three
Would you lock the door?
Will you still need me, will you still feed me
When I'm sixty-four?

You'll be older too
And if you say the word
I could stay with you

I could be handy, mending a fuse
When your lights have gone
You can knit a sweater by the fireside
Sunday mornings go for a ride
Doing the garden, digging the weeds
Who could ask for more?
Will you still need me, will you still feed me
When I'm sixty-four?

Every summer we can rent a cottage
 in the Isle of Wight
If it's not too dear
We shall scrimp and save
Grandchildren on your knee
Vera, Chuck & Dave

Send me a postcard, drop me a line
Stating point of view
Indicate precisely what you mean to say
Yours sincerely, wasting away
Give me your answer, fill in a form
Mine for evermore
Will you still need me, will you still feed me
When I'm sixty-four?
Ho!

Written: Lennon/McCartney

Length: 2'37"

UK Release: *Sgt. Pepper's Lonely Hearts Club Band* album, June 1, 1967

US Release: *Sgt. Pepper's Lonely Hearts Club Band* album, June 2, 1967

WHEN I'M SIXTY-FOUR

LOVELY RITA

Aaaahhh...

Lovely Rita meter maid
Lovely Rita meter maid

Lovely Rita meter maid
Nothing can come between us
When it gets dark I tow your heart away
Standing by a parking meter
When I caught a glimpse of Rita
Filling in a ticket in her little white book
In a cap she looked much older
And the bag across her shoulder
Made her look a little like a military man

Lovely Rita meter maid
May I inquire discreetly (Lovely Rita)
When are you free to take some tea with me?
(Lovely Rita, maid, ah)
Rita!

Took her out and tried to win her
Had a laugh and over dinner
Told her I would really like to see her again
Got the bill and Rita paid it
Took her home I nearly made it
Sitting on the sofa with a sister or two

Oh, lovely Rita meter maid
Where would I be without you
Give us a wink and make me think of you
(Lovely Rita meter maid)
Lovely Rita meter maid, Rita meter maid
(Lovely Rita meter maid)
Oh Lovely Rita meter meter maid (Lovely
Rita meter maid)
Ah da, ah da (Lovely Rita meter maid)

LOVELY RITA

An American friend was visiting Paul and, noticing a female traffic warden (Parking Enforcement Officer), a relatively new British phenomenon, commented: "I see you've got meter maids over here these days." Paul was taken with this alliterative term and began experimenting with it on the piano at his father's home.

The term 'meter maid', according to the *Merriam Webster Dictionary*, was first used in America in 1957 although there had long been female parking inspectors, usually trained police officers with special uniforms and no powers of arrest. The first parking meter in the USA was in Oklahoma City in 1935 but there wouldn't be one in London until 1958. Parking wardens came to the rest of Britain two years later

"I thought it [the term] was great," Paul said. "It got to be 'Rita meter maid' and then 'lovely Rita meter maid'. I was thinking it should be a hate song... but then I thought it would be better to love her." Out of this came the idea for a song about a shy office worker who, having been issued with a parking ticket, seduces the warden in an attempt to get let off the fine. "I was imagining the kind of person I would be to fall for a meter maid," said Paul.

Some years later, a traffic warden by the name of Meta Davies, who had worked in the St John's Wood area of London, claimed she had inspired the song. She hadn't been seduced but, in 1967, she had ticketed Paul for being illegally parked and he'd asked her about her unusual name. "His car was parked on a meter where the time had expired," says Meta, "I had to make out a ticket which, at the time, carried a ten shilling fine. I'd just put it on the windscreen when Paul came along and took it off. He looked at it and read my signature which was in full, because there was another M. Davies on the same unit. As he was walking away, he turned to me and said, 'Oh, is your name really Meta?' I told him that it was. We chatted for a few minutes and he said, 'That would be a good name for a song. Would you mind if I use it?' And that was that. Off he went."

It may be that Paul had already written 'Lovely Rita' and was flattering her a little, for Meta herself was 22 years his senior and the mother of a teenage daughter. "I was never a Beatles' fan," admits Meta. "But you couldn't help hearing their music. My own daughter used to wait outside the Abbey Road Studios to see them."

Written: Lennon/McCartney

Length: 2'42"

UK Release: *Sgt. Pepper's Lonely Hearts Club Band* album, June 1, 1967

US Release: *Sgt. Pepper's Lonely Hearts Club Band* album, June 2, 1967

Paul had a deep affection for the music of the 1920s and 1930s that he'd been introduced to by his father Jim. 'When I'm Sixty-Four' was his tribute to that era.

Good morning, good morning
Good morning, good morning
Good morning ah

Nothing to do to save his life
  call his wife in
Nothing to say but what a day
  how's your boy been
Nothing to do it's up to you
I've got nothing to say but it's OK
Good morning, good morning
Good morning ah

Going to work don't want to go
  feeling low down
Heading for home you start to roam
  then you're in town
Everybody knows there's nothing doing
Everything is closed it's like a ruin
Everyone you see is half asleep
And you're on your own you're in the
street

After a while you start to smile
  now you feel cool
Then you decide to take a walk
  by the old school

Nothing is changed it's still the same
I've got nothing to say but it's OK
Good morning, good morning
Good morning ah

People running round it's five o'clock
Everywhere in town is getting dark
Everyone you see is full of life
It's time for tea and Meet The Wife
Somebody needs to know the time,
  glad that I'm here
Watching the skirts you start to flirt
  now you're in gear
Go to a show you hope she goes
I've got nothing to say but it's OK

Good morning, good morning, good
Good morning, good morning, good
Good morning, good morning, good
Good morning, good morning, good
Good morning, good morning, good
Good morning, good morning, good
Good morning, good morning, good
Good morning, good morning, good
Good morning, good morning, good
Good morning, good morning, good

GOOD MORNING, GOOD MORNING,

Paul dominated *Sgt. Pepper* mainly because John had become a lazy Beatle. He rarely ventured far from home, paid little attention to business and was drawing inspiration not from contemporary art but from the stuff of domestic life – newspapers, school runs, television.

'Good Morning, Good Morning' was an accurate summary of his situation and an admission that he had run out of things to say. It was a song about his indolent life – the result of too many drugs, an exhausted marriage and days measured out in meals, sleep and banal television programmes such as *Meet The Wife*. It bears comparison with 'Nowhere Man', his song about doing nothing and having nothing to say. "When he was at home, he spent a lot of his time lying in bed with a notepad," remembers Cynthia of this period. "When he got up he'd sit at the piano or he'd go from one room to the other listening to music, gawping at television and reading newspapers. He was basically dropping out from everything that was happening. He was thinking about things. Everything he was involved in outside the home was pretty high-powered."

While sitting around in this state of mind, odd sounds and scraps of conversation would trigger ideas. It was a television commercial for Kellogg's Corn Flakes that gave John the title and chorus of 'Good Morning, Good Morning'. The black and white commercial featured nothing more than corn flakes being tipped into a bowl. The four-line jingle went: "Good morning, good morning, The best to you each morning, Sunshine breakfast, Kellogg's Corn Flakes, Crisp and full of fun".

The "walk by the old school" was a reference to taking Julian to Heath House and it's likely that the person he hoped would "turn up at a show" was Yoko Ono who he had met in November 1966. The "show" would therefore most likely have been an art show, not a theatre performance.

GOOD MORNING, GOOD MORNING

Written: Lennon/McCartney

Length: 2'41"

UK Release: *Sgt. Pepper's Lonely Hearts Club Band* album, June 1, 1967

US Release: *Sgt. Pepper's Lonely Hearts Club Band* album, June 2, 1967

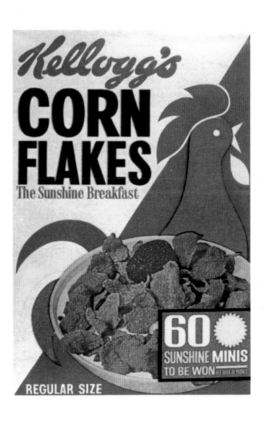

RIGHT: The jingle from a Kellog's Corn Flakes advert gave John the title and chorus for 'Good Morning, Good Morning'.

A DAY IN THE LIFE

For 'She Said She Said', John had combined two of his unfinished songs but here, for the first time, he put together an unfinished song of his own with one of Paul's to build create the most ambitious track on the album.

John's song came from his newspaper reading. The "4,000 holes in Blackburn, Lancashire", was picked from the Far And Near column in the *Daily Mail* dated January 17, 1967, which reported that a Blackburn City Council survey of road surfaces revealed that there was one twenty-sixth of a hole in the road for each resident of the city. When John was stuck for a rhyme for "small" to finish off the line "Now they know how many holes it takes to fill …" his old school friend Terry Doran suggested "the Albert Hall".

The film about the English army winning the war referred to in the lyric was of course *How I Won The War*, which wouldn't be premiered until October 1967 but had been talked about a lot in the press.

The man who "blew his mind out in a car" was Tara Browne, an Irish friend of the Beatles and a well-known socialite, who died in a car accident on December 18, 1966. The coroner's report was issued in January 1967. "I didn't copy the accident," John told Hunter Davies. "Tara didn't blow his mind out. But it was in my mind when I was writing that verse." The details of the accident in the song – not noticing traffic lights and a crowd forming at the scene – were made up. Paul, who contributed lines to this part of the song, says that he didn't know at the time that John had Tara Browne in mind. He thought he was writing about "a stoned politician".

Browne was driving down Redcliffe Gardens in Earls Court after midnight during the early hours, when a Volkswagen emerged from a side street into his path. He swerved and his Lotus Elan ploughed into a stationary van. He was pronounced dead on arrival at a local hospital. The autopsy revealed that his death was the result of "brain lacerations due to fractures of the skull". His passenger, model Suki Potier (Melanie Susan Potier), escaped with bruises and shock. She went on to become Brian Jones's girlfriend. (Ironically, she too died in a car crash – in Portugal in June 1981.)

Tara Browne, great grandson of the brewer Edward Cecil Guinness and son of Lord Oranmore and Browne, was part of a young aristocratic elite who loved to mingle with pop stars. Although only 21 at the time of his death, he would have inherited a £1,000,000 fortune at the age of 25 and was described on his death certificate as a man "of independent means" with a London home in Eaton Row, Belgravia. After schooling at Eton, Browne married Noreen "Nicky" MacSherry in 1963 and fathered two boys (Dorian born in 1963 and Julian born in 1965) before separating and taking up with Potier. He frequented London nightspots such as Sibylla's (in which he had invested) and the Bag O'Nails and had become particularly friendly with Paul and Mike McCartney and Brian Jones. For his 21st birthday in March 1966, he had the Lovin' Spoonful flown to his ancestral home in County Wicklow, Ireland. Mick Jagger, Mike McCartney, Brian Jones and John Paul Getty were amongst the guests. It was at Browne's London home that Paul first took LSD in December 1965 (see 'Got To Get You Into My Life').

Paul's unfinished song, a bright and breezy piece about getting out of bed and setting off for school, was spliced between the second and third verses of John's song. "It was another song altogether but it happened to fit," Paul said. "It was just me remembering what it was like to run up the road to catch a bus to school, having a smoke and going into class … It was a reflection of my

SGT. PEPPER'S LONELY HEARTS CLUB BAND

A DAY IN THE LIFE

I read the news today oh boy
About a lucky man who made the grade
And though the news was rather sad
Well I just had to laugh
I saw the photograph
He blew his mind out in a car
He didn't notice that the lights had changed
A crowd of people stood and stared
They'd seen his face before
Nobody was really sure
If he was from the House of Lords
I saw a film today oh boy
The English Army had just won the war
A crowd of people turned away
But I just had to look
Having read the book
I'd love to turn you on

Woke up, fell out of bed
Dragged a comb across my head
Found my way downstairs and drank a cup
And looking up I noticed I was late
Found my coat and grabbed my hat
Made the bus in seconds flat
Found my way upstairs and had a smoke
And somebody spoke
  and I went into a dream

I read the news today oh boy
Four thousand holes in Blackburn,
  Lancashire
And though the holes were rather small
They had to count them all
Now they know how many holes it takes
  to fill the Albert Hall
I'd love to turn you on

schooldays. I would have a Woodbine [a cheap unfiltered British cigarette] and somebody would speak and I would go into a dream."

The references to having a smoke, dreams and "turn-ons" caused the track to be denied radio airplay in many countries. There were even some who were convinced that the holes in Blackburn, like the holes Paul had been keen to fix, were those of a heroin user.

In 1968 Paul admitted that 'A Day In The Life' was what he called "a turn-on song". "This was the only one on the album written as a deliberate provocation," he said, "but what we want to do is to turn you on to the truth rather than on to pot." George Martin comments: "The 'woke up, got out of bed' bit was definitely a reference to marijuana but 'Fixing A Hole' wasn't about heroin and 'Lucy In The Sky With Diamonds' wasn't about LSD. At the time I had a strong suspicion that 'went upstairs and had a smoke' was a drug reference. They always used to disappear and have a little puff but they never did it in front of me. They always used to go down to the canteen and Mal Evans used to guard it."

The two separate songs – John's about random events as viewed in newspapers, Paul's about going to school in 1950s Liverpool – would have been fairly inconsequential on their own. The genius of the finished production was the stitching together of the two songs to create separate movements and the use of the orchestral glissandi between the sections and at the end. This arrangement changed it into a piece about two levels of consciousness or two ways of viewing the world; the mundane observations about car crashes and early morning routines being interrupted by the sound of approaching transcendence. By "turning on", the world of boring detail ("oh boy") is transformed.

ABOVE RIGHT: Press photo of Tara Browne's crushed Lotus Elan. Browne became the "man who blew his mind out in a car".

INSET RIGHT: Browne was a "gentleman of independent means" who enjoyed the company of pop stars and models.

ABOVE LEFT: When the Beatles stopped touring, John took the opportunity to act in Dick Lester's film *How I Won The War*, and made reference to it in 'A Day In The Life'.

Written: Lennon/McCartney

Length: 5'33"

UK Release: *Sgt. Pepper's Lonely Hearts Club Band* album, June 1, 1967

US Release: *Sgt. Pepper's Lonely Hearts Club Band* album, June 2, 1967

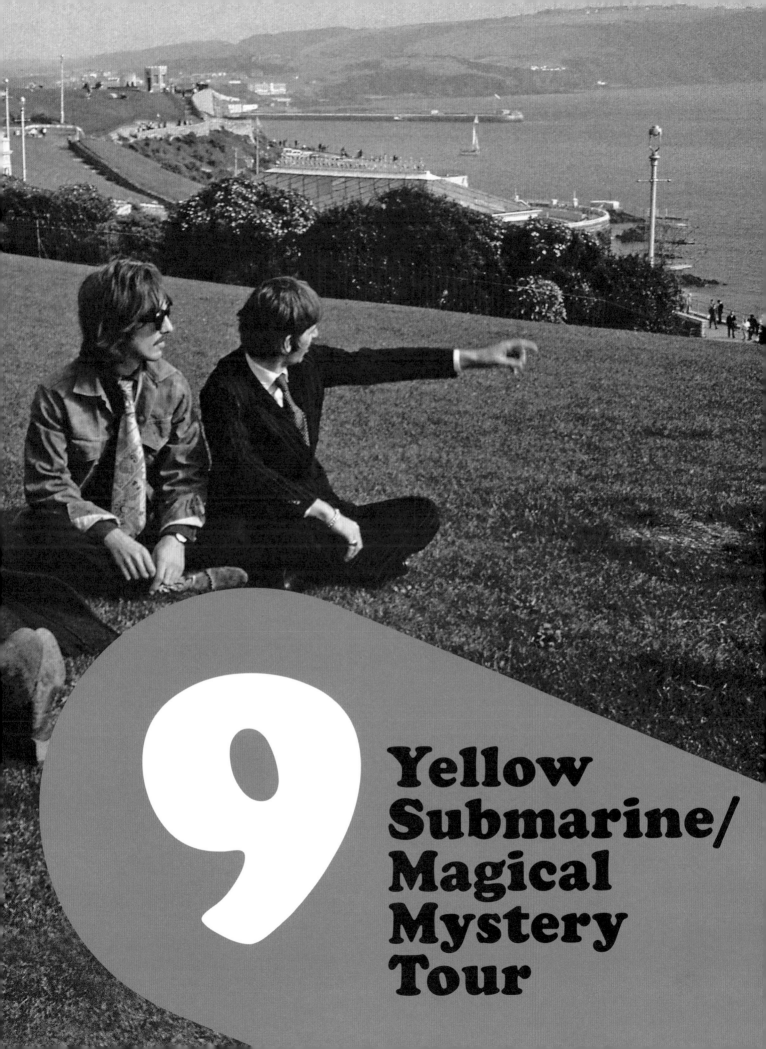

9 Yellow Submarine/Magical Mystery Tour

With *Sgt. Pepper* behind them, the Beatles immediately plunged into recording soundtracks for two very different film projects – *Yellow Submarine* and *Magical Mystery Tour*.

Yellow Submarine, a feature length animation project that fulfilled the three movie deal with United Artists, wasn't initiated by the group but they took a keen interest in its development. The Beatles were happy to see themselves turned into cartoon characters and contributed storylines as well as four original songs. The script was by a team of screenwriters, one of whom was Erich Segal, author of the best-selling novel *Love Story*. A psychedelic fantasy, *Yellow Submarine* concerns a happy kingdom called Pepperland, which is taken over by the villainous Blue Meanies. The Fab Four ride to the rescue in a yellow submarine from Liverpool, eventually conquering the Meanies through the combined power of love and music.

Magical Mystery Tour was an experimental 50-minute colour feature for television. It started off as Paul's project but the whole group was heavily involved in all aspects of production. They financed, directed, cast and scripted the film, as well as appearing in it.

Along with the single 'All You Need Is Love'/'Baby You're A Rich Man', the songs from this period are the most psychedelic of the Beatles' career. *Magical Mystery Tour* was released in America as an album in November 1967 and in Britain as two extended-play discs in December. The *Yellow Submarine* soundtrack, which included an orchestral side from George Martin, wasn't released until January 1968, shortly after *The Beatles* (*The White Album*).

This eclectic bunch of songs would make a fitting farewell to 1967, the year of the Summer of Love, before the more sober reflections of 1968. The new year marked the beginning of a fresh period in the Beatles' song writing; a time when cleaning up, straightening out and getting back to basics became the order of the day.

Magical Mystery Tour, first seen on British television on December 26, 1967, was a critical failure, which consequently received only limited exposure in America. The music was much more successful; the British double EP reached Number 2 in the singles charts and the American album went to Number 1.

The *Yellow Submarine* film was released in July 1968 in Britain and September 1968 in America. The album reached the Number 3 spot in Britain and Number 2 in America.

RIGHT: Ringo and George at the taping of 'All You Need Is Love', dressed in the best Summer of Love gear.

ALL YOU NEED IS LOVE

Early in 1967, the Beatles were approached by the BBC to take part in what would be the first ever live global satellite television link: a 125-minute programme broadcast to 26 countries with contributions from national broadcasting networks in Europe, Scandinavia, North America, Central America, North Africa, Japan and Australia. Each broadcaster that took part was asked to contribute something that contained the essence of all that was best about their country.

The Beatles, being the most visible and admired symbol of Britain's vitality at the time, were asked to compose and record a simple song that would be understood by viewers of all nationalities. Writing began in late May, with Paul and John working on separate compositions, until John's 'All You Need Is Love' emerged as the favourite. The song was not only musically uncomplicated and with a sing-along chorus but also it captured the aspirations of international youth in the summer of 1967. This was the time when the war in Vietnam was at its most intense and the "love generation" was showing its opposition by staging peaceful protests and advocating "Love Not War" on T-shirts and buttons. "It was an inspired song and they really wanted to give the world a message," said Brian Epstein. "The nice thing about it is that it cannot be misinterpreted. It is a clear message saying that love is everything."

'All You Need Is Love' crystallized the message that John had first tried to put across in 'The Word' in 1965. This was a very different love from that of 'Love Me Do', 'All My Loving' and 'She Loves You'. This was spiritual, universal love. Addressing the parents of young Americans, Timothy Leary said, "Close your eyes and listen to the sermon from Liverpool. Learn that it's the oldest message of love and peace and laughter, and trust in God and don't worry."

John was fascinated by the power of slogans to unite people and aspired to compose a song with the timelessness of 'We Shall Overcome' (a labour union song popularized in the Sixties by folk singer Pete Seeger) that could be sung by large crowds. "I like slogans," he once said. "I like advertising. I love the telly." When asked in 1971 whether songs like 'Give Peace A Chance' and 'Power To The People' were propaganda songs, he answered, "Sure. So was 'All You Need Is Love'. I'm a revolutionary artist. My art is dedicated to change."

Yet the although the chorus was memorable and easy to comprehend, the verses were teasingly unclear, appearing to have something to do with the limitless possibilities open to us if we just apply our minds but being so grammatically incorrect as to defy reliable interpretation. This may have been a result of John's own uncertainty – just as he'd shown uncertainty in 'Strawberry Fields Forever' – or it may have been due to his belief that his first thoughts, however apparently incoherent, were his best thoughts. In 1996 Paul admitted "The verse is quite complex. I never really understood it."

What viewers saw in *Our World* on June 25, 1967, when the cameras came to Abbey Road was actually a re-creation of a Beatles studio session rather than the actual session that produced the single. It would have been too complicated and risky to attempt a live recording in front of the world. Rhythm tracks had been laid down on June 14 and the live input was added and instantaneously mixed for transmission. A party atmosphere was created in Studio One by inviting celebrity friends such as Mick Jagger, Marianne Faithfull, Keith Richards, Eric Clapton, Graham Nash and Keith Moon to hold balloons, wave placards and join in on the chorus. The British contribution, which included a broadcast from Scotland, was anchored

Love, love, love
Love, love, love
Love, love, love

There's nothing you can do that can't be done
Nothing you can sing that can't be sung
Nothing you can say but you can learn how
  to play the game
It's easy

Nothing you can make that can't be made
No one you can save that can't be saved
Nothing you can do but you can learn how to
  be you in time
It's easy

All you need is love
All you need is love
All you need is love, love
Love is all you need

Love, love, love
Love, love, love
Love, love, love

All you need is love
All you need is love
All you need is love, love
Love is all you need

Nothing you can know that isn't known
Nothing you can see that isn't shown
Nowhere you can be that isn't where you're
  meant to be
It's easy

RIGHT: The recording of 'All You Need Is Love' was the first global satellite link-up for a TV special.

Written: Lennon/McCartney

Length: 3'48"

UK Release: July 7, 1967

UK Chart position: 1

US Release: July 17, 1967

US Chart position: 1

All you need is love
All you need is love
All you need is love, love
Love is all you need

All you need is love (All together, now!)
All you need is love (Everybody!)
All you need is love, love
Love is all you need
Love is all you need (Love is all you need)
Love is all you need (Love is all you need)
Love is all you need (Love is all you need)
Love is all you need (Love is all you need)
Love is all you need (Love is all you need)
Love is all you need (Love is all you need)
Love is all you need (Love is all you need)
Love is all you need (Love is all you need)
Love is all you need (Love is all you need)
Love is all you need (Love is all you need)
Love is all you need (Love is all you need)
Yee-hai! (Love is all you need)
Love is all you need (Love is all you need)

Yesterday (Love is all you need)
Love is all you need (Love is all you need)
Love is all you need (Love is all you need)
Love is all you need (Love is all you need)
Oh yeah! (Love is all you need)
She loves you, yeah yeah yeah
(Love is all you need)
She loves you, yeah yeah yeah
(Love is all you need)

by veteran BBC broadcaster Cliff Michelmore. The studio segment was introduced from Abbey Road by radio presenter Steve Race and the outside broadcast director was Derek Burrell-Davis. The message of international unity was accentuated when the 13-piece orchestra conducted by Mike Vickers (ex Manfred Mann) opened the song with bars from 'La Marseillaise' (France), and closed with snatches from 'In The Mood' (America), the Brandenburg Concerto (Germany) and 'Greensleeves' (England).

The single was released on July 7, and became the anthem of the Summer of Love, a celebration of peace, love and understanding. "We had been told that we'd be seen recording it by the whole world at the same time," said Paul. "So we had one message for the world – love. We need more love in the world."

BABY YOU'RE A RICH MAN

As with 'A Day In The Life', two unfinished songs – one by John, one by Paul – were brought together to create 'Baby You're A Rich Man', which opens with John's section, originally titled 'One Of The Beautiful People', and then moves up a gear for Paul's "rich man" chorus.

"The beautiful people" was a phrase with a history. In Oscar Wilde's 1895 play *An Ideal Husband* a character at a society party says, "I like looking at geniuses and listening to beautiful people." In 1941 William Saroyan wrote a play called *The Beautiful People*. In 1962, *Vogue* magazine, then edited by Diana Vreeland, began referring to the fashionable circle around the Kennedys as The Beautiful People. By 1964 *Vogue* had extended its meaning to include the wealthy, famous and attractive people who lived gilded lives; the sort of people who'd previously been referred to as the "Jet Set".

An additional meaning was born in the hippie counter-culture, where beauty didn't refer to wealth, looks or fame but to those who lived in a beautiful way and saw the world as beautiful. Because they also tended to wear colourful clothes and possibly even flowers in their hair they became known as the Beautiful People. "At the back of my mind somewhere... there is something which tells me that everything is beautiful," said Paul in an interview with *International Times* in January 1967. "Instead of opposing things like 'Oh, I don't like that television show' or 'No I don't like the theatre' I know really that it's all great and that everything's great and there's no bad ever if I can think of it all as great."

In 1967, San Francisco was regarded as the city of the beautiful people because it was here that the hippie movement was first spotted by the media and where the first psychedelic "happenings" and open-air "tribal gatherings" had taken place. Although the Beatles played San Francisco in 1964, 1965 and 1966, they didn't really get to explore the city until 1967. Paul was the first to visit, on April 4, when he dropped in on a Jefferson Airplane rehearsal and jammed on guitar. George was next when he came to Haight Ashbury, the San Francisco district that had given birth to underground newspapers, psychedelic poster art, communes, crash pads, head shops, free clinics and legions of exotic street people, on August 7. Pattie's sister Jenny was then living in the area. "You are our leader, George," one hippie shouted as he set off walking from the corner of Haight and Masonic with Pattie, Neil Aspinall and Derek Taylor beside him. "You know where it's at."

George was taken aback at the drug-glazed adoration of those who pushed flowers, poems, posters and drugs at him. "It's you who should be leading yourself," he told his would-be followers. "You don't want to be following leaders – me or anyone else." When he arrived at a park, George sat on the grass, listened to other people's songs and then started to sing 'Baby You're A Rich Man'.

It's hard to tell whether John is gently mocking the beautiful people for assuming that they're enlightened or whether he's complimenting them for knowing who they are. The question "How often have you been there?" would appear to be a reference to the LSD trips that, at the time, John thought offered one of the most convenient routes to true knowledge.

The rich man in Paul's section is reputed to be manager Brian Epstein and in a demo version of the song, John maligns him by singing "Baby, you're a rich fag Jew". "The point was," John later said, "stop moaning. You're a rich man and we're all rich men."

BABY YOU'RE A RICH MAN

How does it feel to be
One of the beautiful people?
Now that you know who you are.
What do you want to be?
And have you travelled very far?
Far as the eye can see

How does it feel to be
One of the beautiful people?
How often have you been there?
Often enough to know
What did you see when you were there?
Nothing that doesn't show
Baby you're a rich man
Baby you're a rich man
Baby you're a rich man too
You keep all your money in a big brown
  bag inside a zoo
What a thing to do
Baby you're a rich man
Baby you're a rich man
Baby you're a rich man too

How does it feel to be
One of the beautiful people?
Tuned to a natural E
Happy to be that way
Now that you've found another key
What are you going to play?
Baby you're a rich man
Baby you're a rich man
Baby you're a rich man too
You keep all your money in a big brown
  bag inside a zoo
What a thing to do
Baby, baby you're a rich man
Baby you're a rich man
Baby you're a rich man too
Baby you're a rich man
Baby you're a rich man
Baby, baby you're a rich man too

HELLO GOODBYE

Alistair Taylor, Brian Epstein's assistant, remembered once asking Paul how he wrote his songs, and Paul taking him into his dining room at St John's Wood to give a demonstration on his hand-carved harmonium. As he struck the keys he urged Taylor to shout out the opposite of whatever words he sang. And so it went – black and white, yes and no, stop and go, hello and goodbye. "I've no memory at all of the tune," Taylor later recounted. "You have to remember that melodies are as common around the Beatles as bugs in May. Some grow into bright butterflies and others shrivel and die. I wonder whether Paul really made up that song as he went along or whether it was running through his head already. Anyway, shortly afterwards, he arrived at the office with a demo tape of the latest single – 'Hello Goodbye'."

The last part of the record, where the Beatles repeat the line "Hela, hey, aloha" came about spontaneously in the studio. ("Aloha" is a Hawaiian greeting that means love, affection, mercy or peace.)

Although the song may have evolved from a simple word game it also expressed the Taoist philosophy of yin-yang; the idea that seemingly contrary forces are interconnected and that each gives rise to the other. A large yin-yang symbol was hung overhead in Studio One during the live 'All You Need Is Love' broadcast. "The answer to everything is simple," Paul told *Disc* when discussing the single at the time. "It's a song about everything and nothing. Stop-go, yes-no. If you have black you have to have white. That's the amazing thing about life, all the time."

'Hello Goodbye' was released as a single in November 1967 and topped the charts in both Britain and America. The final "aloha" chorus was used in the *Magical Mystery Tour* film.

Written: Lennon/McCartney

Length: 3'31"

UK Release: November 24, 1967

UK Chart position: 1

US Release: November 27, 1967

US Chart position: 1

HELLO GOODBYE

BABY YOU'RE A RICH MAN

Written: Lennon/McCartney

Length: 3'03"

UK Release: June 1, 1967 as a B-side of 'All You Need Is Love'

US Release: June 17, 1967 as a B-side of 'All You Need Is Love'

LEFT: George in Golden Gate Park, San Francisco on August 7, 1967. He sang 'Baby You're A Rich Man' to a group of gathered hippies.

You say yes, I say no
You say stop and I say go go go, oh, oh no
You say goodbye and I say hello
Hello hello
I don't know why you say goodbye, I say hello
Hello hello
I don't know why you say goodbye, I say hello

I say high, you say low
You say why and I say I don't know, oh,
 oh no
You say goodbye and I say hello
(Hello goodbye hello goodbye) Hello hello
(Hello goodbye) I don't know why you say
 goodbye, I say hello
(Hello goodbye hello goodbye) Hello hello
(Hello goodbye) I don't know why you say
 goodbye
(Hello goodbye) I say hello/goodbye

Why why why why why why do you say
goodbye goodbye, oh no?

You say goodbye and I say hello
Hello hello
I don't know why you say goodbye, I say hello
Hello hello
I don't know why you say goodbye, I say hello

You say yes (I say yes) I say no
 (But I may mean no)
You say stop (I can stay) and I say go go go
(Till it's time to go), oh
Oh no
You say goodbye and I say hello
Hello hello
I don't know why you say goodbye, I say hello
Hello hello
I don't know why you say goodbye, I say hello
Hello hello
I don't know why you say goodbye, I say hello
Hello

Heyla heba helloa
Heyla heba helloa
Heyla heba helloa

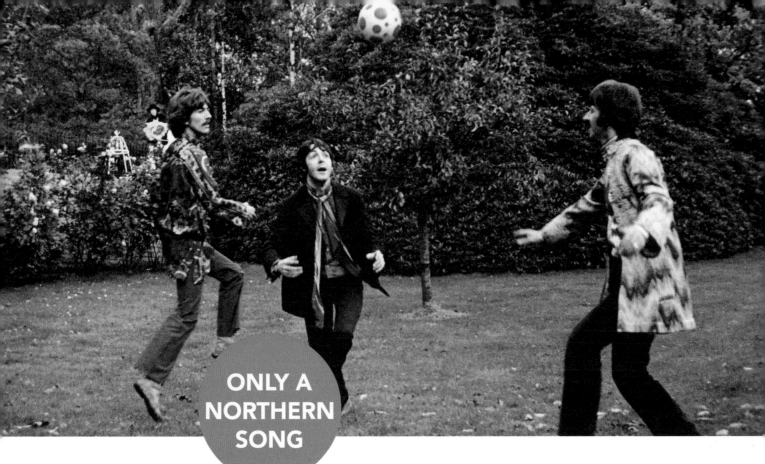

ONLY A NORTHERN SONG

If you're listening to this song
You may think the chords
  are going wrong
But they're not
He just wrote it like that

When you're listening late at night
You may think the band
  are not quite right
But they are
They just play it like that

It doesn't really matter what chords
  I play
What words I say or time of day it is
As it's only a Northern Song

It doesn't really matter what clothes
  I wear
Or how I fare or if my hair is brown
When it's only a Northern song

If you think the harmony
Is a little dark and out of key
You're correct
There's nobody there

And I told you there's no one there

ONLY A NORTHERN SONG

Originally recorded in February 1967 as George's contribution to *Sgt. Pepper's Lonely Hearts Club Band*, 'Only A Northern Song' was first used in *Yellow Submarine*. The song was a sly dig at the business arrangements of the Beatles. Their songs had always been published by Northern Songs Ltd, 30% of whose shares belonged to John and Paul, with Ringo and George owning only 1.6% each. This meant that John and Paul, in addition to being the group's main songwriters, were benefiting again as prime shareholders in the publishing company. As far as Northern Songs was concerned, George was merely a contracted writer.

In 'Only A Northern Song', George complained that it didn't really matter what he wrote because the bulk of the money was going into other people's pockets. Underlying this was his feeling, only expressed publicly after the group had broken up, that his songs were either being ignored or used as a token gesture. "At first it was just great (to get one song on each album), it was like, 'hey, I'm getting in on the act too!'" George commented. "After a while I did (come to resent this), especially when I had good songs. Sometimes I had songs that were better than some of their songs and we'd have to record maybe eight of theirs before they'd listen to one of mine."

It's not surprising that George, who in 1964 claimed that "security is the only thing I want. Money to do nothing with, money to have in case you want to do something", ultimately became the Beatle least keen to resurrect the Beatles.

Written: Harrison

Length: 3'27"

UK Release: *Yellow Submarine* album, January 17, 1969

US Release: *Yellow Submarine* album, January 13, 1969

ALL TOGETHER NOW

'All Together Now' was written in the studio in May 1967 with Paul as main contributor. It was intended as another children's song like 'Yellow Submarine' and John was delighted later, when he heard that British soccer crowds were singing it.

The renewed interest in childhood that resulted from their drug experiences meant that nursery rhymes, comic characters and lullabies began to affect some of their work. Folklorist Iona Opie, editor of *The Oxford Dictionary of Nursery Rhymes*, believed the familiar sounding lines drew more on a shared memory of nursery rhymes than on a specific rhyme. "I can't distinguish any particular influence on 'All Together Now'," she said. "So many ABC rhymes exist and there are counting rhymes like 'One, two, three, four, Mary at the cottage door...' which come pretty close. The song seems to come out of a universal subconscious."

Paul has confirmed that he saw it in the tradition of children's songs ("It's a play-away command song") but that he was also playing with the dual meaning of "all together now" which could be either a music hall style invitation for everyone to join in or a political slogan for world unity. Paul Horn remembers the song being sung while they were in India but instead of singing "H, I, J, I love you" they would sing "H, I, Jai Guru Dev" in honour of the Maharishi's spiritual master.

Written: Lennon/McCartney

Length: 2'13"

UK Release: *Yellow Submarine* album, January 17, 1969

US Release: *Yellow Submarine* album, January 13, 1969

One, two, three, four
Can I have a little more?
Five, six, seven, eight, nine, ten, I love you

A, B, C, D
Can I bring my friend to tea?
E, F, G, H, I, J, I love you

(Boom boom boom boom-ba-boom)
Sail the ship
(Boom-ba-boom) Chop the tree
(Boom-ba-boom) Skip the rope
(Boom-ba-boom) Look at me

(All together now) All together now
(All together now) All together now
(All together now) All together now
(All together now) All together now

Black, white, green, red
Can I take my friend to bed?
Pink, brown, yellow, orange and blue,
I love you

(All together now) All together now
(All together now) All together now
(All together now) All together now
(All together now) All together now
(All together now) All together now
(All together now) All together now
(All together now) All together now
(All together now) All together now

(Boom boom boom boom-ba-boom)
Sail the ship
(Boom boom boom boom-ba-boom)
Chop the tree
(Boom boom boom boom-ba-boom)
Skip the rope
(Boom-ba-boom) Look at me

(All together now) All together now
(All together now) All together now
(All together now) All together now
(All together now) All together now
(All together now) All together now
(All together now) All together now
(All together now) All together now
(All together now) All together now
(All together now) All together now
(All together now) All together now
(All together now) All together now
(All together now) All together now

HEY BULLDOG

Sheepdog
Standing in the rain
Bullfrog
Doing it again
Some kind of happiness is measured out
  in miles
What makes you think you're something
  special when you smile?

Child-like
No one understands
Jack knife
In your sweaty hands
Some kind of innocence is measured out
  in years
You don't know what it's like to listen to
  your fears

You can talk to me
You can talk to me
You can talk to me,
If you're lonely you can talk to me

Big man (Yeah)
Walking in the park
Wigwam
Frightened of the dark
Some kind of solitude is measured out
  in you
You think you know me but you haven't
  got a clue

You can talk to me
You can talk to me
You can talk to me,
If you're lonely you can talk to me
Hey!

Wahoo woof! Woof!

Hey bulldog! Woof! Hey bulldog!
Hey bulldog! Hey bulldog!

[Hey man, what's that noise?

Woof!

What d'you say?

I said woof!

D'you know anymore?

Wooaah ha ha ha!

You got it. That's it. You're brilliant.
That's it, man. That's it. You've got it.

Don't look at me, man. I only have
grandchildren.

Ah ho! Ha ha ha ha ha ha!

Quiet boy, quiet!

OK.]

Hey bulldog!
Hey bulldog!

LEFT: The novelist Erich Segal, author of *Love
Story*, worked on the film *Yellow Submarine*
and thought that he'd had an influence on 'Hey
Bulldog'.

RIGHT: John wasn't afraid to use his music as
propaganda. He wanted to create a song as
powerful and popular as 'We Shall Overcome'.
"My art is dedicated to change," he said.

HEY BULLDOG

'Hey Bulldog' was recorded on February 11, 1968, when the Beatles were at
Abbey Road to make a promotional film for 'Lady Madonna'. Paul suggested
that instead of wasting time pretending to record 'Lady Madonna', they should
tape something new and so John produced some unfinished lyrics he'd written
for *Yellow Submarine*. John explained to the others how he heard the song and
they all threw in suggestions for the words. One line John had written – "Some
kind of solitude is measured out in news" – was misread and came out as
"Some kind of solitude is measured out in you." They decided to keep it.

The bulldog of the title didn't exist before the recording. The original
lyric mentioned a bullfrog and, to make John laugh, Paul started to bark. The
barking was kept on the track and therefore introduced the idea of a bulldog
rather than a bullfrog. John felt that a dog was more appropriate for the lyric
anyway, as it was about a girl worrying someone and trying to pull them
away. Because of the late addition, the song was retitled.

Erich Segal, the author of *Love Story*, and one of the screenwriters on
Yellow Submarine, later claimed that 'Hey Bulldog' had been written for him
because the bulldog was the mascot of Yale University where he was a lecturer
in Classics! Neither John nor Paul ever confirmed this interpretation.

211

Written: Lennon/McCartney

Length: 3'14"

UK Release: *Yellow Submarine* album, January 17, 1969

US Release: *Yellow Submarine* album, January 13, 1969

It's all too much
It's all too much

When I look into your eyes,
Your love is there for me
And the more I go inside,
The more there is to see

It's all too much for me to take
The love that's shining all around you
Everywhere, it's what you make
For us to take, it's all too much

Floating down the stream of time
From life to life with me
Makes no difference where you are
Or where you'd like to be

It's all too much for me to take
The love that's shining all around here
All the world is birthday cake
So take a piece but not too much

Sail me on a silver sun,
Where I know that I'm free
Show me that I'm everywhere,
And get me home for tea

It's all too much for me to see
The love that's shining all around here
The more I learn, the less I know
But what I do is all too much

It's all too much for me to take
The love that's shining all around you
Everywhere, it's what you make
For us to take, it's all too much

It's too much
Ah, it's too much

With your long blond hair
  and your eyes of blue
With your long blond hair
  and your eyes of blue

You're too much, ah
We are getting in touch

Too much, too much, too much
Too much, too much, too much
Too much, too much, too much
Too much, too much, too much
Too much, too much, too much
Too much, too much, too much
Too much, too much, too much
Too much, too much, too much
Too much

Much, much, much, much, much
Much, much, much, much, much
Much, much, much, much, much
Much, much, much, much, much
Much, much, much, much, much

IT'S ALL TOO MUCH

George was the Beatle who most often spoke in spiritual terms about his experience of LSD. 'It's All Too Much', recorded in May 1967, was written, George said, "in a childlike manner from realizations that appeared during and after some LSD experiences and which were later confirmed in meditation."

Through images of silver suns and streaming time, the song attempted to articulate the feeling of personal identity being swallowed up by a benign force. Three months after this recording, George met the Maharishi Mahesh Yogi and began to view his LSD experience as a signpost rather than a destination. "LSD isn't a real answer," he said in September 1967. "It doesn't give you anything. It enables you to see a lot of possibilities that you may never have noticed before but it isn't the answer. It can help you go from A to B, but when you get to B you see C, and you see that to get really high, you have to do it straight. There are special ways of getting high without drugs – with yoga, meditation and all those things."

The line beginning 'With your long blonde hair' is consciously lifted from the song 'Sorrow', a big 1966 hit for the Merseys and originally a 1965 B-side for the American band the McCoys.

IT'S ALL TOO MUCH

Written: Harrison

Length: 6'28"

UK Release: *Yellow Submarine* album, January 17, 1969

US Release: *Yellow Submarine* album, January 13, 1969

MAGICAL MYSTERY TOUR

Flying home to London on April 11, 1967, after visiting Jane Asher in Denver for her 21st birthday party, Paul began to work on an idea for a Beatles television special. The group felt that they had outgrown the "caper" format that had been so successful during Beatlemania and Paul was now taking an active interest in film making (he'd bought an 8mm camera) and composing soundtracks for his own films.

Encouraged by the experimental mood of the times, Paul was excited by the idea of making an unscripted film where characters and locations were chosen in advance, but the story was improvised on camera. His plan was to put the Beatles alongside an assorted collection of actors and colourful characters on a coach that would travel through the English countryside.

As Hunter Davies reported in the *Sunday Times* the day before *Magical Mystery Tour* was shown on British television: "(They had decided that the film) would be *magical*, so that they could do any ideas which came to them, and *mysterious* in that neither they nor the rest of the passengers would know what they were going to do next. 'The whole thing will be a mystery to everyone,' Paul told the rest of the Beatles. 'Including us'."

There were three main inspirations behind *Magical Mystery Tour*. The first was the British working-class custom of the "mystery tour" that was an organized day trip by coach where only the driver knew the destination, which became popular during the early 1950s as wartime fuel rationing ended.

The second was American novelist Ken Kesey's drive through America on a psychedelically painted bus. The sign on the front read "Furthur" (sic) and the one on the back "Caution. Weird load". The bus was full of counter-culture "freaks" who Kesey kept entertained with loud music and drugs. His driver was Neal Cassady, the model for Dean Moriarty in Jack Kerouac's *On The Road*.

ABOVE: The Magical Mystery Tour Coach negotiates a narrow bridge on its way over Dartmoor on September 13, 1967.

MAGICAL MYSTERY TOUR

[Roll up! Roll up for the magical
mystery tour! Step right this way!]

Roll up, roll up for the mystery tour
Roll up, roll up for the mystery tour
Roll up (And that's an invitation),
Roll up for the mystery tour
Roll up (To make a reservation),
Roll up for the mystery tour
The magical mystery tour is
 waiting to take you away
Waiting to take you away

Roll up, roll up for the mystery tour
Roll up, roll up for the mystery tour
Roll up (We've got everything you need),
Roll up for the mystery tour
Roll up (Satisfaction guaranteed),
Roll up for the mystery tour
The magical mystery tour is
 hoping to take you away
Hoping to take you away

Mystery trip

Aaaah... the magical mystery tour
Roll up, roll up for the mystery tour
Roll up (And that's an invitation),
Roll up for the mystery tour
Roll up (To make a reservation),
Roll up for the mystery tour
The magical mystery tour is
 coming to take you away
Coming to take you away
The magical mystery tour is
 dying to take you away
Dying to take you away, take you today

The story of their adventures was eventually told in Tom Wolfe's book *The Electric Kool-Aid Acid Test* (1968) and in the documentary *Magic Trip* (2011) compiled from Kesey's original footage. The Beatles were aware of Kesey's activities and later, when the Apple record label was founded, Kesey visited the office in Savile Row to record a spoken word album for the experimental Zapple label. Unfortunately, Zapple was closed down by Allen Klein in June 1969 and the Kesey album was never made.

The third inspiration was the experimental films of people like Jean-Luc Godard, John Cassavetes, Kenneth Anger, Antony Balch and Bruce Connor that Paul was becoming familiar with through private showings at the apartment of art dealer Robert Fraser. In April 1966 Paul was telling British DJ Alan Freeman that Capitol Records had given the Beatles one of the first domestic video cameras and recorders. "What we're going to do," he announced, "is go out and shoot film – weird shapes and patterns and light – and then record special weird music to go with it. Then we can play it at home on the television."

On April 25 1967, Paul arrived at Abbey Road studios with nothing more than the song title, the first line and a general idea for the tune. He said he wanted the result to be like a commercial for the TV special, letting viewers know what to expect. Mal Evans was dispatched to find some real mystery tour posters from which they could lift phrases but, after visiting coach stations, returned empty-handed. When the backing track had been recorded, Paul asked everyone to shout out words connected with mystery tours for Evans to write down. They came up with "invitation", "reservation", "trip of a lifetime" and "satisfaction guaranteed", but it wasn't enough and so the vocal track was filled with nonsense phrases until Paul returned two days later with a completed lyric.

Paul's words were a mixture of traditional fairground barking and contemporary drug references. To the majority of the audience "roll up, roll up" was the ringmaster's invitation to the show. To Paul it was also an invitation to roll up a joint. *The Magical Mystery Tour* was going to "take you away", on a trip. Even the phrase "dying to take you away" was a deliberate reference to the *Tibetan Book Of The Dead*.

The track was used over an opening sequence of scenes from the film. A voice intones: "When a man buys a ticket for a magical mystery tour, he knows what to expect. We guarantee him the trip of a lifetime, and that's just what he gets – the incredible Magical Mystery Tour."

Written: Lennon/McCartney

Length: 2'51"

UK Release: 'Magical Mystery Tour' EP,
December 8, 1967

US Release: *Magical Mystery Tour* album,
November 27, 1967

Paul, Ringo and George with a *Yellow Submarine* cartoon of John.

THE FOOL ON THE HILL

Paul started work on 'The Fool On The Hill' in March 1967 while he was writing 'With A Little Help From My Friends', although it wasn't recorded until September.

Hunter Davies observed Paul singing and playing "a very slow, beautiful song about a foolish man sitting on the hill." John listened while staring blankly out of the window at Cavendish Avenue. "Paul sang it many times, la la-ing words he hadn't thought of yet. When at last he finished, John said he'd better write the words down or he'd forget them. Paul said it was OK. He wouldn't forget them."

The song was about an *idiot savant*; a person everyone considers to be a fool but who is actually a misunderstood visionary. Paul later said that he thought he'd had the Maharishi in mind ("His detractors called him a fool. Because of his giggle he wasn't taken seriously. It was this idea of a fool on the hill, a guru in a cave, I was attracted to") yet this is unlikely because none of the Beatles had met Maharishi in March 1967. He also said he'd been reminded of a story he'd read about a hermit in Italy who emerged from a cave in the late 1940s and discovered that he'd missed the entire Second World War. The hermit story could refer to the Italian Valerio Ricetti who lived alone for 23 years in a hillside cave in the Australian outback. He built a personal paradise of shelters, gardens, bridges, water cisterns, pathways and a chapel over 16 hectares of Scenic Hill in New South Wales that he named "mia sacra collina" (my sacred hill). He didn't miss the war but was arrested for failing to register and interned. Ricetti died in Italy in 1952. His home is now a heritage site known as Hermit's Cave Lookout.

In his book *Yesterday*, Alistair Taylor, General Manager of Apple Corps, recounts another experience that may have contributed to the song.

He recalls an early morning walk on Primrose Hill with Paul and his dog Martha, where they watched the sun rise and then realized that Martha had gone missing. "We turned round to go and suddenly there he was standing behind us," wrote Taylor. "He was a middle-aged man, very respectably dressed in a belted raincoat. Nothing in that, you may think, but he'd come up behind us over the bare top of the hill in total silence."

Both Paul and Taylor were sure that the man hadn't been there seconds earlier because they'd been searching the area for the dog. He seemed to have appeared miraculously. The three men exchanged greetings, the man commented on the beautiful view and then walked way. When they looked around, he'd vanished. "There was no sign of the man," said Taylor. "He'd just disappeared from the top of the hill as if he'd been carried off into the air! No-one could have run to the thin cover of the nearest trees in the time we had turned away from him, and no-one could have run over the crest of the hill."

What added to the mystery was that immediately before the man's appearance Paul and Taylor had been mulling over the existence of God. "Paul and I both felt the same weird sensation that something special had happened. We sat down rather shakily on the seat and Paul said, 'What the hell do you make of that? That's weird. He was here, wasn't he? We did speak to him?'"

In *Magical Mystery Tour*, the song was used over a sequence with Paul on a hilltop overlooking Nice.

THE FOOL ON THE HILL

Day after day, alone on a hill
The man with the foolish grin
  is keeping perfectly still
But nobody wants to know him
They can see that he's just a fool
And he never gives an answer

But the fool on the hill
Sees the sun going down
And the eyes in his head
See the world spinning around

Well on the way, head in a cloud
The man of a thousand voices talking
  perfectly loud
But nobody ever hears him
Or the sound he appears to make
And he never seems to notice

But the fool on the hill
Sees the sun going down
And the eyes in his head
See the world spinning around

And nobody seems to like him
They can tell what he wants to do
And he never shows his feelings

But the fool on the hill
Sees the sun going down
And the eyes in his head
See the world spinning around

He never listens to them
He knows that they're the fools
They don't like him

The fool on the hill
Sees the sun going down
And the eyes in his head
See the world spinning around

FLYING

The Beatles had recorded two previous instrumentals, 'Cry For A Shadow' in Germany in 1961 (when backing Tony Sheridan as the Beat Brothers) and the unreleased '12-Bar Original' in 1965 (not released until *Anthology 2* in 1996). Flying was the only instrumental to be released on a Beatles' record while the Beatles were still together as a group.

Used as incidental music for *Magical Mystery Tour*, 'Flying' emerged out of a studio jam. Originally titled 'Aerial Tour Instrumental', it was registered as a group composition, although Paul wrote the melody, and featured a basic rhythm track with additional Mellotron (using the trombone setting), backwards organ and vocal chanting. The cloud scenes which 'Flying' was heard over were originally shot by Stanley Kubrick for *2001: A Space Odyssey* but never used.

ABOVE: A firm believer in a strong family life, Paul often found himself spending more time with Julian Lennon than John did.

THE FOOL ON THE HILL

Written: Harrison/Lennon/McCartney

Length: 3'00"

UK Release: 'Magical Mystery Tour' EP, December 8, 1967

US Release: *Magical Mystery Tour* album, November 27, 1967

Written: Harrison/Lennon/McCartney

Length: 2'16"

UK Release: 'Magical Mystery Tour' EP, December 8, 1967

US Release: *Magical Mystery Tour* album, November 27, 1967

BLUE JAY WAY

There's a fog upon LA
And my friends have lost their way
We'll be over soon they said
Now they've lost themselves instead
Please don't be long
Please don't you be very long
Please don't be long for I may be asleep

Well it only goes to show
And I told them where to go
Ask a policeman on the street
There's so many there to meet
Please don't be long
Please don't you be very long
Please don't be long for I may be asleep

Now it's past my bed I know
And I'd really like to go
Soon will be the break of day
Sitting here in Blue Jay Way

Please don't be long
Please don't you be very long
Please don't be long for I may be asleep

Please don't be long
Please don't you be very long
Please don't be long
Please don't be long
Please don't you be very long
Please don't be long
Please don't be long
Please don't you be very long

Please don't be long
Don't be long, don't be long,
  don't be long
Don't be long, don't be long,
  don't be long

BLUE JAY WAY

'Blue Jay Way' was written by George in August 1967 during his visit to California with Pattie, Neil Aspinall and Alex Mardas. On arrival in Los Angeles on August 1, they were driven to a rented house with a pool at 1567 Blue Jay Way, a street in the Hollywood Hills above Sunset Boulevard. It belonged to Robert Fitzpatrick, a music business lawyer who was on vacation in Hawaii.

Derek Taylor, formerly the Beatles' press officer and now a publicist working in Los Angeles, was due to visit them on their first night in town, but he got lost in the narrow canyons on his way to the cottage, and was delayed. There was a small Hammond organ in the corner of the room and George whiled away the time by composing a song about being stuck in a house on Blue Jay Way while his friends were lost in the fog.

Blue Jay Way is a notoriously hard street to find – you can be geographically close and yet separated by a ravine. "By the time we got there the song was virtually intact," said Derek Taylor. "Of course, at the time I felt very bad. Here were these two wretchedly jet-lagged people, and we were about two hours late. But here, indeed, was a song which turned up in *Magical Mystery Tour* (the film) through a prism with about eight images, with George in a red jacket sitting and playing piano on the floor."

Taylor was amused by what people made of the song. One critic thought the line in which George urged his guest not to "be long" was advice to young people telling them not to "belong" (to society, that is). Another acclaimed musicologist believed that, when George said that his friends had "lost their way", he meant that a whole generation had lost direction. "It's just a simple, little song," said Taylor.

BELOW: George at the time of filming the 'Blue Jay Way' sequence for *Magical Mystery Tour*.

YOUR MOTHER SHOULD KNOW

'Your Mother Should Know' by Paul could have been written as early as May 1967, when both John and Paul were working on songs for the *Our World* television special. Like 'When I'm 64', the song was a tribute to the music his father enjoyed singing when he was a young man in Jim Mac's Jazz Band.

Jim McCartney formed his own ragtime band in 1919 and played dates around Liverpool, performing numbers like 'Birth Of The Blues' and 'Stairway To Paradise'. One day, Paul surprised his dad by recording one of his compositions 'Walking In The Park With Eloise', under the alias of the Country Hams.

Paul wrote it at Cavendish Avenue on his harmonium and thinks it was affected by the fact that his Auntie Gin and Uncle Harry were staying with him at the time. He was conscious that it was the sort of song that they would have liked and left open the door of the dining room where he was writing so that they could hear it. Paul also had in mind the idea of "mother knows best", a lament for those who were no longer close to their parents. "I was advocating peace between the generations. I was basically trying to say your mother might know more than you think she does. Give her credit."

'Your Mother Should Know', found its way into *Magical Mystery Tour* in a scene where the four Beatles, in white tail suits, descend a staircase and are joined by teams of formation dancers. Strictly speaking, any hit that Paul's mother would have known would have been a hit before she was born in 1909, in the days when hits were determined not by record sales but by sales of sheet music.

Let's all get up and dance to a song
That was a hit before your mother was born
Though she was born a long, long time ago
Your mother should know
(Your mother should...)
Your mother should know (...yeah)
Sing it again
Let's all get up and dance to a song
That was a hit before your mother was born
Though she was born a long, long time ago
Your mother should know
(Your mother should...)
Your mother should know (...yeah)

Lift up your hearts and sing me a song
That was a hit before your mother was born
Though she was born a long, long time ago
Your mother should know
(Your mother ...yeah)
Your mother should know (...aaaaah)
Your mother should know
(Your mother should...)
Your mother should know (...aaaaah)

Sing it again
Da da da da...
Though she was born a long, long time ago
Your mother should know
(Your mother should...)
Your mother should know (...yeah)
Your mother should know
(Your mother should...)
Your mother should know (...yeah)
Your mother should know
(Your mother should...)
Your mother should know (...yeah)

BLUE JAY WAY

Written: Harrison

Length: 3'56"

UK Release: 'Magical Mystery Tour' EP, December 8, 1967

US Release: *Magical Mystery Tour* album, November 27, 1967

Written: Lennon/McCartney

Length: 2'29"

UK Release: 'Magical Mystery Tour' EP, December 8, 1967

US Release: *Magical Mystery Tour* album, November 27, 1967

I AM THE WALRUS

The sprawling, disjointed nature of 'I Am The Walrus' owes much to the fact that it is an amalgamation of at least three song ideas that John was working on, none of which had come to completion. The first, inspired by hearing a distant police siren while at home in Weybridge, started with the words "Mister c-ity police-man" and fitted the rhythm of the siren. The second was a pastoral melody about his Weybridge garden. The third was a piece of nonsense about sitting on a cornflake.

John told Hunter Davies, who was still researching the Beatles' official biography at the time: "I don't know how it will all end up. Perhaps they'll turn out to be different parts of the same song." The section about sitting in an English garden was John again writing about the experience of being at home in a state of contemplation before inspiration arrives, the same starting point for 'Nowhere Man' and 'Good Morning, Good Morning.' The mention of waiting for the sun or the rain is reminiscent of the thoughts behind his song 'Rain'.

According to Pete Shotton, the catalyst was a letter received from a pupil of Quarry Bank School, which mentioned that an English master was getting his class to analyse Beatles' songs. This was sent to John by Stephen Bayley, who received an answer from John dated September 1, 1967 (sold at auction by Christie's of London in 1992). The idea of Beatles' songs being analyzed as part of a literature course in his old school amused John, who decided to confuse such students by writing a song full of the most perplexing and incoherent clues. He asked Shotton to remind him of a playground rhyme that they'd both enjoyed as children in Liverpool. John wrote it down: "Yellow matter custard, green slop pie, All mixed together with a dead dog's eye, Slap it on a butty, ten foot thick, Then wash it all down with a cup of cold sick."

John proceeded to invent some meaningless images (semolina pilchards, elementary penguins) and nonsense words (texpert, crabalocker), before adding

220

I am he as you are he as you are me
And we are all together
See how they run like pigs from a gun
See how they fly
I'm crying

Sitting on a cornflake
Waiting for the van to come
Corporation tee shirt,
Stupid bloody Tuesday
Man you been a naughty boy.
You let your face grow long
I am the eggman, they are the eggmen
I am the walrus, goo goo g' joob

Mister City Policeman sitting,
Pretty little policemen in a row
See how they fly like Lucy in the sky,
See how they run
I'm crying, I'm crying
I'm crying, I'm crying

Yellow matter custard
Dripping from a dead dog's eye
Crabalocker fishwife
Pornographic priestess
Boy you been a naughty girl,
You let your knickers down
I am the eggman, they are the eggmen
I am the walrus, goo goo g' joob

Sitting in an English garden
Waiting for the sun
If the sun don't come
You get a tan from standing in the
English rain

LEFT: 'I Am The Walrus' was part wind-up and part psychedelic poem by John.

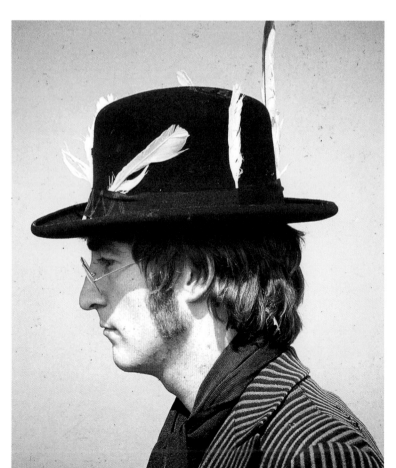

some opening lines he'd written down during an acid trip. He then strung these together with the three unfinished songs he'd already shown Hunter Davies. "Let the fuckers work that one out", he apparently said to Shotton when he'd finished. Asked by *Playboy* to explain 'Walrus' some 13 years later, he remarked that he thought Dylan got away with murder at times and that he'd decided "I can write this crap too."

The only serious part of the lyric, apparently, was the opening line with its vision of the unity behind all things that sounds like a paraphrase of the quote by the spiritual teacher Gurdjieff: "I am Thou. Thou art I. He is ours. We both are His." Of John's line George said "It's true but it's still a joke."

The "elementary penguin" that was "chanting Hare Krishna" was a reference to Allen Ginsberg who, at the time, was chanting the Hare Krishna mantra at public events. The walrus came from Lewis Carroll's poem 'The Walrus And The Carpenter', for which he had drawn an illustration in an exercise book as a schoolboy. (This was sold for £126,500 at an auction in April, 2006.) He may also have been unconsciously influenced by the rhythm of the poem 'Cargoes' by John Masefield who was Poet Laureate from 1930 until June 1967, the month in which *Sgt. Pepper* was released. It was a much-anthologized poem during the period of John's school years. The third verse read:

Dirty British coaster with a salt-caked smoke stack
Butting through the Channel in the mad march days
With a cargo of Tyne coal
Road-rails, pig-lead
Firewood, iron-ware, and cheap tin trays.

The "eggman" supposedly referred to the Animals' vocalist Eric Burdon, who had an unusual practice of breaking eggs over his female conquests while making love and became known amongst his musical colleagues as the "egg man". Marianne Faithfull believes that "semolina pilchard" was a reference to Det. Sgt. Norman Pilcher, the Metropolitan police officer who gained a reputation for targeting pop stars (including John) for drug possession. When John recited the lines beginning "Sitting on a cornflake" Hunter Davies thought he'd said "waiting for the van to come." John had actually said "waiting for the man to come" but preferred the way Davies had mis-heard it and so changed it.

The recording of 'I Am The Walrus' began on September 5. It lasted on and off throughout the month because George Martin was trying to find an equivalent to the flow of images and wordplay in the lyrics by using violins, cellos, horns, clarinet and a 16-voice choir, in addition to the Beatles themselves. On September 29, some lines from a BBC radio broadcast of Shakespeare's *King Lear* (Act IV Scene VI) were mixed in to the song.

Written: Lennon/McCartney

Length: 4'37"

UK Release: November 24, 1967 as a B-side to 'Hello Goodbye'

US Release: November 27, 1967 as a B-side to 'Hello Goodbye'

I am the eggman, they are the eggmen
I am the walrus, goo goo g' joob goo
goo goo g' joob

Expert texpert choking smokers
Don't you think the joker laughs at you?
(Ho ho ho! He he he! Ha ha ha!)
See how they smile like pigs in a sty,
See how they snied
I'm crying

Semolina pilchard
Climbing up the Eiffel Tower
Elementary penguin singing Hare Krishna
Man you should have seen them
Kicking Edgar Allan Poe
I am the eggman, they are the eggmen
I am the walrus, goo goo g' joob goo
    goo g' joob
Goo goo g' joob goo goo g' joob
Goo gooooooooooo jooba jooba jooba
jooba jooba jooba
Jooba jooba
Jooba jooba
Jooba joob

Oompah oompah, stick it up your jumper
(x 3)
Everybody's got one (x at least 12)

[Extract from Shakespeare's *King Lear*,
Act 4, Scene 6 that John taped from
the radio.]

"Slave, thou has slain me;
Villain, take my purse
If ever thou wilt thrive, bury my body
And give the letters which thou find'st
    about me
To Edmund Earl of Gloster; seek him out
Upon the British party: O, untimely
    death"

"I know thee well: a serviceable villain;
As duteous to the vices of thy mistress
As badness would desire."

"What, is he dead?"

"Sit you down, father; rest you."

LADY MADONNA

Lady Madonna, children at your feet
Wonder how you manage
  to make ends meet
Who finds the money when you
  pay the rent?
Did you think that money was
  Heaven sent?
Friday night arrives without a suitcase
Sunday morning creeping like a nun
Monday's child has learned to tie
  his bootlace
See how they run

Lady Madonna, baby at your breast
Wonders how you manage to
  feed the rest

See how they run

Lady Madonna, lying on the bed
Listen to the music playing in your head

Tuesday afternoon is never ending
Wednesday morning papers didn't come
Thursday night your stockings
  needed mending
See how they run

Lady Madonna, children at your feet
Wonder how you manage
  to make ends meet

ABOVE RIGHT: It was this photo and caption from National Geographic that provided the stimulus for Paul's song 'Lady Madonna'.

222

Mountain madonna, with one child at her breast and another laughing into her face, sees her way of life threatened. Her people, of Malayo-Polynesian origin, took refuge in the hills centuries ago. Now they live among thousands of newly settled Vietnamese, who clear tribal areas for themselves, while Viet Cong guerrillas make the highlands a battleground. Thus thrust into the 20th century, the montagnard strives to find his footing in the tides of change.

Stilted, thatched huts shelter some 25 families near the protected hamlet of Gia Vuc (page 61).

LADY MADONNA

'Lady Madonna' was the first single to show that the way forward for the Beatles now lay in returning to the fundamentals of rock 'n' roll. After *Sgt. Pepper's Lonely Hearts Club Band* and *Magical Mystery Tour*, it was assumed that musical progression would mean more complexity, but the Beatles again defied expectations.

The main riff was taken from Johnny Parker's piano playing on the instrumental track 'Bad Penny Blues', a 1956 hit in Britain for jazz trumpeter Humphrey Lyttelton and his band. Officially this single had been produced by Denis Preston but unofficially it was engineer Joe Meek, later to become a star producer himself, who controlled the session. It was released on the Parlophone label when George Martin was its head. "We asked George how they got the sound on 'Bad Penny Blues'," said Ringo. "George told us that they used brushes. So I used brushes and we did a track with just brushes and piano and then we decided we needed an off-beat, so we put an off-beat in."

Lyttelton wasn't offended by the lift because his band's version had been taken from a recording made by Chicago musician Dan Burley. "You can't copyright a rhythm, and rhythm was all that they had borrowed," he said. "I was very complimented. Although none of the Beatles cared for traditional jazz, they all knew and liked 'Bad Penny Blues' because it was a bluesy, skiffley thing rather than a trad exercise." (Dan Burley and His Skiffle Boys, formed in 1946, was the source of the description "skiffle music" first applied to the folk-blues-country style of Lonnie Donegan in Britain during the early 1950s.)

It seems that 'Bad Penny Blues' was made up in the studio as a generic boogie-woogie track. The saxophonist had to leave part way through the session, which meant that only three rhythm players and Lyttelton on trumpet remained. "So what could we do?" remembered Preston. "We had a deadline. So I said, 'Well the best thing is – play the blues. What about one of those Harry James type things like 'Boo-Woo'?' And it worked out a sort of boogie-woogie thing." ('Boo-Woo' was released in 1939 by Harry James and the Boogie Woogie Trio.)

Paul has said of 'Lady Madonna' that "the original concept was the Virgin Mary," thinking back to his childhood in Liverpool when Catholic mothers tended to identify with the Madonna, but that it soon became a song about motherhood in general. "How do they do it?" he asked when interviewed by *Musician* in 1986. "Baby at your breast – how do they get the time to feed them? Where do they get the money? How do you do this thing that women do?"

However, it seems that there was another image of motherhood that may have preceded the thoughts of the Virgin Mary. American singer Richie Havens remembered being with Paul in a Greenwich Village club watching Jimi Hendrix perform when a girl came up to him and asked whether 'Lady Madonna' had been written about America. "No," said Paul. "I was looking through this African magazine and I saw this African lady with a baby. And underneath the picture it said 'Mountain Madonna'. But I said, oh no – Lady Madonna – and I wrote the song."

Paul was essentially right in his recollection except that the magazine was *National Geographic* (January 1965) and the woman with a child was a Montagnard of Polynesian-Malaysian origin living in the central highlands of Vietnam, not an African. The 28-page cover story by *Life* photographer Howard Sochurek was titled 'American Special Forces in Action in Viet Nam'. The photo that caught Paul's eye was on pages 58–59. The opening line of its caption clearly inspired the opening line of Paul's second verse. It read "Mountain Madonna, with one child at her breast and another laughing into her face sees her way of life threatened". Photographer Sochurek died in 1994 at the age of 69.

Released as a single in March 1968, 'Lady Madonna' went to Number 1 in Britain but stalled at Number 4 in America.

THE INNER LIGHT

On September 29, 1967, John and George were guests of David Frost on the live late night television show *The Frost Report*. The subject of this edition was Transcendental Meditation and it included an interview with the Maharishi Mahesh Yogi, filmed earlier the same day at Heathrow Airport.

In the invited audience at the studio in Wembley, north London, was Sanskrit scholar Juan Mascaró, a Cambridge professor who had translated the *Upanishads* into English in 1965 and three years later had translated the *Bhagavad Gita*. The following month, Mascaró wrote to George enclosing a copy of *Lamps Of Fire*, a collection of spiritual wisdom from various traditions that he had edited. He suggested that George might consider putting verses from the *Tao Te Ching* to music, in particular a poem titled 'The Inner Light'.

> *Without going out of my door*
> *I can know all things on earth*

Written: Lennon/McCartney

Length: 2'18"

UK Release: March 15, 1968

UK Chart position: 1

US Release: March 18, 1968

US Chart position: 4

THE INNER LIGHT

Without going out of my door
I can know all things on Earth
Without looking out of my window
I could know the ways of Heaven

The farther one travels
The less one knows
The less one really knows

Without going out of your door
You can know all things on Earth
Without looking out of your window
You could know the ways of Heaven

The farther one travels
The less one knows
The less one really knows

Arrive without travelling
See all without looking
Do all without doing

Written: Harrison

Length: 2'36"

UK Release: March 15, 1968 as a B-side to 'Lady Madonna'

US Release: March 18, 1968 as a B-side to 'Lady Madonna'

Without looking out of my window
I can know the ways of heaven.

For the farther one travels
The less one knows.

The sage therefore
Arrives without travelling,
Sees all without looking,
Does all without doing.

In his preface to *Lamps Of Fire*, first published in 1958, Mascaró wrote: "The passages of this book are lamps of fire. Some shine more and some shine less, but they all merge into that vast lamp called by St John of the Cross 'the lamp of the being of God'." 'The Inner Light' (the song) was essentially an adaptation of this poem, although Mascaro wasn't credited as a co-writer.

When it was released as the B-side of 'Lady Madonna', 'The Inner Light' was the first song of George's to appear on a Beatles' single.

HEY JUDE

Divorce proceedings between John and Cynthia began when John moved in with Yoko. An interim agreement was reached whereby Cynthia and Julian were allowed to stay at Kenwood while the two respondents took up residence in a ground floor flat at 34 Montagu Square, which Ringo had bought in 1965 and which had subsequently been used by Paul and later by Jimi Hendrix.

Paul had always enjoyed a close relationship with John's son Julian, then five years old and, to show support for mother and child during the break-up, he drove down to Weybridge from his home in St John's Wood bearing a single red rose. Paul often used driving time to work out new songs and, on this day, with Julian's uncertain future on his mind, he started singing "Hey Julian" and improvising lyrics on the theme of comfort and reassurance. At some point during the hour-long journey, "Hey Julian" became "Hey Jules" and Paul developed the lines "Hey Jules, don't make it bad, Take a sad song and make it better." It was only later, when he came to flesh out the lyric, that he changed Jules to Jude, feeling that Jude was a stronger sounding name. He had liked the name Jud (Jud Fry) when he'd seen the musical *Oklahoma* as a film in 1955. As the child of a Catholic mother could he also have been aware that Saint Jude is the patron saint of hopeless cases, the one to whom the devout pray when it seems that no help is possible?

The song subsequently became less specific. John believed it was addressed to him, encouraging him to make the break from the Beatles and build a new future with Yoko ("You were made to go out and get her …"). If it was addressed to anyone, Paul felt it was to himself, dealing with the adjustments he knew that he was going to have to make as old bonds were broken within the Beatles.

The music drove the lyric, with sound taking precedence over sense. One line in particular – "the movement you need is on your shoulder" – was intended as a temporary filler. When Paul played the song to John on July 26, 1968, he pointed out that this line needed replacing, saying he knew that it sounded as if he was singing about his parrot. "It's probably

HEY JUDE

Hey Jude, don't make it bad
Take a sad song and make it better
Remember to let her into your heart
Then you can start to make it better

Hey Jude, don't be afraid
You were made to go out and get her
The minute you let her under your skin
Then you begin to make it better

And anytime you feel the pain,
  hey Jude, refrain
Don't carry the world upon your shoulders
For well you know that it's a fool
  who plays it cool
By making his world a little colder
Nah nah nah nah nah nah nah nah nah

Hey Jude, don't let me down
You have found her, now go and get her
Remember to let her into your heart
Then you can start to make it better

So let it out and let it in, hey Jude, begin
You're waiting for someone to
  perform with
And don't you know that it's just you,
  hey Jude, you'll do
The movement you need is on
  your shoulder
Nah nah nah nah nah nah nah nah nah yeah

Hey Jude, don't make it bad
Take a sad song and make it better
Remember to let her under your skin
Then you'll begin to make it
Better better better better better better,
Oh

Nah nah nah nah nah nah, nah nah nah,
Hey Jude
Nah nah nah nah nah nah, nah nah nah,
Hey Jude
Nah nah nah nah nah nah, nah nah nah,
Hey Jude
Nah nah nah nah nah nah, nah nah nah,
Hey Jude
Nah nah nah nah nah nah, nah nah nah,
Hey Jude
Nah nah nah nah nah nah, nah nah nah,
Hey Jude
Nah nah nah nah nah nah, nah nah nah,
Hey Jude
Nah nah nah nah nah nah, nah nah nah,
Hey Jude
Nah nah nah nah nah nah, nah nah nah,
Hey Jude
Nah nah nah nah nah nah, nah nah nah,
Hey Jude
Nah nah nah nah nah nah, nah nah nah,
Hey Jude
Nah nah nah nah nah nah, nah nah nah,
Hey Jude
Nah nah nah nah nah nah, nah nah nah,
Hey Jude
Nah nah nah nah nah nah, nah nah nah,
Hey Jude
Nah nah nah nah nah nah, nah nah nah,
Hey Jude
Nah nah nah nah nah nah, nah nah nah,
Hey Jude

Written: Lennon/McCartney

Length: 7'08"

UK Release: August 30, 1968

UK Chart position: 1

US Release: August 26, 1968

US Chart position: 1

RIGHT: Julian Lennon's situation following the arrival of Yoko Ono in John's life prompted Paul to write 'Hey Jude'.

the best line in the song," said John. "Leave it in. I know what it means."

Julian Lennon grew up knowing the story behind 'Hey Jude' but it wasn't until 1987 that he heard the facts first-hand from Paul, whom he met while staying at the same hotel in New York. "It was the first time in years that we'd sat down and talked to each other," says Julian. "He told me that he'd been thinking about my circumstances all those years ago, about what I was going through and what I would have to go through in the future. Paul and I used to hang out quite a bit – more than Dad and I did. Maybe Paul was into kids a bit more at the time. We had a great friendship going and there seem to be far more pictures of me and Paul playing together at that age than there are pictures of me and Dad."

Paul was right to anticipate that he would have a hard time growing up. "I've never really wanted to know the truth about how Dad was and how he was with me," Julian admits. "I didn't want to know the truth and so I kept my mouth shut. There was some very negative stuff talked about me – like when he said that I'd come out of a whisky bottle on a Saturday night. Stuff like that. That's tough to deal with. You think, where's the love in that? It was very psychologically damaging and for years that affected me. I used to think, how could he say that about his own bloody son!"

Julian hasn't studied the words of 'Hey Jude' for some time but finds it hard to get away from the song. He'll be in a restaurant when he'll hear it played, or it'll come on the car radio when he's driving. "It surprises me whenever I hear it," he says. "It's very strange to think that someone has written a song about you. It still touches me."

At the time of its release Paul scratched the song's title into the white paint then covering the inside of the windows of the Apple boutique on Baker Street. He then received a complaint from a nearby deli owner who mistook it as a translation of the German anti-semitic slogan 'Achtung Juden' that was painted on shops owned by Jews. "I had no idea that 'Jude' meant Jew," said Paul.

'Hey Jude' was the most successful Beatles' single ever. It topped the charts around the world and, by the end, over five million copies had been sold.

10 The Beatles (The White Album)

The Beatles, or *The White Album* as it is commonly referred to, confounded expectations because of its simplicity. It was as if the group had decided to produce the exact opposite of *Sgt. Pepper*. Long album title? Let's just call it *The Beatles*. Multi-coloured cover? Let's go white. Clever overdubs and mixes? Let's use acoustic guitars on a lot of the tracks. Other-worldly subject matter? Let's sing about cowboys, pigs, chocolates and doing it in the road.

The change was in part due to the Beatles' interest in the teachings of Maharishi Mahesh Yogi, the Indian guru. Pattie Harrison had attended a lecture given by him in February 1967 and six months later she encouraged George and the rest of the Beatles to hear him speak at the Hilton Hotel on Park Lane, London. As a result of this meeting, they all embarked on a ten-day TM course at University College, Bangor, in North Wales.

While in Bangor, on Sunday, August 27, 1967, they learned that Brian Epstein had been found dead at his home in Belgravia. The loss of Epstein, who had managed their career since early 1962 and had become something of a father figure, may well have made the Beatles even more open to the guidance of the Maharishi, whom they visited in India in February 1968.

The trip to India not only brought calm and self-reflection to their fraught lives but also rekindled their musical friendships. Paul Horn, an American flautist who was there at the same time, believes that meditation was a great stimulus for them. "You find out more about yourself on deeper levels when you're meditating," he said. "Look how prolific they were in such a relatively short time. They were in the Himalayas away from the pressures and away from the telephone. When you get too involved with life, it suppresses your creativity. When you're able to be quiet, it starts coming up."

On their return from India, the Beatles claimed that they had brought back 30 songs that they would be using on their next album. There were indeed 30 new songs on the Beatles but not all of them were written in India. Some of the Indian songs such as George's 'Sour Milk Sea', 'Dehradun' and 'Circles', Paul's 'Junk' and John's 'Child of Nature' were never recorded by the Beatles. It's fairer to say that about half of the album was written or at least started while they were away. Because they had no access to electric guitars or keyboards, many of these songs were acoustic.

John would later refer to *The Beatles* as being the first unselfconscious album after the Beatles' great period of self-consciousness beginning with *Rubber Soul* and ending with *Magical Mystery Tour* and *Yellow Submarine*. *The Beatles* was released as a double album in November 1968 and rose to the Number 1 spot on both sides of the Atlantic.

John pictured composing a song on the flat roof of a bungalow in Rishikesh, India.

BACK IN THE U.S.S.R.

Friendly rivalry had existed between the Beatles and the Beach Boys, and between 1965 and 1968 each new effort by either band spurred the other on to greater heights. When Brian Wilson heard *Rubber Soul*, he reported that it blew his mind to hear an album of such variety and consistency. "It flipped me out so much," he said, "that I determined to try the same thing – to make an entire album that was a gas." His reply was *Pet Sounds*, the Beach Boys' crowning achievement, which contained 'Sloop John B', 'Caroline No', 'Wouldn't It Be Nice' and 'God Only Knows'. When Paul heard *Pet Sounds*, he was equally impressed and the influence could be heard on *Revolver* and *Sgt. Pepper*.

Although they admired each other, the two groups had little social contact. Carl Wilson and Mike Love had seen the Beatles play in Portland, Oregon, on August 22, 1965, and called by the dressing room after the show. Bruce Johnston had been present at the Waldorf Hotel in London when John and Paul were played a pressing of *Pet Sounds* in April 1966 and in April 1967, Paul dropped by the studio in LA where Brian Wilson was working on the Beach Boys track 'Vegetables'. (Paul was recorded chewing some celery for 'Vegetables'.)

The most prolonged contact came in February 1968, when all four Beatles and their partners travelled to Rishikesh, India, to study Transcendental Meditation under the Maharishi Mahesh Yogi. On the course were three other professional musicians – Scottish singer Donovan, American flautist Paul Horn and Beach Boy Mike Love. The musicians spent a great deal of time together talking, jamming and composing songs.

One of the songs that came out of this encounter between the Beatles and Mike Love was 'Back In The U.S.S.R.', written by Paul as a pastiche of the Beach Boys and Chuck Berry. The genesis of the song was a comment made by Love one morning over breakfast: "Wouldn't it be fun to do a Soviet version of 'Back In The USA'?", referring to Berry's jingoistic 1959 single in which the singer expressed how glad he was to be back home in civilized America with its cafés, drive-ins, skyscrapers, hamburgers and juke boxes. The Beach Boys had earlier drawn on this song and Berry's 'Sweet Sixteen' for their tracks 'California Girls' and 'Surfin' USA', in which they extolled the virtues of local women and surf beaches.

Paul acted on Love's suggestion and came up with a parody that did for the U.S.S.R. what Berry had done for the USA and for Soviet women what the Beach Boys had done for the girls of California. After a decade of lyrics that had made poetry out of the names of places such as Memphis, Chicago and New Orleans, it was striking to hear Moscow mentioned in a rock 'n' roll song. "I just liked the idea of Georgia girls and talking about places like the Ukraine as if it was California," said Paul. As a tribute to Love, the Beatles' eventual recording imitated the vocal harmony style of the Beach Boys.

In a radio interview given in November 1968 Paul said, "In my mind it's just about a (Russian) spy who's been in America for a long time and he's become very American but when he gets back to the U.S.S.R. he's saying 'Leave it 'til tomorrow to unpack my case, Honey, disconnect the phone,' and all that, but to Russian women."

'Back In The U.S.S.R.' disturbed conservative Americans, because at a time of Cold War and conflict in Vietnam it appeared to be celebrating the enemy. Having admitted to drug taking, were these long-haired boys now embracing communism? American anti-rock campaigner David A. Noebel, author of *Communism, Hypnotism and the Beatles*, while unable to produce their party

BACK IN THE U.S.S.R.

Oh, flew in from Miami Beach B.O.A.C.
Didn't get to bed last night
On the way the paper bag was on my knee
Man I had a dreadful flight
I'm back in the U.S.S.R.
You don't know how lucky you are boy
Back in the U.S.S.R.

Been away so long I hardly knew the place
Gee it's good to be back home
Leave it till tomorrow to unpack my case
Honey disconnect the phone
I'm back in the U.S.S.R.
You don't know how lucky you are boy
Back in the U.S.
Back in the U.S.
Back in the U.S.S.R.

Well the Ukraine girls really knock me out
They leave the West behind
And Moscow girls make me sing and shout
That Georgia's always on my my my my my
  my mind

Aw come on!
Ho yeah!
Ho yeah!
Ho ho yeah!
Yeah yeah!

Yeah I'm back in the U.S.S.R.
You don't know how lucky you are boys
Back in the U.S.S.R.

Well the Ukraine girls really knock me out
They leave the West behind
And Moscow girls make me sing and shout
That Georgia's always on my my my my my
  my mind

ABOVE: Beach Boy Mike Love (centre) made the suggestion that led to the writing of 'Back In The U.S.S.R.'.

Oh, show me around the snow-peaked
  mountains way down south
Take me to your daddy's farm
Let me hear your balalaikas ringing out
Come and keep your comrade warm
I'm back in the U.S.S.R.
Hey you don't know how lucky you are boys
Back in the U.S.S.R.

Oh let me tell you, honey
Hey, I'm back!
I'm back in the U.S.S.R.
Yes, I'm free!
Yeah, back in the U.S.S.R.

Written: Lennon/McCartney

Length: 2'43"

UK Release: *The Beatles* album,
November 22, 1968

US Release: *The Beatles* album,
November 25, 1968

membership cards, was sure that they were furthering the cause of revolutionary socialism. "John Lennon and the Beatles were an integral part of the revolutionary milieu and received high marks from the Communist press," he wrote, "especially for the *White Album* which contained 'Back In The U.S.S.R.' and 'Piggies'. One line from 'Back In The U.S.S.R.' left the anti-Communists speechless: 'You don't know how lucky you are boy, Back in the U.S.S.R..'"

Through more diligent research, Noebel would have discovered that the official Soviet line was that the Beatles were evidence of capitalism's decadence. Just as the Nazis declared jazz music and abstract painting "degenerate" so the Communists railed against rock 'n' roll and instead promoted folk music that extolled the virtues of the State. Young people in the Soviet Union were just as excited by the Beatles' music as their Western counterparts but had to rely on bootleg recordings, smuggled imports and radio broadcasts from America, Germany and Britain. For many young Soviets, the Beatles were a representation of the freedom they aspired to. In 1988, with the Cold War about to be consigned to history, Paul paid tribute to his Soviet fans by recording an album of rock 'n' roll standards on the official government label, Melodia. In May 2003 he played a concert in Red Square and had a private meeting at the Kremlin with Vladimir Putin, then President of the Russian Federation, who told him that he had listened to Beatles music as a teenager. "It was very popular," he told Paul. "More than popular. It was a breath of fresh air, a window onto the outside world."

"'Back In The U.S.S.R.' is a hands-across-the-water song," said Paul in 1968. "They like us out there. Even though the bosses in the Kremlin may not, the kids do."

DEAR PRUDENCE

Prudence was Prudence Farrow (younger sister of actress Mia Farrow, daughter of film director John Farrow and actress Maureen O'Sullivan) who attended the same course with the Beatles in India. The song was a plea to her to come out from her excessively long periods of meditation alone in her room and relax with the rest of the students.

At the end of the demo version of 'Dear Prudence', John continues playing guitar and says: "No-one was to know that sooner or later she was to go completely berserk, under the care of Maharishi Mahesh Yogi. All the people around were very worried about the girl because she was going insane. So, we sang to her." Later, John was to explain that Prudence had gone slightly "barmy", locked in her room meditating for three weeks, "trying to reach God quicker than anyone else."

Paul Horn, the American flautist, says that Prudence was a highly sensitive person and that, by jumping straight into deep meditation, against the Maharishi's advice, she had allowed herself to fall into a catatonic state. "She was ashen-white and didn't recognize anybody," he says. "She didn't even recognize her own brother, who was on the course with her. The only person she showed any slight recognition towards was Maharishi. We were all very concerned about her and Maharishi assigned her a full-time nurse."

Prudence, whose living quarters were in the same building as the four Beatles and their partners, denies that she went mad and explains that her failure to recognize people was a result of having lost her glasses but agrees that she was more fanatical about meditating than the Beatles were. "I'd been meditating since 1966 and had tried to get on the course in 1967, so it was like a dream come true for me," she explains. "Being on that course was more important to me than anything in the world. I was very focused on getting in as much meditation as possible, so that I could gain enough experience to teach it myself. I knew that I must have stuck out because I would always rush straight back to my room after lectures and meals so that I could meditate. It was all so fascinating to me. John, George and Paul would all want to sit around jamming and having a good time and I'd be flying into my room. They were all serious about what they were doing but they just weren't as fanatical as me. The song that John wrote was just saying, 'Come out and play with us. Come out and have fun.'"

This she eventually did, and got to know the Beatles well. The Maharishi put her in an after-lecture discussion group with John and George – who he thought would be good for her. "We talked about the things we were all going through," she says. "We were questioning reality, asking questions about who we were and what was going on. I liked them and I think they liked me."

Although the song was written in India, and Prudence overheard various jam sessions between the Beatles, Mike Love and Donovan, John never

Dear Prudence,
Won't you come out to play?
Dear Prudence, greet the brand new day
The sun is up, the sky is blue
It's beautiful and so are you
Dear Prudence,
Won't you come out to play?

Dear Prudence, open up your eyes
Dear Prudence, see the sunny skies
The wind is low, the birds will sing
That you are part of everything
Dear Prudence
Won't you open up your eyes?

Look around round (round round round
 round round round round round)
Look around round (round round round
round round round round round)
Look around (ah, ah, ah, ah)

Dear Prudence, let me see you smile
Dear Prudence, like a little child
The clouds will be a daisy chain
So let me see you smile again
Dear Prudence,
Won't you let me see you smile?

Dear Prudence,
Won't you come out to play?
Dear Prudence, greet the brand new day
The sun is up, the sky is blue
It's beautiful and so are you
Dear Prudence,
Won't you come out to play?

ABOVE: Prudence Farrow (second left, front row) had to be coaxed out of her bungalow by fellow meditators in Rishikesh. John wrote 'Dear Prudence' for her.

DEAR PRUDENCE

Written: Lennon/McCartney

Length: 3'56"

UK Release: *The Beatles* album, November 22, 1968

US Release: *The Beatles* album, November 25, 1968

Written: Lennon/McCartney

Length: 2'17"

UK Release: *The Beatles* album, November 22, 1968

US Release: *The Beatles* album, November 25, 1968

played the song to her. "George was the one who told me about it," she recalls. "At the end of the course, just as they were leaving, he mentioned that they had written a song about me but I didn't hear it until it came out on the album. I was flattered. It was a beautiful thing to have done."

Prudence went on to become the youngest person qualified to teach TM in America as well as gaining a BA, MA and PhD in South Asian Studies and Sanskrit. She authors academic articles on Eastern religion, produces for both cinema and theatre and continues to teach TM in Florida. She has three children and four grandchildren. In October 1983, Siouxie and the Banshees had a British Top 10 hit with their version of 'Dear Prudence'.

GLASS ONION

In an age of rapid social change when old leaders were being deposed and old philosophies discarded, the Beatles were often regarded as prophets and every song was scrutinized for symbols, allusions and messages. Who was the eggman in 'I Am The Walrus'? Was the tea that was mentioned in 'Lovely Rita' really marijuana? Was "Henry the Horse" street slang for heroin?

The Beatles had invited this sort of analysis by mixing poetry and wisdom along with nonsense. John, in particular, had enjoyed obfuscating his point of view, perhaps because of his intellectual insecurity. However, by 1968, he was trying to write more directly and most of the work he brought back from India was less complicated. When a pupil from his old school wrote and asked him to explain the motives behind his writing, John replied that the work was done for fun and laughs. "I do it for me first," he said. "Whatever people make of it afterwards is valid, but it doesn't necessarily have to correspond to my thoughts about it, OK? This goes for anyone's 'creations', art, poetry, song etc. The mystery and shit that is built around all forms of art needs smashing anyway."

'Glass Onion' was a playful response by John to those who pored over his work looking for hidden meanings. He started to piece together the song using lines and images from some of the most enigmatic Beatles' songs – 'Strawberry Fields Forever', 'There's A Place', 'Within You Without You', 'I Am The Walrus', 'Lady Madonna', 'The Fool On The Hill' and 'Fixing A Hole'. In 'Glass Onion', he jokingly claimed that the walrus, from 'I Am The Walrus', was really Paul. (In some primitive cultures the walrus is a symbol of death and this new information was later used as confirmation by those who believed that Paul had been killed in a road accident in 1966, to be replaced by a double.) Finally, he came up with four new tantalizing images for his "literary" fans to pore over – bent back tulips, a glass onion, the Cast-Iron Shore and a dovetail joint.

The bent back tulips, explained former Apple press officer Derek Taylor, was a reference to a particular flower arrangement used in Parkes, a fashionable London restaurant in the Sixties that was at 4 Beauchamp Place in Knightsbridge. "You'd be in Parkes sitting around your table wondering what was going on with the flowers and then you'd realize that they were actually tulips with their petals bent all the way back, so that you could see the obverse side of the petals and also the stamen. This is what John meant about 'seeing how the other half lives.' He meant seeing how the other half of the flower lives but also, because it was an expensive restaurant, how the other half of society lived."

There were simple explanations for the other perplexing references: the Cast-Iron Shore was Liverpool's own beach (also known as the "Cassie"), so-called because it was close to St Michael's Church, Aigburth, built of cast iron by John Cragg of the Mersey Iron Foundry in 1815 and referred to locally as the Cast-Iron Church; a dovetail joint referred to a wood joint using wedge-shaped tenons. A glass onion, besides being just the type of perplexing image that fans would puzzle over while seeking hidden meanings (as they had done with "semolina pilchard" and "elementary penguin" in 'I Am the Walrus'), embraced the concepts of perspicuity (glass is easy to see through) and complexity (an onion has many layers) that the song was addressing.

OB-LA-DI OB-LA-DA

Paul first heard the words "Ob-la-di Ob-la-da" spoken by Nigerian conga player Jimmy Scott, whom he met at the Bag O' Nails club in Soho, London. A flamboyant and unforgettable character in dark glasses and African clothing, Scott was renowned for his catch phrases. His widow Lucrezia says that "ob la di, ob la da" is a phonetic translation of something that his father would say to him in one of the dialects of the Urhobo language used by the Warri people in the Delta region of Southern Nigeria. "It had a special meaning which he never told anyone," she says. "Even the Beatles didn't know what it meant. When I once asked Paul what it meant he said he thought it meant 'Comme ci, comme ça', but that isn't right. To Jimmy it was like a philosophy that he took with him through life."

Jimmy Anonmuogharan Scott Emuakpor was born in Sapele, Nigeria, and came to England in the Fifties, where he found work in the jazz clubs of Soho. He played with Georgie Fame and the Blue Flames in the Sixties, backed Stevie Wonder on his 1965 tour of Britain and later formed his own Ob-la-di Ob-la-da Band. He provided music for some of the dance scenes in the film

GLASS ONION

I told you about Strawberry Fields
You know the place where nothing is real
Well here's another place you can go
Where everything flows
Looking through the bent backed tulips
To see how the other half live
Looking through a glass onion

I told you about the walrus and me, man
You know that we're as close as can be, man
Well here's another clue for you all
The walrus was Paul
Standing on the Cast Iron Shore, yeah
Lady Madonna trying to make ends meet, yeah

Looking through a glass onion

Oh yeah
Oh yeah
Oh yeah
Looking through a glass onion

I told you 'bout the fool on the hill
I tell you man he living there still
Well here's another place you can be
Listen to me
Fixing a hole in the ocean
Trying to make a dovetail joint, yeah
Looking through a glass onion

ABOVE: 'Ob-la-di Ob-la-da' has a distinctively Jamaican flavour yet Jimmy Scott, who supplied the phrase, was born in Nigeria.

OB-LA-DI OB-LA-DA

Desmond has his barrow in the
  market place
Molly is the singer in a band
Desmond says to Molly "Girl I like
  your face"
And Molly says this as she takes him
  by the hand

Ob-la-di ob-la-da life goes on bra
La-la how the life goes on
Ob-la-di ob-la-da life goes on bra
La-la how the life goes on

Desmond takes a trolley to the
  jeweller's store
Buys a twenty carat golden ring
  (Carat ring?)
Takes it back to Molly waiting at the door
And as he gives it to her she begins
  to sing (sing)

Ob-la-di ob-la-da life goes on bra
La-la how the life goes on
Ob-la-di ob-la-da life goes on bra
La-la how the life goes on, yeah

In a couple of years they have built
A home sweet home
With a couple of kids running in the yard
Of Desmond and Molly Jones
(Ah ha ha ha ha ha)

Happy ever after in the market place
Desmond lets the children lend a hand
  (Arm! Leg!)
Molly stays at home and does her
  pretty face
And in the evening she still sings it
  with the band

Yes, ob-la-di ob-la-da life goes on bra
La-la how the life goes on (Ha ha ha)

She (1965), which starred Ursula Andress, Peter Cushing and Christopher Lee. Lucrezia says that the phrase was quite well known because he would shout "Ob la di" to the audience when in concert, the audience would shout back "Ob la da" and Scott would then say "Life goes on."

Paul wrote the song while in India and can remember leading a group of meditators on a walk along the Ganges from the ashram to the heart of Rishikesh while singing the chorus and playing his acoustic guitar. "I think they quite enjoyed it," said Paul. "Maharishi quite liked someone strolling along singing." He developed a ska rhythm and two characters, Desmond and Molly. "Desmond is a very Caribbean name," he later explained. Could it have been a coincidence that the two best known ska singers to have British hits in the 1960s were Desmond (Dekker) and Millie (Small)?

The fact that Paul used Scott's catch phrase as the basis of a song had repercussions. "He got annoyed when I did a song of it because he wanted a cut," Paul told *Playboy* in 1984. "I said 'Come on, Jimmy. It's just an expression. If you'd written the song, you could have had the cut.'"

'Ob-la-di Ob-la-da' has been cited as the first example of white ska. Although the phrase was Urhobo, the song was about Jamaicans. When recording the vocals, Paul made a mistake in singing that Desmond, rather than Molly, "stayed at home and did (his) pretty face". The other Beatles liked the slip and so it was kept. Paul loved the song and wanted it to be a single. John always hated it.

Jimmy Scott played congas on the session (July 5, 1968) – the only time he worked with the Beatles. Lucrezia remembers being called in to hear a playback and taking with her headed notepaper printed for the Ob-la-di Ob-la-da band to show Paul how the phrase was spelt. Later that year, he appeared on the Rolling Stones' *Beggars Banquet* album and in

1969 at the Stones' free concert in Hyde Park. Around this time he was arrested and taken to Brixton prison to await trial on a charge of failing to pay maintenance to his ex-wife. He asked the police to contact the Beatles' office to see if Paul would foot his huge outstanding legal bill. This Paul did, on condition that Scott dropped his case against him over the song.

Scott left England in 1969 and didn't return until 1973, when he immersed himself in the Pyramid Arts project in east London, giving workshops on African music and drumming. In 1983, he joined Bad Manners and was still with them when he died in 1986. "We'd just done this tour of America and he caught pneumonia," remembered Bad Manners' front man Doug Trendle. "When he got back to Britain he was strip-searched at the airport because he was Nigerian. They left him naked for two hours. The next day he was taken into hospital and he died. Nobody is too sure how old he was because he lied about his age when he got his first British passport. He was supposed to be around 64."

In July 1986, a concert featuring Bad Manners, Hi Life International, the Panic Brothers and Lee Perry and the Upsetters was mounted at the Town and Country Club, London, to raise money for the Jimmy Scott Benevolent Fund. He left at least 12 children from two marriages. "Jimmy was essentially a rhythmic, charming, irresistible man with the gift of the gab," Lucrezia wrote in the benefit's programme. "If life was sometimes dull, it shouldn't have been, for his stories of people, of places, of incidents, were an endless stream bubbling with fun."

Paul, who kept in contact with Jimmy, also contributed a comment. "He was a great friend of mine," he wrote. "In the Sixties we used to meet in a lot of clubs and spent many a happy hour chatting until closing time. He had a great positive attitude to life and was a pleasure to work with."

Two British cover versions of 'Ob-la-di Ob-la-da' were recorded and the one by Scottish group Marmalade went to Number 1. The Beatles' version was released as a single only in America, and not until 1976.

Hey, ob-la-di ob-la-da life goes on bra
La-la how the life goes on

In a couple of years they have built
A home sweet home
With a couple of kids running in the yard
Of Desmond and Molly Jones
(Ha ha ha ha ha ha ha ha ha ha)

Yeah, happy ever after in the market place
Molly lets the children lend a hand
Desmond stays at home and does his
    pretty face
And in the evening she's a singer with
    the band

Yeah, ob-la-di ob-la-da life goes on bra
La-la how the life goes on
Yeah, ob-la-di ob-la-da life goes on bra
La-la how the life goes on

And if you want some fun
Take ob-la-di ob-la-da

Written: Lennon/McCartney

Length: 3'08"

UK Release: *The Beatles* album, November 22, 1968

US Release: *The Beatles* album, November 25, 1968

WILD HONEY PIE

The shortest and most repetitive of any Beatles' lyric, 'Wild Honey Pie' emerged from a spontaneous sing-along in Rishikesh.

The recording started with a multi-tracking experiment by Paul that "built up sculpturally" with a lot of vibrato on the guitar strings. The title was a reference to the other 'Honey Pie' on the album contrasting the experimental side of his work ("wild") with the more formal approach.

"It was just a fragment of an instrumental that we weren't sure about," said Paul. "But Pattie Harrison liked it very much, so we decided to leave it on the album."

Mike Love co-wrote a Beach Boys' track entitled 'Wild Honey' with Brian Wilson, which had been released in October 1967.

Written: Lennon/McCartney

Length: 0'52"

UK Release: *The Beatles* album, November 22, 1968

US Release: *The Beatles* album, November 25, 1968

Honey Pie
Honey Pie

Honey Pie
Honey Pie

Honey Pie
Honey Pie
Honey Pie
Honey Pie

I love you

THE CONTINUING STORY OF BUNGALOW BILL

Hey, Bungalow Bill, what did you kill,
Bungalow Bill?
Hey, Bungalow Bill, what did you kill,
Bungalow Bill?

He went out tiger hunting with his
elephant and gun
In case of accidents he always took his
mom
He's the all American bullet-headed Saxon
mother's son
All the children sing

Hey, Bungalow Bill, what did you kill,
Bungalow Bill?
Hey, Bungalow Bill, what did you kill,
Bungalow Bill?

Deep in the jungle where the mighty
tiger lies
Bill and his elephants were taken by
surprise
So Captain Marvel zapped him right
between the eyes, ZAP!
All the children sing

Hey, Bungalow Bill, what did you kill,
Bungalow Bill?
Hey, Bungalow Bill, what did you kill,
Bungalow Bill?

The children asked him if
to kill was not a sin
"Not when he looked so fierce,"
his mummy butted in
If looks could kill it would have been
us instead of him
All the children sing

Hey, Bungalow Bill, what did you kill,
Bungalow Bill?
Hey, Bungalow Bill, what did you kill,
Bungalow Bill?

Oh ho!

Hey, Bungalow Bill, what did you kill,
Bungalow Bill?
Hey, Bungalow Bill, what did you kill,
Bungalow Bill?

Hey, Bungalow Bill, what did you kill,
Bungalow Bill?
Hey, Bungalow Bill, what did you kill,
Bungalow Bill?

Hey, Bungalow Bill, what did you kill,
Bungalow Bill?
Hey, Bungalow Bill, what did you kill,
Bungalow Bill?

[Eh up!]

ABOVE: John dubbed all-American Richard A Cooke III as 'Bungalow Bill', and in his song mocked the fact that he went on a tiger hunt with his mother while on a course exploring spiritual transcendence.

THE CONTINUING STORY OF BUNGALOW BILL

Bungalow Bill, the song says, "Went out tiger hunting with his elephant and gun. In case of accidents he always took his mum." Written by John while in India, it recounts the true story of Richard A. Cooke III, a young American college graduate, who visited his mother Nancy while she was on the course in Rishikesh. Nancy was a glamorous and wealthy socialite who had been a significant figure in spreading the news about TM among trend-setters in America. In Rishikesh she was assigned by the Maharishi to look after the Beatles.

John described Bungalow Bill as "the all-American bullet-headed Saxon mother's son" and Cooke confirms that it was an accurate description of him when he first met the Beatles. He was over 6ft tall, dressed in white and sported

Written: Lennon/McCartney

Length: 3'14"

UK Release: *The Beatles* album, November 22, 1968

US Release: *The Beatles* album, November 25, 1968

a crew cut. "The other Beatles were always real nice to me but John was always aloof," he says. "They epitomized the counter culture and I was the classic good American boy and college athlete. There wasn't a whole bunch that we got to connect on."

The tiger hunt the song refers to took place in Nainital, about three hours from Rishikesh. Once in the region Cooke and his mother travelled by elephant and then hid in a tree on a wooden platform known as a marchand to await the arrival of a tiger. "Rik sat down and I stood behind him," remembers Nancy. "It wasn't long before I saw this flash of yellow and black. I let out a yell and Rik twirled and shot the tiger right through the ear."

"I was pretty excited that I had shot a tiger," remembers Cooke. "But the Texan who organized the shoot came over to me and said, 'You shot it, but don't say a word. As far as the world is concerned you didn't shoot this tiger.' He wanted to be the one who went back home with the skin and the claws as his trophy."

It was when they arrived at the ashram that Cooke began to feel some remorse, wondering whether the killing of the animal would bring him "bad karma". He and his mother had a meeting with Maharishi about the issue, which was also attended by John and Paul.

"It was a fluke that they happened to be sitting there when I had this conversation with Maharishi," says Cooke. "My mother is a very vocal person and she was talking excitedly about killing the tiger and Maharishi looked pretty aghast that his followers could actually go out and do something like this. It was the only time I ever saw him almost angry."

"Rik told him that he felt bad about it and said that he didn't think he'd ever kill an animal again," recalls Nancy. "Maharishi said – 'You had the desire Rik and now you no longer have the desire?'. Then John asked, 'Don't you call that slightly life-destructive?'. I said, 'Well John, it was either the tiger or us. The tiger was jumping right where we were.' That came up in the lyric as 'If looks could kill it would have been us instead of him.'"

The name Bungalow Bill was an allusion to Buffalo Bill, the performing name of American cowboy showman William Frederick Cody (1846–1917) who was a hero in post-war schoolboy comics. John chose "Bungalow" because all the accommodation in Rishikesh was in bungalows. The cartoonish character was also partly inspired by Jungle Jim, hunter Jim Bradley, which began as a cartoon strip in 1934 and in the 1950s became a Dell Comics title, a number of Columbia B-movies starring Johnny Weissmuller and a TV series. Ian MacDonald points out in *Revolution In The Head* that the tune appears to be based on 'Stay As Sweet As You Are', which was written by Mack Gordon and Henry Revel and was used in the 1934 film *College Rhythm*.

Cooke knew nothing of 'Bungalow Bill' until he started getting postcards saying "Hey Bungalow Bill. What did you kill?" from friends who had recognized him in the song. He now lives on the Hawaiian island of Molokai where he was born and works as a photographer for *National Geographic*. He has published two books of his photos for the National Geographic Society: *America's Ancient Cities* and *Blue Ridge Range*. His mother Nancy died in February 2013 at the age of 90.

WHILE MY GUITAR GENTLY WEEPS

I look at you all
 see the love there that's sleeping
While my guitar gently weeps
I look at the floor
 and I see it needs sweeping
Still my guitar gently weeps

I don't know why nobody told you
How to unfold your love
I don't know how
 someone controlled you
They bought and sold you

I look at the world
 and I notice it's turning
While my guitar gently weeps
With every mistake
 we must surely be learning
Still my guitar gently weeps

I don't know how you were diverted
You were perverted too
I don't know how you were inverted
No one alerted you

I look at you all
 see the love there that's sleeping
While my guitar gently weeps
I look at you all
Still my guitar gently weeps

WHILE MY GUITAR GENTLY WEEPS

George was reading the *I Ching*, the Chinese *Book of Changes*, and decided to apply its principles of chance to his writing. At his parents' Lancashire home, he picked a book off the shelf with the intention of writing a song based on the first words that he came across when he opened it at random. The words were "gently weeps" and so George began to write. "The Eastern concept is that whatever happens is all meant to be and that there's no such thing as coincidence," said George.

It could have been the often-anthologized poem 'Rain on the Roof' by American poet Coates Kinney (1826–1904) that caught his eye. The first verse reads:

When the humid shadows hover
Over all the starry spheres,
And the melancholy darkness
Gently weeps in rainy tears,
What a joy to press the pillow
Of a cottage chamber bed,
And to listen to the patter
Of the soft rain overhead!

He started recording it in July 1968 but felt that the other Beatles weren't showing sufficient interest in the song. Some of the lines that he recorded in a demo at his home in Esher, such as "I look at the trouble and see that it's raging" and "The problems you sow are the troubles you are reaping", were not used in the final version. In September, he brought his friend Eric Clapton in to play lead guitar while he played rhythm, the first time another guitarist had been used on a Beatles' recording. When asked to play the part, Clapton was taken aback. "I considered it a funny thing to ask, since he was the Beatles' guitar player, and had always done great work on their records up until then." He used George's guitar to play on the session.

Written: Harrison

Length: 4'45"

UK Release: *The Beatles* album, November 22, 1968

US Release: *The Beatles* album, November 25, 1968

HAPPINESS IS A WARM GUN

For this song John joined together three songs that he had started but which didn't seem to be going anywhere. The first was a series of random images picked up from a night of acid tripping with Derek Taylor, Neil Aspinall and Pete Shotton at a house Taylor was renting from Peter Asher in Newdigate near Dorking in Surrey. "John said he had written half a song and wanted us to toss out phrases while Neil wrote them down," said Taylor. "First of all, he wanted to know how to describe a girl who was really smart and I remembered a phrase of my father's which was 'she's not a girl who misses much'. It sounds like faint praise but on Merseyside, in those days, it was actually the best you could get.

"Then I told a story about a chap my wife Joan and I met in the Carrick Bay Hotel on the Isle of Man. It was late one night drinking in the bar and this local fellow who liked meeting holiday makers and rapping to them suddenly said to us, 'I like wearing moleskin gloves, you know. It gives me a little bit of an unusual sensation when I'm out with my girlfriend.' He then said, 'I don't want to go into details.' So we didn't. But that provided the line, 'She's well acquainted with the touch of the velvet hand'. Then there was 'like a lizard on a window pane'. That, to me, was a symbol of very quick movement. Often, when we were living in LA, you'd look up and see tiny little lizards nipping up the window.

"'The man in the crowd with multi-coloured mirrors on his hobnail boots', was from something I'd seen in a newspaper about a Manchester City soccer fan who had been arrested by the police for having mirrors on the toe caps of his shoes so that he could look up girls' skirts. We thought this was an incredibly complicated and tortuous way of getting a cheap thrill and so that became 'multi-coloured mirrors' and 'hobnail boots' to fit the rhythm. A bit of poetic license. The bit about 'lying with his eyes while his hands were working overtime' came from another thing I'd read where a man wearing a cloak had fake plastic hands, which he would rest on the counter of a shop while underneath the cloak he was busy lifting things and stuffing them in a bag around his waist.

"I don't know where the 'soap impression of his wife' came from but the eating of something and then donating it 'to the National Trust' came from a conversation we'd had about the horrors of walking in public spaces on Merseyside, where you were always coming across the evidence of people having crapped behind bushes and in old air raid shelters. So to donate what you've eaten to the National Trust [a British organization that 'protects special places in Britain for everyone, for ever'] was what would now be known as 'defecation on common land owned by the National Trust.' When John put it all together, it created a series of layers of images. It was like a whole mess of colour."

The second section beginning with "I need a fix" referred to his relationship with Yoko, who played a motherly, and some might say superior, role in his life. For most of their relationship he would refer to her as 'Mother'. He later denied that the "fix" was a reference to heroin, telling *Rolling Stone* that "it wasn't about 'H' at all." However, that is contradicted by his insertion of the word 'junkie' next to this section of the song on his copy of the handwritten lyrics. ("Dirty old man" was inscribed by the first section and "satire of 50s R&R" by the last.) Perhaps he meant that it wasn't an entire song

HAPPINESS IS A WARM GUN

She's not a girl who misses much
Do do do do do do do do, oh yeah
She's well acquainted with the touch
  of the velvet hand
Like a lizard on a window pane
The man in the crowd with the
  multicoloured mirrors
On his hobnail boots
Lying with his eyes while his hands are
  busy working overtime
A soap impression of his wife which he
  ate and donated to the National Trust

Down
I need a fix cos I'm going down
Down to the bits that I left uptown
I need a fix cos I'm going down

Mother Superior jump the gun
Mother Superior jump the gun
Mother Superior jump the gun
Mother Superior jump the gun
Mother Superior jump the gun
Mother Superior jump the gun

Happiness is a warm gun
(Happiness bang, bang, shoot, shoot)
Happiness is a warm gun, mama
(Happiness bang, bang, shoot, shoot)
When I hold you in my arms
  (Oo-oo oh yeah)
And I feel my finger on your trigger
  (Oo-oo oh yeah)

LEFT: Discovered at last – the gun magazine story that George Martin showed to John in the studio and which gave John the title for his song.

I know nobody can do me no harm
  (Oo-oo oh yeah)
Because happiness is a warm gun, mama
(Happiness bang, bang, shoot, shoot)
Happiness is a warm gun, yes it is
(Happiness bang, bang, shoot, shoot)
Happiness is a warm, yes it is, gun
(Happiness bang, bang, shoot, shoot)
Well, don't you know happiness is a
  warm gun, mama?
(Happiness is a warm gun, yeah)

Written: Lennon/McCartney

Length: 2'43"

UK Release: *The Beatles* album,
November 22, 1968

US Release: *The Beatles* album,
November 25, 1968

BELOW: Although Cynthia (far right) accompanied John to India, it was Yoko that was he was thinking of and writing about while he was there.

about heroin, which was true, or even that it wasn't about his own experience of heroin because that didn't come until the following year and would culminate in the experience expressed in 'Cold Turkey'.

The final section was inspired by something in an American gun magazine that George Martin had pointed out to him. It was a copy of the May 1968 copy of *The American Rifleman*, the official journal of the National Rifle Association of America, where there was a single page feature by a writer called Warren W. Herlihy entitled 'Happiness Is A Warm Gun' which detailed the way in which he'd introduced his son to shooting and how much the son (who was by now 18) now loved the sport.

The phrase "happiness is a warm gun", an obvious play on *Peanuts* cartoonist Charles Schulz's 1962 book *Happiness is a Warm Puppy*, was used as a headline but didn't occur in the piece. It was probably created by a sub-editor. The apparently bizarre juxtaposition of killing and pleasure stimulated John's imagination, especially coming at a time when America was involved in a war. "I thought, what a fantastic thing to say," he said. "A warm gun means that you've just shot something."

The music and vocal delivery of this section emulated 'Angel Baby' (1960) by Rosie and the Originals, a track that John always raved about and later covered on his Rock 'n' Roll album. It was recorded by a 15-year old girl in California with a group made up of her friends and was based on a poem she'd written when she was 14. *Rolling Stone* writer Jonathan Cott interviewed John on September 18 1968 and noted that, "Old Fifties 45s were scattered about the floor, and John played Rosie and the Originals' version of 'Give Me Love'." This was the B-side of 'Angel Baby'. Five days later, on September 23, John started recording 'Happiness Is A Warm Gun'.

The Beatles had just started to record this track on the day Linda Eastman arrived in London to begin life with Paul.

241

MARTHA MY DEAR

Martha my dear though I spend my days
  in conversation
Please
Remember me Martha my love
Don't forget me Martha my dear

Hold your head up you silly girl look
  what you've done
When you find yourself in the thick of it
Help yourself to a bit of what is all
  around you
Silly girl

Take a good look around you
Take a good look you're bound to see
That you and me were meant to be for
  each other
Silly girl

Hold your hand out you silly girl
  see what you've done
When you find yourself in the thick of it
Help yourself to a bit of what is
  all around you
Silly girl

Martha my dear you have always been
  my inspiration
Please
Be good to me Martha my love
Don't forget me Martha my dear

RIGHT: Paul with his Old English
sheepdog Martha, who gave her name
to a Beatles song.

THE BEATLES

MARTHA MY DEAR

The name Martha came from Paul's Old English Sheepdog, but this song is a plea to a girl who has always been the singer's muse. He asks her to remember him because he still believes that they were meant for each other. In January 1968, Paul and Jane Asher had announced that they were going to get married during the year but Paul began dating other girls while Jane was away acting and in July she called off the engagement. "We still see each other and love each other, but it hasn't worked out," Jane said at the time. "Perhaps we'll be childhood sweethearts and meet again and get married when we're about 70."

The song began as a two-handed piano exercise, something designed to stretch him musically. The words were no more than a collection of appropriate sounding phrases strung together. Explaining the genesis of the song in 1968 he said: "Mainly I come up with a tune and some words come into my head. In this case these happened to be 'Martha my dear'. They don't mean anything. I don't ever try to make serious social comment. You can read anything you like into it but really it's just a song."

'Martha My Dear' was recorded in October 1968 – by which time Linda Eastman had become Paul's girlfriend. Jane began a relationship with cartoonist Gerald Scarfe in the early Seventies and they married in 1981, the same year that Martha the sheepdog died while at Paul's farm in Scotland.

Written: Lennon/McCartney

Length: 2'28"

UK Release: *The Beatles* album, November 22, 1968

US Release: *The Beatles* album, November 25, 1968

I'M SO TIRED

I'M SO TIRED

During the Beatles' stay in Rishikesh, there were two 90-minute lectures each day and much of the rest of the time was taken up with meditating. Students were expected to build up their periods of meditation slowly as their technique improved. One person on the course reportedly claimed to have clocked up a 42-hour session. John found that this life of stillness and inner absorption meant that he couldn't sleep at night and consequently he began feeling tired during the day.

'I'm So Tired', written after three weeks in India, was also about the things he was beginning to miss. The Academy of Meditation was free of both alcohol and drugs and John's mind was turning to his beloved cigarettes and the possibility of a drink. Sometimes a friend of his would smuggle some wine in. Sir Walter Raleigh (c. 1554–1618) is credited with popularizing tobacco smoking at the English court and a "git" (or "get" as John pronounces it) is, according to the dictionary, British slang for "a foolish or worthless person".

Most of all John was missing Yoko Ono. The couple had not yet begun a full-blown physical affair because John wasn't sure how to end his marriage. He had briefly entertained the idea of inviting her to India but realized that the complications of having Cynthia and Yoko under the same roof would be too great. She is the one he thinks about calling and has set his mind on. He is concerned that she might not take his interest in her seriously – that she'll think he is just "putting her on" (put on – to mislead deliberately). "It's one of my favourite tracks," was John's verdict. "I just like the sound of it, and I sing it well."

Written: Lennon/McCartney

Length: 2'03"

UK Release: *The Beatles* album, November 22, 1968

US Release: *The Beatles* album, November 25, 1968

I'm so tired, I haven't slept a wink
I'm so tired, my mind is on the blink
I wonder should I get up
And fix myself a drink
No, no, no

I'm so tired I don't know what to do
I'm so tired my mind is set on you
I wonder should I call you
But I know what you would do

You'd say I'm putting you on
But it's no joke, it's doing me harm
You know I can't sleep,
I can't stop my brain
You know it's three weeks,
I'm going insane
You know I'd give you everything I've got
For a little peace of mind

I'm so tired, I'm feeling so upset
Although I'm so tired
I'll have another cigarette
And curse Sir Walter Raleigh
He was such a stupid git

You'd say I'm putting you on
But it's no joke, it's doing me harm
You know I can't sleep,
I can't stop my brain
You know it's three weeks,
I'm going insane
You know I'd give you everything I've got
For a little peace of mind
I'd give you everything I've got
For a little peace of mind
I'd give you everything I've got
For a little peace of mind

Paul has always claimed that his best songs have come to him as if already written.

BLACKBIRD

Blackbird singing in the dead of night
Take these broken wings and learn to fly
All your life
You were only waiting for this moment
 to arise.

Blackbird singing in the dead of night
Take these sunken eyes and learn to see
All your life
You were only waiting for this moment
 to be free.

Blackbird fly Blackbird fly
Into the light of the dark black night.

Blackbird fly Blackbird fly
Into the light of the dark black night.

Blackbird singing in the dead of night
Take these broken wings and learn to fly
All your life
You were only waiting for this moment
 to arise
You were only waiting for this moment
 to arise
You were only waiting for this moment
 to arise.

Written: Lennon/McCartney

Length: 2'18"

UK Release: *The Beatles* album,
November 22, 1968

US Release: *The Beatles* album,
November 25, 1968

BLACKBIRD

There are a number of stories surrounding the creation of 'Blackbird'. One says that Paul woke early one morning in Rishikesh to hear a blackbird singing, picked up his guitar to transcribe the bird song and came up with the music. Another suggests that he was inspired by news reports of race riots in America and translated the plight of oppressed racial minorities beginning to flex their muscles into the image of a bird with broken wings struggling to fly.

Paul's step-mother, Angie McCartney, says that it was written for her mother, Edie Stopforth, and that she has a copy of a studio take where Paul says, "This one's for Edie" before recording it. "My mother was staying with Jim and I after a long illness," she says. "During that time Paul visited us and spent some time sitting on mum's bed. She told him that she would often listen to a bird singing at night. Paul eventually took a little tape recorder up to her room and recorded the sound of this bird."

Paul has said that the tune was inspired not by a blackbird's singing but by Bach's 'Bourrée In E Minor' (from the lute suite 'BWV 996') that he had learned as a teenager from a guitar manual. He didn't copy the tune but took direction from his memory. As far as the words were concerned, he was partly thinking of the racial situation in America and wrote it as if offering encouragement to the typical black woman facing oppression.

Although the song was written in 1968, the exact month is difficult to pinpoint since Paul has said that he wrote it not in India but on his Scottish farm. It's possible that he started the music in India, influenced by Donovan, and completed the song between his return to England on March 26 and the demo recordings at George's Esher home in late May. This makes it more likely that the lyric was written in the aftermath of Martin Luther King's death on April 4. On June 11 he performed it for an Apple promotional film that was being directed by Tony Bramwell.

Close to the time of recording he never mentioned the connection with America's racial strife. Speaking to Radio Luxembourg in 1968 he said; "There's nothing to the song. It's just one of those 'pick it and sing it' [songs] and that's it." Nowadays, when performing it in concert, he claims that it was written "when there were troubles in the southern states of America over civil rights and I was hoping that by writing his song I might bring a little hope to the people going through the struggles."

The use of the term "blackbird" to refer to people of African origin dates back to the slave trade and was always used pejoratively. In the Sixties it was appropriated the civil rights campaigners and given a positive spin. A civil rights musical, *Fly Blackbird*, with songs by C. Bernard Jackson and James Hatch, opened off-Broadway in 1962 and went on to win an Obie for Best Musical.

In the summer of 1968, Paul serenaded the fans gathered outside his home with an acoustic version of 'Blackbird'. Margo Bird, a former 'Apple Scruff' (the term for the group of fans who used to congregate outside the Apple offices in Savile Row), remembers: "I think he had a young lady round, Francie Schwartz. We'd been hanging around outside and it was obvious she wasn't going to be leaving. He had a music room right at the top of the house and he opened the sash window, sat on the edge and played it to us. It was the early hours of the morning."

Paul often cites 'Blackbird' as evidence that the best of his songs come spontaneously, when words and music tumble out as if they had already been formulated without conscious effort on his behalf.

PIGGIES

Have you seen the little piggies
  crawling in the dirt?
And for all the little piggies
  life is getting worse
Always having dirt to play around in

Have you seen the bigger piggies
  in their starched white shirts?
You will find the bigger piggies
  stirring up the dirt
Always have clean shirts to play around in

In their styes with all their backing
  they don't care what goes on around
In their eyes there's something lacking
  what they need's a damn good whacking

Everywhere there's lots of piggies
  living piggy lives
You can see them out for dinner
  with their piggy wives
Clutching forks and knives to eat their bacon

PIGGIES

George referred to 'Piggies' as "a social comment" although the song did little more than mock the middle-classes by calling them pigs, a Sixties term of derision usually reserved for the police. The pig was also the animal chosen by George Orwell in *Animal Farm* to represent tyrannical leaders.

The song became notorious in 1971 when it was revealed that Charles Manson, the self-appointed leader of the notorious Manson "family", had interpreted the words as a warning to the white establishment that they were about to be victims of an uprising.

Particularly significant, in Manson's disturbed mind, was the suggestion that the piggies were in need of "a damn good whacking". According to witnesses, this was one of Manson's favourite lines, and one that he quoted frequently before his imprisonment for involvement in the murders that many saw as the final dark chapter in the hippie era.

The clue that eventually linked the eight murders – five at the residence of film-star Sharon Tate, two at Leno LaBianca's and one at Gary Hinman's – was the painting of the word "pig", "pigs" or "piggy" on walls and doors in the victims' blood. The LaBiancas were even stabbed with knives and forks, apparently because these utensils are mentioned in the last verse.

George was horrified by Manson's misguided interpretation of what he felt was a rather tame song, pointing out that the "damn good whacking" line had been suggested by his mother when he was looking for something to rhyme with "backing" and "lacking". "It was nothing to do with American policemen or Californian shagnasties," he said.

Written: Harrison

Length: 2'04"

UK Release: *The Beatles* album, November 22, 1968

US Release: *The Beatles* album, November 25, 1968

ROCKY RACCOON

'Rocky Raccoon' was a musical Western that started off as a talking blues and was written by Paul in India. Set in the "black mountain hills of Dakota" (probably because of the Doris Day song 'Black Hills Of Dakota' from the movie *Calamity Jane*), it tells the tale of young Rocky whose girl, Nancy Magill, runs off with Dan. Rocky pursues Dan and attempts to shoot him down but is beaten to the draw. Afterwards, Rocky is treated in his hotel room by a doctor stinking of gin. "We were sitting on the roof at Maharishi's just enjoying ourselves when I wrote this one," said Paul. "I started laying the chords and originally the title was 'Rocky Sassoon'. Then me, John and Donovan started making up the words and they came very quickly and eventually it became 'Rocky Raccoon' because it sounded more cowboyish."

The lyric bears more that a passing resemblance to Robert Service's popular 'The Shooting of Dan McGrew' (1907), a poem that also tells a story of love and revenge with similar-sounding characters. In both works a shooting takes

Now somewhere in the black mountain
  hills of Dakota
There lived a young boy named Rocky
  Raccoon
And one day his woman ran off with
  another guy
Hit young Rocky in the eye
  Rocky didn't like that
He said I'm gonna get that boy
So one day he walked into town
Booked himself a room in the local saloon

Rocky Raccoon checked into his room
Only to find Gideon's Bible
Rocky had come equipped with a gun
To shoot off the legs of his rival
His rival it seems had broken his dreams
By stealing the girl of his fancy
Her name was Magil and she called
  herself Lil
But everyone knew her as Nancy
Now she and her man who called
  himself Dan
Were in the next room at the hoedown
Rocky burst in and grinning a grin
He said Danny boy this is a showdown
But Daniel was hot,
  he drew first and shot
And Rocky collapsed in the corner, ah

D'da d'da d'da da da da
D'da d'da d'da da da da
D'da d'da d'da da d'da d'da d'da d'da
Do do do do do do

D'do d'do d'do do do do

D'do d'do d'do do do do
D'do d'do d'do do do d'do d'do d'do
  d'do
Do do do do do do

Now the doctor came in stinking of gin
And proceeded to lie on the table
He said Rocky you met your match
And Rocky said doc it's only a scratch
And I'll be better I'll be better doc as
  soon as I am able

And now Rocky Raccoon
He fell back in his room
Only to find Gideon's bible
Gideon checked out
And he left it no doubt
To help with good Rocky's revival, ah
Oh yeah, yeah

D'do d'do d'do do do do
D'do d'do d'do do do do
D'do d'do d'do do do d'do d'do d'do
  d'do
Do do do do do do

D'do d'do d'do do do do,
Come on, Rocky boy
D'do d'do d'do do do do,
Come on, Rocky boy
D'do d'do d'do do do d'do d'do d'do
  d'do
The story of Rocky there

place in a saloon. The *femme fatale* in Rocky's case is described in the line "she called herself Lil…but everyone knew her as Nancy". In Dan McGrew's case the lady is "known as Lou".

Apple Scruff Margo Bird, heard that the character of the doctor was drawn from real life. "Paul had a quad bike that he came off one day towards the end of 1965. He was a bit stoned at the time and cut his mouth and chipped his tooth," she says. "The doctor that came to treat him was stinking of gin and because he was a bit worse for wear he didn't make a very good job of the stitching. That is why Paul had a nasty lump on his lip for a while and he grew a moustache to cover it."

Of the song, Paul said: "I just tried to keep it amusing. It's me writing a play, a little one-act play, giving them most of the dialogue." He said he imagined the main character as wearing a raccoon hat like Davy Crockett.

Written: Lennon/McCartney

Length: 3'32"

UK Release: *The Beatles* album, November 22, 1968

US Release: *The Beatles* album, November 25, 1968

ABOVE: It took Ringo four years to get his first composition on a Beatles album.

DON'T PASS ME BY

'Don't Pass Me By' was Ringo's first complete Beatles' song. Until then, his only contribution to the Beatles' writing had been the titles for 'A Hard Day's Night' and 'Tomorrow Never Knows', plus whatever musical contributions he made to 'Flying' and 'What Goes On'.

Asked in December 1967 whether he had aspirations as a songwriter, Ringo replied: "I try. I have a guitar and a piano and play a few chords, but they're all just chinga-lingas. No great tune comes out as far as I'm concerned."

The truth is he'd been trying to get the Beatles to record 'Don't Pass Me By' for years. During an interview for radio in New Zealand on their June 1964 tour of Australasia, Ringo could be heard urging the others to "sing the song I've written, just for a plug". Paul responded by saying: "Ringo has written a song called 'Don't Pass Me By'. A beautiful melody. This is Ringo's first venture into songwriting."

After Paul and John had sung a verse, Ringo was asked more about it: "It was written as a country and western but Paul and John singing it with that blues feeling has knocked me out. Are the Beatles going to record it? I don't know. I don't think so actually. I keep trying to push it on them every time we make a record."

It was to remain unrecorded for another five years. "Unfortunately there's never enough time to fit Ringo's song on an album," Paul explained in 1964. "He never finishes it."

DON'T PASS ME BY

I listen for your footsteps
Coming up the drive
Listen for your footsteps
But they don't arrive
Waiting for your knock, dear
On my old front door
I don't hear it
Does it mean you don't love me
 any more?

I hear the clock a-tickin'
On the mantel shelf
See the hands a-movin'
But I'm by myself
I wonder where you are tonight
And why I'm by myself
I don't see you
Does it mean you don't love me
 any more?

Don't pass me by, don't make me cry,
Don't make me blue
Cause you know darling I love only you
You'll never know it hurt me so
How I hate to see you go
Don't pass me by, don't make me cry,
(don't make me blue)

I'm sorry that I doubted you
I was so unfair
You were in a car crash
And you lost your hair
You said that you would be late
About an hour or two
I said that's alright I'm waiting here
Just waiting to hear from you

Don't pass me by, don't make me cry,
Don't make me blue
Cause you know darling I love only you
You'll never know it hurt me so
How I hate to see you go
Don't pass me by, don't make me cry

Don't pass me by, don't make me cry,
Don't make me blue
'Cause you know darling I love only you
You'll never know it hurt me so,
How I hate to see you go
Don't pass me by, don't make me cry.

DON'T PASS ME BY

Written: Starr

Length: 3'50"

UK Release: *The Beatles* album, November 22, 1968

US Release: *The Beatles* album, November 25, 1968

WHY DON'T WE DO IT IN THE ROAD?

Written: Lennon/McCartney

Length: 1'41"

UK Release: *The Beatles* album,
November 22, 1968

US Release: *The Beatles* album,
November 25, 1968

Why don't we d-do it in the road? Mm
Why don't we do it in the road? Ah
Why don't we d-do it, do it in the road?
Mm
Why don't we do it in the road? Mm
No one will be watching us
Why don't we do it in the road?

Why don't we do it in the road?
Why don't we do it in the road?
Why don't we do it in the road?
Why don't we do it in the road?
No one will be watching us
Why don't we do it in the road?

Ooh

Why don't we do it in the road?
Why don't we do it in the road?
Why don't we do it, do it in the road?
Why don't we do it in the road?
No one will be watching us
Why don't we do it in the road?

WHY DON'T WE DO IT IN THE ROAD?

One of the great strengths of the Lennon and McCartney team was that, although they now rarely sat down and created a song from scratch together, they did urge each other on to greater heights in what was increasingly to become solo work.

Sometimes they would try to outdo each other by composing in a style more often associated with the other. This explains why *The White Album* contains the sensitive 'Julia' and sentimental 'Goodnight' by John in Paul's style, as well as gritty rock 'n' roll numbers like 'Helter Skelter' and 'Why Don't We Do It In The Road?' from Paul à la Lennon. John was upset by 'Why Don't We Do It In The Road?' because Paul recorded it with Ringo in a separate studio at Abbey Road. What probably irritated him most though was that Paul's chosen style – a risqué lyric and sparse arrangements – was close to the style he had become associated with.

Paul had the idea for the song while in India when he saw two monkeys copulating in the open. (There are many monkeys living around the area of the ashram in Rishikesh.) He was struck by the apparently uncomplicated way in which animals mate compared with the rules, rituals and routines of human sex. He could have been making a libertarian call for a more relaxed attitude to sexual morality ("Hey, let's get naked and have sex in public") or he could have been asking a really profound question about what separates humans from other animals ("Hey, why is that humans have an inborn sense of modesty. What makes us so unique?").

"The Beatles have always been a rock group," he explained in November 1968. "It's just that we're not completely rock 'n' roll. That's why we do 'Ob-La-Di Ob-La-Da' one minute, and this the next. When we played in Hamburg we didn't just play rock 'n' roll all evening because we had these fat old businessmen coming in – and thin old businessmen as well – and they would ask us to play a mambo or a samba. So we had to get into this kind of stuff. I never usually write a song and think: 'Right, now this is going to be about something specific.' It's just that the words happen. I never try to make any serious social point. Just words to go with the music. And you can read anything you like into it."

I WILL

Who knows how long I've loved you
You know I love you still
Will I wait a lonely lifetime
If you want me to, I will

For if I ever saw you
I didn't catch your name
But it never really mattered
I will always feel the same

Love you forever and forever
Love you with all my heart
Love you whenever we're together
Love you when we're apart

And when at last I find you
Your song will fill the air
Sing it loud so I can hear you
Make it easy to be near you
For the things you do endear you to me
Oh, you know I will
I will

Mm mm mm mm mm mm mm mm mm
Da da da da da da da

I WILL

Paul spent 67 takes getting 'I Will' right on September 16, 1968, with Ringo playing on cymbal and maracas and John tapping the rhythm with a piece of wood. It was the first of Paul's songs to be written about Linda and he was still adding and changing lines as it was being recorded.

Unsurprisingly, there's a sense of anticipation in the lyric, provoked no doubt by the knowledge that Linda and her daughter were arriving in London the next week. Paul had previously only met Linda in London during the *Sgt. Pepper* period and on two subsequent visits to America, but he obviously felt he knew enough about her to be confident in offering her his love "forever and forever."

He had started the song in India while sitting playing with Donovan and some others after a day of meditation. Some lyrical ideas were kicked around and a song about the moon was written, but he wasn't completely happy with them, so on his return to England he wrote a fresh lyric. "They're very simple words," he said. "They're straight love song words really. I think they're quite effective. It's still one of my favourite melodies that I've written."

Written: Lennon/McCartney

Length: 1'46"

UK Release: *The Beatles* album, November 22, 1968

US Release: *The Beatles* album, November 25, 1968

You know I love you still

JULIA

Although many of John's lyrics were shaped by the trauma of losing his mother as a teenager, 'Julia' was the first time he directly introduced his mother into a Beatles' song.

Julia Stanley was born in Liverpool in 1914 and married Alfred Lennon in 1938. John was the only child they had together. By the time John was five, Julia gave birth to another man's child, and John was taken into the care of Julia's sister Mimi. His mother was attractive and unconventional. From her John inherited his sense of humour and also his interest in music. She taught him to play banjo and it was through her that John heard his first Elvis Presley records.

Julia's sudden death in a road accident in July 1958 came just when John was becoming close to her again. He'd started using her home in Blomfield Road for band practices with the Quarry Men because Aunt Mimi didn't like loud music in her house. "John took the death really badly," says his childhood friend Nigel Walley, who actually witnessed the accident. "John was always brash on the outside but inside he had a lot of time and love for his mother but he would never want to show it. You had to look hard. But it really hit him. He'd lost his father who'd left home, his Uncle George who'd died and now his mother. What was going to happen next? He didn't seem to be having much luck. All his friends, like myself and Ivan Vaughan, had steady home lives with mothers and fathers and I think the fact that he didn't have that upbringing affected him to some degree."

Although 'Julia' was addressed to his mother, it was also a coded message to his new love, Yoko Ono, who he had taken to referring to as "mother". The "ocean child", who John writes is calling him, is clearly a reference to Yoko whose name in Japanese means "child of the ocean". "It was in India that she began writing to me," John said. "She would write things like 'I am a cloud. Watch for me in the sky.' I would get so excited about her letters."

The first two lines of the song are taken from *Sand And Foam*, a collection of proverbs by the Lebanese mystic Kahlil Gibran, first published in 1927. Gibran wrote: "Half of what I say is meaningless; but I say it so the other half may reach you." The rest of the song, John said, was finished with help from Yoko herself when they met up back in England because, besides being an artist and film maker, she was a poet who wrote in a minimalist style.

The guitar work on 'Julia' was influenced by the way that Donovan played. "John would take particular interest in the finger-style guitar parts I was playing in my songs," says Donovan. "He wanted to know the patterns I was using and I told him I would teach him. John was a diligent student and mastered the complex pattern in a few days. In common with most songwriters, learning a new style meant composing in a different way. In his deep meditation sessions, John had opened up feelings for his mother. He found release for these emotions in 'Julia', the tune he had learned with the new finger style. I remember when I played 'Julia' on my guitar I was struck by how much the images in the song were like the images in my songs. They were very unLennon-like.

Half of what I say is meaningless
But I say it just to reach you, Julia

Julia, Julia, oceanchild, calls me
So I sing a song of love, Julia
Julia, seashell eyes, windy smile, calls me
So I sing a song of love, Julia

Her hair of floating sky is shimmering,
Glimmering
In the sun

Julia, Julia, morning moon, touch me
So I sing a song of love, Julia

When I cannot sing my heart
I can only speak my mind, Julia
Julia, sleeping sand, silent cloud,
 touch me
So I sing a song of love, Julia
Mmm mm mm mm... calls me
So I sing a song of love for Julia, Julia,
 Julia

JULIA

Written: Lennon/McCartney

Length: 2'54"

UK Release: *The Beatles* album,
November 22, 1968

US Release: *The Beatles* album,
November 25, 1968

BIRTHDAY

The songs on *The Beatles* were composed in India on acoustic guitars, because they were the only instruments available at the ashram.

However, 'Birthday' was written in Abbey Road Studios, on September 18, 1968 with Paul thumping out the basic tune on a piano. According to John, Paul had been thinking of 'Happy, Happy Birthday', a 1957 hit in America for the Tuneweavers, but wanted to produce something that sounded contemporary and rock 'n' roll. It was also Linda Eastman's 26th birthday in six days' time and Paul knew that she was arriving in London the following week, just in time to celebrate.

Paul went in the studio late in the afternoon and worked out the basic keyboard riff, the start of which was based on the introduction of Rosco Gordon's 'Just A Little Bit' (1960). Later, George, John and Ringo came in and added a backing track. During the evening, the four of them took a break and went round to Paul's house to watch the British television premiere of *The Girl Can't Help It* (1956), which starred Jayne Mansfield and featured music by Fats Domino, Gene Vincent, the Treniers, the Platters, Little Richard, and Eddie Cochran.

Perhaps inspired by this dose of early rock 'n' roll, the Beatles returned to the studio around 11pm and completed the vocals. Each of the Beatles threw in lines and Yoko Ono and Pattie Harrison helped with the backing. "We just made up the words in the studio," said Paul. "It's one of my favourite tracks on the album because it was instantaneous. It's a good one to dance to."

John's opinion, volunteered 12 years later, was par for the course: "It's a piece of garbage."

Written: Lennon/McCartney

Length: 2'42"

UK Release: *The Beatles* album, November 22, 1968

US Release: *The Beatles* album, November 25, 1968

They say it's your birthday
It's my birthday too, yeah
They say it's your birthday
We're gonna have a good time
I'm glad it's your birthday
Happy birthday to you

Dance, dance, dance
Come on, come on

Yes we're going to a party party
Yes we're going to a party party
Yes we're going to a party party

I would like you to dance (Birthday)
Take a cha-cha-cha-chance (Birthday)
I would like you to dance (Birthday)
Dance yeah

Oh
Come on

I would like you to dance (Birthday)
Take a cha-cha-cha-chance (Birthday)
I would like you to dance (Birthday)
Oh dance! Dance

They say it's your birthday
Well it's my birthday too, yeah
They say it's your birthday
We're gonna have a good time
I'm glad it's your birthday
Happy birthday to you

John and Yoko at the opening of their first joint art exhibition at the Robert Fraser Art Gallery, July 1, 1968.

Yes I'm lonely wanna die
Yes I'm lonely wanna die
If I ain't dead already
Ooh girl you know the reason why

In the morning wanna die
In the evening wanna die
If I ain't dead already
Ooh girl you know the reason why

My mother was of the sky
My father was of the earth
But I am of the universe
And you know what it's worth
I'm lonely wanna die
If I ain't dead already
Ooh girl you know the reason why

The eagle picks my eye
The worm he licks my bone
I feel so suicidal
Just like Dylan's Mr. Jones
Lonely wanna die
If I ain't dead already
Ooh girl you know the reason why

Black cloud crossed my mind
Blue mist round my soul
Feel so suicidal
Even hate my rock 'n' roll
Wanna die yeah wanna die
If I ain't dead already
Ooh girl you know the reason why

Yes I'm lonely wanna die
Yes I'm lonely wanna die
If I ain't dead already
Ooh, girl you know the reason why.

Yes I'm lonely wanna die
Yes I'm lonely wanna die.

YER BLUES

'Yer Blues' was the most despairing song John had written to date, representing an anguished cry to Yoko for help. John felt he was at a crossroads in his life: his career as a concert performing Beatle was over; his manager was dead; and now he was contemplating bringing an end to his marriage.

He felt loyalty to Cynthia and yet he knew that in Yoko he'd met his artistic and intellectual match. She was, he later said, the girl he had always dreamed of meeting, the girl he had imagined when he wrote 'Girl'.

During the stay in Rishikesh, John and Cynthia were often separated because of their different meditation routines and it wasn't until the flight back to London from Delhi that John mentioned to Cynthia his indiscretions during their six-year marriage. She was shocked: "I never dreamt that he had been unfaithful to me during our married life. He hadn't revealed anything to me. I knew of course that touring abroad and being surrounded by all the temptations any man could possibly want would have been impossible to resist. But even so my mind just couldn't and wouldn't accept the inevitable. I had never had anything concrete to go on, nothing tell-tale."

John later said that this dilemma had made him feel suicidal. In this song, he jokingly compares himself to 'Mr Jones', the hapless central character in Dylan's 'Ballad Of A Thin Man' who doesn't comprehend what's going on around him. Musically, 'Yer Blues' was indicative of the direction he would eventually take with his post-Beatle career.

Written: Lennon/McCartney

Length: 4'01"

UK Release: *The Beatles* album, November 22, 1968

US Release: *The Beatles* album, November 25, 1968

Born a poor young country boy,
Mother Nature's son
All day long I'm sitting singing
songs for everyone

Sit beside a mountain stream,
See her waters rise
Listen to the pretty sound
of music as she flies

Doo doo doo doo doo doo doo doo doo
doo doo
Doo doo doo doo doo doo doo doo doo
Doo doo doo

Find me in my field of grass,
Mother Nature's son
Swaying daisies sing a lazy song
beneath the sun

Doo doo doo doo doo doo doo doo doo
doo doo
Doo doo doo doo doo doo doo doo doo
Doo doo doo doo doo doo
Yeah yeah yeah

Mm mm mm mm mm mm mm
Mm mm mm, ooh ooh ooh
Mm mm mm mm mm mm mm
Mm mm mm mm, wah wah wah

Wah, Mother Nature's son

MOTHER NATURE'S SON

Both John and Paul wrote songs after hearing a lecture by the Maharishi about the unity of man and nature, but it was to be Paul's 'Mother Nature's Son' that made the album's final selection.

John's song, 'A Child Of Nature', made similar observations about the sun, sky, wind and mountains but, whereas Paul fictionalized his response by writing in the character of a "poor young country boy", John wrote about himself "on the road to Rishikesh".

A demo of 'A Child Of Nature' was made by John in May 1968, but the Beatles didn't record it. Three years later, and with a new set of lyrics, it became 'Jealous Guy'.

Paul had always been a lover of the countryside and when he wrote 'Mother Nature's Son' he had in mind a song he had heard when he was younger called 'Nature Boy' (1947), made popular by Nat "King" Cole. Although the song was started in India it was completed at his father's house in Heswall, Cheshire.

Written: Lennon/McCartney

Length: 2'48"

UK Release: *The Beatles* album, November 22, 1968

US Release: *The Beatles* album, November 25, 1968

EVERYBODY'S GOT SOMETHING TO HIDE EXCEPT ME AND MY MONKEY

THE BEATLES

EVERYBODY'S GOT SOMETHING TO HIDE EXCEPT ME AND MY MONKEY

Initially known as 'Come On, Come On', the song was built up from its title. John said it was a clear reference to his relationship with Yoko. "That was just a nice line which I made into a song," he said. "Everybody seemed to be paranoid except for us two, who were in the glow of love … everybody was sort of tense around us."

It wasn't until his return from India that the friendship turned into an affair and Cynthia knew what was happening. Yoko started to attend recording sessions for the new album, much to the annoyance of the other Beatles. The British press also found it difficult to accept Yoko and this irked John and was to play a part in his eventual move to America. "In England they think I'm someone who has won the pools and gone off with a Japanese Princess," he once said. "In America, they treat her with respect. They treat her as the serious artist she is."

The rapid "Come on, come on, come on ..." chorus sounds similar to what became known as the "gobble chorus" section of the Fugs' track 'Virgin Forest', which appeared on the band's second album, *The Fugs* (1966). Barry Miles, then running the Indica Bookshop, supplied the Beatles with the latest underground releases from America, including work by the Fugs.

Written: Lennon/McCartney

Length: 2'24"

UK Release: *The Beatles* album, November 22, 1968

US Release: *The Beatles* album, November 25, 1968

Come on come on
Come on come on
Come on is such a joy
Come on is such a joy
Come on let's take it easy
Come on let's take it easy
Take it easy take it easy
Everybody's got something to hide
  'cept for me and my monkey

(Ooh) The deeper you go the higher you fly
The higher you fly the deeper you go
So come on (Come on) come on
Come on is such a joy
Come on is such a joy
Come on let's make it easy
Come on let's make it easy (Oh)
Take it easy (Yeh yeh yeh) take it easy (Hoo)
Everybody's got something to hide
  'cept for me and my monkey

Oh!

Your inside is out and your outside is in
Your outside is in and your inside is out
So come on (Ho) come on (Ho)
Come on is such a joy
Come on is such a joy
Come on let's make it easy
Come on let's make it easy
Make it easy (Hoo) make it easy (Hoo)
Everybody's got something to hide
  'cept for me and my monkey

Hey!

Come on, come on, come on, come on,
  come on
Come on, come on, come on...

Come on, come on, come on, come on,
  come on
Come on, come on, come on...

Sexy Sadie what have you done
You made a fool of everyone
You made a fool of everyone
Sexy Sadie ooh what have you done

Sexy Sadie you broke the rules
You layed it down for all to see
You layed it down for all to see
Sexy Sadie oooh you broke the rules

One sunny day the world was waiting
  for a lover
She came along to turn on everyone
Sexy Sadie (Sexy Sadie) the greatest
  (She's the greatest) of them all

Sexy Sadie how did you know
The world was waiting just for you
The world was waiting just for you
Sexy Sadie oooh how did you know

Sexy Sadie you'll get yours yet
However big you think you are
However big you think you are
Sexy Sadie oooh you'll get yours yet

We gave her everything we owned just
  to sit at her table
Just a smile would lighten everything
Sexy Sadie she's the latest and the
  greatest of them all

She made a fool of everyone
Sexy Sadie

However big you think you are
Sexy Sadie

SEXY SADIE

'Sexy Sadie' appears to be a song about a girl who leads men on, only to make fools of them, but was written about the Maharishi Mahesh Yogi, after John had become disillusioned by him. Knowing that he could never record a potentially libellous song called 'Maharishi', he titled it 'Sexy Sadie', but on the demo recording of the track he let rip with a string of obscenities directed towards his real quarry.

There were two reasons why the Beatles decided to leave Rishikesh. One was that they had been told that the Maharishi was only after their money, and the other was the rumour going around that he had made a sexual advance to one of the women on the course. Although there was never any concrete evidence behind these accusations, it was enough to unnerve them and the three Beatles arranged a meeting with the guru where they informed him that they were leaving. Pressed to explain their decision, John reportedly said, "Well, if you're so cosmic, you'll know why."

Paul Horn, who remembers them leaving, believes they left partly because they had expected too much of the Maharishi and partly because jealousies had developed amongst some hangers-on at the camp. "These courses were really designed for people who wanted to become teachers themselves and who had a solid background in meditation," Horn says. "The Beatles didn't really have the background and experience to be there and I think they were expecting miracles. George was obviously really interested but Ringo wasn't into Eastern philosophy at all. John was on his own trip and always sceptical about anything until it had been proven to him. Paul was easy-going and could have gone either way.

"The big fuss came because there were some people there who were more interested in the Beatles than learning to meditate and they became hangers-on," continues Horn. "There was one girl, a school teacher from New York, who was really into the Beatles and she started all this crap about the Maharishi making passes at her. She told the Beatles this and they got upset about it and left. Basically, there were a lot of rumours, jealousies and triangles going on and she got back at the Beatles through saying this about the Maharishi. The bottom line, though, is that it was time for them to go home anyway. This was just the catalyst."

Both the tune and some of the lyric bears a strong resemblance to Smokey Robinson's 1961 song 'I've Been Good To You', which starts "Look what you've done/ You've made a fool of someone".

Written: Lennon/McCartney

Length: 3'15"

UK Release: *The Beatles* album,
November 22, 1968

US Release: *The Beatles* album,
November 25, 1968

Although Paul was regarded as the ballad-writer of the Beatles, he was responsible for some of the group's loudest and dirtiest-sounding tracks, including 'Helter Skelter'.

HELTER SKELTER

The concept for 'Helter Skelter' came from a music paper's rave review of a new single by the Who. Paul didn't think the single matched the hyperbole and set himself the challenge of writing something that could legitimately be described in that language.

The single was 'I Can See For Miles', which was released in October 1967. *Melody Maker* described it as a "marathon epic of swearing cymbals and cursing guitars (that) marks the return of the Who as a major freak-out force." Rival news weekly *NME* said it was "charged with dynamite" and presented "an ear-shattering wall of sound, with penetrating, rasping guitars, heavy-handed drumming and constant cymbal-crashing."

It's impossible to tell which particular review caught Paul's attention because his description of what he read has changed over the years. In 1968, he reported that this review had said "the group really goes wild with echo and screaming and everything", but 20 years later his memory of it was more fanciful, claiming that it described the Who single as, "the loudest, most raucous rock 'n' roll, the dirtiest thing they'd ever done." His account of the effect that the review had on him hasn't changed, though. "I thought, 'That's a pity. I would like to do something like that.' Then I heard it and it was nothing like it. It was straight and sophisticated. So we did this. I like noise."

Despite being described as having "swearing" cymbals and "cursing" or "rasping" guitars, 'I Can See For Miles' had a discernible melody throughout and could not properly be described as "raucous" or "ear-shattering". Paul wanted to write something that really did 'freak' people out and, when the Beatles first recorded 'Helter Skelter' in July 1968, they did it in a single take almost half an hour long. They returned to it in September "out of their heads", and produced a shorter version. At the end of it, Ringo can be heard shrieking, "I've got blisters on my fingers." Paul commented, "That wasn't a joke put-on. His hands were actually bleeding at the end of the take, he'd been drumming so ferociously."

Most British listeners were aware that a helter skelter was a spiral fairground slide but Charles Manson, who heard *The White Album* in December 1968, apparently thought that the Beatles were warning America of a racial conflict that was "coming down fast". In the scenario that Manson had developed, the Beatles were the four angels mentioned in the New Testament's Book Of Revelations who, through their songs, were telling him and his followers to prepare for the coming holocaust by escaping to the desert. Manson referred to this future uprising as 'Helter Skelter' and it was the daubing of these words in blood at the scene of one of the murders that became another vital clue in the subsequent police investigation. It was because of the song's significance that Vincent Bugliosi, the Los Angeles District Attorney who prosecuted at Manson's trial, named his best-selling account of the murders *Helter Skelter*.

When I get to the bottom I go back
  to the top of the slide
Where I stop and I turn and I go for a ride
Till I get to the bottom and I see you again
Yeah yeah yeah hey

Do you, don't you want me to love you
I'm coming down fast but
  I'm miles above you
Tell me tell me tell me come on
  tell me the answer
Well you may be a lover but
  you ain't no dancer

Now helter skelter helter skelter
Helter skelter yeah ooh!

Will you, won't you want me to make you
I'm coming down fast but
  don't let me break you
Tell me tell me tell me the answer
You may be a lover but
  you ain't no dancer

Look out helter skelter helter skelter
Helter skelter ooh

Look out, cos here she comes

When I get to the bottom
　I go back to the top of the slide
And I stop and I turn and I go for a ride
And I get to the bottom
　and I see you again
Yeah yeah yeah

Well do you, don't you want me
　to make you
I'm coming down fast but
　don't let me break you
Tell me tell me tell me the answer
You may be a lover but
　you ain't no dancer

Look out helter skelter helter skelter
Helter skelter

Look out helter skelter
She's coming down fast
Yes she is
Yes she is coming down fast

(My head is spinning, ooh...
Ha ha ha, ha ha ha, alright!
I got blisters on my fingers!)

The song appears to be a song about furious sex but when talking to Barry Miles for the 1996 book *Many Years From Now* Paul suggested a more serious intention. "I was using the symbol of a helter skelter as a ride from the top to the bottom – the rise and fall of the Roman Empire – and this was the fall, the demise, the going down."

Written: Lennon/McCartney

Length: 4'29"

UK Release: *The Beatles* album,
November 22, 1968

US Release: *The Beatles* album,
November 25, 1968

ABOVE: George was the first to show an interest in Eastern religion and he maintained his studies throughout his life. He even became reconciled to the Maharishi late in his life.

LONG LONG LONG

It's been a long long long time
How could I ever have lost you
When I loved you

It took a long long long time
Now I'm so happy I found you
How I love you

So many tears I was searching
So many tears I was wasting, oh oh

Now I can see you, be you
How can I ever misplace you
How I want you
Oh I love you
You know that I need you
Ooh I love you

LONG LONG LONG

More than any other Beatle, George was inspired to write by hearing other songs. The chords of 'Long Long Long' were suggested to him by Bob Dylan's haunting track 'Sad Eyed Lady Of The Lowlands', which had taken up one whole side of one of the discs on Dylan's 1966 double album *Blonde On Blonde*. George was fascinated with the movement from D to E minor to A and back to D and wanted to write something that sounded similar. He scribbled the lyric out in the pages of an empty week-at-a-glance diary for 1968 and called it 'It's Been A Long Long Long Time', which became the working title.

'Long Long Long' sounds like a straightforward love song written by someone who has lost and regained the object of his affections but, according to George, the "you" in question here is God. He was the first Beatle to show an interest in Eastern religion and the only one to carry on with it after the others became disenchanted with the Maharishi following their visit to India. George did, however, alter his allegiances, distancing himself from Maharishi and Transcendental Meditation and becoming publicly identified with the International Society for Krishna Consciousness, later producing their 'Hare Krishna' mantra as a hit single.

Written: Harrison

Length: 3'04"

UK Release: *The Beatles* album, November 22, 1968

US Release: *The Beatles* album, November 25, 1968

REVOLUTION 1

Written: Lennon/McCartney

Length: 4'15"

UK Release: *The Beatles* album, November 22, 1968

US Release: *The Beatles* album, November 25, 1968

REVOLUTION 1

The Summer of Love was followed by the Spring of Revolution. In March 1968, thousands marched on the American Embassy in London's Grosvenor Square to protest against the war in Vietnam. In May, students rioted in Paris and barricades were erected. Unlike Mick Jagger, who made an appearance at Grosvenor Square, John surveyed these events from the comfort of his Weybridge home, keeping in touch through the news media and the underground press. He began work on 'Revolution' while in India and completed it at home when Cynthia was away in Greece. He took it to Paul as a potential single but Paul said the song wasn't commercial enough.

As with 'Back In The U.S.S.R.', the title was deceptive. It wasn't the song of a revolutionary but rather the song of someone under pressure from revolutionaries to declare his allegiance. Easily the most politically conscious of the Beatles and unapologetically left-wing in outlook, John had become a target for various Leninist, Trotskyist and Maoist groups, who felt he should lend both moral and financial support to their causes.

'Revolution' was John's reply to these factions, informing them that, while

Right. Take 2
OK!

You say you want a revolution
Well you know
We all want to change the world
You tell me that it's evolution
Well you know
We all want to change the world
But when you talk about destruction
Don't you know that you can
   count me out
Don't you know it's gonna be (shooby doo
   wah) alright (shooby doo wah)
Don't you know it's gonna be (shooby doo
   wah) alright (shooby doo wah)
Don't you know it's gonna be (shooby doo
   wah) alright (shooby doo wah)

You say you got a real solution
Well you know
We'd all love to see the plan
You ask me for a contribution
Well you know
We're all doing what we can
But if you want money for people with
   minds that hate
All I can tell you is
   brother you have to wait
Don't you know it's gonna be (shooby doo
   wah) alright (shooby doo wah)
Don't you know it's gonna be (shooby doo
   wah) alright (shooby doo wah)
Don't you know it's gonna be (shooby doo
   wah) alright (shooby doo wah)

You say you'll change The Constitution
Well you know
We'd all love to change your head
You tell me it's the institution
Well you know
You'd better free your mind instead
But if you go carrying pictures of
   Chairman Mao
You ain't going to make it with anyone
   anyhow
Don't you know it's gonna be (shooby doo
   wah) alright (shooby doo wah)
Don't you know it's gonna be (shooby doo
   wah) alright (shooby doo wah)
Don't you know it's gonna be (shooby doo
   wah) alright (shooby doo wah)

Oh, oh, oh, oh, oh, oh, oh, oh, oh, oh
Alright, alright, alright, alright, alright
Alright, alright, alright, alright, alright
Oh, oh, oh, oh, oh, oh
Alright, alright, alright
Alright
Alright

he shared their desire for social change, he believed that the only worthwhile revolution would come about through inner change rather than revolutionary violence. However, he was never absolutely sure of his position, hedging his bets on the slow version of the song on the album. After admitting that destruction can come with revolution, he sang "you can count me out/in", obviously unsure of which side of the debate to come down on. On the fast version, recorded six weeks later and released as the B-side of 'Hey Jude', he omitted "in". Of this Yoko said, "His spirit was in, but his body was out."

The omission provoked much hand-wringing in the underground press. The American magazine *Ramparts* called it a "betrayal" and the *New Left Review*: "a lamentable petty bourgeois cry of fear". *Time* devoted a whole article to the song saying that it "criticized radical activists the world over".

The nature of John's dilemma was revealed in an exchange of letters published in a Keele University magazine. In an open letter, student John Hoyland said of 'Revolution': "That record was no more revolutionary than *Mrs Dale's Diary* [a BBC radio soap]. In order to change the world, we've got to understand what's wrong with the world. And then – destroy it. Ruthlessly. This is not cruelty or madness. It is one of the most passionate forms of love. Because what we're fighting is suffering, oppression, humiliation – the immense toll of unhappiness caused by capitalism. And any 'love' which does not pit itself against these things is sloppy and irrelevant. There is no such thing as a polite revolution."

In his reply, John wrote: "I don't remember saying that 'Revolution' was revolutionary. Fuck Mrs Dale. Listen to all three versions of Revolution – 1, 2 and 9 and then try again, dear John [Hoyland]. You say 'in order to change the world, we've got to understand what's wrong with the world and then destroy it. Ruthlessly'. You're obviously on a destruction kick. I'll tell you what's wrong with it – people. So, do you want to destroy them? Ruthlessly? Until you/we change your/our heads – there's no chance. Tell me one successful revolution. Who fucked up communism, Christianity, capitalism, Buddhism etc? Sick heads, and nothing else. Do you think all the enemy wear capitalist badges so that you can shoot them? It's a bit naive, John. You seem to think it's just a class war."

Interviewed later by journalists from the same magazine, John (Lennon) said: "All I'm saying is I think you should do it by changing people's heads, and they're saying we should smash the system. Now the system-smashing scene has been going on forever. What's it done? The Irish did it, the Russians did it and the French did it and where has it got them? It's got them nowhere. It's the same old game. Who's going

to run this smashing up? Who's going to take over? It'll be the biggest smashers. They'll be the ones to get in first and, like in Russia, they'll be the ones to take over. I don't know what the answer is but I think it's down to people."

It was a position John was to hold to. In 1980, he said that 'Revolution' still stood as an expression of his politics. "Count me out if it's for violence. Don't expect me on the barricades unless it's with flowers."

The single version of the track was much faster than the version on *The Beatles*. John was becoming attracted to the idea of songs used in the cause of propaganda and also songs that were like newspaper reports of his own life and thinking. This would come to fruition with his work with the Plastic Ono Band and his album recorded with Elephant's Memory, *Some Time In New York*.

Significant to the background of this song was the so-called Cultural Revolution taking place in China. Starting in September 1965 Chairman Mao (Mao Tse Tung) fired up young people to go back to the basics of Chinese Communism and resist the changes being talked about by liberals. The revolution is reckoned to have been complete by October 1968.

Some Western political radicals – particularly those who opposed the war in Vietnam – were appreciative of Mao's uncompromising stance and would wear the caps of the Red Guard in a show of solidarity.

The words of the single were the same as the album track with the exception of not singing the word "in" after "count me out", dropping the "shooby doo wah" backing vocals on the chorus and saying "we all want to change your head" rather than "we'd all love to change your head".

Speaking to Tariq Ali in 1971 John said: "On the version released as a single I said, 'when you talk about destruction you can count me out.' I didn't want to get killed. I didn't really know that much about the Maoists, but I just knew that they seemed to be so few [in the West] and yet they painted themselves green and stood in front of the police waiting to get picked off.

"I just thought it was unsubtle, you now. I thought the original Communist revolutionaries coordinated themselves a bit better and didn't go around shouting about it. That was how I felt. I was really asking a question."

The single version was released as the B-side of Paul's 'Hey Jude.'

HONEY PIE

'Honey Pie' was a tribute to Jim McCartney from his son. "My dad's always played fruity old songs like this, and I like them," Paul said. "I would have liked to have been a writer in the Twenties because I like the top hat and tails thing."

Paul's inspirations were music hall, the music he'd heard growing up on TV shows like *The Billy Cotton Band Show* and songs like 'Cheek to Cheek' by Fred Astaire. "I very much liked the old crooner style, so 'Honey Pie' was me writing one of them to an imaginary woman, across the ocean, on the silver screen, who was called Honey Pie. It's another of my fantasy songs. We put a sound on my voice to make it sound like a scratchy old record. So it's not a parody, it's a nod to the vaudeville tradition that I was raised on."

HONEY PIE

She was a working girl
North of England way
Now she's hit the big time
In the USA
And if she could only hear me
This is what I'd say

Honey pie you are making me crazy
I'm in love but I'm lazy
So won't you please come home

Oh honey pie my position is tragic
Come and show me the magic
Of your Hollywood song

You became a legend of the silver screen
And now the thought of meeting you
Makes me weak in the knee

Oh honey pie you are driving me frantic
Sail across the Atlantic
To be where you belong

Honey pie come back to me, oh

Yeah
I like it like that, oh ah
I like this kind of hot kind of music
Hot kind of music
Play it to me honey, we're blue

Will the wind that blew her boat
Across the sea
Kindly send her sailing back to me

Now honey pie you are making me crazy
I'm in love but I'm lazy
So won't you please come home
Come, come back to me, honey pie

Ooooooooooooh oh
Oh oh oh oh oh oh oh
Honey pie, honey pie

Just as he believed 'Helter Skelter' was written for him personally, Charles Manson found further instructions in 'Honey Pie'. After all, it was addressed to people in the USA, inviting them to display the magic of their 'Hollywood song'? Manson lived near Los Angeles. What could be clearer?

Written: Lennon/McCartney

Length: 2'41"

UK Release: *The Beatles* album, November 22, 1968

US Release: *The Beatles* album, November 25, 1968

SAVOY TRUFFLE

George had been friendly with Eric Clapton since meeting him in April 1966 and 'Savoy Truffle' was a playful song by him about Clapton's love of chocolate. This habit contributed to tooth decay and George was warning him that one more soft-centred chocolate and he'd have to have his teeth pulled out.

The song's lyric is made up of the exotic names then given to individual chocolates in Mackintosh's Good News assortment such as Crème Tangerine, Montelimart, Ginger Sling and Coffee Dessert. Savoy Truffle was another authentic name, whereas Cherry Cream and Coconut Fudge were invented to fit the song.

Derek Taylor helped with the middle eight by suggesting the title of a semi-documentary film about the San Francisco hippie scene that had just been released called *You Are What You Eat*. It had been made by two American friends, Alan Pariser and Barry Feinstein. The phrase didn't scan properly, so George changed it to "you know that what you eat you are".

LEFT: The names of the chocolates in the Mackintosh's Good News selection filled George's song 'Savoy Truffle'.

SAVOY TRUFFLE

Crème Tangerine and Montelimart
A Ginger Sling with a pineapple heart
A Coffee Dessert, yes, you know it's
   Good News
But you'll have to have them all pulled out
After the Savoy Truffle

Cool cherry cream, nice apple tart
I feel your taste all the time we're apart
Coconut fudge really blows down
   those blues
But you'll have to have them all pulled out
After the Savoy Truffle

You might not feel it now
But when the pain cuts through
You're gonna know and how
The sweat is going to fill your head
When it becomes too much
You'll shout aloud
But you'll have to have them all pulled out
After the Savoy Truffle.

You know that what you eat you are
But what is sweet now, turns so sour
We all know Ob-La-Di-Bla-Da
But can you show me, where you are?

Crème Tangerine and Montelimart
A Ginger Sling with a pineapple heart
A Coffee Dessert, yes, you know it's
   Good News
But you'll have to have them all pulled out
After the Savoy Truffle
Yes you'll have to have them all pulled out
After the Savoy Truffle

Written: Harrison

Length: 2'54"

UK Release: *The Beatles* album, November 22, 1968

US Release: *The Beatles* album, November 25, 1968

CRY
BABY
CRY

Cry baby cry, make your mother sigh
She's old enough to know better
The King of Marigold was in the kitchen
Cooking breakfast for the queen
The queen was in the parlour
Playing piano for the children of the king
Cry baby cry, make your mother sigh
She's old enough to know better
So cry baby cry

The king was in the garden
Picking flowers for a friend who
  came to play
The queen was in the playroom

Painting pictures for the
  children's holiday
Cry baby cry, make your mother sigh
She's old enough to know better
So cry baby cry

The Duchess of Kirkaldy always smiling
And arriving late for tea
The duke was having problems
With a message at the local bird and bee
Cry baby cry, make your mother sigh
She's old enough to know better
So cry baby cry

At twelve o'clock a meeting round
  the table
For a séance in the dark
With voices out of nowhere
Put on specially by the children for a lark
Cry baby cry, make your mother sigh
She's old enough to know better
So cry baby cry cry cry
Cry baby, make your mother sigh
She's old enough to know better
Cry baby cry
Cry cry cry, make your mother sigh
She's old enough to know better
So cry baby cry

Can you take me back where I came
  from, can you take me back?
Can you take me back where I came
  from, brother can you take me back
Can you take me back home?
Can you take me back where I came
  from, can you take me back?

CRY BABY CRY

In 1968, as Hunter Davies was finishing his biography of the Beatles, John told him: "I've got another (song) here, a few words, I think I got them from an advert – 'Cry baby cry, make your mother buy'. I've been playing it over on the piano. I've let it go now. It'll come back if I really want it."

The lines came back to him while he was in India, where Donovan remembered him working on it. "I think the eventual imagery was suggested by my own songs of fairy tales. We had become very close in exchanging musical vibes."

Partly based on the nursery rhyme 'Sing A Song Of Sixpence' and, via the advert, partly on the playground taunt 'Cry, baby, cry/ Stick a finger in your eye/ And tell your mother it wasn't I' (and other variations), the song includes John's own creations the Duchess of Kirkaldy and the King of Marigold. Kirkaldy is in Fife, Scotland, and the Beatles played there at the Carlton Theatre on October 5, 1963, just as Beatlemania was breaking.

On the recording the song is followed by a ditty from Paul known as 'Can You Take Me Back', which isn't listed as a track. It came out of a jam session on September 16 after recording 'I Will', which also produced the seeds of his song for Cilla Black, 'Step Inside Love'. The full-length version goes on for almost two minutes with a series of improvised lines. The version on the record lasts for only 28 seconds and is used as a soft intro to 'Revolution Number 9'.

Cynthia can recall being in the house as John was finishing it up with Paul. "They were both doing it in our lounge," she says. Julian was standing her whistling to them." Oddly enough, when asked about the song by David Sheff for the 1980 *Playboy* interview John said, "Not me. A piece of rubbish."

Written: Lennon/McCartney

Length: 3'01"

UK Release: *The Beatles* album, November 22, 1968

US Release: *The Beatles* album, November 25, 1968

266

THE BEATLES

REVOLUTION 9

'Revolution 9' was neither a Lennon and McCartney song nor a Beatles' recording but an 8 minute and 15 second-long amalgamation of taped sounds that John and Yoko mixed together.

The album track of 'Revolution' originally clocked in at over 10 minutes; more than half of it consisting of John and Yoko screaming and moaning over a range of discordant sounds, created to simulate the rumblings of a revolution. Subsequently, they decided to extract the chaotic section and use it as the basis of another track, which turned into 'Revolution 9'.

At this point, home-made tapes of crowd disturbances were brought in and other sound effects were found in EMI's library. Due to the lack of sophisticated multi-track recording, all three Abbey Road studios had to be commandeered, with machines being specially linked together and tape loops held in place with pencils. John operated the faders to create a live mix.

With so many overlapping sounds, it is almost impossible to identify all the individual noises and spoken comments. Mark Lewisohn, who studied the original four-track recording, divided these into: a choir; backwards violins; a backwards symphony; an orchestral overdub from 'A Day In The Life'; banging glasses; applause; opera; backwards mellotron; humming; spoken phrases by John and George, and a cassette tape of Yoko and John screaming the word "right" from 'Revolution'.

The most memorable tape, which supplied part of the title, was the sonorous voice intoning "Number Nine, Number Nine". This was apparently discovered on a library tape, which may have formed part of a taped examination question for students of the Royal Academy of Music.

Once again, Charles Manson thought that John was speaking personally to him through the hubbub, taking the number nine as a reference to *Revelation* chapter 9 with its vision of the coming apocalypse. Manson thought John was shouting "rise", rather than "right", and interpreted it as an incitement to the black community to rise against the white middle class. "Rise" became one of Manson's key phrases and was found painted in blood at one of the murder scenes.

Paul was in America when 'Revolution 9' was put together and was disappointed at its inclusion on *The Beatles*, particularly as he had been making sound collages at home since 1966 and realized that John would now be seen as the innovator in this area.

REVOLUTION 9

Written: Lennon/McCartney

Length: 8'22"

UK Release: *The Beatles* album, November 22, 1968

US Release: *The Beatles* album, November 25, 1968

(Bottle of Claret for you if I had realised

Well, do it next time.

I forgot about it, George, I'm sorry.
Will you forgive me?

Yes.)

Number 9, number 9, number 9,
number 9, number 9, number 9,
number 9, number 9, number 9,
number 9, number 9, number 9,
number 9, number 9, number

Then there's this Welsh Rarebit wearing
  some brown underpants
About the shortage of grain in
  Hertfordshire
Everyone of them knew that as time
  went by they'd get a little bit older and
  a little bit slower but it's all the same
  thing, in this case manufactured by
  someone who's always
Umpteen your father's giving it diddly-i-
  dee
District was leaving, intending to pay for

Number 9, number 9

Who's to know?
Who wants to know?

Number 9, number 9, number 9,
number 9, number 9, number 9, number 9

I sustained nothing worse than
Also for example
Whatever you're doing
A business deal falls through
I informed him on the third night
  but fortunately

Number 9, number 9, number 9

People ride, people ride
Right! Right! Right!
Right! Right!
Riiight! Riiight!

9, number 9
I've missed all of that

It makes me a few days late
Compared with, like, wow!
And weird stuff like that
Taking our sides sometimes
Floral bark
Rouge doctors have brought this
specimen

I have nobody's daughter, aha

9, number 9

With the situation

They are standing still

The plan, the telegram

Ooh ooh

Number 9, number

Ooh

A man without terrors from beard to
  false as the headmaster reported to me
My son he really can try as they do to
  find function
Tell what he was saying, and his voice
  was low and his hive high
And his eyes were low

Alright!

Number 9, number 9, number 9,
number 9, number 9, number 9,
number 9, number 9, number 9,
number 9, number 9

So the wife called and we better go to
  see a surgeon
Or whatever to price it yellow
  underclothes
So, any road, we went to see the dentist
  instead
Who gave her a pair of teeth which
  wasn't any good at all
So instead of that, joined the bloody
  navy and went to sea

In my broken chair, my wings are broken
  and so is my hair

I'm not in the mood for wearing

Um da
Aaah

How?
Dogs are for dogging, cats are for
  catting
Birds for birding and fish for fishing
Lems are for lemming, men are for
women

Only to find the night-watchman
Unaware of his presence in the
  building

Onion soup

Number 9, number 9, number 9,
number 9, number 9, number 9

Industrial output
Financial imbalance

Thrusting it between his shoulder
  blades

The Watusi
The twist

Eldorado

Take this brother, may it serve you
  well

Maybe it's not that, it's
Ahh
Maybe even then exposure is
  something
– a difficult thing
I'll be alright. I'll be alright.

Exposure
It's almost like being naked
I'll be alright. I'll be alright. I'll be
  alright.

If, you become naked.

REVOLUTION
9

GOOD NIGHT

Now it's time to say good night
Good night, sleep tight
Now the sun turns out his light
Good night, sleep tight
Dream sweet dreams for me
(Dream sweet)
Dream sweet dreams for you

Close your eyes and I'll close mine
Good night, sleep tight
Now the moon begins to shine
Good night, sleep tight
Dream sweet dreams for me
(Dream sweet)
Dream sweet dreams for you

Mmmmmm
Mmmmmm
Mmmmmmmmmm

Close your eyes and I'll close mine
Good night, sleep tight
Now the sun turns out his light
Good night, sleep tight
Dream sweet dreams for me
(Dream sweet)
Dream sweet dreams for you

Good night everybody
Everybody everywhere
Good night

Written: Lennon/McCartney

Length: 3'11"

UK Release: *The Beatles* album, November 22, 1968

US Release: *The Beatles* album, November 25, 1968

GOOD NIGHT

'Good Night' is certainly the most schmaltzy song ever written by John. If it had been one of Paul's songs, he would probably have dismissed it as "garbage", but his final comment was only that it was possibly "over-lush". It was given to Ringo to sing, in Paul's view, because John thought it might not be good for his image to be the vocalist.

It was written for Julian as a bedtime song just as, 12 years later, he would write 'Beautiful Boy' for his second son Sean. The melody appears to have been "inspired" by Cole Porter's 'True Love' (1956) a song from the musical *High Society* which became a hit for Bing Crosby and Grace Kelly. The Beatles included 'True Love' in their Hamburg set. "John rarely showed his tender side, but my key memories of John are when he was tender. That's what has remained with me – the moments where he showed himself to be a very generous, loving person. I always cite 'Good Night' as an example of the John beneath the surface that we only saw occasionally," suggests Paul.

Julian wasn't aware that John had written the song for him until he was interviewed for this book. This was probably due to the fact that his parents split up within a few weeks of its composition.

ABOVE: Perhaps aware that he was about to leave his family, John wrote the lullaby 'Good Night' for Julian.

11 Let It Be

The recording of *Let It Be* preceded *Abbey Road* but its release came after, making it the final album of their career. Most often thought of as the soundtrack to the film of the same name, it was originally planned as a live album called *Get Back*, to be recorded in an unusual location (a Roman ampitheatre in Tunisia, the deck of the *QE2* and the Roundhouse in London were mentioned) and have a film made of the concert and the preparations. However, disagreements over where and whether to play on stage meant that the project disintegrated. What remained was an 80-minute colour documentary of the group rehearsing at Twickenham Film Studios, recording in the studio and playing live on the roof of the Apple office in London.

The filming was completed in January 1969 but the film wasn't released until May 1970. At this time the album and a 160-page book titled *The Beatles Get Back* (with photos by Ethan Russell and text by *Rolling Stone* writers Jonathan Cott and David Dalton) was packaged as a box set. The title of the book and the fact that the publishing date on he content page is given as 1969 is evidence of the failed ambitions and delays involved in the project. The album wasn't available separately until November 1970.

Intended to be a record of a group at the height of its powers the film instead became a drama about a group finally falling apart. To get them in the mood during the filming, they played over 400 favourite songs recorded by other artists. There were also early versions of all but four of the songs that would be included on *Abbey Road* and songs that John, Paul and George would later use on their solo albums.

The artists whose songs they covered were almost exactly the same as they had been in 1962 with the one exception that the artist with the most songs covered was now Bob Dylan. Beneath him, in descending order, were Chuck Berry, Elvis, Buddy Holly, Ray Charles, Little Richard, Lonnie Donegan, Carl Perkins, Johnny Cash, The Everly Brothers, Bo Diddley and Gene Vincent. To get the album finished, Paul assumed control, pushing and prodding where necessary, while John and George sulked, openly displaying their resentment.

Rows over the album then contributed to the group's final break-up.

Let

Because it was the soundtrack of what was essentially a live performance either in a film studio, a recording studio or on the roof of Apple, and wasn't expected to require extensive mixing or overdubbing, they only employed an engineer, Glyn Johns, making it their first album without George Martin at the helm. In June 1969 John was quoted as saying the album would be ready for release in July and would be called *Get Back, Don't Let Me Down And 12 Other Songs*. In July it was said that the release had been delayed until September. In September, the time when *Abbey Road* was released, the delay was extended to December.

When Allen Klein came in to manage their business affairs he wasn't happy with the versions of the album offered by Johns from mixes made at Olympic Studios and so in March 1970 he brought in Phil Spector to give it some polish. When Paul heard the strings that Spector had added to 'The Long And Winding Road', he requested that it be restored to its original form. When his request was ignored, Paul announced his departure from the Beatles.

By the time *Let It Be* was released, the Beatles were no more and the title sounded like an appropriate valediction. Paul had already released his first solo album (*McCartney* – April 17, 1970) although the union wasn't officially dissolved until the end of the year following Paul's lawsuit. *Let It Be* reached the top of the British and American album charts after, the advance orders of almost 4 million in the US being the largest for any album ever.

In 2003 a remixed version of the album, *Let It Be…Naked*, was released with an additional disc of musical and conversational outtakes from the filmed sessions. The running order was completely altered, two tracks were left off ('Maggie Mae' and 'Dig It') and one was added ('Don't Let Me Down'). The goal was to restore it to the way it was originally intended to be heard before Klein and Spector got involved. Said Paul. "It's just the bare tapes; just the bare truth and the great thing now about the re-mixed versions is that, with today's technology, they sound better than ever."

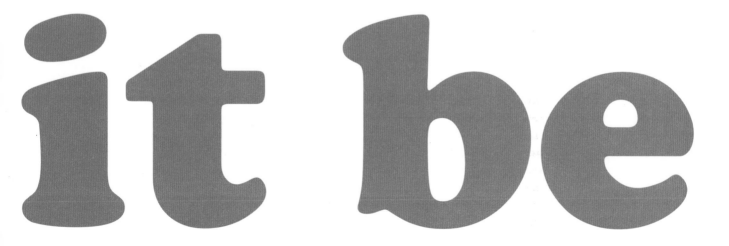

TWO OF US

[I Dig A Pygmy by Charles
Hawtree and the Deaf Aids.
Phase one, in which Doris gets
  her oats.]

Two of us riding nowhere
Spending someone's
Hard earned pay
You and me Sunday driving
Not arriving
On our way back home
We're on our way home
We're on our way home
We're going home

Two of us sending postcards
Writing letters
On my wall
You and me burning matches
Lifting latches
On our way back home
We're on our way home
We're on our way home
We're going home

You and I have memories
Longer than the road that
  stretches out ahead

Two of us wearing raincoats
Standing so low
In the sun
You and me chasing paper
Getting nowhere
On our way back home
We're on our way home
We're on our way home
We're going home

You and I have memories
Longer than the road that
  stretches out ahead

Two of us wearing raincoats
Standing solo
In the sun
You and me chasing paper
Getting nowhere
On our way back home
We're on our way home
We're on our way home
We're going home

[We're going home, you better believe
  it. Goodbye.]

TWO OF US

Performed in the film by John and Paul on acoustic guitars, with George playing electric bass, 'Two Of Us' sounds like a song about their Liverpool teenage years together – burning matches, lifting latches and going home to Paul's house to write songs. But the "two of us" in question were not Paul and John but Paul and Linda. To Paul one of the most attractive things about his new girlfriend was her lack of pretension and her down-to-earth approach to life. In a world where he was hemmed in by work schedules, public expectations and contractual obligations, he relished being with someone who seemed consistently laid-back; someone with whom he could temporarily forget he was a Beatle.

Soon after they met in London during the autumn of 1968, Linda introduced Paul to the joyous wonder of getting completely lost. She would drive him out of the city with no destination in mind and with the sole intention of ending up miles from anywhere. To a Beatle, who was constantly told where and when he was needed, this was an exhilarating return to freedom. "As a kid I loved getting lost," explained Linda. "I would say to my father – 'Let's get lost.' But you could never seem to be able to get really lost. All signs would eventually lead back to New York or wherever we were staying! Then, when I moved to England to be with Paul, we would put the dog Martha in the back of the car and drive out of London. As soon as we were on the open road, I'd say 'Let's get lost' and we'd keep driving without looking at any signs. Hence the line in the song 'two of us riding nowhere'.

"Paul wrote 'Two Of Us' on one of those days out. It's about us. We just pulled off in a wood somewhere and parked the car. I went off walking while Paul sat in the car and started writing. He also mentions the postcards because we used to send a lot of postcards to each other."

Written: Lennon/McCartney

Length: 3'54"

UK Release: *Let It Be* album, May 8, 1970

US Release: *Let It Be* album, May 18, 1970

ABOVE: John and Yoko, seen here with David Bowie, were engrossed in each others' lives at the time of *Let It Be*. Yoko was present at most of the sessions, and John's songs were directly or indirectly about her.

ABOVE LEFT: It was Linda Eastman who helped Paul through his "hour of darkness" and introduced him to the simple pleasure of "Sunday driving, not arriving," as he put it in 'Two Of Us'.

DIG A PONY

I dig a pony
Well you can celebrate anything you want
Yes you can celebrate anything you want
Oh!
I do a road hog
Well you can penetrate any place you go
Yes you can penetrate any place you go
I told you so
All I want is you
Everything has got to be just like you
  want it to because
I pick a moon dog
Well you can radiate everything you are
Yes you can radiate everything you are
Oh now
I roll a stoney
Well you can imitate everyone you know
Yes you can imitate everyone you know
I told you so
All I want is you
Everything has got to be just like you
  want it to
Because...

Ooh now
I feel the wind blow
Well you can indicate everything you see
Yes you can indicate anything you see
Oh now
I, load a lorry
Well you can syndicate any boat you row
Yeah you can syndicate any boat you row
I told you so,
All I want is you
Everything has got to be just like you
  want it to
Because...

DIG A PONY

'Dig A Pony' was largely composed in the studio and the words make very little sense. At one point it was called 'Con A Lowry' (possibly a reference to the Lowry organ used in the studio), but John changed it to 'Dig A Pony', "because 'I con a Lowry' didn't sing well ... It's got to be d's and p's, you know."

Similarly, the line "I do a road hog" started as "I dig a skylight" and then became "I did a groundhog." "It had to be rougher," John argued. "I don't care if skylight was prettier." The chorus was taken from a separate song of John's written about Yoko called 'All I Want Is You'. The original track-listing for the album used this as its title.

In January 1969 when the song was recorded, John explained, "I just make it up as I go along". In 1972 he expanded on this to say; "I was just having fun with words. It was literally a nonsense song. You just take words and you stick them together, and you see if they have any meaning. Some of them do, some of them don't." In September 1980, he laconically concluded, "(just) another piece of garbage."

Written: Lennon/McCartney

Length: 3'54"

UK Release: *Let It Be* album,
May 8, 1970

US Release: *Let It Be* album,
May 18, 1970

Words are flowing out like endless rain
  into a paper cup
They slither wildly as they slip away
  across the universe
Pools of sorrow, waves of joy are
  drifting through my opened mind
Possessing and caressing me
Jai Guru Deva OM

Nothing's gonna change my world
Nothing's gonna change my world
Nothing's gonna change my world
Nothing's gonna change my world

Images of broken light which dance
  before me like a million eyes
They call me on and on
  across the universe
Thoughts meander like a restless wind
  inside a letter box
They tumble blindly as they make their
  way across the universe
Jai Guru Deva OM

Nothing's gonna change my world
Nothing's gonna change my world
Nothing's gonna change my world
Nothing's gonna change my world

Sounds of laughter, shades of life are
  ringing through my opened ears
Inciting and inviting me
Limitless undying love which shines
  around me like a million suns
And calls me on and on, across the
universe
Jai Guru Deva OM

Nothing's gonna change my world
Nothing's gonna change my world
Nothing's gonna change my world
Nothing's gonna change my world

Jai Guru Deva
Jai Guru Deva
Jai Guru Deva
Jai Guru Deva
Jai Guru Deva

ACROSS
THE
UNIVERSE

ACROSS THE UNIVERSE

The oldest song on the *Let It Be* album, 'Across The Universe' was recorded in February 1968 and first featured on *No One's Gonna Change Our World*, a charity album put together by Spike Milligan for the World Wildlife Fund and released in December 1969.

It is a song about composing, or at least about the mysteries of the creative process, and John frequently referred to it as one of his favourite Beatles' songs because the lyric was so inspired. The words had come to him at Kenwood. He had been arguing in bed with Cynthia and, as he tried to sleep, the phrase "pools of sorrow, waves of joy" came to him and wouldn't leave until he got up and started writing.

"It drove me out of bed," John said. "I didn't want to write it. I was just slightly irritable and I couldn't go to sleep. She must have been going on and on about something and she'd gone to sleep and I kept hearing these words over and over, flowing like an endless stream. I went downstairs and it turned into a sort of cosmic song rather than an irritated song. I've looked at it and said, 'Can I write another one with this meter?' It's so interesting. 'Words are flowing out like endless rain into a paper cup/ They slither wildly as they slip away across the universe.' Such an extraordinary meter and I can never repeat it! It's not a matter of craftsmanship – it wrote itself. It's like being possessed; like a psychic or a medium. You have to… make it into something, and then you're allowed to sleep. That's always in the middle of the night when you're half-awake or tired and your critical facilities are switched off."

Written after having met the Maharishi Mahesh Yogi in England but before studying with him in India, the chorus mentions Guru Dev, who was Maharishi's guru. John wanted this to be a single to be released while they were in Rishikesh but 'Lady Madonna' was chosen instead.

Although 'Across The Universe' remained one of his favourite Beatles' songs, he was unhappy with both the original recording (which was why he allowed it to be used on the WWF album) and the way in which Phil Spector had slowed down the tape in April 1970 and added an orchestra and choir for the version included on *Let It Be*. "The guitars are out of tune and I'm singing out of tune," he said in 1980. "The song was never done properly."

Written: Lennon/McCartney

Length: 3'48"

UK Release: *Let It Be* album, May 8, 1970

US Release: *Let It Be* album, May 18, 1970

I ME MINE

As George became more deeply involved in Hindu philosophy, he felt the need to reconcile his position as a rock star with the religious demands of attaining enlightenment by relinquishing the ego. The demands of being a Beatle were not conducive to the ascetic life.

He believed that our preoccupation with our individuality and personal desire – what "I" want, what belongs to "me", what's "mine" – is what prevents us from achieving a higher level of consciousness. "There is nothing that isn't part of the complete whole," he said. "When the little 'i' merges into the big 'I', then you are really smiling!"

He was no doubt influenced by the words of Krishna as recorded in the *Bhagavad Gita* (2.72): "They are forever free who renounce all selfish desires and break away from the ego cage of 'I,' 'Me,' 'Mine' to be united with the Lord. This is the supreme state."

George said that he was being driven "crackers" by his ego at the time. "I hated everything about my ego. It was a flash of everything false and impermanent. Later, I learned from it. I learned to realize that there is somebody else in here apart from old blabbermouth. 'Who am I?' became the order of the day. Anyway, that's what came out of it – 'I Me Mine'. It's about the ego, the eternal problem."

The waltz-time tune was inspired by background music he'd heard the night before on a BBC 2 documentary called *Europa: The Titled and the Unentitled*. The music, played by the Vienna Philharmonic Orchestra conducted by Willi Boskovsky was 'Kaiser Walzer' ('Emperor Waltz') composed by Johan Strauss II in 1889. The extract used was only 60-seconds long and the music for 'I Me Mine' was based on what George remembered of it.

Written: Harrison

Length: 2'25"

UK Release: *Let It Be* album,
May 8, 1970

US Release: *Let It Be* album,
May 18, 1970

All through the day
I Me Mine, I Me Mine, I Me Mine
All through the night
I Me Mine, I Me Mine, I Me Mine
Now they're frightened of leaving it
Everyone's weaving it
Coming on strong all the time
All through the day
I Me Mine

All I can hear
I Me Mine, I Me Mine, I Me Mine
Even those tears
I Me Mine, I Me Mine, I Me Mine
No-one's frightened of playing it
Everyone's saying it
Flowing more freely than wine
All through the day
I Me Mine

All I can hear
I Me Mine, I Me Mine, I Me Mine
Even those tears
I Me Mine, I Me Mine, I Me Mine
No-one's frightened of playing it
Everyone's saying it
Flowing more freely than wine
All through your life
I Me Mine

LET IT BE

LEFT: Following his time of devotion to Maharishi Mahesh Yogi, George switched his attention to the Krishna Consciousness movement, helping the organization financially and recording their chant for a single on the Apple label.

DIG IT

This is a 49-second extract from a jam that lasted for over 13 minutes. It had started with the group playing Dylan's 'Like A Rolling Stone' and had then drifted into improvisation. The idea of calling out random names and responding to them by shouting things like "Get off", "Yes", "Can you dig it?", or "Come on" had been around for a few days. In one long version they called out over 50 names, ranging from James Brown and Cassius Clay to old Liverpool friends like Jeff Mohammed, Tony Carricker, Eric Griffiths and Ivan Vaughn. The verb "to dig" was a hipster term loosely meaning "to understand, appreciate, enjoy."

When they recorded, a lot of time was spent hanging around reading newspapers, which might account for the references to the FBI and CIA. Transcripts of studio conversations reveal George talking about blues guitarist B B King and distinguishing him from fellow blues man Freddie King. Matt Busby was the heroic manager of Manchester United, one of England's most popular and successful football teams. Busby would have been in the news because he had recently announced his retirement after 24 years with the club.

Although the song was what John would term a "throwaway", it embraced the thought that the Beatles had been developing since 1965 of appreciating everything with an enlightened consciousness. Everything was to be dug! John was familiar with the writing of Alan Watts, who in 1960 published his book *This Is It*, which put forward the argument that "the immediate, everyday, and present experience" was "the entire and ultimate point for the existence of a universe." He said that to an enlightened individual "it appears as a vivid and overwhelming certainty that the universe, precisely as it is at this moment, as a whole and in every one of its parts, is so completely right as to need no explanation or justification beyond what simply is."

While at art school in Liverpool, John had read the Beat literature anthology *Protest* (1959), edited by Gene Feldman and Max Gartenberg. In the preface to one of two extracts from the work of Jack Kerouac the authors wrote; "It was Kerouac who named his generation 'beat'. In two novels, *The Town And The City* and *On The Road*, he gave it also its Creed – DIG EVERYTHING."

Like a rolling stone
Like a rolling stone
Like a rolling stone
Like the FBI and the CIA
And the BBC, BB King
And Doris Day
Matt Busby
Dig it, dig it, dig it
Dig it, dig it, dig it, dig it, dig it, dig it,
  dig it, dig it

[That was 'Can You Dig It' by Georgie Wood. And now we'd like to do 'Hark The Angels Come']

Written: Harisson/Lennon/McCartney/Starr

Length: 0'50"

UK Release: *Let It Be* album, May 8, 1970

US Release: *Let It Be* album, May 18, 1970

LET IT BE

'Let It Be' sounded as if it had been written as the Beatles' swansong but when it was recorded, in January 1969, no-one had any idea that the end was near. John later said it was an attempt to emulate 'Bridge Over Troubled Water', but this couldn't be so because the Simon and Garfunkel single wasn't released until January 1970.

Paul had written 'Let It Be' out of his general feelings of despair as the Beatles began to unravel. John preferred spending time with Yoko, whose presence at the studio was not welcomed by everyone. George was discouraged by the way his songs were rarely given serious consideration by John or Paul and had threatened to leave. Even Ringo had taken off for a short holiday during the recording of *The White Album* when the atmosphere got really bad.

Paul had put himself in the driving seat because he felt that without organization and discipline nothing of value would be achieved. "I think we've been very negative since Mr. Epstein passed away," Paul says in the film. "We haven't been positive. That's why all of us in turn have been sick of the group. There's nothing positive in it. It's a bit of a drag. The only way for it not to be a bit of a drag is for the four of us to think – should we make it positive or should we forget it?"

Although the role was necessary, it didn't make Paul popular. The others began to resent being told what to do. 'Let It Be' was written as a response to these pressures: "I wrote it when all those business problems started to get me down," he said. "I really was passing through my 'hour of darkness' and writing the song was my way of exorcizing the ghosts." Written in the style of a modern hymn, the religious feeling was heightened by Billy Preston's gospel chords and the mention of "Mother Mary", which appeared to reference the Virgin Mary but in this case alluded to Paul's mother, Mary McCartney, who he was imagining as offering support from beyond the grave. At one point, John suggested changing it to Brother Malcolm in honour of Mal Evans.

"I used to lie in bed and wonder what was going on and feel quite paranoid," he said. "I had a dream one night about my mother. She had died when I was 14, so I hadn't heard from her in quite a while and it was very good. It gave me some strength. In my darkest hour, mother Mary had come to me." In the dream she had told him that everything would be all right.

Paul later said that he was aware that it had become a "quasi-religious thing" although that hadn't been his intention. The chorus not only shares an affinity with the Virgin Mary's words of submission to God's will as quoted in *Luke* 1v38, but also the words of Buddha when he advocates relinquishment of possessions. At the January 26 session, John declared, "Country & Gospel it is. C&G."

LET IT BE

Written: Lennon/McCartney
Length: 4'03"
UK Release: March 6, 1970
UK Chart Position: 2
US Release: March 11, 1970
US Chart Position: 1

When I find myself in times of trouble
Mother Mary comes to me
Speaking words of wisdom, let it be
And in my hour of darkness
She is standing right in front of me
Speaking words of wisdom, let it be
Let it be, let it be
Let it be, let it be
Whisper words of wisdom, let it be

And when the broken-hearted people
Living in the world agree
There will be an answer, let it be
For though they may be parted
There is still a chance that they will see
There will be an answer, let it be
Let it be, let it be
Let it be, let it be
Yeah, there will be an answer, let it be

Let it be, let it be
Let it be, let it be
Whisper words of wisdom, let it be

Let it be, let it be
Ah, let it be, yeah, let it be
Whisper words of wisdom, let it be

And when the night is cloudy
There is still a light that shines on me
Shine until tomorrow, let it be
I wake up to the sound of music,
Mother Mary comes to me
Speaking words of wisdom, let it be
Let it be, let it be
Let it be, yeah, let it be
Oh, there will be an answer, let it be
Let it be, let it be
Let it be, yeah, let it be
There will be an answer, let it be
Let it be, let it be,
Let it be, yeah, let it be
Whisper words of wisdom, let it be

The arrival of Yoko Ono in 1968 turned John's attention away from the Beatles and played a part in the ending of the Lennon-McCartney songwriting partnership.

MAGGIE MAE

MAGGIE MAE

'Maggie Mae' (usually spelt 'Maggie May') was one of those songs the Beatles played when reminiscing. It had warm associations both with their home city and with their own musical roots. Ringo played on it in 1957 when he was part of the Eddie Clayton Skiffle Group and the same year John sang it with the Quarry Men at the church fête where he met Paul for the first time.

Its roots are in the early nineteenth century and there have been many versions with many additional verses. The central story is that Maggie May is a Liverpool prostitute charged with robbing a client of his wages as a merchant seaman. As punishment she is sent to an Australian penal colony. (The story is truncated on *Let It Be* because it halts abruptly at the start of the second verse.)

John may well have learned it from his mother Julia. Michael Fishwick, who lodged at 251 Menlove Avenue as a young student, recalls the following incident: "Julia was very vivacious. She was an in-your-face type of person, very extrovert. I remember she came over one day in 1957 and John was there. She gave us an unexpurgated version of 'Maggie May' that she had probably learned from Freddy [Lennon] or from her father. She even had to translate some of the Liverpuddlian for me."

Although included on *Let It Be* as a spot of light relief it nevertheless contains elements of songwriting that the Beatles would incorporate into their future work. It was about a Liverpool girl – as were 'Eleanor Rigby' and 'Polythene Pam' – and in the longer versions included references to actual places (Lime Street, Canning Place, Park Lane) as 'Strawberry Fields Forever' and 'Penny Lane' would do.

The storytelling approach of the song is extended in Beatles' songs such as 'Rocky Raccoon,' 'Ob-la-di, Ob-la-da,' and 'Maxwell's Silver Hammer' and the sing-along style in 'All Together Now,' 'Yellow Submarine' and 'The Continuing Story of Bungalow Bill.'

Alun Owen, screenwriter of *A Hard Day's Night*, wrote the book for a musical based on the song, which was premiered in 1964 and had songs written by Lionel Bart, who'd made his name with *Oliver!*.

Oh, dirty Maggie May
They have taken her away
And she'll never walk down Lime Street
  any more
Well, the judge he guilty found her
Robbin' a homeward bounder
That dirty no good robbin'
  Maggie May...

'Tis the Port of Liverpool
They returned me to
Two pound ten a week that was my
pay...

Written: Traditional, arranged by Lennon/McCartney/Harrison/Starkey

Length: 0'38"

UK Release: *Let It Be* album, May 8, 1970

US Release: *Let It Be* album, May 18, 1970

I'VE GOT A FEELING

I've got a feeling, a feeling deep inside
Oh yeah, oh yeah, that's right
I've got a feeling, a feeling I can't hide
Oh no no, oh no, oh no
Yeah yeah I've got a feeling yeah

Oh please believe me,
I'd hate to miss the train
Oh yeah, yeah, oh yeah
And if you leave me
I won't be late again
Oh no, oh no, oh no
Yeah yeah I've got a feeling yeah
I've got a feeling

All these years I've been wandering
  around
Wondering how come nobody told me
All that I was looking for was somebody
Who looked like you

I've got a feeling, that keeps me on
  my toes
Oh yeah, oh yeah
I've got a feeling, I think that
  everybody knows
Oh yeah, oh yeah, oh yeah
Yeah yeah I've got a feeling yeah
Yeah

Everybody had a hard year
Everybody had a good time
Everybody had a wet dream
Everybody saw the sunshine
Oh yeah, (oh yeah) oh yeah, oh yeah

Everybody had a good year
Everybody let their hair down
Everybody pulled their socks up
Everybody put their foot down
Oh yeah

Everybody had a good year
(I got a feeling)
Everybody had a hard time
(A feeling deep inside, oh yeah)
Everybody had a wet dream
(Oh yeah)
Everybody saw the sunshine
(I've got a feeling)
Everybody had a good year
(A feeling I can't hide)
Everybody let their hair down
(Oh no)
Everybody pulled their socks up
(Oh, no no no)
Everybody put their foot down
Oh yeah.
I've got a feeling
I've got a feeling
I've got a feeling

[Oh, my soul! It's so hard]

I'VE GOT A FEELING

'I've Got A Feeling' was again two unfinished songs strung together, this time Paul's 'I've Got A Feeling' and John's 'Everybody's Had A Hard Year'. Paul's song, optimistic as ever, was presumably written for Linda to tell her that she was the girl he'd always been looking for. John's song was a litany where each line began with the word "everybody".

John had indeed been through a hard year. His marriage to Cynthia had ended, he was separated from his son Julian, Yoko had suffered a miscarriage, he had been arrested on a charge of drug possession, and he reckoned his personal fortune had dwindled to about £50,000.

During the filming of *Let It Be*, John ran through 'Everybody Had A Hard Year' and said, somewhat tongue in cheek, that it was something he had started writing the night before. If this were true, it would date the song's origin to January 1969, but there is BBC film of him shot in December 1968, where he is singing the song with an acoustic guitar in the garden of his Ascot home.

This was one of the most rehearsed songs of the whole *Let It Be* album. They first played it through on January 2, and worked on it in nine other sessions, finally finishing on January 30.

ABOVE: On October 18, 1968, John and Yoko appeared at Marylebone Magistrate Court charged with possession of marijuana and obstructing the police. John admitted to possession.

Written: Lennon/McCartney

Length: 3'37"

UK Release: *Let It Be* album, May 8, 1970

US Release: *Let It Be* album, May 18, 1970

THE LONG AND WINDING ROAD

Like 'Yesterday', 'The Long And Winding Road' evokes loss. The images of wind and rain suggest abandonment in a wilderness, while the road to "her door" gives hope.

The imagery came from High Park, Paul's farm in Scotland. The long and winding road is the 16 miles of twisting lanes that wind down Kintyre into Campbeltown, the town closest to the farm.

Paul had Ray Charles in mind when he wrote it, which influenced the use of jazzy chords. "It's a sad song," he once said, "because it's all about the unattainable, the door you never quite reach. This is the road that you never quite get to the end of."

It was released as a US single in May 1970, reaching Number 1. In rehearsal, George Martin asked if strings were going to be added. "Dunno," said Paul. "This particular song doesn't need it," Martin said. "It needs something more clinical." Paul saw it as a quiet song "with almost no energy". Phil Spector felt otherwise and for the controversial re-mix added strings that were arranged by Richard Hewson. Paul removed them for *Let It Be … Naked*.

The long and winding road
That leads to your door
Will never disappear
I've seen that road before
It always leads me here
Lead me to your door

The wild and windy night
 that the rain washed away
Has left a pool of tears crying for the day
Why leave me standing here,
Let me know the way

Many times I've been alone
 and many times I've cried
Anyway you'll never know the many ways
 I've tried
And still they lead me back to the long
 winding road
You left me standing here a long,
 long time ago
Don't leave me waiting here,
 lead me to you door

But still they lead me back
To the long winding road
You left me standing here
A long, long time ago
Don't keep me waiting here
Lead me to you door
Yeah, yeah, yeah, yeah

Written: Lennon/McCartney

Length: 3'40"

UK Release: *Let It Be* album, May 8, 1970

US Release: *Let It Be* album, May 18, 1970

LEFT: The rugged landscape, inclement weather and winding roads of Kintyre in Scotland supplied Paul with the imagery for his song 'The Long And Winding Road'.

ONE AFTER 909

'One After 909' could well be the oldest Lennon and McCartney song ever to be recorded by the Beatles. It was one of the songs that they wrote long before recording 'Love Me Do' and goes back to the time that the two of them wrote together in the front room at Forthlin Road.

The Beatles first recorded 'One After 909' in March 1963 during the session that produced 'From Me To You' but George Martin wasn't impressed with it and it wasn't released. It had been an attempt to write an American railroad song in the style of such skiffle hits as 'Last Train To San Fernando' by Johnny Duncan, 'Cumberland Gap' and 'Rock Island Line' by Lonnie Donegan and 'Freight Train' by the Chas McDevitt Skiffle Group. The "one after 909" was meant to be the train leaving after the nine minutes past nine departure.

"We used to sag off [play truant from] school, go back to my house and the two of us would write," Paul recalled. "There are a lot of songs from back then that we've never reckoned on because they're all very unsophisticated songs... We always hated the words to 'One After 909', but they're great."

When they came to play around with it during the sessions there was chat between John and Paul where they mentioned how they had originally dropped it because they'd always considered the lyrics illogical and unfinished.

ONE AFTER 909

Written: Lennon/McCartney

Length: 2'55"

UK Release: *Let It Be* album, May 8, 1970

US Release: *Let It Be* album, May 18, 1970

My baby says she's trav'ling
  on the one after 909
I said move over honey
  I'm travelling on that line
I said move over once, move over twice
Come on baby don't be cold as ice
She said she's trav'ling on the one
  after 909

I begged her not to go
  and I begged her on my bended knees
You're only fooling around,
  only fooling around with me
She said move over once,
  move over twice
Come on baby don't be cold as ice
She said I'm trav'ling on the one after 909

Pick up my bag, run to the station
Railman says you've got the the wrong
  location
Pick up the bag, run right home
Then I find I got the number wrong

She said she's trav'ling
  on the one after 909
I said move over honey
  I'm travelling on that line
I said move over once, move over twice
Come on baby don't be cold as ice
She said she's trav'ling on the one after 909

Pick up my bag, run to the station
Railman says you've got the wrong
  location
Well, pick up my bag, run right home
Then I find I got the number wrong

She said she's trav'ling
  on the one after 909
I said move over honey
  I'm travelling on that line
I said move over once, move over twice
Come on baby don't be cold as ice
I said we're trav'ling on the one after 90
I said we're trav'ling on the one after 90
I said we're trav'ling on the one after 909

(Oh Danny Boy, the old summer is
calling)

FOR YOU BLUE

George wanted to create a rough-edged 12-bar blues. John played slide guitar, and the piano was stuffed with paper to make it sound more like an old-fashioned honky-tonk piano. On January 25, the day the song was introduced, George explained, "The main thing with this, in my head, is that it's influenced by those old fellows, where nothing was professional at all. So it's really like a one-take wonder, but we may have a four-take wonder."

At one point George said that the song, written with Pattie in mind, had been influence by 'Corrina, Corrina', an old blues song first recorded by Bo Carter in 1928. "They must have done it all in five minutes," he said. "That's how I'd rather do it." John replied, "Well, you've got another three minutes to go."

Written: Harrison

Length: 2'32"

UK Release: *Let It Be* album, May 8, 1970

US Release: *Let It Be* album, May 18, 1970

(Queen says no to pot-smoking FBI members)

Because you're sweet and lovely girl I love you
Because you're sweet and lovely girl it's true
I love you more than ever girl I do
I want you in the morning girl I love you
I want you at the moment I feel blue
I'm living every moment girl for you

(Walk, walk cat walk.
Go Johnny go.
Same old 12-bar blues.

Elmore James got nothin' on this baby)

I loved you from the moment I saw you
You looked at me that's all you had to do
I feel it now I hope you feel it too
Because you're sweet and lovely girl I love you
Because you're sweet and lovely girl it's true
I love you more than ever girl I do

GET BACK

'Get Back' started out on January 7, 1969 as little more than a riff with the line "Get back, get back, get back to where you once belonged'", the rest of the song being filled with nonsense sounds. Over the next three weeks it grew incrementally into the track we now know as the sounds were replaced with words and then the outline of a plausible story was built up.

"Think of some words if you can," said Paul on January 11. "I don't know what it's about. It's about going away and then the chorus says 'get back.' Actually, it's not about anything." George liked the idea of the song not being about anything. "Well, just have those words," he said. "Just like that 'Caledonia Mission' [by the Band]. They're just nothing about anything. They're just like rubbish."

On January 12, they fooled around with a separate idea inspired by the policies of Conservative MP Enoch Powell who was in favour of what he termed "the encouragement of re-emigration" because he believed the stability and traditions of Britain were under threat by unprecedented levels of immigration from Commonwealth countries. Paul began singing the word "commonwealth" with John responding "Yes" and then Paul sang, "Hear me talkin' Commonwealth/ If you don't want trouble/ Then you better go back home." On January 13 the Enoch Powell satire had been incorporated into a verse of 'Get Back' with Paul singing, "Meanwhile back at home there's 20 Pakistanis, living in a council flat/ Candidate for Labour tells them what the

Written: Lennon/McCartney

Length: 3'18"

UK single release: April 11, 1969

US single release: May 5, 1969

Jojo was a man who thought he was
  a loner
But he knew it wouldn't last
Jojo left his home in Tucson, Arizona
For some California grass
Get back, get back
Get back to where you once belonged
Get back, get back
Get back to where you once belonged
Get back Jojo
Go home
Get back, get back
Get back to where you once belonged
Get back, get back
Get back to where you once belonged
Get back Jo

Sweet Loretta Martin thought she was
  a woman
But she was another man
All the girls around her say she's got it
  coming
But she gets it while she can
Oh get back, get back
Get back to where you once belonged
Get back, get back
Get back to where you once belonged
Get back Loretta
Go home
Oh get back, yeah get back
Get back to where you once belonged
Get back, get back
Get back to where you once belonged

Ooh, oh, oh,
Get back Loretta
Your mama's waiting for you
Wearing her high-heel shoes
And a low-neck sweater
Get back home Loretta
Get back
Oh, get back
Get back to where you once belonged
Oh, get back
Get back, get back, oh yeah,
Jojo, oh yeah.

[I'd like to thank you on behalf of the
group and ourselves and I hope we've
passed the audition.]

plan is/ Then he tells them where it's at". However, it was quickly dropped. "It started off as a protest song," he explained to George, "but it'll work just as these two [verses], you know, without the verse about Pakistanis and that. I was never struck on that. I like the word 'Pakistanis' but it'll work out with just those two verses."

At one point Paul says of a verse "it sings right" and it was this feeling rather than any sense that dictated the words. When John sang "JoJo Jackson left his home in Arizona/ But he knew it couldn't last", Paul says the second line is "no good" and substitutes "Looking for his (something) last". Ringo suggested, "Looking for a blast from the past." Paul tried "looking for a blade of grass", then "Looking for the greener grass."

When it became "California grass" Paul said, "It's daft really, but we'll straighten it out." Paul then introduced "Tucson, Arizona" in the first line because it was a nice phrase to sing. Asked who JoJo was, he said "It's a drag queen, y'know?"

Musically, Paul wanted 'Get Back' to sound more rock 'n' roll. He wanted "Rock 'n' roll changes. That's the only thing I feel about this song. Like A to D." He said he wanted the chords to be "very strident" and illustrated what he meant by playing the chords and shouting "Bam! Bam!" to emphasize the sound he wanted between each line of the chorus.

When tapes of the session were leaked, those who heard the "Pakistani" version alone assumed the Beatles had been making up racist songs for fun while recording 'Get Back'. "(The verses) were not racist at all," explained Paul when asked about it. "They were anti-racist … If there was any group that was not racist, it was the Beatles. All our favourite people were always black."

BELOW: The last ever Beatles public appearance – on the roof of the Apple office in London, January 30, 1969.

Although the "get back" of the song came with no idea attached, it conveniently suggested a return to musical roots and simplicity of recording, a meaning that Apple exploited when it came to advertising the single in April 1969 with the slogan "The Beatles as nature intended". The attached copy said, "'Get Back' is the Beatles' new single. It's the first Beatles' record which is as live as can be, in this electronic age. There's no electronic watchamacallit. 'Get Back' is a pure spring-time rock number."

Paul's summary of its creation was: "We were sitting in the studio and we made it up out of thin air … we started to write words there and then … when we finished it, we recorded it at Apple Studios and made it into a song to rollercoast by."

In the film, the Beatles are famously seen playing it on the roof of the Apple building in Savile Row, with Billy Preston on keyboards. The version released on the album, almost a year after the single, is a different mix. 'Get Back' sold over two million copies and was a hit around the world. It reached the Number 1 spot in Britain, America, Australia, Canada, West Germany and France.

DON'T LET ME DOWN

John had repeatedly expressed fears of being let down by those he had put his trust in. 'If I Fell' was the template for songs in which he confessed his need to be loved and also his almost paralyzing anxiety over the possibility of being rejected.

Written about Yoko, whom he was to marry two months later, this same old concern was expressed with a sound that was as painful as the emotions it expressed. As John was getting ready to sing it he instructed Ringo to really crash the cymbals "to give me the courage to come out screaming." Paul has since said that it was a "genuine plea" for help and that he was saying to Yoko, "I'm really stepping out of line on this one. I'm really just letting my vulnerability be seen, so you must not let me down."

When the group started rehearsing it on January 6, 1969, Paul and George were working on vocal responses to John's lines, singing "For the first time in my life", "Don't you know it's going to last", "I'll never let it get away", and "It lasts forever and a day".

Paul was concernd that some of the lines they were coming up with were corny, but John insisted: "I think the words should be corny, because there's no clever words in it." However, those lyrical phrases were soon dropped.

Although it was released as the B-side of 'Get Back' in April 1969 and was played during the rooftop concert used in the film, Phil Spector dropped the track from the *Let It Be* album. It was reinstated for the remixed *Let It Be… Naked* in 2003.

Written: Lennon/McCartney

Length: 3'18"

UK single release: April 11, 1969, as B-side of 'Get Back'

US single release: May 5, 1969, as B-side of 'Get Back'

Don't let me down, don't let me down
Don't let me down, don't let me down

Nobody ever loved me like she does
Ooh, she does, yeah, she does
And if somebody loved me like she do me
Ooh, she do me, yes, she does

Don't let me down, don't let me down
Don't let me down, don't let me down

I'm in love for the first time
Don't you know it's gonna last
It's a love that lasts forever
It's a love that has no past

Don't let me down, don't let me down
Don't let me down, don't let me down

And from the first time that she really
 done me
Ooh, she done me, she done me good
I guess nobody ever really done me
Ooh, she done me, she done me good

Don't let me down,
Hey don't let me down
Heeeee, don't let me down

Don't let me down
Don't let me down,
Don't let me let down
Can you dig it? Don't let me down

DON'T LET ME DOWN

THE BALLAD OF JOHN AND YOKO

'The Ballad Of John And Yoko' – in which John related the details of his marriage to Yoko in Gibraltar and their subsequent "honeymoon" – was recorded in mid-April 1969 and released before the end of May. Paul helped with the final verse. It was consciously written in the ballad tradition, specifically the broadside, where songs are used to relay news, a style he was to return to on his *Some Time In New York City* album in 1972. The song portrayed the couple as victims about to be "crucified": the two are turned back at Southampton docks; can't get a wedding licence in France; then they're misunderstood as they lie in bed "for peace" and laughed at when they sit in a bag.

Something John failed to mention was the fact that they were turned back at Southampton dock not for reasons of notoriety but because they were trying to exit the country without passports. The plane they "finally made" into Paris was not a scheduled airliner but a private jet that John requested when he realized that a wedding ceremony wasn't possible on a cross-Channel ferry.

John's decision to marry appears to have been made suddenly, on March 14, 1969, when he and Yoko were being driven to Poole in Dorset to visit his Aunt Mimi. This was two days after Paul's registry office wedding to Linda. John asked his chauffeur Les Anthony to go to Southampton and enquire about the possibility of their being married at sea. When this was found to be impossible, he asked his office to see if a wedding in Paris was possible. Peter Brown, a director of Apple who had taken over many of the Beatles' day-to-day management affairs since the death of Brian Epstein, learned that this couldn't be arranged at short notice but that they could marry in Gibraltar because it was a British protectorate and John was a British citizen.

The couple flew by private plane to Gibraltar on March 20, where they were married by the local registrar Cecil Wheeler in a ten-minute ceremony held at the British Consulate. Peter Brown was best man. They were on the ground for less than an hour before flying to Amsterdam, where they had booked the Presidential Suite at the Hilton. Their stay in the city was to be an extraordinary "honeymoon". Instead of requesting the usual privacy, they invited the world's press to invade their bedroom daily between 10 am and 10 pm during which time, they said, they would be staying in bed "for peace".

Naturally, the world's press hoped that John and Yoko might be intending to consummate their marriage in public. After all, they'd exposed their naked bodies on the cover of their album *Two Virgins* and had recorded the heartbeat of the child that Yoko later miscarried. There seemed to be no area of their lives that they weren't willing to turn into art for the public to consume.

The sight that actually greeted the media in suite 902 was John and Yoko in neatly pressed pyjamas sitting upright in bed doing nothing more than talking about the end of wars. It was the perfect deal. The press had an insatiable appetite for the Beatles and John wanted to spread a message of peace. The Amsterdam "Bed In" meant that all parties went away satisfied.

They held court for seven days, and the coverage was extensive. They did interviews with American radio stations, produced a sixty-minute documentary and the image of the couple in bed appeared on the front pages of newspapers around the world. "Yoko and I are quite willing to be the world's clowns, if by doing it we do some good," said John. "For reasons known only to themselves people do print what I say. And I'm saying peace. We're not pointing a finger

THE BALLAD OF JOHN AND YOKO

Standing in the dock at Southampton
Trying to get to Holland or France
The man in the mac said,
"You've got to go back"
You know they didn't even give us
   a chance
Christ you know it ain't easy
You know how hard it can be
The way things are going
They're gonna crucify me

Finally made the plane into Paris
Honeymooning down by the Seine
Peter Brown called to say
"You can make it OK
You can get married in Gibraltar,
   near Spain"
Christ you know it ain't easy
You know how hard it can be
The way things are going
They're gonna crucify me

Drove from Paris to the
   Amsterdam Hilton
Talking in our beds for a week
The newspeople said,
"Say what you doing in bed?"
I said, "We're only trying to get us
   some peace"
Christ you know it ain't easy
You know how hard it can be
The way things are going
They're gonna crucify me

at anybody. There are no good guys and bad guys. The struggle is in the mind. We must bury our own monsters and stop condemning people. We are all Christ and all Hitler. We want Christ to win. We're trying to make Christ's message contemporary. What would he have done if he had advertisements, records, films, TV and newspapers? Christ made miracles to tell his message. Well, the miracle today is communications, so let's use it."

From Amsterdam, they went to Vienna, where they stopped overnight at the Hotel Sacher and ate some of its famous Sacher Torte (a rich chocolate cake with apricot jam filling) before watching the television premiere of their film *Rape*.

On April 1, they arrived back in London and gave a press conference at the airport. John expected a hostile reception because Yoko, as a foreign divorcée, was not considered the ideal partner for a British-born Beatle. To his surprise, the welcome was warm. The "fifty acorns" refers to a stunt they organized where acorns were mailed to world leaders with the request that they "plant an acorn for peace". Some of the leaders wrote back to John and Yoko. The idea had started in 1968 when the pair was asked to contribute to the Exhibition of British Sculpture being hosted by Coventry Cathedral. They entered a circular white seat and, beneath it, they planted two acorns as symbols of peace. Unfortunately, these acorns were subsequently stolen.

Paul was initially apprehensive about John's references to being crucified, and the use of "Christ" as an expletive reminded him of the problems the Beatles had encountered in America less than three years before when John had compared the current popularity of the Beatles with the currently popularity of Jesus and Christianity. He didn't want to ignite the wrath of Christian fundamentalists and other conservatives.

'The Ballad Of John And Yoko' was recorded at Abbey Road on the same day it was written at Paul's house with Paul playing bass, piano, maracas and drums, while John played lead and acoustic guitars and sang the vocals. In order not to create controversy ahead of its release, John ordered that it be kept under wraps and that advance publicity shouldn't draw attention to the "Christ" and "crucify" references. It was released as a single in Britain on May 30, 1969, six weeks after its writing and recording, a fast turnaround for the Beatles.

Saving up your money for a rainy day
Giving all your clothes to charity
Last night the wife said
"Oh boy, when you're dead
You don't take nothing with you
But your soul. Think!"

Made a lightning trip to Vienna
Eating chocolate cake in a bag
The newspapers said,
"She's gone to his head
They look just like two gurus in drag"
Christ you know it ain't easy
You know how hard it can be
The way things are going
They're gonna crucify me

Caught the early plane back to London
Fifty acorns tied in a sack
The men from the press said,
"We wish you success
It's good to have the both of you back"
Christ you know it ain't easy
You know how hard it can be
The way things are going
They're gonna crucify me
The way things are going
They're gonna crucify me

Written: Lennon/McCartney

Length: 2'55"

UK Release: May 30, 1969

UK Chart Position: 1

US Release: June 4, 1969

US Chart Position: 8

You know my name, look up the number
You know my name, look up the number
You you know you know my name
You you know you know my name

Good evening and welcome to Slaggers
Featuring Denis O'Bell
Come on Ringo, let's hear it for Denis

Good evening, you know my name
Well then look up my number
You know my name
That's right, look up my number
You you know you know my name
You you know you know my name
You know my name
Ba ba ba ba ba ba ba ba ba
Look up the number
You know my name
That's right, look up the number
Oh you know you know
  you know my name
You know you know
  you know my name
Huh huh huh huh, you know my name
Ba ba ba bum, look up the number
You know my name, look up the number
You-a you know you know my name
Baby you-a you know you know my name
You know you know my name
You know you know my name

Let's hear it. Go on Denis let's hear it for
Denis O'Bell

You know my name
You know you know my name
You know you know my name
Prrr you know my name and the number
You know my name and the number
You know you know my name
Look up me number
You know my name
You know my number too
You know my number three
 You know my number four
Oh you know my name
  you know my number too
You know my name you know my number
What's up with you?
You know my name
That's right?
Yeah

YOU KNOW MY NAME

Released as the B-side of 'Let It Be', 'You Know My Name' was the most unusual song ever released on a single by the Beatles and remains one of their least-known officially released tracks.

It had first been recorded shortly after the completion of *Sgt. Pepper*, after John arrived at Abbey Road wanting to record a song called 'You Know My Name, Look Up The Number'. When Paul asked to see the lyric, John told him that *was* the lyric. He wanted it repeated in the style of the chorus of the Four Tops' hit of the year before, 'Reach Out, I'll Be There', until it sounded like a mantra. The line was a variation on a slogan John had seen on the front cover of the Post Office's London telephone directory for 1967 which read: "You have their NAME? Look up their NUMBER".

For three days in May and June 1967, the Beatles worked on the song but it rapidly departed from the original intention of a song in the style of the Four Tops and became a comical ramble reminiscent of *Goon Show* radio comedy or the Bonzo Dog Doo-Dah Band. It was then abandoned until April 1969, when the track was revisited for some added vocal parts and a drastic editing down from over 20 minutes to 4 minutes and 19 seconds.

The only departure from the words of the title came when John twice asked for a big hand for "Denis O'Bell", a reference to the Irish-born film producer Denis O'Dell who had been Associate Producer on *A Hard Day's Night* and who had become director of Apple Films and Apple Publicity.

None of the Beatles told O'Dell that they had referred to him in the song and so it came as a shock to him when he started receiving anonymous telephone calls at his home in St George's Square, Pimlico.

"There were so many of them my wife started going out of her mind," says O'Dell. "Neither of us knew why this was suddenly happening. Then I happened to be in one Sunday and picked up the phone myself. It was someone on LSD calling from a candle-making factory in Philadelphia and they just kept saying, 'We know your name and now we've got your number.'

"It was only through talking to the person that I established what it was all about. Then Ringo, who I'd worked with on the film *The Magic Christian*, played me the track and I realized why I'd been getting all these mysterious phone calls. It was because of this experience that I first went ex-directory. We were starting to get people turn up on the doorstep. Once there were 10 or 12 of these people who'd tracked me down and they arrived thinking they could all come and live with us!

"I still don't know why they put my name in the song. I wasn't in the studio with them at the time as far as I can remember. They never mentioned it since!"

Written: Lennon/McCartney

Length: 4'19"

UK Release: March 6, 1970 as B-side of 'Let It Be'

US Release: March 11, 1970 as B-side of 'Let It Be'

YOU KNOW MY NAME

OLD BROWN SHOE

George introduced 'Old Brown Shoe' on January 28, saying he had no title for the song. In *I Me Mine,* he said that it started as a piano exercise, and words emerged by playing with opposites. "The duality of things – yes-no, up-down, left-right, right-wrong etc." The title was taken from a line in the first verse that says, "I'm stepping out this old brown shoe".

Because George presented it with a spiritual subtext it seemed reasonable to assume that the "brown shoe" was materialism, which he sought to escape. However, while rehearsing it, George was talking to Mal Evans about getting new shoes from a "groovy" shop on Bond Street. Pushed for time, he needed Mal to get a selection of slip-on shoes that he could pick from.

None of the other Beatles linked the "old brown shoe" of the song and the black leather shoes George was after. Mal asked whether he wanted patent leather. "I'm fed up with them," said George. "I've got about 18 pairs. I just want ... black slip-on shoes, size eights."

It was finally recorded in April 1969 and released as the B-side of 'The Ballad Of John and Yoko'. Much later it appeared on the compilation albums *Hey Jude* and *The Beatles 1967–1970*.

LET IT BE

Written: Harrison

Length: 3'16"

UK Release: May 30, 1969 as B-side of 'The Ballad of John and Yoko'

US Release: June 4, 1969 as B-side of 'The Ballad of John and Yoko'

I want a love that's right
  but right is only half of what's wrong
I want a short-haired girl
  who sometimes wears it twice as long
Now I'm stepping out this old brown shoe
Baby I'm in love with you
I'm so glad you came here
  it wont be the same now, I'm telling you

You know you pick me up
  from where some try to drag me down
And when I see your smile
  replacing every thought less frown
You got me escaping from this zoo
Baby I'm in love with you
I'm so glad you came here
  it wont be the same now, when I'm with you

If I grow up I'll be a singer
  wearing rings on every finger
Not worrying what they or you say
I'll live and love and maybe someday
Who knows baby? You may comfort me

I may appear to be imperfect
But my love is something you can't reject
I'm changing faster than the weather
If you and me should get together
Who knows baby? You may comfort me

I want that love of yours
To miss that love is something I'd hate
I'll make an early start
I'm making sure that I'm not late
For your sweet top lip I'm in the queue
Baby I'm in love with you
I'm so glad you came here
It wont be the same now, when I'm with you

Yes, I'm so glad you came here
It wont be the same now, when I'm with you

During the sessions for *Let It Be*, George confided to John that he had written enough songs to make a solo album. John encouraged him to do it.

12 Abbey Road

Seven years on from their first recordings at the Abbey Road Studios, the Beatles returned for what proved to be their final sessions. Back in June 1962, they were wide-eyed provincial lads keen to make their mark on the music business. By July 1969, they had become world-weary sophisticates, their lives blighted by struggles over power and money.

The songs on *Abbey Road* reflected their frustrations. They're about legal negotiations, unpaid debts, being ripped off, bad karma and generally bearing the weight of the world on their shoulders. There was even a mock-jolly song about a silver hammer (namely Maxwell's) that is waiting to come down hard on you just when things appear to be getting better.

Despite this mood – or perhaps because of it – *Abbey Road* was an outstandingly inventive farewell offering. It featured two of George's best songs, 'Here Comes The Sun' and 'Something', a stand-out track by John, 'Come Together', and a fascinating medley of half-finished songs skilfully woven together by Paul.

George Martin remembered that after *Let It Be*, Paul came to him and asked him to produce a Beatles album with the kind of feeling they used to generate together. Martin agreed to help out if the Beatles were prepared to give him their co-operation. "That's how we made *Abbey Road*. It wasn't quite like the old days because they were still working on their own songs and they would bring in the other people to work as kind of musicians for them rather than being a team."

The fundamental problem now affecting the Beatles was that they were no longer able to startle themselves. What had once appeared to be magic was now craft and hard slog. In January 1969, during the *Let It Be* sessions, John had turned to Paul, George and Ringo and said "The end result of the records now isn't enough because now we know so clearly how we arrived at it and what it was. Before, it was always a surprise. We weren't so aware of how we reached it, so when something came out like *Revolver* there was still an element of surprise. We didn't know where it came from. But now we know exactly where it came from and how it arrived and how it could have been better, or needn't have been at all. The only way to do it satisfactorily for yourself is to do it on your own, and then that's too hard."

In Britain, *Abbey Road* was released in September 1969 and stayed at Number 1 for 18 weeks. In America, it was released in October and was at Number 1 for 11 weeks.

COME TOGETHER

'Come Together' began as a campaign song for Timothy Leary, when he decided in 1969 that he was going to run as Governor of California against America's future president Ronald Reagan. At the time Leary was best known as the psychologist and Harvard professor who had left academic life to promote what he saw as the benefits of LSD and who became known as the "acid guru". He was an enthusiastic fan of the Beatles, who he believed were taking the message of consciousness transformation to the masses. He likened them to the four evangelists – Matthew, Mark, Luke and John – who spread the gospel passed on by Jesus.

Leary and his wife Rosemary were invited up to Montreal, where John and Yoko were between the sheets for another major "bed in" on the 19th floor of the Queen Elizabeth Hotel. They arrived on June 1, 1969, and were promptly coaxed into singing on the chorus of John's song 'Give Peace A Chance', which was recorded in the hotel bedroom. Leary and his wife were rewarded for their participation by having their names included in the lyric ("Everybody's talking 'bout John and Yoko, Timmy Leary, Rosemary, Tommy Smothers, Bobby Dylan…")

The next day, John asked Leary if there was anything that he could do to help him in his political campaign and Leary suggested he write a song to be used in commercials and performed at rallies. Leary's slogan was "come together, join the party" – the "come together" part coming from the *I Ching*, the Chinese book of changes, possibly from Hexagram 13 T'ung Jen – T'ung meaning "gathering together", "fellowship" or "harmony", Jen meaning "humanity". "There was obviously a double meaning there," said Leary. "It was come together and join 'the party' – not a political party but a celebration of life."

John immediately picked up his guitar and began building on the phrase: "Come together right now, Don't come tomorrow, Don't come alone, Come together right now over me, All that I can tell you, Is you gotta be free." After coming up with a few more versions along the same lines, he made a demo tape and handed it to Leary.

Leary had the song played on alternative radio stations throughout California and began to think of it as his own. However, unknown to him, John had returned to England and within seven weeks had recorded a version with the Beatles. In October, it was released on the flip side of 'Something', the first single to be taken from *Abbey Road*.

Shoot. Shoot. Shoot. Shoot.
Here come old flat top,
He come grooving up slowly
He got juju eyeball, he want holy roller
He got hair down to his knee
Got to be a joker he just do what he please

Shoot. Shoot. Shoot. Shoot.
He wear no shoeshine,
He got toe-jam football
He got monkey finger,
He shoot coca-cola
He say "I know you, you know me"
One thing I can tell you is
  you've got to be free
Come together right now over me

Shoot. Shoot. Shoot.
He Bag production,
He got walrus gumboot
He got Ono sideboard,
He want spinal cracker
He got feet down below his knee
Hold you in his arms, yeah
  you can feel his disease
Come together right now over me

(Right!
Come, oh, come, come, come)

He roller-coaster,
He got early warning
He got muddy water,
He want mojo filter
He say "One and one and one is three"
Got to be good-looking
  cos he's so hard to see
Come together right now over me

Shoot. Shoot. Shoot
Oh,
Come together, yeah
Come together, yeah
Come together, yeah
Come together, yeah
Come together, yeah
Come together, yeah
Come together, yeah
Ah. Come together, yeah
Come together, yeah

LEFT: John borrowed a line from Chuck Berry and had to pay his publishers for the loan.

Leary's campaign to become Governor of California came to an abrupt halt in December 1969, when he was charged with possessing marijuana and eventually imprisoned. It was while in prison, that Leary first heard *Abbey Road* on a local rock station and the completed 'Come Together' came as a total surprise to him. "Although the new version was certainly a musical and lyrical improvement on my campaign song, I was a bit miffed that Lennon had passed me over in this way. When I sent a mild protest to him, he replied with typical Lennon charm and wit that he was a tailor and I was a customer who had ordered a suit and never returned. So he sold it to someone else."

The recorded version, with its semi-nonsense lyric, was largely made up in the studio, the 'swampy' New Orleans bass added by Paul. Two of the song lines referring to the "old flat top" were lifted from Chuck Berry's 'You Can't Catch Me' and John was later sued for plagiarism. It was hard to deny that the words had come from this source, although, in this new context, they were no more than an affectionate tribute. John strenuously denied any musical theft.

The conflict was resolved when John promised to record three songs belonging to the publisher of 'You Can't Catch Me'. He fulfilled this promise when he recorded Berry's 'Sweet Little Sixteen' and 'You Can't Catch Me' for his rock 'n' roll album and Lee Dorsey's 'Ya Ya' on *Walls and Bridges*.

'Come Together' was released as a single in October 1969 and topped the American charts. Teamed up with 'Something' as a double A-side in Britain, it only reached Number 4.

Written: Lennon/McCartney

Length: 4'20"

UK Release: *Abbey Road* album, September 26, 1969

US Release: *Abbey Road* album, October 1, 1969

SOMETHING

'Something' was the first Beatles' A-side to be written by George. Its sources of inspiration were Ray Charles, who he imagined singing it, and a 1968 album track by James Taylor titled 'Something In The Way She Moves'.

James Taylor, an American, was signed to the Apple label and his first album (*James Taylor*) produced between July and October 1968 by Peter Asher. Paul played bass on one track. 'Something In The Way She Moves' was the last track on the first side of the album and the opening lines were: "There's something in the way she moves, Or looks my way or calls my name, That seems to leave this troubled world behind."

The White Album was being recorded at Abbey Road at exactly the same time as Taylor was recording at Trident Studios in London's Soho. Indeed, on October 3, George was at Trident recording 'Savoy Truffle' with Paul and Ringo and probably heard the track then.

"I've always assumed George must have heard it but I never actually spoke to him about it," says Taylor. "I'd written 'Something In The Way She Moves' about two years before I recorded it and, strangely enough I'd wanted to call it 'I Feel Fine', but of course that was a Beatles' track.

"I often notice traces of other people's work in my own songs," Taylor continues. "If George either consciously or unconsciously took a line from one of my songs, then I find it very flattering. It's certainly not an unusual thing to happen. I'd made a tape of 'Something In The Way She Moves' and about seven other songs about a couple of months before I met Peter Asher. I know Paul listened to it at Apple but I'm not sure who else listened to it."

The basic writing of 'Something' probably took place in October. When George introduced it on January 28, 1969, he said he'd been working on it "for, like, six months." Even though he'd had it that long he still had problems with the opening lines. He had 'Something in the way she moves attracts me like...' but admitted, "I can't think of what attracts me at all."

John said, "Just say whatever comes into your head each time – 'Attracts me like a cauliflower...' – until you get the words." George suggested a pomegranate, but was worried about working with nonsense. John said, "If you try to make sense of it every time in every line, you'll have to stop every time," he said. "You should go on and on and on and then go back over it."

George first offered 'Something' to Joe Cocker and Jackie Lomax but then, in May 1969, decided to record it for Abbey Road. It was an enormously successful song, becoming the second most covered Beatles' song after 'Yesterday' and giving him his first US Top 10 hit.

It had always been assumed that he wrote the song about Pattie but in a 1996 interview George said, "I didn't. I just wrote it and then somebody put together a video that used some footage of me and Pattie, Paul and Linda, Ringo and Maureen and John and Yoko. So then everybody presumed I wrote it about Pattie but, actually, when I wrote it I was thinking of Ray Charles." However, Pattie still believes that he had her in mind. "He always told me that it was about me," she says. In her autobiography *Wonderful Tonight* she said that George first played it to her while *The White Album* was being recorded. Back in 1969, when asked who the song was about, George answered, "Maybe Pattie. Probably."

Something in the way she moves
Attracts me like no other lover
Something in the way she woos me

I don't want to leave her now
You know I believe and how

Somewhere in her smile she knows
That I don't need no other lover
Something in her style that shows me

I don't want to leave her now
You know I believe and how

You're asking me will my love grow
I don't know, I don't know
You stick around now it may show
I don't know, I don't know

Something in the way she knows
And all I have to do is think of her
Something in the things she shows me

I don't want to leave her now
You know I believe and how

Written: Harrison

Length: 3'03"

UK Release: *Abbey Road* album, September 26, 1969

US Release: *Abbey Road* album, October 1, 1969

Joan was quizzical, studied pataphysical
  Science in the home
Late nights all alone with a test-tube
Ohh oh oh oh
Maxwell Edison majoring in medicine
Calls her on the phone
Can I take you out to the pictures, Joan?
But as she's getting ready to go
A knock comes on the door

Bang, bang, Maxwell's silver hammer
  came down upon her head
Bang, bang, Maxwell's silver hammer
  made sure that she was dead

Back in school again
  Maxwell plays the fool again
Teacher gets annoyed
Wishing to avoid an unpleasant scene
She tells Max to stay
  when the class has gone away
So he waits behind
Writing 50 times "I must not be so"
  Oh oh oh
But when she turns her back on the boy
He creeps up from behind

Bang, bang, Maxwell's silver hammer
  came down upon her head
Do do do do do
Bang, bang, Maxwell's silver hammer
  made sure that she was dead

P.C. 31 said "We caught a dirty one"
Maxwell stands alone
Painting testimonial pictures
Ohh oh oh oh
Rose and Valerie
  screaming from the gallery
Say he must go free
  (Maxwell must go free)
The judge does not agree and he tells
  them so oh oh oh
But as the words are leaving his lips
A noise comes from behind

Bang, bang, Maxwell's silver hammer
came down upon his head
Do do do do do
Bang, Bang, Maxwell's silver hammer
  made sure that he was dead
Wow wow wow oh!
Do do do do do
Silver hammer Man

MAXWELL'S SILVER HAMMER

Written: Lennon/McCartney

Length: 3'27"

UK Release: *Abbey Road* album,
September 26, 1969

US Release: *Abbey Road* album,
October 1, 1969

RIGHT ABOVE: Pattie Harrison always thought 'Something' was written for her, but George never publicly commented about who, if anyone, he had in mind.

RIGHT BELOW: Peter Sellers with Ringo. It was while sailing on the actor's yacht that Ringo had the idea for 'Octopus's Garden'.

MAXWELL'S SILVER HAMMER

A song driven by strong rhymes in which medical student Maxwell Edison uses his silver hammer to kill first his girlfriend, then a lecturer and finally a judge. It was delivered in a jaunty, vaudevillian style, the only indication of Paul's recent avant-garde interests being the mention of pataphysics, a concept invented by Alfred Jarry (1873–1907), the French pioneer of absurdist theatre, to describe a philosophy that was beyond metaphysics. He defined it as "the science of imaginary solutions."

"John told me that 'Maxwell's Silver Hammer' was about the law of karma," says former Apple employee Tony King. "We were talking one day about 'Instant Karma' [John's 1970 single with Yoko Ono and the Plastic Ono Band] because something had happened where he'd been clobbered and he'd said that this was an example of instant karma. I asked him whether he believed that theory. He said that he did and that 'Maxwell's Silver Hammer' was the first song that they'd made about that. He said that the idea behind the song was that the minute you do something that's not right, Maxwell's silver hammer will come down on your head."

Paul said at the time that the song, "epitomizes the downfalls of life. Just when everything is going smoothly, 'bang bang' down comes Maxwell's silver hammer and ruins everything." The hammer was "silver" for no other reason than that it scanned better than 'Maxwell's hammer'. Many of the lines were composed in the studio during the *Let It Be* sessions.

John later said that the song had taken three whole days of overdubbing, because Paul imagined it could be a future single. "He did everything to make it into a single and it never was and it never could have been."

OH! DARLING

Paul wanted his voice to sound raw on 'Oh Darling', so he sang it through again and again each day for a week at the start of the *Abbey Road* sessions before finally recording it. During that time he experimented with different microphones to get the precise sound that he had in mind. "I wanted it to sound as though I'd been performing it on stage all week," he said.

In 1969 George described it as "a typical 1950s–1960s period song because of its chord structure." In particular it appears to draw from the genre of Southern Louisiana music known as swamp pop typified by songs such as 'Raining In My Heart' by Slim Harpo, 'Please Come Home For Christmas' by Charles Brown and 'This Should Go On Forever' by Rod Bernard. Swamp pop producer Floyd Soileau said "When 'Oh! Darling' came out, people around here swore that someone from South Louisiana did it. It was so typical of the sound, the rhythm patterns and the arrangements that you find in a lot of this area's music."

Significantly, Paul used the term "swampy" to describe his bass line on 'Come Together' and John Fred Gourrier (of John Fred and the Playboys) discovered when he met them in June 1968 that the Beatles had a good knowledge of swamp pop. "They were very familiar with a lot of records like 'Irene' by Guitar Gable. That freaked me out! I didn't think that song ever left Mamou. I knew what it was because we played 'Irene' all the time. The Beatles were very familiar with South Louisiana music."

Despite all of Paul's hard work in front of the microphone John was dismissive of the result, claiming that he could have done better. "It was more my style than his," he said.

Written: Lennon/McCartney

Length: 3'26"

UK Release: *Abbey Road* album, September 26, 1969

US Release: *Abbey Road* album, October 1, 1969

Oh! Darling, please believe me
I'll never do you no harm
Believe me when I tell you
I'll never do you no harm

Oh! Darling, if you leave me
I'll never make it alone
Believe me when I thank you, ooo
Don't ever leave me alone

When you told me
You didn't need me anymore
Well you know I nearly broke down
  and cried
When you told me
You didn't need me anymore
Well you know I nearly broke down
  and died

Oh! Darling, if you leave me
I'll never make it alone
Believe me when I tell you
I'll never do you no harm
Believe me darling

When you told me
You didn't need me anymore
Well you know I nearly broke down
  and cried
When you told me
You didn't need me anymore
Well you know I nearly broke down
  and died

Oh! Darling, please believe me
I'll never let you down
Oh, believe me darling
Believe me when I tell you, ooo
I'll never do you no harm

OCTOPUS'S GARDEN

Ringo's second (and last) Beatles' song as a writer was inspired by a family holiday in Sardinia which he took in 1968 on board Peter Sellers' yacht, *Amelfis*. After Ringo had turned down the offer of an octopus lunch, the vessel's captain started to tell him all he knew about the life of octopi.

"He told me how they go around the sea bed picking up stones and shiny objects to build gardens with," said Ringo. "I thought this was fabulous because at the time I just wanted to be under the sea too. I wanted to get out of it for a while."

To most listeners, it was a children's seaside song in the vein of 'Yellow Submarine' but, in 1969, George revealed that he thought there were hidden dimensions. "I find very deep meaning in the lyrics which Ringo probably doesn't see," he said. "Like 'resting our heads on the sea' and 'we'll be warm beneath the storm', which is really great because it's like this level is a storm and if you get deep into your consciousness, it's very peaceful. So Ringo's writing his cosmic songs without really noticing it!"

Written: Starr

Length: 2'51"

UK Release: *Abbey Road* album, September 26, 1969

US Release: *Abbey Road* album, October 1, 1969

I'd like to be under the sea
In an octopus's garden in the shade
He'd let us in, knows where we've been
In his octopus's garden in the shade

I'd ask my friends to come and see
An octopus's garden with me
I'd like to be under the sea
In an octopus's garden in the shade

We would be warm below the storm
In our little hideaway beneath the waves
Resting our heads on the sea bed
In an octopus's garden near a cave

We would sing and dance around
Because we know we can't be found
I'd like to be under the sea
In an octopus's garden in the shade

We would shout and swim about
The coral that lies beneath the waves
(Lies beneath the ocean waves)
Oh what joy for every girl and boy
Knowing they're happy and they're safe
(Happy and they're safe)

We would be so happy you and me
No one there to tell us what to do
I'd like to be under the sea
In an octopus's garden with you
In an octopus's garden with you
In an octopus's garden with you

I want you
I want you so bad
I want you
I want you so bad
It's driving me mad
It's driving me mad

I want you
I want you so bad, babe
I want you
I want you so bad
It's driving me mad
It's driving me mad

I want you
I want you so bad, babe
I want you
I want you so bad
It's driving me mad
It's driving me mad

I want you
I want you so bad
I want you
I want you so bad
It's driving me mad
It's driving me mad

She's so heavy
Heavy, heavy, heavy

She's so heavy
She's so heavy
Heavy, heavy, heavy

I want you
I want you so bad
I want you
I want you so bad
It's driving me mad
It's driving me mad

I want you
You know I want you so bad, babe
I want you
You know I want you so bad
It's driving me mad
It's driving me mad
Yeah

She's so...

I WANT YOU (SHE'S SO HEAVY)

Consisting only of the repeated title line and the information that he wants his "babe" so bad that it's driving him mad, the lyric of John's 'I Want You' was once read out on BBC TV's current affairs programme *24 Hours*, as an example of the banalities of pop music. One reviewer said that it showed that he had lost his talent as a lyricist.

For John it was an experiment in minimalism, perhaps affected by Yoko's poetry. "That's all it says but to me that's a damn sight better than 'Walrus' or 'Eleanor Rigby' lyric-wise because it's a progression to me. If I want to write a song with no words or one word then maybe that's Yoko's influence." (A 1964 poem of Yoko's consisted of the single word "water".)

The adjective "heavy" is of its era and had such a multiplicity of meanings. Loud music was heavy, bad situations were heavy, intellectual discussions were heavy, violence was heavy and esoteric facts were heavy. However, as the song was "about Yoko" he almost certainly was using the word heavy to mean "really good, excellent", "unbelievable, out of the ordinary" or "profound", probably a combination of all three.

His intention was to strip away all unnecessary words and invest those that were left with the maximum of emotion. "She (Yoko) was very heavy and there was nothing else I could say about her other than 'I want you' and 'she's so heavy'... When it gets down to it, when you're drowning you don't say, 'I would be incredibly pleased if someone would have the foresight to notice me drowning and come and help me.' You just scream."

Written: Lennon/McCartney

Length: 7'47"

UK Release: *Abbey Road* album, September 26, 1969

US Release: *Abbey Road* album, October 1, 1969

I WANT YOU (SHE'S SO HEAVY)

HERE COMES THE SUN

Here comes the sun,
Here comes the sun
And I say it's alright

Little darling, it's been a long cold lonely
winter
Little darling, it feels like years
since it's been here
Here comes the sun,
Here comes the sun
And I say it's alright

Little darling, the smile's returning to
their faces
Little darling, it seems like years
since it's been here
Here comes the sun,
Here comes the sun
And I say it's alright

Sun, sun, sun, here it comes
Sun, sun, sun, here it comes
Sun, sun, sun, here it comes
Sun, sun, sun, here it comes
Sun, sun, sun, here it comes

Little darling, I feel that ice is slowly
melting
Little darling, it seems like years
since it's been clear
Here comes the sun,
Here comes the sun
And I say it's alright
Here comes the sun,
Here comes the sun
It's alright, it's alright

HERE COMES THE SUN

In January 1969, John and Yoko met with music industry manager Allen Klein and shortly afterwards declared that he would be looking after their business affairs, despite the fact that New York lawyer John Eastman, brother of Linda, had recently been brought in to represent the Beatles collectively. This was the beginning of a bitter drawn-out conflict over who should manage the Beatles and what should be done about the chaotic state of their finances. Despite the tremendous sales of Beatles' music over the past six years, John claimed, "all of us could be broke in six months."

Klein offered to restructure Apple, organize a takeover bid for the shares the Beatles didn't own in Northern Songs and renegotiate a better royalty deal with EMI. He was able to persuade John, George and Ringo of his ability to do these things but Paul remained loyal to Eastman. As a result, the existence of the Beatles was now under threat and the frequent meetings at Apple were fraught with tension. One morning in the early spring, George decided it was all getting a bit too much like school, and so he took a day off from the round table routine and went to see his friend Eric Clapton at his country home in Ewhurst, Surrey.

Borrowing one of Eric's acoustic guitars, George took a walk around the gardens and, basking in the first real sunshine of the year, he felt a sudden flush of optimism and started to write 'Here Comes The Sun'. "It was such a great release for me simply being out in the sun," said George at the time. "The song just came to me."

In his eponymous autobiography Eric Clapton remembers the same moment: "It was a beautiful spring morning and we were sitting at the top of a big paddock at the bottom of the garden. We had our guitars and were just strumming away when he started singing 'Da da de de, it's been a long cold lonely winter,' and bit by bit fleshed it out, until the first verse was finished and it was time for lunch." The song was completed in Sardinia where George and Pattie holidayed in June 1969.

Written: Harrison

Length: 3'05"

UK Release: *Abbey Road* album, September 26, 1969

US Release: *Abbey Road* album, October 1, 1969

BECAUSE

John was relaxing on a sofa at home, while Yoko played the first movement of Beethoven's Piano Sonata No 14 in C Sharp Minor ('Moonlight Sonata') on the grand piano. John has said that he asked her if she could play the same chords in reverse order. This she did, and it proved to be the inspiration for 'Because'.

The similarity between the opening of 'Moonlight Sonata' and 'Because' is striking although it appears to be a straightforward borrowing rather than a reversal of the notes. Musicologist Wilfrid Mellers, author of *Twilight Of The Gods: The Music of the Beatles*, said, "The affinity between the enveloping, arpeggiated C sharp minor triads, with the sudden shift to the flat supertonic, is, in the Lennon and Beethoven examples, unmistakable."

There was irony in the idea of the Beatles borrowing from Beethoven because at the time they were seen as the polar opposites of culture. Chuck Berry's 'Roll Over Beethoven', which the Beatles had recorded, offered the irreverent advice that classical composers should step aside and make way for rock 'n' roll.

One of the first questions the Beatles were asked in America was, 'What do you think of Beethoven?' It was Ringo who answered. "I love him, especially his poems." But it was John, in particular, who later came to respect Beethoven as a fellow composer and would often include him along with Picasso, Van Gogh and Dylan Thomas in his pantheon of great artists with whom he identified.

Music critics, keen to stress the seriousness and significance of the Beatles, often drew not entirely convincing parallels between them and the great composers. In a celebrated *Observer* (London) review of *The White Album*, critic and film maker Tony Palmer declared the Beatles to be "the greatest songwriters since Schubert" and promised that the double album would "surely see the last vestiges of cultural snobbery and bourgeois prejudice swept away in a deluge of joyful music making, which only the ignorant will not hear and only the deaf will not acknowledge."

George said of the song in 1969, "'Because' is one of the most beautiful tunes. There's three-part harmony right throughout … I think this is possibly my favourite one on the album. The lyrics are so simple. The harmony was pretty difficult to sing. We had to really learn it. But I think that's one of the tunes that will impress most people. It's really good."

Aaaaaahhhhh...
Because the world is round
It turns me on
Because the world is round...
aaaaaahhhhhh

Because the wind is high
It blows my mind
Because the wind is high...aaaaaaaahhhh

Love is old, love is new
Love is all, love is you

Because the sky is blue,
It makes me cry
Because the sky is blue...aaaaaaaahhhh

Aaaaahhhhhhhhhh...
Aaaaahhhhhhhhhh...
Aaaaahhhhhhhhhh...

Written: Lennon/McCartney

Length: 2'45"

UK Release: *Abbey Road* album, September 26, 1969

US Release: *Abbey Road* album, October 1, 1969

BECAUSE

You never give me your money
You only give me your funny paper
And in the middle of negotiations
You break down

I never give you my number
I only give you my situation
And in the middle of investigation
I break down

Out of college, money spent
See no future, pay no rent
All the money's gone, nowhere to go
Any job got the sack
Monday morning, turning back
Yellow lorry slow, nowhere to go
But oh, that magic feeling, nowhere to go
Oh, that magic feeling, nowhere to go
Nowhere to go

Aaaaahhhhhhhhhh...
Aaaaahhhhhhhhhh...
Aaaaahhhhhhhhhh...

One sweet dream
Pick up the bags and get in the limousine
Soon we'll be away from here
Step on the gas and wipe that tear away
One sweet dream came true today
Came true today
Came true today (Yes it did)

One two three four five six seven
All good children go to Heaven
One two three four five six seven
All good children go to Heaven
One two three four five six seven
All good children go to Heaven
One two three four five six seven
All good children go to Heaven
One two three four five six seven
All good children go to Heaven
One two three four five six seven
All good children go to Heaven
One two three four five six seven
All good children go to Heaven
One two three four five six seven
All good children go to Heaven

YOU NEVER GIVE ME YOUR MONEY

'You Never Give Me Your Money' announced the medley of short or unfinished songs which dominate the second side of *Abbey Road*. Paul collected the pieces and worked out a way of linking them together. Linda McCartney remembered Paul asking John and George if they had anything to contribute. "Then I remember him at home writing down on a notepad the ways in which he could out them together and then I took a photo of them together at the studio where Paul is showing his notes to John. That was them working it out, and that was what the relationship was really about. That was it right there."

'You Never Give Me Your Money' itself is made up of three distinct fragments written by Paul in New York. The first, which develops the line in the title, was an allusion to the Beatles' financial problems saying that instead of money all they ever seemed to get was "funny paper".

"That's what we get," said George. "We get bits of paper saying how much is earned and what this and that is but we never actually get it in pounds, shillings and pence. We've all got a big house and a car and an office but to actually get the money we've earned seems impossible."

The next fragment, which mentions being penniless after leaving college, may have referred to the same problems but was written in the jolly, nostalgic style of Paul's "woke up/ got out of bed" section of 'A Day In The Life'. The final piece was about the freedom of Paul's new life with Linda, where he could just pack the car and drive out of town leaving his worries behind.

Written: Lennon/McCartney

Length: 4'02"

UK Release: *Abbey Road* album, September 26, 1969

US Release: *Abbey Road* album, October 1, 1969

ABOVE: The guitar style of Peter Green of Fleetwood Mac had an effect on George's playing on tracks such as 'Sun King'.

Aaaaahhhhhhhhhh...
Here comes the sun king
Here comes the sun king
Everybody's laughing
Everybody's happy
Here comes the sun king

Cuando para mucho mi amore
de felice corazòn
Mondo paparazzi mi amore chica
verde parasol
Questo obrigado tanta mucho
que can eat it carousel

Written: Lennon/McCartney

Length: 2'26"

UK Release: *Abbey Road* album,
September 26, 1969

US Release: *Abbey Road* album,
October 1, 1969

SUN KING

SUN KING

As with his opinions on 'Being For The Benefit Of Mr Kite!', John's verdict on 'Sun King' came to alter over the years – but in this instance, changing from good to bad. In 1969 he said, "It was just half a song I had and this was just one way of getting rid of it without ever finishing it." In 1971, he referred to it as something that had come to him in a dream, implying that it was an inspired piece of work. By 1980, it had been reassessed as just another piece of "garbage".

Historically, the Sun King (*le Roi-Soleil*) was Louis XIV of France, who was so-called because of the splendour of his court at Versailles, and it could have been he whom John dreamt about, a dream wherein the King entered his palace to find all his guests were laughing and happy. Nancy Mitford had recently published a biography of Louis, *The Sun King*, and John may have come across it. It may also have been a jokey reference to George's song 'Here Comes The Sun'.

The closing lines of the song are composed of tourist Italian, Spanish and Portuguese words, strung together in no particular order – "paparazzi", "obrigado", "parasol", "mi amore". The original title of the song was 'Los Paranoias', a jokey reference to the Paraguayan singer Luis Alberto Del Parana who toured Britain with his group Los Paraguayos in the early 1960s and appeared on the same bill as the Beatles for the 1963 *Royal Variety Performance*. John said that they were joking around and started to throw in other foreign words and phrases. "Paul knew a few Spanish words from school that sounded vaguely like something."

According to George, Fleetwood Mac's 'Albatross', an instrumental hit early in 1969 on which Peter Green had used a lot of reverb on his guitar, was an influence on the sound. "We said 'Let's be Fleetwood Mac doing "Albatross"' just to get going. It never really sounded like Fleetwood Mac but that was the point of origin."

RIGHT: Royston Ellis (in glasses and beard) lands in Guernsey with the Beatles on August 8, 1963. It was that night that John had his polythene experience.

MEAN MR MUSTARD

John said that 'Mean Mr Mustard' was about a miser who concealed his paper money in order to prevent people forcing him to spend it. The line about stuffing a "ten bob note" (a British ten shilling note) up his nose John admitted was his own invention, claiming that it had absolutely nothing to do with snorting cocaine.

"I wrote it India," said John in 1969, "and it was from some newspaper clipping the title of which was 'Mean Mister Mustard' which was about some guy who'd done something or other and of course the story (in the song) is nothing like it. It was just the newspaper heading. It was another half a song that I never finished so I put it in there."

Mr Mustard sounds like a comic creation, maybe because of Colonel Mustard in the board game *Cluedo* that was created in 1949, but it is an actual British surname dating back at least to the 13th century. There are currently 72 British Mr Mustards registered to vote.

Tony Bramwell believes another colourful London character also provided John with inspiration for this song. "There was an old 'bag lady' who used to hang around the Knightsbridge end of Hyde Park, close to the army barracks," he remembers. "She had all her possessions in plastic bags and slept in the park. I'm sure that she had something to do with the song."

The reference to a "dirty old man" in the last line may have alluded to the character of Albert Steptoe in the BBC TV situation comedy *Steptoe And Son* (1962–1974), who was always referred to by his son Harold as "You dirty old man". It became a catchphrase in Britain around the same time that the actor who played the senior Steptoe, Wilfrid Brambell, played Paul's grandfather in *A Hard Day's Night*. (This explains the many references in the movie to Paul's granddad being "very clean").

'Mean Mr Mustard' was recorded with 'Sun King' as a continuous piece. In the original lyric, Mr Mustard had a sister called Shirley but John changed the name to Pam to form continuity with 'Polythene Pam'.

Mean Mister Mustard sleeps in the park
Shaves in the dark trying to save paper
Sleeps in a hole in the road
Saving up to buy some clothes
Keeps a ten-bob note up his nose
Such a mean old man
Such a mean old man

His sister Pam works in a shop
She never stops, she's a go-getter
Takes him out to look at the queen
Only place that he's ever been
Always shouts out something obscene
Such a dirty old man
Dirty old man

MEAN MR MUSTARD

311

Written: Lennon/McCartney

Length: 1'06"

UK Release: *Abbey Road* album, September 26, 1969

US Release: *Abbey Road* album, October 1, 1969

POLYTHENE PAM

Although John initially insisted that 'Polythene Pam' was about "a mythical Liverpool scrubber [coarse and promiscuous woman] dressed up in her jackboots and kilt", the song was actually based on two people he had known. The phrase "killer diller" was jazz slang for "terrific".

The name came from Pat Hodgetts (now Pat Dawson), one of a circle of original Beatles' fans during the Cavern Club era who knew the group well. She had an odd habit of chewing polythene and so became known to them as Polythene Pat. "I started going to see the Beatles in 1961 when I was 14 and I got quite friendly with them," she remembers. "If they were playing out of town they'd give me a lift back home in their van. It was about the same time that I started getting called Polythene Pat. It's embarrassing really. I just used to eat polythene all the time. I'd tie it in knots and then eat it. Sometimes I even used to burn it and then eat it when it got cold. Then I had a friend who got a job in a polythene bag factory, which was wonderful because it meant I had a constant supply."

But Polythene Pat never dressed in a polythene bag as the song describes. That little quirk was taken from another incident involving a girl called Stephanie, whom John met in the Channel Islands while on tour in August 1963.

Although John didn't identify her by name when he spoke to *Playboy* in 1980, he supplied a few clues. "('Polythene Pam') was me remembering a little event with a woman in Jersey, and a man who was England's answer to Allen Ginsberg, who gave us our first exposure."

England's answer to American beat poet Ginsberg was Royston Ellis, who first met the Beatles in June 1960 when he was invited to read his poetry at a Liverpool University arts festival, and what he exposed the Beatles to was the drug Benzedrine. It was the first drug they had been confronted with.

The "little event with a woman", as John described it, took place on Guernsey, not Jersey, when John met up with Ellis, who at that time had a summer job on the island as a ferryboat engineer. After the Beatles' concerts at the Auditorium in Guernsey on August 8, Ellis and his girlfriend Stephanie went back with John to the attic flat Ellis was renting and this is where the polythene came into the story. "[Ellis] said Miss X (a girl he wanted me to meet) dressed up in polythene," John later remembered. "She did. She didn't wear jackboots and kilts. I just sort of elaborated. Perverted sex in a polythene bag! I was just looking for something to write about."

Ellis, who now lives in Sri Lanka and writes travel books, can't recall any "perverted sex", but remembers the night spent in a bed with Stephanie and John. "We'd read all these things about leather and we didn't have any leather but I had my oilskins and we had some polythene bags from somewhere," he says. "We all dressed up in them and wore them in bed. John stayed the night with us in the same bed. I don't think anything very exciting happened and we all wondered what the fun was in being 'kinky'. It was probably more my idea than John's. It could have all happened because in a poetry booklet of mine which I had dedicated to the Beatles there was a poem with the lines: 'I long to have sex between black leather sheets, and ride shivering motorcycles between your thighs.'

"I can't really remember everything that happened. At the time, it meant nothing to me. It was just one event during a very eventful time of my life," Ellis adds. Besides being a poet, Ellis was a pundit on teenage life and a chronicler of emergent British rock 'n' roll. At the time of their first meeting, he

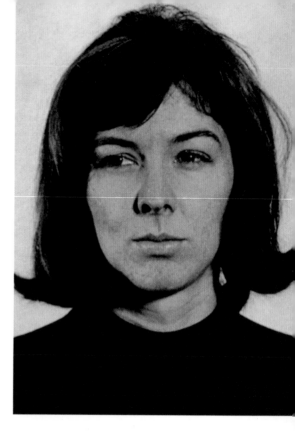

ABOVE: Stephanie, girlfriend of poet Royston Ellis, was part of the inspiration for the character of Polythene Pam.

Well you should see Polythene Pam
She's so good-looking but she looks like
  a man
Well you should see her in drag
  dressed in her polythene bag
Yes you should see Polythene Pam
Yeah yeah yeah

Get a dose of her in jackboots and kilt
She's killer-diller when she's dressed to
  the hilt
She's the kind of a girl that makes the
  "News of the World"
Yes you could say she was attractively
  built
Yeah yeah yeah

POLYTHENE
PAM

had just completed *The Big Beat Scene*, an excellent survey of late Fifties British beat music. (This book was republished in 2011 by Music Mentor Books with an afterword that details his experiences with the Beatles.)

Ellis intrigued John because he stood at the juncture of rock 'n' roll and literature. He arranged for the Beatles to back him early on at a beat music and poetry event at the Jacaranda Club. In July 1960, the *Record Mirror* reported that "the bearded sage" was thinking of bringing a Liverpool group called the Beetles to London to play behind him as he performed his poetry. "I was quite a star for them at that time because I had come up from London and that was a world they didn't really know about," says Ellis. "I stayed with them for about a week in their flat at Gambier Terrace during that 1960 visit. John was fascinated by the fact that I was a poet and that led to deep conversations."

Shortly after introducing John to the delights of polythene, Ellis left England and has spent much of the time since travelling. So far removed has he been from the British pop scene, that he had never even heard 'Polythene Pam' until contacted for this book. He does recall with some pride, though, that in 1973 John wrote to the alternative newspaper *International Times* to correct them about the circumstances of the Beatles' first drug experiences: "The first dope, from a Benzedrine inhaler, was given the Beatles (John, George, Paul and Stuart) by an English cover version of Allen Ginsberg – one Royston Ellis, known as 'beat poet'" said John. "So, give the saint his due."

SHE CAME IN THROUGH THE BATHROOM WINDOW

This song was inspired by the activities of an Apple Scruff who climbed into Paul's house in St John's Wood when he was away for the day. "We were bored, he was out and so we decided to pay him a visit," remembers Diane Ashley. "We found a ladder in his garden and stuck it up at the bathroom window, which he'd left slightly open. I was the one who climbed up and got in."

Once she was inside the house, she opened the front door and let the rest of the girls in. Fellow Apple Scruff Margo Bird remembers: "They rummaged around and took some clothes. People didn't usually take anything of real value but I think this time a lot of photographs and negatives were taken. There were really two groups of Apple Scruffs – those who would break in and those who would just wait outside with cameras and autograph books. I used to take Paul's dog for a walk and got to know him quite well. I was eventually offered a job at Apple. I started by making the tea and ended up in the promotions department working with Tony King."

Paul asked Margo if she could retrieve any of his belongings. "I knew who had done it and I discovered that a lot of the stuff had already gone to America," she said. "But I knew that there was one picture he particularly wanted back – a colour-tinted picture of him in a Thirties frame. I knew who had taken this and got it back for him."

Paul completed 'She Came In Through The Bathroom Window' in June 1968 during a trip to America to do business with Capitol Records. It was here that he resumed his relationship with Linda Eastman, whom he'd been introduced to the previous summer in London and had since met in New York.

One line was apparently inspired by the name of a New York cab driver.

Written: Lennon/McCartney

Length: 1'12"

UK Release: *Abbey Road* album, September 26, 1969

US Release: *Abbey Road* album, October 1, 1969

SHE CAME IN THROUGH THE BATHROOM WINDOW

(Gonna come out now, ha ha ha, wow look out)

She came in through
  the bathroom window
Protected by a silver spoon
But now she sucks her thumb
  and wanders
By the banks of her own lagoon

Didn't anybody tell her?
Didn't anybody see?
Sunday's on the phone to Monday
Tuesday's on the phone to me

She said she'd always been a dancer
She worked at 15 clubs a day
And though she thought I knew
  the answer
Well I knew but I could not say

And so I quit the police department
And got myself a steady job
And though she tried her best to
  help me
She could steal but she could not rob

Didn't anybody tell her?
Didn't anybody see?
Sunday's on the phone to Monday
Tuesday's on the phone to me
Oh yeah

"Paul and Heather and I were in New York going to the airport to come back to England," said Linda. "The name of the taxi driver talking to us was Eugene Quits, so then Paul wrote the line 'So I quit the police department'." Paul said, "This was the great thing about the randomness of it all. If I hadn't been in this guy's cab, or if it had been someone else driving, the song would have been different. Also I had a guitar there, so I could solidify it into something straight away."

According to Carol Bedford, an Apple Scruff who wrote the book *Waiting For The Beatles*, Paul later said to her: "I've written a song about the girls who broke in. It's called 'She Came In Through The Bathroom Window'." Diane was surprised to have become the subject of a Beatles' song. "I didn't believe it at first because he'd hated it so much when we broke in," she says. "But then I suppose anything can inspire a song, can't it? I know that all his neighbours rang him when they saw we'd got in and I'm sure that gave rise to the lines, 'Sunday's on the phone to Monday/Tuesday's on the phone to me'."

Now married with four teenage children, Diane keeps a framed photo of herself with Paul on her kitchen shelf and looks back on her days as an Apple Scruff with affection. "I don't regret any of it. I had a great time, a really great time."

GOLDEN SLUMBERS

Paul was at his father's house in Cheshire tinkering around on the piano. Flicking through a songbook belonging to his step-sister Ruth (Jim McCartney had since remarried), he came across the traditional lullaby 'Golden Slumbers'. Unable to read the music, he went ahead and made up his own melody adding new words as he went along.

The original version read:

Golden slumbers kiss your eyes
Smiles awake you when you rise;
Sleep, pretty wantons, do not cry,
And I will sing a lullaby;
Rock them, rock them, lullaby.

Care is heavy, therefore sleep you,
You are care, and care must keep you;
Sleep pretty wantons, do not cry,
And I will sing a lullaby;
Rock them, rock them, lullaby.

'Golden Slumbers' was written by the English writer and dramatist Thomas Dekker (c. 1572–1632), a contemporary of Shakespeare. The song was first published in *The Pleasant Comedy of Old Fortunatus* (1600).

A Londoner, Dekker was the author of *The Shoemaker's Holiday* (1600), *The Honest Whore* (1604), *The Gull's Hornbook* (1609), *The Roaring Girl* (1611) and the posthumously published *The Syn's Darling* (1656).

GOLDEN SLUMBERS

Once there was a way
  to get back homeward
Once there was a way to get back home
Sleep pretty darling do not cry
And I will sing a lullabye

Golden slumbers fill your eyes
Smiles awake you when you rise
Sleep pretty darling do not cry
And I will sing a lullabye

Once there was a way
  to get back homeward
Once there was a way to get back home
Sleep pretty darling do not cry
And I will sing a lullabye

Written: Lennon/McCartney

Length: 1'31"

UK Release: *Abbey Road* album, September 26, 1969

US Release: *Abbey Road* album, October 1, 1969

Written: Lennon/McCartney

Length: 1'57"

UK Release: *Abbey Road*'album, September 26, 1969

US Release: *Abbey Road* album, October 1, 1969

HER MAJESTY

Written by Paul on his farm in Scotland, 'Her Majesty' was originally part of the medley, coming between 'Mean Mr Mustard' and 'Polythene Pam' but, on hearing a playback, Paul didn't like it and asked for it to be edited out.

The engineer who cut it out then tagged it to the end of the tape so that it wouldn't be destroyed. Paul must have heard another playback with 'Her Majesty' appearing as an apparent afterthought and liked it enough to keep it there. Because the edit was only meant to be rough, the last chord of 'Mean Mr Mustard' was pressed into service to start 'Her Majesty', which ends abruptly because its own final note was left behind at the beginning of 'Polythene Pam'.

When he was ten years old, Paul was one of 60 Liverpool children to win a Coronation essay competition – his entry, entitled 'Coronation Day', compared the crowning of Elizabeth with that of William the Conqueror 900 years before. "But on the Coronation Day of our lovely young queen, Queen Elizabeth II, no rioting nor killing will take place, because present-day royalty rules us with affection rather than force."

The Beatles met Queen Elizabeth to receive their MBEs on October 26, 1965. Afterwards, asked what they thought of her, Paul answered: "She's lovely. She was very friendly. She was just like a mum to us." Years later Paul confessed to having had a crush on the young Elizabeth when he was a boy. Of the song Paul has said, "It's quite funny because it's basically monarchist, with a mildly disrespectful tone, but it's very tongue in cheek. It'd almost like a love song to the Queen."

In January 1997, it was announced that Paul would be honoured with a knighthood. He received it from the Queen on March 11, 1997 at Buckingham Palace, watched by his children James, Stella and Mary.

'Her Majesty' has the dubious distinction of being the final track on the last album the Beatles ever recorded.

Her Majesty's a pretty nice girl
But she doesn't have a lot to say
Her Majesty's a pretty nice girl
But she changes from day to day
I wanna tell her that I love her a lot
But I gotta get a belly full of wine
Her Majesty's a pretty nice girl
Some day I'm gonna make her mine
Some day I'm gonna make her mine.

Written: Lennon/McCartney

Length: 0'23"

UK Release: *Abbey Road* album, September 26, 1969

US Release: *Abbey Road* album, October 1, 1969

CARRY THAT WEIGHT

Although 'Carry That Weight' appears to be just another song in the medley and is credited as such on the album, it was in fact recorded with 'Golden Slumbers' as a single piece. It brought the medley back to where it started with the subject of money, business and the burdens of being a superstar.

The lyric expressed Paul's fears about the Beatles in their twilight days. He later said that the arguments over finance and management plunged him into the "darkest hours" of his life. The atmosphere around the Beatles had changed. "At certain times things get to me so much that I can't be upbeat any more and that was one of the times," he told his biographer Barry Miles. "In this heaviness there was no place to be. It was serious, paranoid heaviness and it was just very uncomfortable."

The song was recorded as a single by Apple signing Trash (formerly known as White Trash) under producer Tony Meehan, former drummer with the Shadows.

Boy, you're gonna carry that weight,
Carry that weight a long time
Boy, you're gonna carry that weight
Carry that weight a long time

I never give you my pillow
I only send you my invitations
And in the middle of the celebrations
I break down

Boy, you're gonna carry that weight
Carry that weight a long time
Boy, you're gonna carry that weight
Carry that weight a long time

Written: Lennon/McCartney

Length: 1'36"

UK Release: *Abbey Road* album, September 26, 1969

US Release: *Abbey Road* album, October 1, 1969

LEFT: Some fans were content to mob Paul. Others gathered outside his house and office at Apple and became quite friendly with him. Some came in through his bathroom window (*see* page 313).

RIGHT: The final photo session for the Beatles, August 22, 1969, in the grounds of John's Ascot mansion.

THE END

As the final proper track on the last album recorded by the Beatles, 'The End' was to become the song that signed off their studio career. Paul says that ultimately the love you "take" is equal to the love you "make". He may have been saying no more than "you take out what you put in", but John was sufficiently impressed to declare it a "very cosmic line" proving that "if Paul wants to, he can think."

Paul saw the couplet as a musical equivalent of the rhyming couplets with which Shakespeare ended some of his plays, a summary and also a signal that the events of the drama were now ended.

It certainly provided a neat symmetry to their recording career – which started with the gawky pleadings of lovesick teenagers in 'Love Me Do', and matured to reveal enigmatic words of wisdom from the group who transformed popular music.

THE END

Oh yeah, all right
Are you going to be in my dreams
Tonight?

And in the end
The love you take
Is equal to the love
You make

Written: Lennon/McCartney

Length: 2'19"

UK Release: *Abbey Road* album, September 26, 1969

US Release: *Abbey Road* album, October 1, 1969

I'LL BE ON MY WAY

In 1982 Kevin Howlett looked through the BBC's archives of radio sessions with the Beatles and produced a programme called *Beatles At The Beeb*. It was the first time that most of this material had been heard since the original broadcasts aired between 1962 and 1965. Shortly afterwards discussions began between EMI and the BBC to get the material released. However, it wasn't until 1994 that the project was realized.

The BBC's tapes were then taken to Abbey Road, where George Martin digitally remastered the 58 songs which had survived from a total of 88 which the Beatles had played live on BBC radio. In fact, only 57 of the tracks had survived in the BBC archives. The 58th was secured from a fan who had contacted Howlett in 1988, during the transmission of another Beatles series, to see if he would be interested in hearing some recordings he had made of the Beatles from radio programmes.

"The series was virtually over by then," says Howlett. "It was a bit too late to include anything else but I kept his letter on file and when the question of the album came up we had him come down to London where we took him along to EMI with his tapes. Fortunately he had a copy of 'Keep Your Hands Off My Baby' that didn't exist anywhere else. If you listen to it, you can tell that it's an off-air recording."

These robust live performances, captured by programmes with cute period names like *Easy Beat* and *Top Gear*, didn't have the benefit of multi-track recording facilities, overdubs or remixes and so provide an unvarnished example of what the Beatles sounded like during the peak of their performing career.

John and Paul learned to write songs by emulating the great singles of their youth. Trying these cover versions out on audiences taught them what worked and helped them to understand why. Bit by bit they began to drop the cover versions in favour of their own songs that created the same mood until most of their stage show was made up of Beatles originals.

Live At The BBC illustrates this growth. Of the songs they cover, 76% were from between 1954 and 1959, the period when they were serving their apprenticeship in Liverpool. Almost half the cover songs were written by the handful of writers they particularly revered: Chuck Berry, Little Richard, Carl Perkins, Goffin and King and Leiber and Stoller.

One of the advantages the Beatles and their contemporaries had over succeeding generations of rock musicians was that they had been musically literate since the earliest days of rock 'n' roll. When they played songs by Little Richard or Chuck Berry they weren't saluting a glorious past but playing music that had thrilled them at the time it was released. None of the songs on *Live At The BBC* was a decade old at the time of taping.

The double album *Live At The BBC* was released in November 1994 and went on to sell over 8 million copies in its first year.

The sun is fading away
That's the end of the day
As the June light turns to moonlight
I'll be on my way

Just one kiss and I'll go
Don't hide the tears that don't show
As the June light turns to moonlight
I'll be on my way

To where the winds don't blow
And golden rivers flow
This way will I go

They were right I was wrong
True love didn't last long
As the June light turns to moonlight
I'll be on my way hey

To where the winds don't blow
And golden rivers flow
This way will I go

They were right I was wrong
True love didn't last long
As the June light turns to moonlight
I'll be on my way hey
I'll be on my way oh
I'll be on my way oh
I'll be on my way

Written: Lennon/McCartney

Length: 1'57"

UK Release: *Live At The BBC* album, November 30, 1994

US Release: *Live At The BBC* album, November 30, 1994

I'LL BE ON MY WAY

'I'll Be On My Way' was the only unreleased Lennon-McCartney song to be included on *Live At The BBC* and, as such, the first Lennon-McCartney song played by the Beatles to be released since May 1970.

Written by Paul in 1961 in emulation of Buddy Holly, it was included in the group's repertoire over the next two years but wasn't played at the Decca audition, an indication that it had already fallen out of favour. It was given to their stable mate Billy J Kramer, who used it as the flip side of 'Do You Want To Know A Secret?' in April 1963.

The lyrics serve as a reminder that the Beatles didn't start out as artistic visionaries but simply rearranged existing cliches. Here "June light" turns to "moon light" (naturally) and the lovelorn narrator is forced into exile where "golden rivers flow" and "the winds don't blow". It sounds like the rim of an active volcano, but maybe Paul had something else in mind. John, typically, poured scorn on the song when asked about it in 1980 because it was precisely the sort of pop that had always made him uncomfortable by stifling individual points of view with a raft of stock phrases. Paul wasn't quite so harsh when he looked back. It was "a bit too June-moon" he conceded, but it had "worked out quite well" for the group in their early shows.

Billy J Kramer and the Dakotas recorded their version at Abbey Road on March 14, 1963, the Beatles' version was taped for the BBC programme *Side by Side* on April 4 and Kramer's single was released on April 21.

13
Live at the BBC

The three double albums that make up the *Anthology* set owe their genesis to an exercise in 1984 when engineer John Barrett was given the task of collating all the Beatles material in EMI's archives. Out of hundreds of hours of recordings he identified 13 unreleased tracks. EMI made test pressings and approached the remaining Beatles with the suggestion of an album. At the time, no agreement on a release could be reached.

Five years later, in an unrelated move, Apple's long-time manager Neil Aspinall revived a documentary idea he'd had in 1969 to collect all the best film footage of the Beatles for a television series that would tell their story, in their words. He wanted the remaining Beatles to come together and record

some new incidental music. The project would be called *The Long And Winding Road*.

The album of unreleased songs and the documentary series eventually coalesced into *Anthology*. The planned incidental music was dropped in favour of recording two new Beatles tracks. "As the thought of the three of us sitting down in a studio got nearer, I got cold feet about it," said Paul. "I thought, 'Does the world need a three-quarter Beatle record?' But what if John was on – the three of us and John – like a real new record? If only we could pull off the impossible, that would be more fun, a bigger challenge."

When Yoko agreed to let the remaining Beatles use two demo cassettes of unfinished songs by John as the basis for the new tracks, the seemingly impossible

Anthology
1-3

14

was achieved. These eventually became singles that helped to promote both the six-hour TV documentary series and the *Anthology* albums.

Anthology was not a soundtrack to the documentary series but an aural counterpart made up of alternative takes, unreleased tracks, live performances, early demos and brief snatches of interview. Out of the 139 songs on the collection, 28 were cover versions.

The greatest interest was naturally in the 21 new Beatles compositions, some of which had only previously been heard performed by other artists or on rare bootlegs. These ranged from poor quality home recordings that were purely of historical value to completed studio tracks that hadn't been included on the albums for which they'd been recorded.

The general critical response to these rarities was that the Beatles original judgment to drop them or give them away had been sound. They could probably have had a hit with 'Come And Get It' and it's hard to see why 'Not Guilty' didn't find a place on *The White Album* but otherwise none of these "new" songs enhanced their reputation. They merely confirmed what we had assumed, which was that the Beatles had already given us their best. Their original choices had been good.

ABOVE: Fielding questions at the launch of *Anthology 1* were (left to right) EMI's Rupert Perry, Derek Taylor, Jeff Lynne, George Martin and Neil Aspinall.

FREE AS A BIRD

'Free As A Bird' was essentially a novelty single designed to attract attention to the *Anthology* project. The novelty was that it would be the first new Beatles single in 25 years and would, in sound at least, reunite the most popular pop group the world has known.

There was feverish media excitement surrounding the release of the record, which was encouraged by EMI's publicity department. An early press release read: "The single, copies of which are currently under armed guard outside the UK, will be released worldwide on MONDAY DECEMBER 4."

Nothing could hope to live up to these expectations but, in the event, 'Free As A Bird' was plausibly Beatles-sounding (circa 1969) although obviously hampered by the restraints of having been built around a discarded fragment of a John Lennon song that had been taped on a cassette machine.

The events that led to the recording began on January 1, 1994 when Paul called Yoko to wish her a happy new year. This act of reconciliation led to further conversations and then a meeting when Paul attended John's induction into the Rock 'n' Roll Hall of Fame. During this time together they discussed the possibility of the remaining Beatles working on John's home demos. Yoko offered three tracks for consideration – 'Real Love', 'Grow Old With Me' and 'Free As A Bird'.

"I liked 'Free As A Bird' immediately," Paul said. "I liked the melody. It had strong chords and it really appealed to me … The great thing was that John hadn't finished it. On the middle eight he was just blocking out lyrics that didn't have yet. That meant that we had to come up with something, and that now I was actually working 'with John'."

John probably first worked on the song at home in New York during the latter part of 1977. On October 4 of that year he and Yoko held a press conference in Japan to announce that they were both putting their careers on hold to concentrate on raising their son Sean.

Several of the songs he began during this period dealt with his new life as a house-husband. In 'I'm Stepping Out', "Watching The Wheels', 'Beautiful Boy' and 'Cleanup Time' he wrote of the strange sense of freedom he felt in abandoning the life of a celebrity for domestic duties.

Like many people psychologically wounded in early life, John craved attention and then spurned it when it came. Interviewed by *Rolling Stone* in 1970 his first comment was: "If I had the capabilities of being something other than I am, I would. It's no fun being an artist." His final comment, after being asked how he saw himself at 64, was in a similar vein. "I hope we're a nice old couple living off the coast of Ireland or something like that – looking at our scrapbook of madness."

For John, a stable family home had been the one thing that had always eluded him. With Sean and Yoko, he was determined to hang on to what he had got. 'Free As A Bird' was written to express his delight at being set free from the demands of celebrity and from the artistic pressure of having to compete with his earlier selves. He was, as he sings, "home and dry."

For the middle section of the song John had only the couplet "Whatever happened to/The life that we once knew?", lines reminiscent of the belief he had expressed in 'Help!', 'Strawberry Fields Forever' and 'In My Life' that his early childhood was the most idyllic time of his life. Paul's additional lines subvert this train of thought, turning it into a longing for healed relationships – presumably his own with John.

Free as a bird
It's the next best thing to be
Free as a bird

Home, home and dry
Like a homing bird fly
As a bird on wings

Whatever happened to
The lives that we once knew?
Can we really live without each other?

Where did we lose the touch
That seemed to mean so much?
It always made me feel so...

Free as a bird
Like the next best thing to be
Free as a bird

Home, home and dry
Like a homing bird I'll fly
As a bird on wings

Whatever happened to
The life that we once knew?
Always made me feel so free

Ah...
Ah...
Ah...

Free as a bird
It's the next best thing to be
Free as a bird
Free as a bird
Free as a bird
Oooooo

Free...

FREE AS A BIRD

ABOVE: Sean Lennon, Yoko Ono and Paul at the Rock and Roll Hall of Fame in January 1994. Bridges were rebuilt between Paul and Yoko that have allowed Beatles projects to flow.

Written: Original version – Lennon; Beatles version – Lennon/McCartney/Harrison/Starr.

Length: 4'24"

UK single release: December 4, 1995

UK chart position: 2

US single release: December 4, 1995

US chart position: 6

Recording took place in February and March of 1994 at Paul's studio in Sussex with production credits being shared between the Beatles and former Electric Light Orchestra vocalist/guitarist Jeff Lynne. John's original cassette was transferred to tape and the sound digitally remastered. "We then took the liberty of beefing the song up with different chord changes and different arrangements," said George Harrison.

The project was approached as if John was still alive and that he and Paul were still working on each other's unfinished songs. "We came up with this holiday scenario," said Paul. "I rang up Ringo and said let's pretend that John's gone on holiday and he's sent us a cassette and said, 'Finish it up for me.'"

George Martin, although not involved, gave it a cautious blessing but felt that it lacked dynamics because they hadn't been able to successfully separate the piano and vocals on the original cassette and had put it in a rigid time beat to make overdubbing easier.

"They stretched it and compressed it and put it around until it got to a regular waltz control click and then they were done," he said. "The result was that in order to conceal the bad bits they had to plaster it fairly heavily so that what you ended up with was quite a thick homogeneous sound that hardly stops."

'Free As A Bird' reached Number 2 in the British charts and Number 6 in America.

All my little plans and schemes
Lost like some forgotten dreams
Seems that all I really was doing
Was waiting for you

Just like little girls and boys
Playing with their little toys
Seems like all they really were doing
Was waiting for love

No need to be alone
No need to be alone
It's real love, it's real
Yes it's real love, it's real

From this moment on I know
Exactly where my life will go
Seems that all I really was doing
Was waiting for love

No need to be afraid
No need to be afraid
It's real love, it's real
Yes it's real love, it's real

Thought I'd been in love before
But in my heart, I wanted more
Seems like all I really was doing
Was waiting for you

No need to be alone
Don't need to be alone

It's real love, it's real
It's real love, it's real
Yes it's real love, it's real
It's real love, it's real
Yes it's real love, it's real
It's real love, it's real
Yes it's real love, it's real
It's real love, it's real

Written: Lennon

Length: 3'54"

UK single release: March 4, 1996

UK chart position: 4

US single release: March 4, 1996

US chart position: 11

REAL LOVE

'Real Love' was a song that John had worked on for at least two years and, although many people weren't aware of it, a version was used in the 1988 soundtrack to Andrew Solt's documentary film *Imagine*.

It began as a song called 'Real Life', the verses of which later became 'I'm Stepping Out', posthumously released on *Milk And Honey*. He obviously thought the remaining chorus – "It's real life/Yes, it's real life" – too good to throw away. The theme of the song, 'I have got back to what really counts in life', was the essential theme of all his post-Beatles work. He was still stripping away myths, dispensing with the unnecessary and in this case, getting down to the reality of kitchens, cigarettes, babies, news papers and early morning blues.

The revamped song, still called 'Real Life', was coming closer to the version that the Beatles would work on. The references to "little girls and boys" and "little plans and schemes" were there but the verses were not yet in the final order.

When he finally changed the chorus from "real life" to "real love" the theme became the transforming love of Yoko Ono. He said many times in interview that he felt that she was the woman that all his longings for love and acceptance had been directed towards even before he met her. She was the "girl with kaleidoscope eyes". She was, as he wrote in an essay titled 'The Ballad Of John And Yoko', "Someone who I had already known, but somehow had lost."

During February 1995 producer Jeff Lynne worked at deleting any extraneous noises on John's cassette copy of 'Real Love' and then transferred the mono recording to two 24-track analogue tapes at Paul's Sussex studio. Paul, George and Ringo then added guitars, drums, bass, percussion and backing vocals. At one point Paul even used the upright bass he owns which once belonged to Bill Black and was used on Elvis Presley's 'Heartbreak Hotel'.

'Real Love' made it to Number 4 in the British charts and 11 in America.

BELOW: A freshly shorn John with Yoko at the Watergate hearings in June 1973.

REAL LOVE

CHRISTMAS TIME (IS HERE AGAIN)

Particularly for the British, the Beatles became inextricably linked to the Christmases of the 1960s. Six of their albums were released to take advantage of the Christmas market and four of their singles were Christmas Number 1s. In 1963 and 1964 they presented special Christmas shows in London theatres that were a mixture of music and pantomime and had support acts ranging from the Yardbirds to Rolf Harris.

Between 1963 and 1969 they produced a flexi disc (a record pressed on paper thin vinyl especially used for giveaways in magazines) exclusively for members of their official fan club that offered spoken greetings from each Beatle and some lighthearted conversation. The earliest messages were clearly scripted but as their music developed in its imaginative scope, so did the discs. In 1965 they fooled around with a version of 'Auld Lang Syne' and the next year Paul wrote a mini pantomime for the group.

'Christmas Time (Is Here Again)', the only original song written for fan club members, came out in 1967, the year that *Magical Mystery Tour* was being screened on Boxing Day. The unedited version, recorded on November 28, was over six minutes long and parts of it were used to punctuate a satirical sketch written by all four Beatles.

Although it largely consists of a single line repeated like a musical mantra, 'Christmas Time (Is Here Again)' is illustrative of their fascination with children's songs and rhymes which began with 'Yellow Submarine' in 1966. This in part reflected nostalgia for the Liverpool of the 1940s but was also part of the psychedelic tendency to regress to simpler states of mind where it wasn't out of place for an adult to wear ripped jeans, blow bubbles and think buttercups were "far out".

BELOW: During the 1960s Beatles albums and singles were frequently timed for the Christmas market. For seven consecutive years they produced a special recording for members of the official fan club.

CHRISTMAS TIME (IS HERE AGAIN)

Here's the fan's new remix. Take 444

Christmas time is here again
Christmas time is here again
Christmas time is here again
Christmas time is here again

Ain't been 'round since you know when
Christmas time is here again
O U T spells out

Christmas time is here again
Christmas time is here again
Christmas time is here again
Christmas time is here again

Ain't been 'round since you know when
Christmas time is here again
O U T spells out

Christmas time is here again
Christmas time is here again
Christmas time is here again
Christmas time is here again

Ain't been 'round since you know when
Christmas time is here again
O U T spells out

Christmas time is here again
Christmas time is here again
Christmas time is here again
Christmas time is here again

Written: Harrison/Lennon/McCartney/Starr

Length: 3'03"

UK single release: December 4, 1995 on 'Free As A Bird' EP

US single release: December 4, 1995 on 'Free As A Bird' EP

In spite of all the danger
In spite of all that may be
I'll do anything for you
Anything you want me to
If you'll be true to me

In spite of all the heartache
That you may cause me
I'll do anything for you
Anything you want me to
If you'll be true to me

I'll look after you
Like I've never done before
I'll keep all the others
From knocking at your door

In spite of all the danger
In spite of all that may be
I'll do anything for you
Anything you want me to
If you'll be true to me

Yeah!

In spite of all the heartache
That you may cause me
I'll do anything for you
Anything you want me to
If you'll be true to me
I'll do anything for you
Anything you want me to
If you'll be true to me

IN SPITE OF ALL THE DANGER

Written: Harrison/McCartney

Length: 2'44"

UK release: *Anthology 1* album, November 21, 1995

US release: *Anthology 1* album, November 21, 1995

IN SPITE OF ALL THE DANGER

A rough recording transferred from a slightly worn 78 rpm shellac disc cut in the spring or summer of 1958, this has historical value in that it is the earliest taping of the soon-to-be Beatles as well as being the group's first writing effort to make it into the archives.

It was recorded on a £400 portable tape recorder at a small studio housed in the terraced home of a 63-year-old electrical goods shop owner in the Kensington district of Liverpool. The Quarry Men, which then consisted of John, Paul, George, pianist John Duff Lowe and drummer Colin Hanton, paid 17 shillings and six pence (87p) to cut two songs.

The first song they chose was 'That'll Be The Day', a September 1957 hit in Britain for the Crickets (with Buddy Holly), and the second was the McCartney-Harrison number 'In Spite Of All The Danger'. "It says on the label that it was me and George but I think it was written by me and George played the guitar solo," said Paul in 1995. "It was my song. It was very similar to an Elvis song."

It was in fact very similar to a particular Elvis song – 'Trying To Get To You' – which was written by Rose Marie McCoy and Margie Singleton and recorded by Elvis on July 11, 1955. It was the only Sun recording by Elvis to use a piano and was released as a single in September 1956.

John Duff Lowe remembers 'In Spite Of All The Danger' as being the only original song the Quarry Men played at the time. "I can well remember even at the rehearsal at his house in Forthlin Road Paul was quite specific about how he wanted it played and what he wanted the piano to do," he says. "There was no question of improvising. We were told what we had to play. There was a lot of arranging going on even back then."

It was recorded on a single microphone and Lowe thinks that it must have gone straight to disc because he can't recall waiting around for it to be transferred from tape and there are mistakes in John's vocal which would otherwise have been corrected. The disc was then passed on from member to member and eventually came down to Lowe, who kept it in a sock drawer until 1981 when a colleague suggested to him that it might have some commercial value. He had it valued by Sotheby's, which led to the discovery of the disc being reported by *Sunday Times* columnist Stephen Pile in July 1981.

"Before mid-day on that Sunday Paul McCartney had called my mum in Liverpool," says Lowe. "I eventually spoke to him on the 'phone and we had long conversations over the next few days because he wanted to buy it from me. I was living in Worcester at the time and he sent his solicitor and his business manager up. I deposited the disc in a small brief case at the local Barclay's Bank and we met up in a small room the bank kindly let me use. The deal was done, I handed the record over and we all went home."

Although Paul didn't have a specific project in mind at the time, part of the deal was that Lowe had to assign over all rights to the track and promise not to perform the song for the next 15 years. "That took us up to August 1996," says Lowe. "Isn't it strange that two months later the final album in the *Anthology* set came out?"

YOU'LL BE MINE

Recorded in the summer of 1960 on a borrowed tape machine at Paul's family home at Forthlin Road, this is the first recording of a Lennon and McCartney song, although that's the extent of its interest. It sounds like nothing more than a couple of minutes of musical hilarity put together by teenagers in awe of the sound of their own voices.

Without a drummer but with the addition of fourth guitarist Stuart Sutcliffe, the group was rehearsing for their upcoming stint in Hamburg and decided on an Inkspots parody with John delivering a melodramatic spoken section that owed a lot to his fascination with the Goons. Appropriately the whole track concludes with a wild squeal of laughter. You can almost picture them wetting themselves as they played it back again and again.

Written: Lennon/McCartney

Length: 1'38"

UK release: *Anthology 1* album, November 21, 1995

US release: *Anthology 1* album, November 21, 1995

Well darling all that night
You'll be mine and I know
You'll be mine
Every time
You'll be mine

And so all at night
You'll be mine
You'll be mine
And the stars
Never die
You'll be mine
Oh

(My darling. When you
brought me that toast the other morning
I, I looked into you eyes and I could see
your National Health eyeball
And I loved you, like I never done,
I've never done before!)

As the stars
Never die
And you'll be mine
You will be mine
You'll be mine
As the stars and so
You'll be mine

YOU'LL BE MINE

CAYENNE

Paul has said that the instrumental 'Cayenne', or 'Cayenne Pepper' as it was originally titled, was written before he met John, probably at the age of 14 when he got his first £15 guitar. Another instrumental he wrote during the same period, 'Cat's Walk', was recorded by the Chris Barber Band in 1967 as 'Cat Call'.

When Paul committed 'Cayenne' to tape in the summer of 1960, rock 'n' roll instrumentals were a regular chart phenomenon. Since the January of that year there had been hit singles by Johnny and the Hurricanes, the Ventures, Duane Eddy, Bert Weedon, Sandy Nelson, Jerry Lordan, the John Barry Seven and The Shadows.

"It's not brilliant," Paul has said of 'Cayenne', "But when you listen to it you can hear a lot of stuff I'm going to write. So, it's interesting from that point of view."

Written: McCartney

Length: 1'13"

UK release: *Anthology 1* album, November 21, 1995

US release: *Anthology 1* album, November 21, 1995

CAYENNE

CRY FOR A SHADOW

When this track was recorded in June 1961, Cliff Richard and the Shadows were Britain's premier pop act. Since his first hit with 'Move It' in October 1958 Cliff had enjoyed ten Top Ten hits and the Shadows were now making their own instrumental hits.

Although the Beatles found Cliff a bit too tame for their liking, they were early admirers of the Shadows. Paul learned the opening chords of 'Move It' from watching lead guitarist Hank Marvin's finger movements on the *Oh Boy!* TV show and when Cliff first played the Liverpool Empire with the Shadows on October 12, 1958, Paul was in the audience.

'Cry For A Shadow', an instrumental intended to sound like the Shadows, was credited to Harrison-Lennon. It was the Beatles first composition to make it onto record when it appeared on Tony Sheridan's 1962 German album *My Bonnie*, where the "backing group" was listed as the Beat Brothers.

The story is that the composition came about by accident. Rory Storm was in Germany and had asked George to play him a recent British hit by the Shadows – 'Apache' or 'Frightened City' – and George came up with something new, either because he couldn't remember the Shadows' tunes or as a joke on Storm. At first he was going to title it 'Beatle Bop' but then, out of homage to his original inspiration, he called it 'Cry For A Shadow'. "It doesn't sound like 'Frightened City' or 'Apache'," says Shadows guitarist Bruce Welch. "What it has in common with the Shadows is that it has the same instrumentation that we used but melodically it's nowhere near either of them. What I had heard was that it was done as a piss-take because at that time we had a stranglehold on the British group scene and we'd never been to Germany as almost every other group did."

It was recorded in Germany when the orchestra leader and record company producer Bert Kaempfert hired the Beatles for 300 Marks to back Sheridan on a Polydor record. Norwich-born Sheridan, a veteran of London's 2 I's coffee bar, had spent a lot of time in Germany and Kaempfert wanted him to do rocked-up versions of such standards as 'My Bonnie' and 'When The Saints Go Marching In'. The Beatles were allowed their own spot on 'Ain't She Sweet' and 'Cry For A Shadow'.

Brian Epstein, who was responsible for getting the Beatles out of leather jackets and into tailored suits, encouraged them to emulate the Shadows in their attire and on-stage courtesies. The two groups first met in 1963 at a party in London and in June of that year Hank, Bruce and new bass player Brian 'Licorice' Locking came to Paul's 21st in Liverpool.

ABOVE: The Shadows: (left to right) Bruce Welch, Tony Meehan, Hank Marvin and Jet Harris. In 1961 they were the British rock group to contend with.

CRY FOR A SHADOW

Written: Harrison/Lennon

Length: 2'22"

UK release: *Anthology 1* album, November 21, 1995

US release: *Anthology 1* album, November 21, 1995

LIKE DREAMERS DO

I, I saw a girl in my dreams
And so it seems that I will love her
Oh you, you are that girl in my dreams
And so it seems that I will love you
And I waited for your kiss
Waited for the bliss
Like dreamers do
And I,
Oh I'll be there, yeah
Waiting for you, you, you, you, you, you

You, you came just one dream ago
And now I know that I will love you
Oh I knew when you first said hello
That's how I know that I will love you
And I waited for your kiss
Waited for the bliss
Like dreamers do
And I
Oh I'll be there, yeah
Waiting for you, you, you, you, you

You, you came just one dream ago
And now I know that I will love you
Oh I knew when you first said hello
That's how I know that I will love you
And I waited for your kiss
Waited for the bliss
Like dreamers do
Oh like dreamers do
Like dreamers do

Written: Lennon/McCartney

Length: 2'35"

UK release: *Anthology 1* album, November 21, 1995

US release: *Anthology 1* album, November 21, 1995

LIKE DREAMERS DO

The sound that was dubbed "Merseybeat" started out largely as covers of recent American hits and selections from Buddy Holly, Chuck Berry, Ray Charles and Jerry Lee Lewis. The Beatles stood out initially by discovering unknown acts and obscure B-sides but even these were soon copied and became standard fare on Merseyside.

It was this situation that propelled them into serious song writing. Their goal was to come up with material that not only went down well with their audiences but which remained unique to their act. Paul has said that 'Like Dreamers Do' was one of the first of his own compositions that he tried out at the Cavern. This implies that he wrote it for the Cavern audience, but the Quarry Men were performing it as far back as 1958. What he probably meant was that it was one of the first songs from his back catalogue that he felt confident enough to slip into the Beatles' regular set.

The early arrangement of the song was weak, he thought, although "certain of the kids" at the Cavern liked it. When the Beatles came to audition for Decca on January 1, 1962 it was one of three Lennon-McCartney songs that they included in a 15-song set (the others were 'Hello Little Girl' and 'Love Of The Loved').

By the time of their EMI audition nine months later, all of these songs had been replaced by better material. Shortly afterwards these new compositions were offered to other artists, 'Like Dreamers Do' to the Applejacks, a Birmingham six-piece group with a female bassist, who reached Number 20 with it in July 1964.

'Like Dreamers Do' is a typically optimistic McCartney song. He dreams about a girl, meets a girl who resembles the girl of his dreams and knows that he will love her. There is no mention of whether the girl will love him. Paul's foregone conclusion was that his feelings would be reciprocated.

329

ANTHOLOGY 1–3

BELOW: The restored living room of Paul's childhood home. It was by this fireplace that several early Beatles songs were composed by John and Paul.

HELLO LITTLE GIRL

John frequently referred to 'Hello Little Girl' as his earliest composition. Written in 1958, it became the first of his songs to be performed by the Quarry Men.

He credited its origin to the Cole Porter song 'It's De-Lovely', with its chorus of "It's delightful, it's delicious, it's de-lovely", which was first sung by Bob Hope in the 1936 stage musical *Red, Hot and Blue* and was recorded in Britain by Carroll Gibbons and the Savoy Hotel Orpheans in 1938.

"That song always fascinated me for some reason or another," John said. "It was possibly connected to my mother. She used to sing that one. It's all very Freudian. So I made 'Hello Little Girl' out of it. It was supposed to be a Buddy Holly-style song."

There is no similarity between the two songs other than the device of repeating the title as a chorus. It may have been more the playful spirit of the song and, as with 'Please Please Me', the association with his mother's musical interests. The imprint of Buddy Holly is more easily detectable. In its earliest incarnation the middle eight was apparently swiped wholesale from 'Maybe Baby'.

Just as Paul's early songs always bore the hallmark of optimism, John's bore the hallmark of pessimism. Paul assumed acceptance and love where John braced himself for rejection. In 'Hello Little Girl' he attempts to attract a girl's attention but she remains unaware of him. He sends her flowers but she is unmoved. He ends up lonely about to "lose my mind".

Recorded for the Decca audition in January 1962 'Hello Little Girl' was already off their set-list by the time they signed for EMI later in the year. "It was then offered to Gerry and the Pacemakers," remembers Tony Bramwell. "It was considered as the follow up to 'How Do You Do It?'. They recorded a demo of it [included on *Gerry and the Pacemakers: The Best of the EMI Years*, 1992] but by that time Mitch Murray had come up with 'I Like It'."

The song was then offered to the Fourmost, another Liverpool group managed by Brian Epstein. After a Sunday concert in Blackpool in which the two groups had appeared, John invited the Fourmost to his house to see the lyrics. The following morning they were sent a demo tape. "We had to record on the Wednesday and so we only had two days to record it," said bass guitarist Billy Hatton. "As a matter of fact, when we were recording, we were just learning the song as we went along."

The record was a hit for the Fourmost after its release on August 23 and reached Number 7 in the British charts. It was released in America on September 16.

Hello little girl
Hello little girl
Hello little girl

When I see you everyday
I say, "Mm mm hello little girl"
When you're passing on your way
I say, "Mm mm hello little girl"
When I see you passing by
I cry, "Mm mm hello little girl"
When I try to catch your eye
I cry, "Mm mm hello little girl"

I send you flowers, but you don't care
You never seem to see me
   standing there
I often wonder what you're thinking of
I hope it's me and love love love
So I hope there'll come a day
When you'll say, "Mm you're my little
   girl"

It's not the first time that it's
   happened to me,
It's been a long lonely time
It's so funny, funny to see that I'm
   about to lose my my-my-my-mind

So I hope there'll come a day
When you say, "Mm mm
You're my little girl, mm mm mm
You're my little girl, mm mm mm"
You're my little girl, oh yeah
You're my little girl

Do do do do do

HELLO
LITTLE GIRL

Written: Lennon/McCartney

Length: 1'40"

UK release: *Anthology 1* album, November 21, 1995

US release: *Anthology 1* album, November 21, 1995

When I see you
I just don't know what to say
I like to be with you
Every hour of the day
So if you want me
Just like I need you
You know what to do

I watched you walking by
And you looked alone
I hope that you won't mind
If I walk you back home
But if you want me
Just like I need you
You know what to do

Just call on me
When you're lonely
I'll keep my love
For you only
I'll call on you
If I'm lonely too

Understand I'll stay
With you every day
Make you love me more
In every way
So if you want me
Just like I want you
You know what to do

Just call on me
When you're lonely
I'll keep my love
For you only
I'll call on you
If I'm lonely too

Understand I'll stay
With you every day
Make you love me more
In every way
So if you want me
Just like I need you
You know what to do

YOU KNOW WHAT TO DO

YOU KNOW WHAT TO DO

This is a languid country-flavoured song written by George and recorded on June 3, 1964. Ringo had been taken ill that morning, on the verge of a tour, and so the studio time booked to record a fourteenth and final song for the *A Hard Day's Night* album had to be used to rehearse substitute drummer Jimmy Nicol. As a result only three new demos were recorded that day – Paul's 'It's For You' (later given to Cilla Black), John's 'No Reply' and this new song from George.

Being the youngest Beatle, George always had a hard time getting his ideas to be taken seriously. This was only the second song of his to be taped by the group (the first being 'Don't Bother Me') but it was never developed and, due to misfiling, was lost for the next three decades. If it had been worked on by the group, it would surely have been a contender for *Beatles For Sale*.

Although it is a formulaic song with no deep revelation at the core, what is interesting to note is that George was just 12 weeks into his courtship of Pattie Boyd. Could he have written a song at the time about wanting to be with his girl "every hour of the day" without having her in mind?

Written: Harrison

Length: 1'58"

UK release: *Anthology 1* album, November 21, 1995

US release: *Anthology 1* album, November 21, 1995

BELOW: Brian Epstein's "Stable of Stars" – the Beatles, Gerry and the Pacemakers, and Billy J Kramer and the Dakotas. This was the cream of "Merseybeat".

IF YOU'VE GOT TROUBLE

If you've got trouble
Then you got less trouble than me
You say you're worried
You can't be as worried as me (Oh oh)

You're quite content to be bad
With all the advantage you had over me
Just cause you're trouble
Then don't bring your troubles to me

I don't think it's funny
When you ask for money and things
Especially when you're standing there
Wearing diamonds and rings (Oh oh)

You think I'm soft in the head
Well try someone softer instead anything
It's not so funny
When you know what money can bring

You better leave me alone
I don't need a thing from you
You better take yourself home
Go and count a ring or two

If you've got trouble
Then you got less trouble than me
You say you're worried
You can't be as worried as me

You're quite content to be bad
With all the advantage you had over me
Just cause you're trouble
Then don't bring your troubles to me

(Ah rock on, anybody.)

You better leave me alone,
I don't need a thing from you
You better take yourself home
Go and count a ring or two

If you've got trouble
Then you got less trouble than me
You say you're worried
You can't be as worried as me (Oh oh)

You're quite contend to be bad
With all the vantage you had over me
Just cause you're trouble
And don't bring your troubles to me
Just cause you're trouble
And don't bring your troubles to me

IF YOU'VE GOT TROUBLE

John and Paul never gave Ringo their best songs but neither did they give him their worst. However, 'If You've Got Trouble' must rate as the worst one they ever expected him to sing. Melodically, it's uninspiring. Lyrically, it's embarrassing. It's hard to believe that the team that had just written 'Ticket To Ride' and 'You've Got To Hide Your Love Away' could come up with this. Recorded in one take, it sounds as though it was also composed in one take.

The theme of the song could be roughly summarized as "If you think you've got problems – you should see mine!". The vitriol in the song sounds like John. Did it start out as a barbed attack on Cynthia, telling her to quit complaining about his abilities as a husband and a father and to be grateful for the luxuries afforded by the Beatles new stardom?

An interview that year in the *Saturday Evening Post* conducted by Al Aronowitz suggests such a context for the song: "Their friends say that she [Cynthia] was in awe of John when they first met and she still is; a feeling, in fact, which has grown as his stardom rockets him further into the entertainment heavens, troubling her with the occasional thought that she might be left behind. When the Beatles are on tour, she often is left behind. 'Well, she certainly doesn't seem to mind spending the money I'm making,' John says."

Intended for the *Help!* album, it was never worked on again or considered for any other album.

Written: Lennon/McCartney

Length: 2'48"

UK release: *Anthology 2* album, March 18, 1996

US release: *Anthology 2* album, March 18, 1996

A friend says that your love
Won't mean a lot
But you know that your love
Is all you've got
At times things are so fine
And at times they're not
But when she says she loves you
That means a lot

A friend says that a love
Is never true
But you know that this
Can't apply to you
A touch can mean so much
When it's all you've got
And when she says she loves you
That means a lot

Love can be deep inside
Love can be suicide
Can't you see you can't hide
What you feel when it's real

A friend says that your love
Won't mean a lot
But you know that your love
Is all you've got
A touch can mean so much
When it's all you've got
But when she says she loves you
That means a lot

Can't you see, yeah
Can't you see, yeah
Can't you see, yeah
Can't you see, yeah
Can't you see, yeah
Can't you see, yeah
Can't you see, yeah
Can't you see, yeah (fade out)

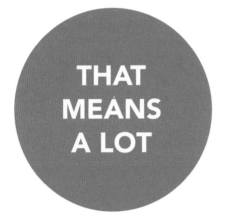

THAT MEANS A LOT

THAT MEANS A LOT

Written primarily by Paul, this was another song intended to appear on *Help!* for which the Beatles weren't able to record a definitive version. During sessions on February 20 and March 30, 1965 they attempted it 24 times before finally abandoning it.

The song takes the point of view of a third party looking in on a relationship, a device first used in 'She Loves You'. The shift in viewpoint opened up the possibility of writing in voices other than their own and expressing attitudes that were not necessarily their own.

"We found that we just couldn't sing it," summarized John some time later. "In fact, we made such a hash of it that we thought we'd better give it to someone who could do it well." That someone was P J Proby, an American singer who'd been invited to Britain by Brian Epstein in April 1964 to take part in a Beatles TV special, and who had become friendly with the group. Proby recorded 'That Means A Lot' and it made Number 30 in the British charts in October 1965.

Written: Lennon/McCartney

Length: 2'26"

UK release: *Anthology 2* album, March 18, 1996

US release: *Anthology 2* album, March 18, 1996

BELOW: George, John and Paul in the back yard of Paul's family home in Liverpool, 1963.

12-BAR ORIGINAL

Written: Harrison/Lennon/McCartney/Starr

Length: 2'55"

UK release: *Anthology 2* album, March 18, 1996

US release: *Anthology 2* album, March 18, 1996

Motorcars
Handlebars
Bicycles for two
Broken hearted jubilee

Parachutes
Army boots
Sleeping bags for two
Nah nah nah nah jamboree

Buy buy...

Motorcars
Handlebars
Bicycles for two
Broken hearted jubilee

Parachutes
Army boots
Sleeping bags for you
Nah nah nah jamboree

La la la la la
Why why, says the sign
In the yard

Buy buy, says the sign
In the shop window
Why why, says the junk
In the yard

12-BAR ORIGINAL

Recorded between 'What Goes On' and 'I'm Looking Through You' in November 1965, was this the soul intended for *Rubber Soul?* Two takes were recorded and one of them was mixed but neither was ever released.

It is one of the least typical Beatles' tracks and appears to be an attempt to mimic the Memphis soul sound. The obvious template is Booker T. & the MG's – keyboard player Booker T. Jones, drummer Al Jackson, bass player Donald "Duck" Dunn and guitarist Steve Cropper – the Stax Records session musicians who played behind such soul greats as Otis Redding, Sam and Dave and Eddie Floyd. They had enjoyed a string of instrumental hits under their own name beginning with 'Green Onions' in 1962.

'12-Bar Original', which is credited to all four Beatles, sounds like a pastiche of 'Green Onions' and its follow-up 'Jellybread', minus the distinctive keyboard playing.

In March 2966 there were tentative plans for the Beatles to record at Stax Studios with Steve Cropper producing. Brian Epstein even went to Memphis to make advance preparations and check out accommodation but nothing came of it.

JUNK

Paul wrote 'Junk' while in India and first recorded it in May 1968 when all four Beatles met up at George's home on Claremont Drive, Esher, Surrey. It's this version, an acoustic demo with unfinished lyrics, which appears on *Anthology 3*. Paul hoped to complete it for inclusion on *Abbey Road* and rehearsed it during the *Let It Be* sessions but instead recorded it for his first solo album, *McCartney*, which was released in April 1970.

The demo is nothing more than a rough sketch. An unfinished verse is repeated twice, he is still thinking up words for the chorus and the gaps are filled with humming and giggling.

It's impossible to determine the story because Paul's way of composing at the time was to fit interesting words to a tune he had hit upon, in this case words to do with a scrap yard and a junk shop. In the press release that went out with his solo album his only comment was: "Originally written in India, at Maharishi's camp, and completed bit by bit in London."

Written: McCartney

Length: 2'24"

UK release: *Anthology 3* album, October 28, 1996

US release: *Anthology 3* album, October 28, 1996

NOT GUILTY

Recorded during *The White Album* sessions in August 1968, George had already spent two months in the studio with only one of his songs – 'While My Guitar Gently Weeps' – having been picked up by the group. Over 100 takes and rehearsals of this song were produced between August 7 and August 12 but for some reason it wasn't included in the final track list.

The song didn't surface until 1979 when a re-recorded version was used on the album *George Harrison*. Structurally the song remained the same, with the exception of the addition of the lines: "Not guilty for being on your street/ Getting underneath your feet".

Around this time George explained the song as being about the problems that were beginning to affect him as a part of the Beatles in 1968: "Paul, John, Apple, Rishikesh, Indian friends, etc." Written at a time when he was starting to be regarded as the freaky, mystical Beatle, he seems to be saying: "Don't blame me for getting you involved with freak culture. Hey, I'm not asking for too much. I just want to do my job and get a bit of respect." It's hard not to see such lines as "I'm not trying to be smart/ I only want what I can get" as a bitter comment on his inability to increase his presence within the group and become regarded as a songwriting equal to John and Paul. Maybe that's why it didn't get on the album.

Written: Harrison

Length: 3'22"

UK release: *Anthology 3* album, October 28, 1996

US release: *Anthology 3* album, October 28, 1996

Not guilty
For getting in your way
While you're trying to steal the day

Not guilty
And I'm not here for the rest,
I'm not trying to steal your vest

I am not trying to be smart
I only want what I can get

I'm really sorry for your ageing head,
But like you heard me said
Not guilty

No use handing me a writ
While I'm trying to do my bit

I don't expect to take your heart
I only want what I can get

I'm really sorry that you're underfed
But like you heard me said
Not guilty

Not guilty
For looking like a freak
Making friends with every Sikh

Not guilty
For leading you astray
On the road to Mandalay

I won't upset the apple cart
I only want what I can get

I'm really sorry that you've been misled
But like you heard me said
Not guilty

NOT GUILTY

WHAT'S THE NEW MARY JANE?

She looks as an African Queen
She eating twelve chapatis and cream
She tastes as Mongolian lamb
She coming from out of Bahran
What a shame Mary Jane had a pain at
the party
What a shame Mary Jane what a shame
Mary Jane had a pain at the party

She like to be married with Yeti
He grooving such cookie spaghetti
She jumping as Mexican bean
To make that her body morphine
What a shame Mary Jane had a pain at
the party
What a shame Mary Jane what a shame
Mary Jane had a pain at the party

She catch Patagonian pancake
With that one and gin party make
She having always good contact
She making with Apple and contract
What a shame Mary Jane had a pain at
the party
What a shame Mary Jane what a shame
Mary Jane had a pain at the party
All together now
What a shame Mary Jane had a pain at
the party
What a shame what what a shame Mary
Jane had a pain at the party
What a shame what a shame what a
shame what a shame
Mary Jane had a pain at the party
What a shame what a shame what a
shame what a shame
Mary Jane had a pain at the party
What a shame what a shame Mary Jane
had a pain at the party
What a shame what a shame what a
shame
Mary Jane had a pain at the party

What a shame Mary Jane Mary Jane had
a pain at the party
What a shame Mary Jane what a shame
Mary Jane had a pain at the party
What a shame Mary Jane what a shame

She looks as an African Queen
She tastes as Mongolian lamb

What a shame Mary Jane what a shame
Mary Jane had a pain at the party
All together now
What a shame Mary Jane had a pain at
the party
What a shame what what a shame Mary
Jane had a pain at the party
What a shame what a shame what a
shame what a shame

(That's it. Before we get taken away!)

Written: Lennon/McCartney

Length: 6'12"

UK release: *Anthology 3* album, October 28, 1996

US release: *Anthology 3* album, October 28, 1996

WHAT'S THE NEW MARY JANE?

"This was a thing I wrote half with our electronic genius Alex," said John in 1969. "It was called 'What A Shame Mary Jane Had A Pain At The Party' and it was meant for *The Beatles* album."

Written in India when John Alexis Mardas paid a visit, it was demoed at George's home in May 1968. At this stage it was two and a half minutes long and as the Beatles improvised towards the end one shouted, "Ooh. What's the news? ...What are you saying? What a shame Mary Jane had a pain at the party. What's the new Mary Jane ... Oh, my God! Mary! Mary!" This gave rise to the unusual title. The studio version, recorded by John and George with help from Yoko and Mal Evans, went on for over six minutes with a two-minute "freak out" before the final verse. The lyric remained the same as demoed in May except for the line "He grooving such cookie spaghetti" which came out, whether by accident or creative play, as "He groovy such cooking spaghetti."

The syntax of the lyric is unorthodox. There is a deliberate use of wrong tenses and wrong words that suggest that John may have been imitating the way that Indians often speak English when it is their second language. The story told is either deliberate or a coded putdown of someone in Maharishi's circle. Significantly, John had been recording 'Sexy Sadie' the day before.

"It was real madness," said John describing the track in 1969. "I'd like to do it again."

STEP INSIDE LOVE

Cilla Black, real name Priscilla White, was a Liverpool typist and Cavern club cloakroom girl, signed by Brian Epstein and given a contract with Parlophone. Her first single, released in February 1963, was 'Love Of The Loved', an old Quarry Men song written by Paul and used by the Beatles at their Decca Records audition. Paul turned up for the recording.

In 1964 he wrote 'It's For You' for her and then in 1968, after hearing that she was to front her own BBC TV series, he offered to write the theme song for her. Entertainment shows of the time were traditionally bookended by big band numbers but Cilla wanted to change that.

"Paul understood what I felt," she said. "He said to me: 'I know what they're doing. They're sending you these Billy Cotton Band type of numbers and that's not you. You're the kind of person that should invite people into your house. You should have a song that that starts off very quietly and then builds up.'"

Paul recorded a demo of 'Step Inside Love' at his home in Cavendish Avenue and double tracked it with his own voice. "All he had given us was one verse and a chorus with him playing on guitar," remembers director and producer Michael Hurll. "We played it that way for the first couple of weeks and then decided that we needed a second verse. Paul came over to the BBC Theatre in Shepherd's Bush and sat with me and Cilla and worked on a second verse. It starts off with the line "You look tired love" because Cilla was tired after a lot of rehearsing and most of what he wrote related to what was going on that day."

The version of the song included on *Anthology* was captured in September 1968 while the Beatles were waiting to record 'I Will'. Paul begins with the chorus and slips straight into the second verse that he forgets, singing "kiss me goodnight" instead of "love me tonight", leaving a line out and concluding with the last line of what should have been the third verse.

'Step Inside Love' became a Top Ten hit for Cilla in Britain, was released in America in May and earned her a ban in South Africa where it was considered to be a play on a prostitute's invitation. It could have been worse. Tony Bramwell remembers that Paul's initial idea was "Come Inside Love".

"I quite like the song," said Paul. " It was just a welcoming song for Cilla. It was very cabaret. It suited her voice."

LOS PARANOIAS

This was nothing more than an extended studio joke initiated by Paul when, at the end of his bossa nova version of 'Step Inside Love', he announced in the voice of an MC, "Joe Prairie and the Prairie Wall Flyers." John responded with "Los Paranoias", which was enough to get Paul improvising a South American spoof about Los Paranoias.

The likely inspiration was the Paraguayan group Trio Los Paraguayas led by Luis Alberto Del Parana (see 'Sun King') who appeared in variety shows on British TV during the 1950s with their Latin American rhythms and released a *Best Of* album in 1957.

Written: Lennon/McCartney

Length: 1'06"

UK release: *Anthology 3* album, October 28, 1996

US release: *Anthology 3* album, October 28, 1996

Step inside love and stay
Step inside love
Step inside love
Step inside love
I want you to stay

You look tired, love
Let me turn down the light
Come in out of the cold
Rest your head on my shoulder
And kiss me goodnight
We are together
Now and forever, come my way

Step inside love and stay
Step inside love
Step inside love
Step inside love
I want you to stay

STEP INSIDE LOVE

Written: Lennon/McCartney

Length: 1'22"

UK release: *Anthology 3* album, October 28, 1996

US release: *Anthology 3* album, October 28, 1996

Joe Prairies and the Prairie Wall Flyers.
Los Paranoias.

Los Paranoias invite you to
  to just enjoy us.
Come on you can do
  it baby,
Come on and join Los Paranoias.
Just enjoy us.
Los Paranoias,
Los Paranoias.
Come on enjoy us.
Harmony.

Los Paranoias,
Come on enjoy us.
We're Los Paranoias.
We're here to sing for you
And whatever you want us to
We will sing a little song for you.

This is the story
Of a boy named Ted
If his mother said
"Ted, be good (Be good, Ted),"
he would (alright)

She told him tales
About his soldier dad
But it made her sad
And she cried, oh my

Ted used to tell her
He'd be twice as good
And he knew he could
Cos in his head he said
"Mama don't worry
Your Teddy boy's here
Taking good care of you
Mama don't worry
Your Teddy boy's here
Teddy's gonna see you through"

And she said
"Teddy don't worry
Your Mama is here
Taking good care of you"
She said, "Teddy don't worry
Your mummy's here
Teddy's gonna see you through"

He said, "Ta da da..."

Then came the day
She found herself a man
Teddy turned and ran
Oh far away, oh yeah

He couldn't stand it
Just to be around
So he left the town far away, yeah yeah

Ted used to tell her
He'd be twice as good
And he knew he could
Cos in his head he said
"Mama don't worry
Now Teddy boy's here
Taking good care of you
Mama don't worry
Your Teddy boy's here
Teddy's gonna see you through"

TEDDY BOY

"Another song started in India," announced Paul in 1970 when 'Teddy Boy' was included on his first solo album. "It was recorded for the *Get Back* album *(Let It Be)* but later not used." It was started during one at the Maharishi's lectures at Rishikesh when Paul turned to John and sung the first line in his ear and was then finished in Scotland and London.

Strictly speaking, it was never "recorded" by the Beatles because there was no final take, no mixing, and in January 1969 Paul had still not completed the lyric. What is presented on *Anthology* is a rough sketch of a song offered by Paul in the hopes that John, George and Ringo would like it. The atmosphere is so informal that Paul laughs in parts, whistles over the unwritten patches and John can be clearly heard talking to others in the studio as he played along.

This inconsequential tale of a boy called Ted who is told to be good by his mother is not one that would have warmed John's heart. He once referred to Paul's story songs as being about "boring people doing boring things". This is probably why as the song ended during this session John picked up the rhythm on his guitar and turned it into a clunky square dance song; "Take your partners do-si-do/ Hold them tight and don't let go." That was his none-too-subtle comment about where 'Teddy Boy' fitted into Sixties rock culture.

And she said
"Teddy don't worry
Now your mummy is here
Taking good care of you
Teddy don't worry
Your mummy's here
Mummy's gonna see you through"

And he said
"Mummy mummy don't worry
Your Teddy boy's here
Taking good care of you
Mummy don't worry
Now Teddy boy's here
Teddy's gonna see you through"

Take your partners
And dosi-do
Hold them tight
And don't let go
When you've got it. Jump up

Take your partners
And dosi-do
When you got it
Then let it go
Hold them tight and

Now Ted used to tell her
He'd be twice as good
And he knew he could
Cos in his head, he said

TEDDY BOY

Written: McCartney

Length: 3'18"

UK release: *Anthology 3* album, October 28, 1996

US release: *Anthology 3* album, October 28, 1996

ALL THINGS MUST PASS

In November 1968, after finishing up his work on *The White Album*, George had gone to Woodstock to stay with Bob Dylan. Here he also spent time with the Band, Dylan's former backing group, who had just recorded *Music From Big Pink*.

This album was seen at the time as a reaction against the excesses of psychedelia and a return to the mainstream of American music. The bluntness of the group's name and the rustic simplicity of their publicity photographs suggested a swing away from surrealism and a return to the roots of American culture.

Their music was particularly appealing to seasoned musicians weary of the demands of fan hysteria – which had been instrumental in the break-up of Cream, for example. "I got the tapes of *Music From Big Pink* and I thought this is what I want to play – not extended solos and maestro bullshit but just good, funky songs," he explained in 1974.

George's song 'All Things Must Pass', which he played during Beatles' recording sessions in January 1969 and then recorded alone on February 25, was an attempt to capture the feeling that The Band had captured on their single 'The Weight'. In fact, when George first played it through to John and Paul he openly enthused about The Band and their music.

The lyric was based on a poem from Timothy Leary's *Psychedelic Prayers After The Tao Te Ching* (Poets Press, New York, 1966). The poem was a "translation from English to psychedelese" of part of the 23rd chapter of the *Tao* that Leary had titled 'All Things Pass'; "All things pass/ A sunrise does not last all morning/ All things pass/ A cloudburst does not last all day...' As George was to admit: "I remembered one of these prayers and it gave me the idea for this thing."

Despite George's frequent references to the song while the others were recording it wasn't considered for either *Let It Be* or *Abbey Road*. Instead it became the title track of his debut solo album in December 1970, which reached nNumber 4 in the British album charts and topped the American charts.

BELOW: Bob Dylan and the Beatles were the great rock innovators of the 1960s. George became particularly close to Dylan, playing with him in the Traveling Wilburys.

ALL THINGS MUST PASS

Sunrise doesn't last all morning
A cloudburst doesn't last all day
Seems my love is up
And has left you with no warning
It's not always been this grey

All things must pass
All things must pass away

Sunset doesn't last all evening
A mind can blow those clouds away
After all this my love is up
And must be leaving
It's not always been this grey

All things must pass
All things must pass away

All things must pass
None of life's strings can last
So I must be on my way
And face another day

Darkness only stays at nighttime
In the morning it will fade away
Daylight is good
At arriving at the right time
It's not always going to be this grey

All things must pass
All things must pass away
All things must pass
All things must pass away

Written: Harrison

Length: 3'05"

UK release: *Anthology 3* album, October 28, 1996

US release: *Anthology 3* album, October 28, 1996

If you want it, here it is
Come and get it
Make your mind up fast
If you want it anytime I can give it
But you better hurry 'cause it may not last

Did I hear you say that there must be
  a catch?
Will you walk away from a fool and
  his money?

If you want it, here it is
Come and get it
But you better hurry 'cause it's going fast

If you want it, here it is
Come and get it
Make your mind up fast
If you want it anytime I can give it
But you'd better hurry 'cause it may
  not last

Did I hear you say that there must be
  a catch?
Will you walk away from a fool and
  his money?

Sonny, if you want it, here it is
Come and get it
But you'd better hurry 'cause it's going fast
You'd better hurry 'cause it's going fast

Woo, fool and his money

Sonny, if you want it, here it is
Come and get it
But you'd better hurry 'cause it's going fast
You'd better hurry 'cause it's going fast
You'd better hurry 'cause it's going fast

COME AND GET IT

Apple Films, which was being run by Denis O'Dell, were planning a film of Terry Southern's 1958 novel *The Magic Christian* and O'Dell asked Paul to do the music. Paul agreed, reluctantly it now seems, and with a shooting script in hand began to write.

He started with a song to be used over a scene where Sir Guy Grand, the world's richest man (played by Peter Sellers), throws banknotes into a vat of filth and gets pleasure from seeing respectable people wallowing in slime in the hopes of grabbing some free cash. The idea came to him late at night while at Cavendish Avenue and he came downstairs and taped it in a whisper so as not to wake Linda. When he played it back the next day he believed that he had come up with "a very catchy song".

On July 5, 1969 one of the Apple label signings, the Iveys, gave an interview to *Disc & Music Echo* in which they complained of being neglected by the Beatles. Three weeks later Paul contacted the group and on July 29 he met them at their home and offered them 'Come And Get It', which he'd recorded alone with engineer Phil MacDonald five days previously at Abbey Road. He also suggested that they might make other contributions to the film soundtrack as he was trying to put his energies into recording the *Abbey Road* album.

Paul produced the group on August 2, choosing Tom Evans to do the lead vocal and encouraging them to stick to the simplicity of his demo on which he'd played only piano, drums, bass and maracas. He told them that if they did it right he could guarantee them a hit and if they didn't do it right then he'd keep it for a Beatles single. "That challenge really made us work hard," said Evans.

By the time 'Come And Get It' came out the Iveys were Bad Finger (after John's 'Badfinger Boogie'). The single reached the top five and the group could no longer say they were neglected. The soundtrack to *The Magic Christian* contained three Badfinger songs and in a move to capitalize on this they titled their next album *Magic Christian Music*.

Asked whether 'Come And Get It' was a veiled message to those squabbling over the Beatles fortune in 1968, Paul said, "It was just a straightforward pop song with all the old innuendoes. Come and get what?".

Written: McCartney

Length: 2'29"

UK release: *Anthology 3* album, October 28, 1996

US release: *Anthology 3* album, October 28, 1996

Discography

UK RELEASES

SINGLES

'Love Me Do'/'PS I Love You', October 5, 1962,
Parlophone 45-R 4949.

'Please Please Me'/'Ask me Why', January 11, 1963,
Parlophone 45-R 4983.

'From Me To You'/'Thank You Girl', April 11, 1963,
Parlophone R 5015.

'She Loves You'/'I'll Get You', August 23, 1963, Parlophone R
5055.

'I Want To Hold Your Hand'/'This Boy', November 29, 1963,
Parlophone R 5084.

'Can't Buy Me Love'/'You Can't Do That', March 20, 1964.
Parlophone R 5114.

'A Hard Day's Night'/'Things We Said Today', July 10, 1964,
Parlophone R 5160.

'I Feel Fine'/'She's A Woman', November 27, 1964, Parlophone
R 5200.

'Ticket To Ride'/'Yes It Is', April 9, 1965, Parlophone R 5265.

'Help!'/'I'm Down', July 23, 1965, Parlophone R 5305.

'We Can Work It Out'/'Day Tripper', December 3, 1965,
Parlophone R 5389.

'Paperback Writer'/'Rain', June 10, 1966, Parlophone R 5452.

'Eleanor Rigby'/'Yellow Submarine', August 5, 1966,
Parlophone R 5493.

'Strawberry Fields Forever'/'Penny Lane', February 17, 1967,
Parlophone R 5570.

'All You Need Is Love'/'Baby, You're A Rich Man', July 7, 1967,
Parlophone R 5620

'Hello, Goodbye'/'I Am The Walrus', November 24, 1967,
Parlophone R 5655.

'Lady Madonna'/'The Inner Light', March 15, 1968,
Parlophone R 5675.

'Hey Jude'/'Revolution', August 30, 1968, Apple [Parlophone]
R 5722.

'Get Back'/'Don't Let Me Down', April 11, 1969, Apple
[Parlophone] R 5777.

'The Ballad Of John And Yoko'/'Old Brown Shoe', May 30, 1969,
Apple [Parlophone] R 5786.

'Something'/'Come Together', October 31, 1969, Apple
[Parlophone] R 5814.

'Let It Be'/'You Know My Name (Look Up The Number)', March 6,
1970, Apple [Parlophone] R 5833.

'Free As A Bird'/'I Saw Her Standing There'/'This Boy'/ 'Christmas
Time (Is Here Again)', December 4 1995, Apple [Parlophone]
CDR 6422

'Real Love'/'Baby's In Black'/'Yellow Submarine'/'Here, There And
Everywhere', March 4, 1996, Apple [Parlophone] CDR 6425

EPS

Twist And Shout, July 12, 1963, Parlophone GEP 8882 (mono)–
'Twist And Shout'; 'A Taste Of Honey'/ Do You Want To Know A
Secret'; 'There's A Place'.

The Beatles' Hits, September 6, 1963, Parlophone GEP 8880
(mono) – 'From Me To You'; 'Thank You Girl'/'Please Please Me';
'Love Me Do'.

The Beatles (No 1), November 1, 1963, Parlophone GEP 8883
(mono) – 'I Saw Her Standing There'; 'Misery'/'Anna (Go To Him)';
'Chains'.

All My Loving, February 7, 1964, Parlophone GEP 8891(mono) –
'All My Loving'; 'Ask Me Why'/'Money (That's What I Want)'/'PS
I Love You'.

Long Tall Sally, June 19, 1964, Parlophone GEP 8913 (mono) –
'Long Tall Sally'; 'I Call Your Name'/'Slow Down'; 'Matchbox'.

Extracts From The Film A Hard Day's Night, November 6, 1964,
Parlophone GEP 8920 (mono) – 'I Should Have Known Better'; 'If
I Fell'/'Tell Me Why'; 'And I Love Her'.

Extracts From The Album A Hard Day's Night, November 6,
1964, Parlophone GEP 8924 (mono) – 'Any Time At All'; 'I'll Cry
Instead'/'Things We Said Today'; 'When I Get Home'.

Beatles For Sale, April 6, 1965, Parlophone GEP 8931 (mono) – 'No
Reply'; 'I'm A Loser'/'Rock And Roll Music'; 'Eight Days A Week'.

Beatles For Sale (No 2), June 4, 1965, Parlophone GEP 8938
(mono) – 'I'll Follow The Sun'; 'Baby's In Black'/'Words Of Love'; 'I
Don't Want To Spoil The Party'

The Beatles' Million Sellers, December 6, 1965, Parlophone GEP
8946 (mono) –
'She Loves You'; 'I Want To Hold Your Hand'/'Can't Buy Me Love';
'I Feel Fine'.

Yesterday, March 4, 1966, Parlophone GEP 8948 (mono only)–
'Yesterday'; 'Act Naturally'/'You Like Me Too Much'; 'It's Only Love'.

Nowhere Man, July 8, 1966, Parlophone GEP 8948 – 'Nowhere
Man'; 'Drive My Car'/'Michelle'; 'You Won't See Me'.

Magical Mystery Tour, December 8, 1967, Parlophone MMT-
1 (mono), SMMT-1 (stereo) – 'Magical Mystery Tour'; 'Your
Mother Should Know'/'I Am The Walrus'; 'The Fool On The Hill';
'Flying'/'Blue Jay Way'.

ALBUMS

Please Please Me, March 22, 1963, Parlophone PMC 1202 (mono),
PCS 3042 (stereo) – 'I Saw Her Standing There'; 'Misery'; 'Anna (Go
To Him)'; 'Chains'; 'Boys'; 'Ask Me Why'; 'Please Please Me'/'Love
Me Do'; 'PS I Love You'; 'Baby It's You'; 'Do You Want To Know A
Secret'; 'A Taste Of Honey'; 'There's A Place'; 'Twist And Shout'.

With The Beatles, November 22, 1963, Parlophone PMC 1206
(mono), PCS 3045 (stereo) – 'It Won't Be Long'; 'All I've Got To
Do'; 'All My Loving'; 'Don't Bother Me'; 'Little Child'; 'Till There
Was You'; 'Please Mister Postman'/ 'Roll Over Beethoven'; 'Hold

Me Tight'; 'You Really Got A Hold On Me'; 'I Wanna Be Your Man'; '(There's A) Devil In Her Heart'; 'Not A Second Time'; 'Money (That's What I Want)'.

A Hard Day's Night, July 10, 1964, Parlophone PMC 1230 (mono), PCS 3058 (stereo) – 'A Hard Day's Night'; 'I Should Have Known Better'; 'If I Fell'; 'I'm Happy Just To Dance With You'; 'And I Love Her'; 'Tell Me Why'; 'Can't Buy Me Love'/'Any Time At All'; 'I'll Cry Instead'; 'Things We Said Today'; 'When I Get Home'; 'You Can't Do That'; 'I'll Be Back'.

Beatles For Sale, December 4, 1964, Parlophone PMC 1240 (mono), PCS 3062 (stereo) – 'No Reply'; 'I'm A Loser'; 'Baby's In Black'; 'Rock And Roll Music'; 'I'll Follow The Sun'; 'Mr Moonlight'; 'Kansas City'/'Hey-Hey-Hey!'/'Eight Days A Week'; 'Words Of Love'; 'Honey Don't'; 'Every Little Thing'; 'I Don't Want To Spoil The Party'; 'What You're Doing'; 'Everybody's Trying To Be My Baby'.

Help!, August 6, 1965, Parlophone PMC 1255 (mono), PCS 3071 (stereo) – 'Help!'; 'The Night Before'; 'You've Got To Hide Your Love Away'; 'I Need You'; 'Another Girl'; 'You're Going To Lose That Girl'; 'Ticket To Ride'/'Act Naturally'; 'It's Only Love'; 'You Like Me Too Much'; 'Tell Me What You See'; 'I've Just Seen A Face'; 'Yesterday'; 'Dizzy Miss Lizzy'.

Rubber Soul, December 3, 1965, Parlophone PMC 1267 (mono), PCS 3075(stereo) – 'Drive My Car'; 'Norwegian Wood (This Bird Has Flown)'; 'You Won't See Me'; 'Nowhere Man'; 'Think For Yourself'; 'The Word'; 'Michelle'/'What Goes On'; 'Girl'; 'I'm Looking Through You'; 'In My Life'; 'Wait'; 'If I Needed Someone'; 'Run For Your Life'.

Revolver, August 5, 1966, Parlophone PMC 7009 (mono), PCS 7009 (stereo) – 'Taxman'; 'Eleanor Rigby'; 'I'm Only Sleeping'; 'Love You To'; 'Here, There And Everywhere'; 'Yellow Submarine'; 'She Said She Said'/'Good Day Sunshine'; 'And Your Bird Can Sing'; 'For No One'; 'Doctor Robert'; 'I Want To Tell You'; 'Got To Get You Into My Life'; 'Tomorrow Never Knows'.

A Collection Of Beatles Oldies, December 9, 1966, Parlophone PMC 7016 (mono), PCS 7016 (stereo) – 'She Loves You'; 'From Me To You'; 'We Can Work It Out'; 'Help!'; 'Michelle'; 'Yesterday'; 'I Feel Fine'; 'Yellow Submarine'/'Can't Buy Me Love'; 'Bad Boy'; 'Day Tripper'; 'A Hard Day's Night'; 'Ticket To Ride'; ' Paperback Writer'; 'Eleanor Rigby'; 'I Want To Hold Your Hand'.

Sgt. Pepper's Lonely Hearts Club Band, June 1, 1967, Parlophone PMC 7017 (mono), PCS 7027 (stereo) – 'Sgt. Pepper's Lonely Hearts Club Band'; 'With A Little Help From My Friends'; 'Lucy In The Sky With Diamonds'; 'Getting Better'; 'Fixing A Hole'; 'She's Leaving Home'; 'Being For The Benefit Of Mr. Kite!'/ 'Within You Without You'; 'When I'm Sixty Four'; 'Lovely Rita'; 'Good Morning Good Morning'; 'Sgt. Pepper's Lonely Hearts Club Band (Reprise)'; 'A Day In The Life'.

The Beatles, November 22, 1968, Apple [Parlophone] PMC 7067-7068 (mono), PCS 7067-7068 (stereo) – 'Back In The U.S.S.R.'; 'Dear Prudence'; 'Glass Onion'; 'Ob-La-Di, Ob-La-Da'; 'Wild Honey Pie'; 'The Continuing Story Of Bungalow Bill'; 'While My Guitar Gently Weeps'; 'Happiness Is A Warm Gun'/'Martha My Dear'; 'I'm So Tired'; 'Blackbird'; 'Piggies'; 'Rocky Raccoon'; 'Don't Pass Me By'; 'Why Don't We Do It In The Road'; 'I Will'; 'Julia'/'Birthday'; 'Yer Blues'; 'Mother Nature's Son'; 'Everybody's Got Something To Hide Except Me And My Monkey'; 'Sexy Sadie'; 'Helter Skelter'; 'Long Long Long'/'Revolution 1'; 'Honey Pie'; 'Savoy Truffle'; 'Cry Baby Cry'; 'Revolution 9'; 'Good Night'.

Yellow Submarine, January 17, 1969, Apple [Parlophone] PMC 7070 (mono), PCS 7070 (stereo) – 'Yellow Submarine'; 'Only A Northern Song'; 'All Together Now'; 'Hey Bulldog'; 'It's All Too Much'; 'All You Need Is Love'/ [Seven soundtrack instrumental cuts by the George Martin Orchestra].

Abbey Road, September 26, 1969, Apple [Parlophone] PCS 7088 (stereo only) – 'Come Together'; 'Something'; 'Maxwell's Silver Hammer'; 'Oh! Darling'; 'Octopus's Garden'; 'I Want You (She's So Heavy)'/'Here Comes The Sun'; 'Because'; 'You Never Give Me Your Money'; 'Sun King'/'Mean Mr Mustard'; 'Polythene Pam'/'She Came In Through The Bathroom Window'; 'Golden Slumbers'/'Carry That Weight'; 'The End'; Her Majesty'.

Let It Be, May 8, 1970, Apple [Parlophone] PCS 7096 (stereo only) – 'Two Of Us'; 'Dig A Pony'; 'Across The Universe'; 'I Me Mine'; 'Dig It'; 'Let It Be'; 'Maggie Mae'/'I've Got A Feeling'; 'The One After 909'; 'The Long And Winding Road'; 'For You Blue'; 'Get Back'.

Live At The BBC, November 30, 1994, Apple [Parlophone] CDPCSP 726 TC (mono) – 'From Us To You'; 'I Got A Woman'; 'Too Much Monkey Business'; 'Keep Your Hands Off My Baby'; 'I'll Be On My Way'; 'Young Blood'; 'A Shot Of Rhythm And Blues'; 'Sure To Fall (In Love With You)'; 'Some Other Guy'; 'Thank You Girl'; 'Baby It's You'; 'That's All Right (Mama)'; 'Carol'; 'Soldier Of Love'; 'Clarabella'; 'I'm Gonna Sit Right Down And Cry (Over You)'; 'Crying, Waiting, Hoping'; 'You Really Got A Hold On Me'; 'To Know Her Is To Love Her'; 'A Taste Of Honey'; 'Long Tall Sally'; 'I Saw Her Standing There'; 'The Honeymoon Song'; 'Johnny B Goode'; 'Memphis, Tennessee'; 'Lucille'; 'Can't Buy Me Love'; 'Till There Was You'; 'A Hard Day's Night'; 'I Wanna Be Your Man'; 'Roll Over Beethoven'; 'Things We Said Today'; 'She's A Woman'; 'Sweet Little Sixteen'; 'Lonesome Tears In My Eyes'; 'Nothin' Shakin''; 'The Hippy Hippy Shake'; 'Glad All Over'; 'I Just Don't Understand'; 'So How Come (No One Loves Me)'; 'I Feel Fine'; 'I'm A Loser'; 'Everybody's Trying To Be My Baby'; 'Rock And Roll Music'; 'Ticket To Ride'; 'Dizzy Miss Lizzy'; 'Kansas City/'Hey! Hey! Hey!'; 'Matchbox'; 'I Forgot To Remember To Forget'; 'I Got To Find My Baby'; 'Ooh! My Soul'; 'Don't Ever Change'; 'Slow Down'; 'Honey Don't'; Love Me Do'.

Anthology 1, November 21, 1995, Apple [Parlophone] CDPCSP 727 – 'Free As A Bird'; 'That'll Be The Day'; 'In Spite Of All The Danger'; 'Hallelujah, I Love Her So'; 'You'll Be Mine'; 'Cayenne'; 'My Bonnie'; 'Ain't She Sweet'; 'Cry For A Shadow'; 'Searchin''; 'Three Cool Cats'; 'The Sheik Of Araby'; 'Like Dreamers Do'; 'Hello Little Girl'; 'Besame Mucho'; 'Love Me Do'; 'How Do You Do It'; 'Please Please Me'; 'One After 909'; 'Lend Me Your Comb'; 'I'll Get You'; 'I Saw Her Standing There'; 'From Me To You'; 'Money (That's What I Want)'; 'You Really Got A Hold On

Me'; 'Roll Over Beethoven'; 'She Loves You'; 'Till There Was You'; 'Twist And Shout'; 'This Boy'; 'I Want To Hold Your Hand'; 'Moonlight Bay'; 'Can't Buy Me Love'; 'All My Loving'; 'You Can't Do That'; 'And I Love Her'; 'A Hard Day's Night'; 'I Wanna Be Your Man'; 'Long Tall Sally'; 'Boys'; 'Shout'; 'I'll Be Back', 'You Know What To Do'; 'No Reply' (Demo); 'Mr Moonlight'; 'Leave My Kitten Alone'; 'No Reply'; 'Eight Days A Week'; 'Kansas City'/'Hey! Hey! Hey!'.

Anthology 2, March 18, 1996, Apple [Parlophone] CDPCSP 728 – 'Real Love'; 'Yes It Is'; 'I'm Down'; 'You've Got To Hide Your Love Away'; 'If You've Got Trouble'; 'That Means A Lot'; 'Yesterday'; 'It's Only Love'; 'I Feel Fine'; 'Ticket To Ride'; 'Yesterday'; 'Help!'; 'Everybody's Trying To Be My Baby'; 'Norwegian Wood (This Bird Has Flown)'; 'I'm Looking Through You'; '12-Bar Original'; 'Tomorrow Never Knows'; 'Got To Get You Into My Life'; 'And Your Bird Can Sing'; 'Taxman'; 'Eleanor Rigby' (Strings Only); 'I'm Only Sleeping' (rehearsal); 'I'm Only Sleeping' (take 1); 'Rock And Roll Music'; 'She's A Woman'; 'Strawberry Fields Forever' (Demo); 'Strawberry Fields Forever' (Take 1); 'Strawberry Fields Forever' (Take 7); 'Penny Lane'; 'A Day In The Life'; 'Good Morning Good Morning'; 'Only A Northern Song'; ' Being For The Benefit Of Mr. Kite! (Takes 1 and 2)'; 'Being For The Benefit Of Mr. Kite!' (Take 7); 'Lucy In The Sky With Diamonds', 'Within You Without You' (Instrumental); 'Sgt. Pepper's Lonely Hearts Club Band' (Reprise); 'You Know My Name (Look Up The Number)'; 'I Am The Walrus'; 'The Fool On The Hill' (Demo); 'Your Mother Should Know'; 'The Fool On The Hill' (Take 4); 'Hello, Goodbye'; 'Lady Madonna'; 'Across The Universe'.

Anthology 3, October 28, 1996, Apple [Parlophone] CDPCSP 729 – 'A Beginning'; 'Happiness Is A Warm Gun'; 'Helter Skelter'; 'Mean Mr Mustard'; 'Polythene Pam'; 'Glass Onion'; 'Junk'; 'Piggies'; 'Honey Pie'; 'Don't Pass Me By'; 'Ob-La-Di, Ob-La-Da'; 'Good Night'; 'Cry Baby Cry'; 'Blackbird'; 'Sexy Sadie'; 'While My Guitar Gently Weeps'; 'Hey Jude'; 'Not Guilty'; 'Mother Nature's Son'; 'Glass Onion'; 'Rocky Raccoon'; 'What's The New Mary Jane'; 'Step Inside Love'/'Los Paranoias'; 'I'm So Tired'; 'I Will'; 'Why Don't We Do It In The Road'; 'Julia'; 'I''ve Got A Feeling'; 'She Came In Through The Bathroom Window'; 'Dig A Pony'; 'Two Of Us'; 'For You Blue'; 'Teddy Boy'; 'Rip It Up'/'Shake, Rattle and Roll'/ 'Blue Suede Shoes'; 'The Long And Winding Road'; 'Oh! Darling'; 'All Things Must Pass'; 'Mailman, Bring Me No More Blues'; 'Get Back'; 'Old Brown Shoe'; 'Octopus's Garden'; 'Maxwell's Silver Hammer'; 'Something'; 'Come Together'; 'Come And Get It'; 'Ain't She Sweet'; 'Because'; 'Let It Be'; 'I Me Mine'; 'The End'.

US RELEASES
SINGLES

'Please Please Me'/'Ask Me Why', February 25, 1963, Vee Jay VJ 498.

'From Me To You'/'Thank You Girl', May 27, 1963, Vee Jay VJ 522.

'She Loves You'/'I'll Get You', September 16, 1963, Swan 4152.

'I Want To Hold Your Hand'/'I Saw Her Standing There',

December 26, 1963, Capitol 5112.

'Please Please Me'/'From Me To You', January 30, 1964, Vee Jay VJ 581.

'Twist And Shout'/'There's A Place', March 2, 1964, Tollie 9001.

'Can't Buy Me Love'/'You Can't Do That', March 16, 1964, Capitol 5150.

'Do You Want To Know A Secret'/'Thank You Girl', March 23, 1964, Vee Jay VJ 587.

'Love Me Do'/'PS I Love You', April 27, 1964, Tollie 9008.

'Sie Liebt Dich'/'I'll Get You', May 21, 1964, Swan 4182.

'A Hard Day's Night'/'I Should Have Known Better', July 13, 1964, Capitol 5222.

'I'll Cry Instead'/'I'm Happy Just To Dance With You', July 20, 1964, Capitol 5234.

'And I Love Her'/'If I Fell', July 20, 1964, Capitol 5235.

'Matchbox'/'Slow Down', August 24, 1964, Capitol 5255.

'I Feel Fine'/'She's A Woman', November 23, 1964, Capitol 5327.

'Eight Days A Week'/'I Don't Want To Spoil The Party', February 15, 1965, Capitol 5371.

'Ticket To Ride'/'Yes It Is', April 19, 1965, Capitol 5407.

'Help!'/'I'm Down', July 19, 1965, Capitol 5476.

'Yesterday'/'Act Naturally', September 13, 1965, Capitol 5498.

'We Can Work It Out'/'Day Tripper', December 6, 1965, Capitol 5555.

'Nowhere Man'/'What Goes On', February 21, 1966, Capitol 5587.

'Paperback Writer'/'Rain', May 30, 1966, Capitol 5651.

'Eleanor Rigby'/'Yellow Submarine', August 8, 1966, Capitol 5715

'Strawberry Fields Forever'/'Penny Lane', February 13, 1967, Capitol 5810.

'All You Need Is Love'/'Baby, You're A Rich Man', 17 July 1967, Capitol 5964.

'Lady Madonna'/'The Inner Light', March 18, 1968, Apple [Capitol] 2138.

'Hey Jude'/'Revolution', August 26, 1968, Apple [Capitol] 2276.

'Get Back'/'Don't Let Me Down', May 5, 1969, Apple [Capitol] 2490.

'The Ballad Of John And Yoko'/'Old Brown Shoe', June 4, 1969. Apple [Capitol] 2531.

'Something'/'Come Together', October 6, 1969, Apple [Capitol] 2654.

'Let It Be'/'You Know My Name (Look Up The Number)', March 11, 1970, Apple [Capitol] 2764.

'The Long And Winding Road'/'For You Blue', May 11, 1970, Apple [Capitol] 2832.

'Free As A Bird'/'I Saw Her Standing There'/'This Boy'/'Christmas Time (Is Here Again)', December 4, 1995, Apple [Capitol] C2 7243 8 584 972

'Real Love'/'Baby's In Black'/'Yellow Submarine'/'Here, There And Everywhere', March 4, 1996, Apple [Capitol] C2 7243 8 585 442

ALBUMS

Introducing The Beatles, July 22, 1963, Vee Jay VJLP 1062 (mono), SR 1062 (stereo) – 'I Saw Her Standing There'; 'Misery';

'Anna (Go To Him)'; 'Chains'; 'Boys'; 'Love Me Do'/'PS I Love You'; 'Baby It's You'; 'Do You Want To Know A Secret'; 'A Taste Of Honey'; 'There's A Place '; 'Twist And Shout'.

Meet The Beatles!, January 20, 1964, Capitol T-2047 (mono), ST-2047 (stereo) – ' I Want To Hold Your Hand'; 'I Saw Her Standing There'; 'This Boy'; 'It Won't Be Long'; 'All I've Got To Do'; 'All My Loving'/'Don't Bother Me'; 'Little Child'; 'Till There Was You'; 'Hold Me Tight'; 'I Wanna Be Your Man'; 'Not A Second Time'.

Introducing The Beatles, January 27, 1964, Vee Jay VJLP 1062 (mono; no stereo release) – 'I Saw Her Standing There'; Misery'; 'Anna (Go To Him)'; 'Chains'; 'Boys'; 'Ask Me Why'/'Please Please Me'; 'Baby It's You'; 'Do You Want To Know A Secret'; 'A Taste Of Honey'; 'There's A Place'; 'Twist And Shout'.

The Beatles' Second Album, April 10, 1964, Capitol T-2080 (mono), ST-2080 (stereo) – 'Roll Over Beethoven'; 'Thank You Girl'; 'You Really Got A Hold On Me'; '(There's A) Devil In Her Heart'; 'Money (That's What I Want)'; 'You Can't Do That'/ 'Long Tall Sally'; 'I Call Your Name'; 'Please Mister Postman'; 'I'll Get You'; 'She Loves You'.

A Hard Day's Night, June 26, 1964, United Artists UA 6366 (mono), UAS 6366 (stereo) – 'A Hard Day's Night'; 'Tell Me Why'; 'I'll Cry Instead'; 'I'm Happy Just To Dance With You'; plus two soundtrack instrumental cuts by George Martin & Orchestra/ I Should Have Known Better'; 'If I Fell'; 'And I Love Her'; 'Can't Buy Me Love'; plus two soundtrack instrumental cuts by George Martin & Orchestra.

Something New, July 20, 1964, Capitol T-2108 (mono), ST-2108 (stereo) – 'I'll Cry Instead'; 'Things We Said Today'; 'Any Time At All'; 'When I Get Home'; 'Slow Down'; 'Matchbox'/'Tell Me Why'; 'And I Love Her'; 'I'm Happy Just To Dance With You'; 'If I Fell'; 'Komm, Gib Mir Deine Hand'.

The Beatles' Story, November 23, 1964, Capitol TBO-2222 (mono), STBO-2222 (stereo) – 'Interviews plus extracts from 'I Want To Hold Your Hand'; 'Slow Down'; 'This Boy'/Interviews plus extracts from 'You Can't Do That'; 'If I Fell'; 'And I Love Her'/Interviews plus extracts from 'A Hard Day's Night'; 'And I Love Her'/Interviews plus extracts from 'Twist And Shout' (live); 'Things We Said Today'; 'I'm Happy Just To Dance With You'; 'Little Child'; 'Long Tall Sally'; 'She Loves You'; 'Boys'.

Beatles '65, December 15, 1964, Capitol T-2228 (mono), ST-2228 (stereo) – 'No Reply'; 'I'm A Loser'; 'Baby's In Black'; 'Rock And Roll Music'; 'I'll Follow The Sun'; 'Mr Moonlight'/ 'Honey Don't'; 'I'll Be Back'; 'She's A Woman'; 'I Feel Fine'; 'Everybody's Trying To Be My Baby'.

The Early Beatles, March 22, 1965, Capitol T-2309 (mono), ST-2309 (stereo) – 'Love Me Do'; 'Twist And Shout'; 'Anna (Go To Him)'; 'Chains'; 'Boys'; 'Ask Me Why'/'Please Please Me'; 'PS I Love You'; 'Baby It's You'; 'A Taste Of Honey'; ' Do You Want To Know A Secret'.

Beatles VI, June 14, 1965, Capitol T-2358 (mono), ST-2358 (stereo) – 'Kansas City'/'Hey-Hey-Hey-Hey!'; 'Eight Days A Week'; 'You Like Me Too Much'; 'Bad Boy'; 'I Don't Want To Spoil The Party'; 'Words Of Love'/ 'What You're Doing'; 'Yes It Is'; 'Dizzy Miss Lizzy'; 'Tell Me What You See'; 'Every little Thing'.

Help! August 13, 1965, Capitol MAS-2386 (mono), SMAS-2386 (stereo) – 'Help!'; 'The Night Before'; 'You've Got To Hide Your Love Away'; 'I Need You'; plus three soundtrack instrumental cuts by George Martin & Orchestra/'Another Girl'; 'Ticket To Ride'; 'You're Going To Lose That Girl'; plus three soundtrack instrumental cuts by George Martin & Orchestra.

Rubber Soul, December 6, 1965, Capitol T-2442 (mono), ST-2442 (stereo) – 'I've Just Seen A Face'; Norwegian Wood (This Bird Has Flown)'; 'You Won't See Me'; 'Think For Yourself'; 'The Word'; 'Michelle'/ 'It's Only Love'; 'Girl'; 'I'm Looking Through You'; 'In My Life'; 'Wait'; 'Run For Your Life'.

"Yesterday"…And Today, June 20, 1966, Capitol T-2553 (mono), ST-2553 (stereo) – 'Drive My Car'; 'I'm Only Sleeping'; 'Nowhere Man'; 'Doctor Robert'; 'Yesterday'; 'Act Naturally'/'And Your Bird Can Sing'; 'If I Needed Someone'; 'We Can Work It Out'; 'What Goes On'; 'Day Tripper'.

Revolver, August 8, 1966, Capitol T-2576 (mono), ST-2576 (stereo) – 'Taxman'; 'Eleanor Rigby'; 'Love You To'; 'Here, There And Everywhere'; 'Yellow Submarine'; 'She Said She Said'/'Good Day Sunshine'; 'For No One'; 'I Want To Tell You'; 'Got to Get You Into My Life'; 'Tomorrow Never Knows'.

Sgt. Pepper's Lonely Hearts Club Band, June 2, 1967, Capitol MAS-2653 (mono), SMAS-2653 (stereo) – tracks as UK release

Magical Mystery Tour, November 27, 1967, Capitol MAL-2835 (mono), SMAL-2835 (stereo) – 'Magical Mystery Tour'; 'The Fool On The Hill'; 'Flying'; 'Blue Jay Way'; 'Your Mother Should Know'; 'I Am The Walrus'/'Hello, Goodbye'; 'Strawberry Fields Forever'; 'Penny Lane'; 'Baby, You're A Rich Man'; 'All You Need Is Love'.

The Beatles, November 25, 1968, Apple [Capitol] SWBO-101 (stereo) – tracks as UK release

Yellow Submarine, January 13, 1969, Apple [Capitol] SW-153 (stereo) – tracks as UK release

Abbey Road, October 1, 1969, Apple [Capitol] SO-383 (stereo) – tracks as UK release

Hey Jude, February 26, 1970, Apple [Capitol] SW-385 (stereo) – 'Can't Buy Me Love'; 'I Should Have Known Better'; 'Paperback Writer'; 'Rain'; 'Lady Madonna'; 'Revolution'/ 'Hey Jude'; 'Old Brown Shoe'; 'Don't Let Me Down'; 'The Ballad Of John And Yoko'.

Let It Be, May 18, 1970, Apple [Capitol] AR-34001 (stereo) – tracks as UK release

Live At The BBC, November 30, 1994, Apple [Capitol] (mono) – tracks as UK release

Anthology 1, November 21, 1995, Apple [Capitol] – tracks as UK release

Anthology 2, March 18, 1996, Apple [Capitol] – tracks as UK release

Anthology 3, October 28, 1996, Apple [Capitol] – tracks as UK release

Bibliography

BOOKS ABOUT THE BEATLES

Bacon, David and Maslov, Norman. *The Beatles' England.* Columbus Books, London, 1982; 910 Books, San Francisco, 1982.

Baird, Julia. *John Lennon My Brother.* Grafton, London, 1988.

The Beatles Lyrics. MacDonald, London, 1969.

Bedford, Carol. *Waiting For The Beatles,* Blandford Press, Newton Abbot, 1984.

Braun, Michael. *Love Me Do.* Penguin, London, 1964.

Brown, Peter. *The Love You Make.* MacMillan, London, 1983.

Coleman, Ray. *Lennon.* McGraw Hill, New York, 1984.

Dalton, David and Cott, Jonathan. *The Beatles Get Back.* Apple, London, 1969.

Davies, Hunter. *The Beatles.* Heinemann, London 1968.

Elson, Howard. *McCartney: Songwriter.* W.H.Allen, London, 1986.

Freeman, Robert. *The Beatles: A Private View.* Pyramid, London, 1992.

Fulpen, H.V. *The Beatles: An Illustrated Diary.* Plexus, London, 1982.

Giuliano, Geoffrey. *Blackbird.* Smith Gryphon, London, 1991.

Goldman, Albert. *The Lives Of John Lennon.* Bantam Press, London, New York.

Harrison, George. *I Me Mine.* W.H.Allen, London, 1980.

Harry, Bill (Editor). *Mersey Beat; The Beginnings Of The Beatles.* Columbus Books, London, 1977. The Ultimate Beatles Encyclopaedia. Virgin, London, 1992.

Leigh, Spencer. *Drummed Out!* Northdown Publishing, Hampshire, 1998.

Lennon, Cynthia. *A Twist Of Lennon.* W.H. Allen, London 1978.

Lennon, John. *In His Own Write.* Jonathan Cape, London,1964.

Lewisohn, Mark. *The Complete Beatles Recording Sessions.* Hamlyn, London, 1988.

The Complete Beatles Chronicle. Pyramid, London, 1992.

MacDonald, Ian. *Revolution In The Head.* Fourth Estate, London, 1994.

McCabe, Peter and Schonfeld, Robert. *Apple To The Core.* Sphere Books, London, 1972.

McCartney, Mike. *Thank U Very Much.* Weidenfeld & Nicholson, London, 1982.

Mellers, Wilfrid. *Twilight Of The Gods.* Schirmer Books, New York, 1973.

Miles, Barry. *Paul McCartney: Many Years From Now.* Secker & Warburg, London, 1997.

Norman, Philip. *Shout,* Elm Tree, London, 1981.

Rolling Stone magazine. *The Ballad Of John And Yoko.* Michael Joseph, London, 1982.

Salewicz, Chris. *McCartney: The Biography.* MacDonald, London, 1986.

Schaffner, Nicholas. *The Beatles Forever.* MSF Books, New York, 1978.

Schultheiss,Tom. *A Day In The Life.* Pierian Press, Ann Arbor, 1980.

Sheff, David. *The Playboy Interviews With John Lennon And Yoko Ono.* New English Library, London, 1981; Playboy Press, Chicago, 1981.

Shepherd, Billy. *The True Story Of The Beatles.* Beat Publications, London, 1964.

Shotton, Pete. *John Lennon In My Life.* Stein & Day, New York, 1983.

Stuart Ryan. David, *John Lennon's Secret.* Kozmik Press Center, New York, 1982.

Taylor, Alistair. *Yesterday.* Sidgwick and Jackson, London; Pioneer Books, Las Vegas, 1989.

Wenner, Jann. *Lennon Remembers.* Straight Arrow Books, San Francisco, 1971.

Wiener, Jon. *Come Together: John Lennon In His Time.* Faber & Faber, London, 1984; Random House, New York, 1984.

GENERAL BOOKS

Anthony, Gene. *Summer Of Love.* Celestial Arts, Berkeley,1980.

Buglioso, Vincent. *Helter Skelter.* Bantam, New York, 1974.

Fein, Art. *The LA Musical History Tour.* Faber & Faber, Boston, 1990.

Gaines, Steven. *Heroes and Villains.* MacMillan, London,1986; New American Library, New York, 1986.

Gibran, Kahlil. *Sand And Foam,* 1927.

Gillett, Charlie. *The Sound Of The City.* Sphere Books, London, 1970.

Goodman, Pete. *The Rolling Stones: Our Own Story.* Bantam, New York, 1965.

Guinness Book of Rock Stars. Guinness, London, 1989.

Hotchner, A.E. *Blown Away.* Simon and Schuster, London, 1990.

Leary, Timothy. *Flashbacks.* Heinemann, London, 1983.

Maharishi Mahesh Yogi,. *The Science of Being And The Art Of Living.* International SRM Publications, London, 1963.

Mascaró, Juan. *Lamps Of Fire,* Methuen, London 1958.

Matovina, *Dan. Without You: The Tragic Story Of Badfinger.* Frances Glover Books, San Mateo, 1997.

Marsh, Dave. *The Heart Of Rock And Roll.* Penguin, London, 1989; New American Library, New York, 1989.

Smith, Joe. *Off The Record.* Sidgwick and Jackson, London, 1989.

Stein, Jean. *Edie.* Jonathan Cape, London, 1982.

Turner, John M. *A Dictionary Of Circus Biography* (unpublished).

White, Charles. *Little Richard.* Pan, London, 1984.

Wolfe, Tom. *The Electric Kool-Aid Acid Test.* Bantam, New York, 1968.

Worth, Fred and Tamerius, Steve. *Elvis: His Life from A-Z.* Contemporary Books, New York, 1988.

Wyman, Bill. *Stone Alone.* Viking, London, 1990.

Index of Song Titles

Credits & Acknowledgements

PHOTOGRAPHS

The publishers would like to thank the following sources for their kind permission to reproduce the pictures in this book.

Key: t = Top, b = Bottom, c = Centre,
l = Left & r = Right

Michael Ochs Archives/Getty Images, 6. Steve Turner, 8-9. Terry O'Neill/Getty Images, 10. Sipa Press/Rex, 11. Mike Forster/Daily Mail/Rex, 12. Paul Popper/Popperfoto/Getty Images, 13. Christopher Furlong/Getty Images, 14. Terry O'Neill/Rex, 15. UPPA/Photoshot, 16. Harry Benson/Express/Hulton Archive/Getty Images, 17. TS Productions/Getty Images, 18. Michael Ward/Getty Images, 19. Keystone/Getty Images, 21. Hulton-Deutsch Collection/Corbis, 27. David Redfern/Redferns/Getty Images, 29-32. Harry Hammond/V&A Images/Getty Images, 34-35. Redferns/Getty Images, 37. (top) David Redfern/Redferns/Getty Images, 37. (bottom) Paul Popper/Popperfoto/Getty Images, 38. Redferns/Getty Images, 40-41. Terry O'Neill/Getty Images, 43. Hulton-Deutsch Collection/Corbis, 45. David Redfern/Redferns/Getty Images, 48. Central Press/Hulton Archive/Getty Images, 50. Michael Ochs Archives/Getty Images, 53. Popperfoto/Getty Images, 57. CBS Photo Archive/Getty Images, 59. Harry Benson/Express/Getty Images, 60. Val Wilmer/Redferns/Getty Images, 61. Pictorial Press, 63. Keystone-France/Gamma-Keystone via Getty Images, 64-65. Moviestore collection Ltd/Alamy, 69. Michael Ochs Archives/Getty Images, 71, Popperfoto/Getty Images, 72. Keystone-France/Gamma-Keystone via Getty Images, 74. Mirrorpix, 75. Michael Ochs Archives/Getty Images, 76-77. Michael Ochs Archives/Getty Images, 79. Bettmann/Corbis, 80. Daily Sketch/Rex, 81. Evening Standard/Hulton Archive/Getty Images, 83. (left) Michael Ochs Archives/Getty Images, 83. (right) David Farrell/Redferns/Getty Images, 84-85. Bettmann/Corbis, 89. AP/Press Association Images, 90. Bob Whitaker/Getty Images, 91. David Magnus/Rex, 97. Bob Gomel/The LIFE Images Collection/Getty Images, 98. Michael Ochs Archives/Getty Images, 99 Robert Whitaker/Getty Images, 100-101. Michael Ochs Archives/Getty Images, 105. REX, 107. David Redfern/Redferns/Getty Images, 108. Starstock/Photoshot, 111. (top) Topfoto (bottom) Press Association Images/AP, 113. Michael Ochs Archives/Getty Images, 114. Everett Collection/REX, 117. Michael Ochs Archive/Getty Images, 118. Redferns/Getty Images, 119. Keystone/Getty Images, 120-121. Keystone-France/Gamma-Keystone via Getty Images, 123. Max Scheler - K & K/Redferns/Getty Images, 124-125. Les Lee/Express/Getty Images, 127. Bob Whitaker/Getty Images, 129. David Montgomery/Getty Images, 131. Mirrorpix, 135. ITV/REX, 136. Hulton-Deutsch Collection/Corbis, 137. Bob Whitaker/Getty Images, 140. JazzSign/Lebrecht Music & Arts/Lebrecht Music & Arts/Corbis, 146. Keystone/Getty Images, 148. Robert Whitaker/Hulton Archive/Getty Images, 152, (left) Robert Whitaker/Hulton Archive/Getty Images, (right) Private Collection, 156. (left) Steve Turner, (right & bottom) Private Collection, 158. Keystone USA/REX, 161. GAB Archive/Redferns/Getty Images, 164. Frederic Lewis/Getty Images, 166. Private Collection, 168. GAB Archive/Redferns/Getty Images, 169. Jack Ramsey/REX, 171. (top) Kent Gavin/Keystone/Getty Images, (bottom) Keystone USA/REX, 172-173 John Pratt/Keystone/Getty Images, 176. Jim Dyson/Getty Images, 177. & 182. Steve Turner, 184. Popperfoto/Getty Images, 187. Private Collection, 188-189. David Redfern/Redferns/Getty Images, 190. Getty Images, 191 (top) Private Collection, 192. Mirrorpix, 196. Keystone/Getty Images, 197. Private Collection, 199. (left) Michael Ochs Archives/Getty Images, (top right) Mirrorpix, Solo Syndication (right), 200-201. David Redfern/Redferns/Getty Images, 205. Cummings Archives/Redferns/Getty Images, 205. David Redfern/Redferns/Getty Images, 206. Bettman/Corbis, 208. Lillian Evans/REX, 210. Fred Sweets/The Washington Post via Getty Images, 211. David Magnus/REX, 213. David Redfern/Redferns/Getty Images, 215. Popperfoto/Getty Images, 217. Central Press/Getty Images, 218. John Williams/BIPs/Getty Images, 220. David Redfern/Redferns/Getty Images, 222. National Geographic Stock/Howard Sochurek, 225. David Magnus/REX, 226-227. Hulton Archive/Getty Images, 229. Keystone-France/Gamma-Keystone via Getty Images, 231. Bettmann/Corbis, 233. Colin Harrison, 235. Jimmy Scott Benevolent Fund, 237. Steve Turner, 240. Private Collection, 241. Corbis, 242. Keystone-France/Gamma-Keystone via Getty Images, 244. David Redfern/Redferns/Getty Images, 248. David Redfern/Redferns/Getty Images, 253. David Magnus/REX, 258-259. AP/Press Association Images, 261. Keystone Features/Hulton Archive/Getty Images, 265. Private Collection, 269. Hulton Archive/Getty Images, 270-271. Daily Sketch /REX, 274. Bentley Archive/Popperfoto/Getty Images, 275. Ron Galella/WireImage/Getty Images, 278. Keystone-France/Gamma-Keystone via Getty Images, 282. Larry Ellis/Express/Hulton Archive/Getty Images, 285. Keystone-France/Gamma-Keystone via Getty Images, 286. Steve Turner, 289. Express/Express/Getty Images, 295. Keystone/Getty Images, 296. pwe Verlag GmbH/ullstein bild via Getty Images, 300. Jeff Albertson/Corbis, 303. (top) Michael Webb/Keystone/

Getty Images, (bottom) Cummings Archives/Redferns/Getty Images, 306. Daily Mail/REX, 310. Jan Persson/Redferns/Getty Images, 311. Royston Ellis, 312. Steve Turner, 316. REX, 317. Alamy/Zuma Wire Service, 319. Cummings Archives/Redferns/Getty Images, 320-321. Sue Moore/Empics Entertainment/Press Association Images, 323. Time Life Pictures/DMI/The LIFE Picture Collection/Getty Images, 324. Corbis/Bettmann, 325. Redferns/Getty Images, 328. Getty Images, 331. Hulton Archive/Getty Images, 333. Keystone/Getty Images, 339. Bill Ray/The LIFE Picture Collection/Getty Images

Every effort has been made to acknowledge correctly and contact the source and/or copyright holder of each picture and Carlton Books Limited apologises for any unintentional errors, or omissions which will be corrected in future editions of this book.

ACKNOWLEDGEMENTS

For interviews carried out specifically for this book I thank: Al Aronowitz, Diane Ashley, David Ashton, Marc Behm, Margo Bird, Pattie Boyd, Tony Bramwell, Prudence Bruns, Tony Carricker, Iris Caldwell, Allan Clarke, Maureen Cleave, Melanie Coe, Richard A. Cooke, Nancy Cooke de Herrera, Meta Davis, Rod Davis, Pat Dawson, Richard DiLello, Royston Ellis, Peter Fonda, Roger Greenaway, Johnny Guitar, Paul Horn, Kevin Howlett, Michael Hurll, Stephen James, Rod Jones, Tony King, Timothy Leary, Donovan Leitch, Julian Lennon, Dick Lester, John Duff Lowe, Kenny Lynch, Angie McCartney, Roger McGough, Thelma McGough, Elliot Mintz, Rod Murray, Delbert McClinton, Denis O'Dell, Lucy O' Donnell (Vodden), Alun Owen, Viv Prince, Little Richard, Jimmy Savile, John Sebastian, Helen Shapiro, Don Short, Joel Schumacher, Lucrezia Scott, Derek Taylor, James Taylor, Doug Trendle, Dr John Turner, Jan Vaughan, Gordon Waller and Nigel Walley.

I also drew on past interviews with Lionel Bart, Hunter Davies, John Dunbar, Cynthia Lennon, John Lennon, George Martin, Linda McCartney, Paul McCartney, Barry Miles, Spike Milligan, Roy Orbison, Ravi Shankar, Bruce Welch and Muriel Young.

For supplying information or setting up interviews I thank: Tony Barrow, Penny Bell, Gloria Boyce, Eleanor Bron, Lynne DeBernardis, Liz Edwards, Mile Edwards, Peggy Ferguson, Roberta Freymann, Sarah Jane Freymann, Lynda Gilbert, David Gilmour, Matt Godwin, Jack Good, Adrian Henri, Corinna Honan, Shelagh Jones, Andrew King, Martha Knight, Carol Lawrence, Mark Lewisohn, Brian Patten, Mrs Juan Mascaro, Mike McCartney, Robby Montgomery, Pete Nash, Iona Opie, Peter Rhone, Bettina Rose, Juliet Rowe, Phil Spangenberger, Alvin Stardust, Jean Stein, Sue Turner, Lisa Ullmann, Linda Watts and Paul Wayne.

I used facilities supplied by the following organizations: American Federation of Musicians, ASCAP, BMI, Beatles Shop (Liverpool), Bristol Library, Bristol Old Vic, British Library, Chiswick Library, Highland Bookshop and Wildlife Art Gallery (Traverse City, Michigan), National Newspaper Library, National Sound Archives, Nigerian High Commission, Performing Rights Society, Rochdale Library, Theatre Museum, UCLA Library and Westminster Library.

Finally, I would like to thank Piers Murray Hill and Jonathan Goodman at Carlton Books.

SONG CREDITS

I Saw Her Standing There Words and Music by John Lennon & Paul McCartney © 1963, Reproduced by permission of Sony/ATV Music Publishing (UK) Ltd/ Sony/ATV Tunes LLC, London W1F 9LD

Misery Words and Music by John Lennon & Paul McCartney © 1963, Reproduced by permission of Sony/ATV Music Publishing (UK) Ltd/ Sony/ATV Tunes LLC, London W1F 9LD

Ask Me Why
(50% USA and Canada) Words and Music by John Lennon and Paul McCartney. Copyright © 1963 UNIVERSAL/DICK JAMES MUSIC LTD. and DOWNTOWN DMP SONGS. Copyright Renewed. All Rights for UNIVERSAL/DICK JAMES MUSIC LTD. Controlled and Administered by UNIVERSAL - SONGS OF POLYGRAM INTERNATIONAL, INC. All Rights Reserved. Used by Permission. Reprinted with Permission of Hal Leonard Corporation.
(50% USA and Canada) Writers: John Lennon and Paul McCartney Publisher: Lenono Music (GMR).
(Rest of world) Words & Music by John Lennon & Paul McCartney © Copyright 1963 Dick James Music Limited. Universal/Dick James Music Limited. All Rights Reserved. International Copyright Secured. Used by permission of Music Sales Limited.

Please Please Me
(50% USA and Canada) Words and Music by John Lennon and Paul McCartney. Copyright © 1962, 1964 UNIVERSAL/DICK JAMES MUSIC LTD. Copyright Renewed and Assigned to UNIVERSAL/DICK JAMES MUSIC LTD., JULIAN LENNON, SEAN ONO LENNON and YOKO ONO LENNON. All Rights for UNIVERSAL/DICK JAMES MUSIC LTD. in the U.S. and Canada Administered by UNIVERSAL - SONGS OF POLYGRAM INTERNATIONAL, INC. All Rights Reserved. Used by Permission. Reprinted with Permission of Hal Leonard Corporation.
(50% USA and Canada) Writers: John Lennon and Paul McCartney. Publisher: Lenono Music GMR.
(Rest of world) Words & Music by John Lennon & Paul McCartney. © Copyright 1962 Dick James Music Limited. Universal/Dick James Music Limited. All Rights Reserved. International Copyright Secured. Used by permission of Music Sales Limited.

Love Me Do
(UK) Words and Music by John Lennon and Paul McCartney. © 1962 (Renewed) Beechwood Music Corp. Administered in the UK by MPL Communications, Inc. All Rights Reserved. Used By Permission.
(Rest of world) Words and Music by John Lennon & Paul McCartney © 1962. Reproduced by permission of Sony/ATV Music Publishing (UK) Ltd/ Sony/ATV Tunes LLC, London W1F 9LD

P.S. I Love You
(UK) Words and Music by John Lennon and Paul McCartney. © 1962 (Renewed) Beechwood Music Corp. Administered in the UK by MPL Communications, Inc. All Rights Reserved. Used By Permission.
(Rest of world) Words and Music by John Lennon & Paul McCartney © 1962, Reproduced by permission of MPL Communications Inc/ EMI Music Publishing Ltd, London W1F 9LD

Do You Want To Know A Secret Words and Music by John Lennon & Paul McCartney © 1963, Reproduced by permission of Sony/ATV Music Publishing (UK) Ltd/ Sony/ATV Tunes LLC, London W1F 9LD

There's A Place Words and Music by John Lennon & Paul McCartney © 1963, Reproduced by permission of Sony/ATV Music Publishing (UK) Ltd/ Sony/ATV Tunes LLC, London W1F 9LD

From Me To You Words and Music by John Lennon & Paul McCartney © 1963, Reproduced by permission of Sony/ATV Music Publishing (UK) Ltd/ Sony/ATV Tunes LLC, London W1F 9LD

Thank You Girl Words and Music by John Lennon & Paul McCartney © 1963, Reproduced by permission of Sony/ATV Music Publishing (UK) Ltd/ Sony/ATV Tunes LLC, London W1F 9LD

She Loves You Words and Music by John Lennon & Paul McCartney © 1963, Reproduced by permission of Sony/ATV Music Publishing (UK) Ltd/ Sony/ATV Tunes LLC, London W1F 9LD

I'll Get You Words and Music by John Lennon & Paul McCartney © 1963, Reproduced by permission of Sony/ATV Music Publishing (UK) Ltd/ Sony/ATV Tunes LLC, London W1F 9LD

It Won't Be Long Words and Music by John Lennon & Paul McCartney © 1963, Reproduced by permission of Sony/ATV Music Publishing (UK) Ltd/ Sony/ATV Tunes LLC, London W1F 9LD

All I've Got To Do Words and Music by John Lennon & Paul McCartney © 1963, Reproduced by permission of Sony/ATV Music Publishing (UK) Ltd/ Sony/ATV Tunes LLC, London W1F 9LD

All My Loving Words and Music by John Lennon & Paul McCartney © 1963, Reproduced by permission of Sony/ATV Music Publishing (UK) Ltd/ Sony/ATV Tunes LLC, London W1F 9LD

Little Child Words and Music by John Lennon & Paul McCartney © 1963, Reproduced by permission of Sony/ATV Music Publishing (UK) Ltd/ Sony/ATV Tunes LLC, London W1F 9LD

Don't Bother Me
(USA and Canada) Words and Music by George Harrison. Copyright © 1963 UNIVERSAL/DICK JAMES MUSIC LTD. Copyright Renewed. All Rights in the U.S. and Canada Controlled and Administered by UNIVERSAL - SONGS OF POLYGRAM INTERNATIONAL, INC. All Rights Reserved. Used by Permission. Reprinted with Permission of Hal Leonard Corporation.
(Rest of world) Words & Music by George Harrison. © Copyright 1963 Dick James Music Limited. Universal/Dick James Music Limited. All Rights Reserved. International Copyright Secured. Used by permission of Music Sales Limited.

Hold Me Tight Words and Music by John Lennon & Paul McCartney © 1963, Reproduced by permission of Sony/ATV Music Publishing (UK) Ltd/ Sony/ATV Tunes LLC, London W1F 9LD

Not A Second Time Words and Music by John Lennon & Paul McCartney © 1963, Reproduced by permission of Sony/ATV Music Publishing (UK) Ltd/ Sony/ATV Tunes LLC, London W1F 9LD

I Wanna Be Your Man Words and Music by John Lennon & Paul McCartney © 1963, Reproduced by permission of Sony/ATV Music Publishing (UK) Ltd/ Sony/ATV Tunes LLC, London W1F 9LD

I Want To Hold Your Hand
(USA and Canada) Words and Music by John Lennon and Paul McCartney. Copyright © 1963 NORTHERN SONGS LTD. Copyright Renewed. All Rights in the United States and Canada Controlled and Administered by SONGS OF UNIVERSAL, INC. All Rights Reserved Used by Permission. Reprinted by Permission of Hal Leonard Corporation.
(Rest of world) Words and Music by John Lennon & Paul McCartney © 1963, Reproduced by permission of Sony/ATV Music Publishing (UK) Ltd/ Sony/ATV Tunes LLC, London W1F 9LD

This Boy Words and Music by John Lennon & Paul McCartney © 1963, Reproduced by permission of Sony/ATV Music Publishing (UK) Ltd/ Sony/ATV Tunes LLC, London W1F 9LD

I Call Your Name Words and Music by John Lennon & Paul McCartney © 1963, Reproduced by permission of Sony/ATV Music Publishing (UK) Ltd/ Sony/ATV Tunes LLC, London W1F 9LD

A Hard Day's Night Words and Music by John Lennon & Paul McCartney © 1964, Reproduced by permission of Sony/ATV Music Publishing (UK) Ltd/ Sony/ATV Tunes LLC, London W1F 9LD

I Should Have Known Better Words and Music by John Lennon & Paul McCartney © 1964, Reproduced by permission of Sony/ATV Music Publishing (UK) Ltd/ Sony/ATV Tunes LLC, London W1F 9LD

If I Fell Words and Music by John Lennon & Paul McCartney © 1964, Reproduced by permission of Sony/ATV Music Publishing (UK) Ltd/ Sony/ATV Tunes LLC, London W1F 9LD

And I Love Her Words and Music by John Lennon & Paul McCartney © 1963, Reproduced by permission of Sony/ATV Music Publishing (UK) Ltd/ Sony/ATV Tunes LLC, London W1F 9LD

I'm Happy Just To Dance With You Words and Music by John Lennon & Paul McCartney © 1964, Reproduced by permission of Sony/ATV Music Publishing (UK) Ltd/ Sony/ATV Tunes LLC, London W1F 9LD

Tell Me Why Words and Music by John Lennon & Paul McCartney © 1964, Reproduced by permission of Sony/ATV Music Publishing (UK) Ltd/ Sony/ATV Tunes LLC, London W1F 9LD

Can't Buy Me Love Words and Music by John Lennon & Paul McCartney © 1964, Reproduced by permission of Sony/ATV Music Publishing (UK) Ltd/ Sony/ATV Tunes LLC, London W1F 9LD

Any Time At All Words and Music by John Lennon & Paul McCartney © 1964, Reproduced by permission of Sony/ATV Music Publishing (UK) Ltd/ Sony/ATV Tunes LLC, London W1F 9LD

I'll Cry Instead Words and Music by John Lennon & Paul McCartney © 1964, Reproduced by permission of Sony/ATV Music Publishing (UK) Ltd/ Sony/ATV Tunes LLC, London W1F 9LD

Things We Said Today Words and Music by John Lennon & Paul McCartney © 1964, Reproduced by permission of Sony/ATV Music Publishing (UK) Ltd/ Sony/ATV Tunes LLC, London W1F 9LD

When I Get Home Words and Music by John Lennon & Paul McCartney © 1964, Reproduced by permission of Sony/ATV Music Publishing (UK) Ltd/ Sony/ATV Tunes LLC, London W1F 9LD

You Can't Do That Words and Music by John Lennon & Paul McCartney © 1964, Reproduced by permission of Sony/ATV Music Publishing (UK) Ltd/ Sony/ATV Tunes LLC, London W1F 9LD

I'll Be Back Words and Music by John Lennon & Paul McCartney © 1964, Reproduced by permission of Sony/ATV Music Publishing (UK) Ltd/ Sony/ATV Tunes LLC, London W1F 9LD

I Feel Fine Words and Music by John Lennon & Paul McCartney © 1964, Reproduced by permission of Sony/ATV Music Publishing (UK) Ltd/ Sony/ATV Tunes LLC, London W1F 9LD

She's A Woman Words and Music by John Lennon & Paul McCartney © 1964, Reproduced by permission of Sony/ATV Music Publishing (UK) Ltd/ Sony/ATV Tunes LLC, London W1F 9LD

Eight Days A Week Words and Music by John Lennon & Paul McCartney © 1964, Reproduced by permission of Sony/ATV Music Publishing (UK) Ltd/ Sony/ATV Tunes LLC, London W1F 9LD

I'm A Loser Words and Music by John Lennon & Paul McCartney © 1964, Reproduced by permission of Sony/ATV Music Publishing (UK) Ltd/ Sony/ATV Tunes LLC, London W1F 9LD

No Reply Words and Music by John Lennon & Paul McCartney © 1964, Reproduced by permission of Sony/ATV Music Publishing (UK) Ltd/ Sony/ATV Tunes LLC, London W1F 9LD

I Don't Want To Spoil The Party Words and Music by John Lennon & Paul McCartney © 1964, Reproduced by permission of Sony/ATV Music Publishing (UK) Ltd/ Sony/ATV Tunes LLC, London W1F 9LD

I'll Follow The Sun Words and Music by John Lennon & Paul McCartney © 1964, Reproduced by permission of Sony/ATV Music Publishing (UK) Ltd/ Sony/ATV Tunes LLC, London W1F 9LD

Baby's In Black Words and Music by John Lennon & Paul McCartney © 1964, Reproduced by permission of Sony/ATV Music Publishing (UK) Ltd/ Sony/ATV Tunes LLC, London W1F 9LD

Every Little Thing Words and Music by John Lennon & Paul McCartney © 1964, Reproduced by permission of Sony/ATV Music Publishing (UK) Ltd/ Sony/ATV Tunes LLC, London W1F 9LD

What You're Doing Words and Music by John Lennon & Paul McCartney © 1964, Reproduced by permission of Sony/ATV Music Publishing (UK) Ltd/ Sony/ATV Tunes LLC, London W1F 9LD

Yes It Is Words and Music by John Lennon & Paul McCartney © 1965, Reproduced by permission of Sony/ATV Music Publishing (UK) Ltd/ Sony/ATV Tunes LLC, London W1F 9LD

I'm Down Words and Music by John Lennon & Paul McCartney © 1965, Reproduced by permission of Sony/ATV Music Publishing (UK) Ltd/ Sony/ATV Tunes LLC, London W1F 9LD

Help! Words and Music by John Lennon & Paul McCartney © 1965, Reproduced by permission of Sony/ATV Music Publishing (UK) Ltd/ Sony/ATV Tunes LLC, London W1F 9LD

The Night Before Words and Music by John Lennon & Paul McCartney © 1965, Reproduced by permission of Sony/ATV Music Publishing (UK) Ltd/ Sony/ATV Tunes LLC, London W1F 9LD

You've Got To Hide Your Love Away Words and Music by John Lennon & Paul McCartney © 1965, Reproduced by permission of Sony/ATV Music Publishing (UK) Ltd/ Sony/ATV Tunes LLC, London W1F 9LD

I Need You Words and Music by George Harrison © 1965, Reproduced by permission of Sony/ATV Music Publishing (UK) Ltd/ Sony/ATV Tunes LLC, London W1F 9LD

Another Girl Words and Music by John Lennon & Paul McCartney © 1965, Reproduced by permission of Sony/ATV Music Publishing (UK) Ltd/ Sony/ATV Tunes LLC, London W1F 9LD

You're Going To Lose That Girl Words and Music by John Lennon & Paul McCartney © 1965, Reproduced by permission of Sony/ATV Music Publishing (UK) Ltd/ Sony/ATV Tunes LLC, London W1F 9LD

Ticket To Ride Words and Music by John Lennon & Paul McCartney © 1965, Reproduced by permission of Sony/ATV Music Publishing (UK) Ltd/ Sony/ATV Tunes LLC, London W1F 9LD

Tell Me What You See Words and Music by John Lennon & Paul McCartney © 1965, Reproduced by permission of Sony/ATV Music Publishing (UK) Ltd/ Sony/ATV Tunes LLC, London W1F 9LD

You Like Me Too Much Words and Music by George Harrison © 1965, Reproduced by permission of Sony/ATV Music Publishing (UK) Ltd/ Sony/ATV Tunes LLC, London W1F 9LD

It's Only Love Words and Music by John Lennon & Paul McCartney © 1965, Reproduced by permission of Sony/ATV Music Publishing (UK) Ltd/ Sony/ATV Tunes LLC, London W1F 9LD

I've Just Seen A Face Words and Music by John Lennon & Paul McCartney © 1965, Reproduced by permission of Sony/ATV Music Publishing (UK) Ltd/ Sony/ATV Tunes LLC, London W1F 9LD

Yesterday Words and Music by John Lennon & Paul McCartney © 1965, Reproduced by permission of Sony/ATV Music Publishing (UK) Ltd/ Sony/ATV Tunes LLC, London W1F 9LD

Day Tripper Words and Music by John Lennon & Paul McCartney © 1965, Reproduced by permission of Sony/ATV Music Publishing (UK) Ltd/ Sony/ATV Tunes LLC, London W1F 9LD

We Can Work It Out Words and Music by John Lennon & Paul McCartney © 1965, Reproduced by permission of Sony/ATV Music Publishing (UK) Ltd/ Sony/ATV Tunes LLC, London W1F 9LD

Drive My Car Words and Music by John Lennon & Paul McCartney © 1965, Reproduced by permission of Sony/ATV Music Publishing (UK) Ltd/ Sony/ATV Tunes LLC, London W1F 9LD

351